THE PERFECT PASTOR?

(Understanding and Relating to the Life and Work of a Pastor)

—m—

D. T. Owsley

D. Thomas Owsley

XULON PRESS

TABLE OF CONTENTS

ACKNOWLEDGEMENTS

—ᴍ—

There are several individuals worthy of acknowledgement who have contributed, either directly or indirectly, in the formation of this work, but more specifically in the formation of my life. I begin by thanking Kent Hughes, who faithfully discipled high school and college men as a youth pastor, of which I was one. A seminarian at the time, Kent led me to Christ and mentored me in the faith. I am indebted to him for giving me a solid start in my walk with Christ.

I also am indebted to Andy Strachan, my first pastor-friend who gave me an inside glimpse into the life and work of a pastor.

Thanks is extended to Joey Pipa, who, as a pastor put fourteen ministerial interns and me through a well-rounded program that provided a wide range of opportunities to question our calls, apply our training, test our gifts, and hone our skills.

To Richard Ganz who modeled how to be bold, strong and loving, I give my heartfelt appreciation. He taught me to confront legalism and to measure life by God's Word. He showed me how to live by grace, and then led me by the ear into Christ's freedom for which we have been set free.

To Dominic Aquila, good professor and friend whose patient and wise advise has helped me more than he will ever know. His teaching has edified me, his counsel has rescued me, and his wisdom has directed me to where I am today. God used this man to keep me in the ministry.

My long-time friend Linda Eagon, is also worthy of tribute. Her prudent, candid and encouraging words during times of deep discouragement were like sweet golden apples in settings of silver. Her great sense of humor frequently balanced the heaviness of my heart with the lighter side of life, and in fact often tipped the scales so I could laugh again.

I wish to thank another good friend, Carole Thaxton of Konos Connection. This wife, mother, author, curriculum writer, teacher, missionary, and conference speaker - a renaissance woman - graciously applied her skills to edit this work and make it clearer.

My love and appreciation also extends to our two beautiful, precious daughters who have loved me as their father, even though I am a pastor. What's more, I could never be grateful enough for the loving wife of my youth whom I cherish. In her I have found a good thing and favor from the Lord. She has faithfully been with me in the wild ride of life, in poverty and adversity, in sickness and in health, in sorrow and in joy. Indeed, she is my crown.

Above all, I am most thankful for Jesus Christ who has graciously given me life as Creator, new life as Savior, and then blessed me with the privilege of serving him as Lord.

FOREWORD

—ɯ—

Ministry is people intensive. We may romanticize ministry but we must recognize that we are dealing with sinners, people with real needs. And because people are needy and require careful attention, ministry can appear like herding cats.

What does the perfect pastor look like? Is he a good shepherd, preacher, administrator, counselor, teacher, discipler, evangelist? Are all of these characteristics wrapped up in one man? Are most of them? A clear "no" is the right answer.

No man is a perfect pastor. He may be godly pastor, a good pastor, a faithful pastor and a patient pastor—but not a perfect pastor. Yet church members keep looking for the perfect pastor. Why this compulsion, this constant search when we know there is no such pastor? There are a number of reasons, some of which flow from the expectations of pastors and people.

Pastors Have Faulty Definitions and Expectations of Themselves, Their Calling and Their Task

Pastors have developed a type of messianic complex, at least partly due to attempting to fulfill faulty expectations. Pastors by nature are fixers; they think they can do it all and they try hard to do it all. Then sprinkle in a good dose of idealism and we have a mixture ready for distortion and exploitation.

Have you heard of Blue Mondays? It is a distinctly pastoral malady. This weekly low point is characterized by a depressed, sullen sense of inadequacy and unfulfilled goals. Why the regularity of Blue Mondays? Because pastors tend to have a silver bullet mentality. They prepare their sermon for Sunday as if it were a silver bullet and then mount the pulpit with the expectation that this is the sermon that will bring about the next Great Awakening. Yet, as normally happens, not only is there no Great Awakening, there isn't even a mild ripple or earthquake. So Monday comes and pastors go into a blue mood asking, "Why didn't anyone or anything change?"

At some point in a pastor's life he awakens to the realization that he is not perfect and cannot do it all. In fact, he may even sense that he has let God down because of the faulty notion that his "calling" should have immunized him from ministry failure. He may feel abandoned by God. Jeremiah felt all of these emotions numerous times in his ministry. At one point he said this:

> O LORD, you deceived me, and I was deceived; you overpowered me and prevailed. I am ridiculed all day long; everyone mocks me. Whenever I speak, I cry out proclaiming

violence and destruction. So the word of the LORD has brought me insult and reproach all day long. But if I say, "I will not mention him or speak any more in his name," his word is in my heart like a fire, a fire shut up in my bones. I am weary of holding it in; indeed, I cannot (Jeremiah 20:7-9).

Notice that while Jeremiah felt deceived, that is, called into something that was set for failure, he still acknowledged that he was called to proclaim God's Word. Even in the middle of his struggle with his call, Jeremiah knew that the Word was so much a part of his being that it was like fire in his bones.

The good pastor is not perfect; he is faithful to his calling. God's Word burns in his heart and he cannot hold it in. He is aware of his gifts and calling, which gives a sense of his abilities and his limitations. The more he is comfortable with this self understanding, with the strong sense of calling, the more he will minister with confidence. The focus of a pastor's ministry should not be so much on his performance, as important as that is, but on his beliefs that undergird his life. Paul told Timothy:

Be diligent in these matters [the proper exercise of his ministry]; give yourself wholly to them, so that everyone may see your progress. Watch your life and doctrine closely. Persevere in them, because if you do, you will save both yourself and your hearers (I Timothy 4:15-16).

Pastors become their own worst enemy when they allow themselves to believe they have messianic, fixer attributes. It is only when they come to a sane estimate of themselves and live within the context of their calling and seek to be faithful to it that they will find security in their ministries.

People Have Faulty Expectations of Pastors, Their Calling and Their Tasks

Church members have expectations for ministry and ministers framed more by experience and desire than by biblical teaching. These faulty notions are fanned by tradition and experience and are rarely challenged. These expectations create competing agendas which often place pastor and people on a collision course.

Church members hire pastors to be the consummate professional, the preacher, visitor, counselor, administrator, financial advisor, problem solver, healer, cultural commentator, and spiritual advisor. And pastors are expected to do all of these tasks flawlessly, without grumbling, without assistance, on a shoestring budget, and with smiles on their faces.

Obviously, the pastor's job description is commonly understood. The issue becomes the perception of how these tasks are to be performed. Pastors and people have different expectations of pastoral performance and it is because of this that conflict comes.

The perfect pastor? There is no such creature. But there are godly and faithful pastors whole-heartedly committed to fulfilling their calling.

What is able to satisfy the disparate views of pastors and people? At base, our hearts must be bathed in the gospel of grace and our minds transformed by the power of God Word and Spirit.

Dr. Dominic Aquila
President
New Geneva Theological Seminary
Colorado Springs, CO

INTRODUCTION

—⁓⁓—

London/Wiseman: What about the ways a congregation can take care of the pastor?

Bob: Congregational care of the pastor is more likely to happen if key laypeople are trained to know the unique strains, as well as the blessings, of being a pastor. For example, most laypeople don't understand how many pastors have a Monday adrenaline loss after a busy Sunday. They have no experience with the constant demands, the frequent role changes, the willingness of parishioners to drop everything emotionally on the pastor. The 'ain't it awful' syndrome we hear so often in the church; the peripheral issues that people bring to the pastor; the accumulative load from a thousand tiny parasites, like self-centeredness, control, pride and intolerance – these seem multiplied on Sundays, and they take their toll on many pastors the following day.[1]

****

Twenty-nine-year-old Paul served as a youth director before taking on his first pastorate. He, his wife and three little children entered the small town church with high hopes and abundant enthusiasm. The little church was started by a conservative group who had broken away from a mainline denomination. Initially, they maintained their denominational name, style of worship and form of government. Paul, agreed to take the call since many of the members were fairly comfortable with his theology.

However, only a few months into his ministry he encountered the first real challenge. During a regular board meeting, Paul was informed that he was not fulfilling his duties. Without a formal or written job description, the board, nevertheless, had particular expectations of Paul as the sole pastor. Paul, too, had expectations largely informed by the pastor of the church in which he grew up whom he considered a model and mentor. With his seminary training still fresh on his mind, he was operating on the assumption that what he had been taught was indeed the right and biblical way to minister. He was also enough of an idealist to think that the congregation and the board would follow his lead because he believed he was operating on biblical principles.

The board was composed of business and retired military men and women. Some were charter members. A few of them had purchased the acreage and built the facility with their own generous funds. They liked their old Southern denominational roots and church traditions. In the minds of these board members, the pastor was an employee of the board, a submissive servant hired to do their bidding. Any job description would be determined by them and adjusted as they saw fit. This young man's recoiling at their demands surprised and angered them.

Paul was baffled and became frustrated with the board. How could they insist that he was failing to measure up? After all, they had failed to communicate their expectations, and he was working very hard as the new pastor. It was an even greater challenge for him because previous pastors willingly submitted to the board. A precedent had been set and the board liked what they had before. Now he was kicking himself because he did not ask more probing questions during the interview process. How could they ask him to do all that a pastor is to do and also serve as the youth minister, church custodian and groundskeeper?

After wrestling through these issues, Paul and the board were able to come to a workable solution. A man was hired part-time to clean the church and different people signed up to take care of the lawn. The rest of the facility maintenance would take place during workdays. But the initial conflict was not without a cost. Paul's refusal to keep house and mow lawns led most of the board members to believe that he lacked humility and was lazy. Sadly, the tension between the two parties lasted the entire three years Paul served in the church.

Paul was the first pastor with whom I developed a friendship. My wife and I entered the church a couple of weeks after he and his family started at the church. Though I was still in the military, Paul came to treat me as his very part-time, unofficial and unpaid assistant. I was more of a confidant, gopher and yes-man than anything else. The role was easy because we shared a heart and service for the Lord, biblical convictions, youthful idealism, and a philosophy of ministry. Paul provided me with many opportunities to gaze into the world of pastoral ministry. Upon sharing his first ministerial challenge, I was likewise angered. The trouble was neither of us comprehended the heart of the matter. It was not so much about who was in control, though there was some of that to be sure. Rather, both parties were operating on different presuppositions and paradigms. Both sides defined and described ministry differently. What's more, each board member had in mind his or her own personal perspective as to what a pastor is and does, which at times conflicted with the other members. The board seemingly lacked an objective or absolute standard upon which to define and describe the person and role of a pastor.

Over the years, in many different churches, I have observed and experienced this dynamic again and again. Conflict between members in the congregation and the pastor or between the governing body of the church and the pastor has often times resulted from divergent expectations. People place expectations on the pastor and the pastor places expectations on the people. Most often these expectations are unspoken or at least poorly communicated; and too often these expectations are broken.

Most church members have good intentions toward their pastor. However, their often unrealistic understanding of what a pastor is supposed to be and do is based on an ignorance of the Bible's teaching. Thus, I resolved to research the Scriptures' teaching on the relationship and role between a pastor and his people.

The purpose of this book is not merely to address conflict between people and pastors, per se. Other books and resources are available to help resolve conflict between pastors and church people. The purpose is not even merely to define and describe the qualifications and work of a pastor. There are many good books which speak to that subject too. My purpose is to provide a tool to improve relationships between church members and their pastors, and bring them into greater proximity to God's purposes.

Such a tool is not only useful, but necessary. This conclusion is borne out of thirty-six years as an active member in various churches (independent, Baptist, and now conservative Presbyterian). This includes two years as a church board member, one year as youth director, four years as an elder, and eleven years as a pastor. In other words, God has blessed me with many years on both sides of the proverbial fence.

Before becoming a pastor I had a strong admiration for a few pastors, was ambivalent about a few, and also had little trust or respect for a few. The latter were those with whom I had some conflict. Hindsight has taught me that the conflict was often because they disappointed my expectations. Admittedly, most of those expectations were at best, personal, and at worst, unbiblical.

After I became a pastor, I encountered people who were disappointed or angry with me. Why? Some of the time I missed the biblical mark as a pastor, but most of the time I had disappointed their expectations. For them, I failed or violated their personal preferences. Time has taught me that a significant portion of the interpersonal problems and conflicts between a member of the church and me as pastor, centered upon misguided or even sinful expectations we had of each other.

There is much written about pastors, particularly their role and duties toward God's people. Yet, nearly all of it is addressed to ministerial students or pastors. On the other hand, virtually nothing is written about the member's role and duties toward the pastor. The Bible is the God-given authority for all matters pertaining to life and godliness (2 Peter 3:1-11). Since this is true, the Bible is the standard against which to evaluate a pastor's call, character and competency. It is also the authority on a congregant's service to his pastor and other church members.

So, this book is designed to be a tool. The questions at the end of each chapter are designed to provoke personal reflection or group discussion. The lessons embedded in each chapter and the appendices at the back of this book are intended to teach or incite further interest in studying God's Word about the various subjects addressed. It is my heartfelt desire that church members will be better equipped to choose a pastor, to relate to him and to support him. Pastors, likewise, will find ways to relate to the varieties of people in their church.

At the same time, this book is also a story. It's about a fictional pastor named Dan, and his family who live in a fictional small town. Yet, it tells the realistic, practical, humorous, exasperating real-life experiences of a pastor. Dan attempts to apply the Bible's requirements, roles and responsibilities of every pastor to his own strengths and shortcomings and to a diverse, and sometimes difficult, body of believers.

1

UNQUALIFIED APPLICANTS
NEED NOT APPLY

—〰—

Daniel's head was buried in his hands, elbows sunk into his knees when the part-time secretary bolted into the office. "I'm sorry," she apologized, "I didn't mean to interrupt your praying."

Practically in tears the thirty-seven-year-old pastor dismissed her interruption with a polite, "No problem. What do you need?" Melissa was impressed that Dan was so passionate in his prayers, but he felt guilty for not being honest enough to correct her. He was not praying; he was wallowing in pity and self-doubt about his role as pastor.

"Ms. Dumpleton is here to see you again. She's pretty upset." When isn't she? Dan thought. The woman was the bewitched Gladys Kravitz, Little House's Harriet Oleson and Cinderella's wicked step-mother balled up into one powerful matriarch of the church. The silver-haired woman made a fortune being a tough businesswoman, and wielded all kinds of influence because of it, and because of her family's long history in town. Since she inherited the town's original hardware store that serviced nearly all county contractors, her deep pockets financed the construction of the picturesque facility, complete with red brick, white pillars and a handsome steeple. Given that she financed the loan for the acreage and built the structure with her money, she believed she was entitled to respect, which in her dictionary meant power and control. She was an example of what G. Lloyd Rediger wrote, "A general sense of entitlement is growing in the church, as well as in society. Church members feel entitled to comfort and privilege. If a pastor does not please them, they feel free to criticize and punish. The business mentality that pervades the church says if the CEO (pastor) does not produce, he should be fired."[1]

Her heels hammered the creaky wood floor until she came to the office door. Irma Dumpleton impatiently barged in, barreling, "Mr. Lee! Mr. Lee, I tried all day yesterday to get you. Where were you?"

"Yesterday was my only day off, Ms. Dumpleton," he replied with restraint.

"Well, I left you plenty of messages and you should have returned them. Pastors are supposed to be available any time they are needed!" she rebuked as if he was one of her young employees. She had no time to sit, and as usual got right to the punch line. "I'm here to tell you that my brother is finally going to deal with you! Everyone is disappointed in you. It's about time something is done about your inability to pastor this church!" That was nothing new. In fact it was almost a mantra with the woman. For some reason, about every ten days, she had this apparent need to make clear the pastor's job description or his failures. She insisted on telling him at the office because he successfully avoided her after church on Sunday. Without waiting for him to reply, not that his reply was important to her, she announced that her brother was going to deal with him at the elders' next meeting. Her brother was an important elder, she reminded him. Having done her duty she rushed out as quickly as she blustered in.

He got up from his desk and pulled on the new door knob. The old wood door meowed until it was firmly shut. He didn't know whether to throw something and cuss or have an emotional meltdown. He chose to sulk in a stupor. It was barely twenty minutes when the matriarch's brother called. "Yes, Mr. Dumpleton? What can I do for you today?" the minister said with all the composure he could muster. Bernie Dumpleton had served as elder for over forty years. In fact, he was a founding member of the church. Most of the members feared the Dumpletons.

Even though Bernie Dumpleton had a dry sense of humor and seemed personable enough, he was controlling and critical. He nearly always got his way. "The elders and I have been talking. We just want you to know that your preaching is not good and it is certainly not great. What we need in the pulpit is a great preacher. So we have a plan. I'm going to teach you how to preach. I'm going to teach you good grammar because your grammar is terrible. The elders will critique you on a weekly basis. You will submit your sermons to me, I will edit them, and you will then preach what we approve. Later in the week the elders and I will meet with you to tell you how to better communicate. Now, we hope this plan is acceptable to you. We will discuss it Thursday night. Do you have any questions?"

Too stunned to respond, Dan automatically replied, "Not at this time."

"Very well. Good day!"

I would have never thought pastoring would be such a challenge, Dan thought. He wondered what happened to his long-held dream. No sooner had Dan become a Christian when he had this impulse to be a pastor. He could visualize doing what his first pastor did: preaching, discipling, teaching, counseling, spending time with people, serving others, and helping to oversee church activities. Other pastors he personally knew seemed to make a difference, and he wanted his life to make a difference too; an eternal difference. Those pastors were also as happy and fulfilled as his first pastor. Their lives and ministries made a big impression on Dan, so that the more he thought about becoming one the more excited he got.

Years later his dream came true. Dan was filled with exhilaration when his first church called him to serve. He entered the pastorate thinking he could have an incredible impact upon the lives of the church members, and take the town for Jesus. He worked tirelessly and enthusiastically at his sermons, Sunday School and Bible study lessons, along with all of the other pastoral tasks. When his dream fell apart after four years, he was crushed. He was ready to give up his passion altogether. However, a new opportunity availed itself, and Dan believed the second church could not be any more challenging than the first. So he took it. But thanks to people like Irma and Bernie he was dead wrong.

At first Irma's abrupt imposition and Bernie's arrogant dictate stunned him. Now Dan was hot. With his secretary next door and others within earshot, he confined his tirade to the arena of his mind. What to do? He is supposed to be submissive to his fellow elders, but this did not seem right. On the surface it appeared they were well-intentioned, yet he doubted his preaching was that bad.

Dan walked the half block home for lunch. There his wife prodded him into revealing why he was so obviously angry. Dan was not in the habit of bringing such matters home, but under this latest challenge he gave in. She tried to comfort her Danny, but he didn't want comfort. He wanted action. As far as he was concerned the old man's apparent display of pious aid was really camouflaged manipulation. After inhaling half of his meal he escaped to the home office and called the first of three seasoned pastors. No answer, so he shot off a two-page email describing the recent encounters. He sent another email to his pastor friend and mentor before dialing the third man. Thankfully he reached his old pastor and was calmed by the discussion. His counsel seemed wise, but Daniel would wait for replies from the others before formulating any action plan.

Late that evening he heard from the other pastors. Each had a different perspective on the matter, but all agreed on the crucial points. First, this was indeed a form of manipulation, and if the pastor gave in, he would forever after be expected to cater to the Bernie's and the other elders' every wish and whim. So Dan could not submit to them in this way. Secondly, he needed to demonstrate humility by admitting that he was not a great preacher. That he knew. It was, in fact, a major part of his personal turmoil as pastor. Third, he needed to formulate and present a counter plan. Such an admission would show he agreed with the need for improvement, though not on their terms. None of Dan's advisors had ever heard of an elder editing or rewriting the sermons for the pastor. Unable to sleep, Dan put on paper an alternate plan, and the approach he would take at the elders' meeting.

A short night of sleep does not make it easy to grasp the obvious or to evaluate things with a level perspective. Daniel tried hard anyway. He mentally rehearsed similar events of his five years as an ordained minister.

When the embattled man settled into his desk chair he picked up the page Melissa had typed for him. She was a very organized and efficient part-time secretary. The twenty-five-year-old single woman grew up in town and stayed after graduating from the local community college to help her widowed mother. She often typed excerpts from books or magazines that Dan had highlighted to help him with his research or sermons. The page was what he had been reading the day before when he was interrupted. It was on the state of the contemporary American pastorate, and it astounded him. He read that each month over 1500 pastors leave the ministry each month due to conflict in churches, burnout or moral failure. Eighty percent of Bible school or seminary graduates leave the ministry within the first five years of entering. Half of all pastors are so discouraged and disillusioned with ministry would seek other work if they could. A majority of pastors believe they are unqualified, and overworked. Most believe they did not receive the kind of training really needed to pastor in today's church.[2] "Man, I can relate!" Dan mumbled to himself.

As a whole the previous congregation had no problems with Dan's sermons. With the exception of one family and regular Sunday complaints from two well-meaning men most of the people seemed to receive his messages well and were challenged or comforted by them. The two men were on opposite sides of a theological debate on preaching. The one man complained Dan did not have enough law or application. The other carped on Dan for using application. After all, preaching with application was supposedly usurping the Holy Spirit's role.

The local leadership at his first pastorate failed to inform the new kid on the block of their philosophy of ministry, but neither had Dan asked. Since that experience, Dan learned that it is good to come to the interview at a prospective church with a list of hard questions (see Appendix A). Meeting after meeting the church leadership revealed the kinds of ministries or programs acceptable to them, but very few were acceptable to Dan. Nevertheless, he figured that over time he would change his views and comply with their desires, they would change their views and comply with his, or both parties would come to a compromise. He was a poor mathematician. During that time they informed him that his vision and mission for the church was wrong. This amused him since he formulated the vision and mission largely from notes he took at seminary, which they respected, and a book on the church by Edmund Clowney, whom they admired.[3] Dan ended up leaving because neither he nor they would change their views of ministry.

One intervening denominational leader determined that it was a case of bad leadership on Dan's part. At a meeting of the oversight board an elder told him, "You know, some men aren't cut out to be pastors." The implication was obvious. The chair of the oversight board tried hard to steer the discussion in a different direction, but the insinuation seemed clear: Dan was not competent enough to be a pastor, and as an appointed leader he was a big reason for the church's problems. Months later in another meeting, they surprised him by asking him to resign.

Dan and his family came to Grace Church with high hopes and expectations. It was a new start. A little less idealistic, he still expected things would go well, particularly since the candidating process, a unanimous vote and a great installation service appeared to indicate a good and long term of service. In spite of these foretastes, he quickly learned about clusters of people with allegiances to former pastors, and about the critical spirit among the leadership and a small, but vocal faction. Dan was quickly measured against each and every one of the previous pastors and fell short on many, many points. He did not preach like any of them, and certainly lacked the quality of those radio and television celebrities. He did not lead like Pastor S., or teach as well as Pastor B. There was no question he was not the door-to-door evangelist like Pastor K.

Even though Dan allowed the jibes and cuts to get him down, he came to his senses when his wife wisely posed, "If all those previous pastors were so great, and this church is so fantastic, then why aren't any of them here today? Why have so many pastors come and gone over the years? Danny boy, I don't think it's all about you."

Still, it was not easy to be the brunt of relentless criticisms, deserved or otherwise. Neither was it easy to have 6 percent of the congregation behaving as if the church was theirs to own and rule.

Monday was fun day. Tuesday was quiet and productive administratively. A pastoral visit was planned. Dan would take along his young seminary intern. After a delightful supper and a slice of Mona's heavenly, pudding-saturated devil's food cake Dan kissed the children good night and took off for the visit. It was his goal to visit a family a week in their home, but it turned out more realistic to visit two a month. He often went alone, though from time to time one of the other elders went with him. The elders frequently reminded him that a good shepherd visits once a week and expressed disappointment when he did not. They even suggested visiting two families in one night. Dan tried that but found people liked to talk longer than the allotted thirty minutes. Besides, he was more interested in getting to know the people than merely marking off one of his assigned duties. Twenty minutes accomplished little other than to read a verse, pray and offer a few platitudes. It did not count for the elders that he and Mona got to know people when they hosted at least one family a week in their home for supper or dessert.

Thus far, pastoral visits had gone well and were enjoyable. It did provide him some insight into the home life, which was often much different than what he witnessed at church. Dan learned from the pastor under whom he interned how to conduct a pastoral visit. He would go to each home in a role like that of a physician to conduct a spiritual checkup. He used a form he kept tucked in his personal Bible that he would fill out right after the visit (see Appendix B). It was a form he compiled from his internship lessons.[4]

If applicable, Pastor Dan would address the children first to get a sense of who and what they are and to assess, if possible, their spiritual condition. He would ask them about their walk with God, life at school, any interests, and if they had any questions of the pastor. Dan would pray for them and then dismiss them so he could have a relatively private time with the parent(s). If the husband or father was present he would start with him, inquiring about his spiritual condition, how he spent his Sundays, whether or not he was pastoring his family, meaning whether he led in family devotions, had times of prayer with them, taught them spiritual truths, etc. Afterward he'd inquire about other essential matters. Then the pastor would turn his attention to the wife or mother and ask her relevant questions.

Of course every family unit, as they are called, is different. A visit could be with a single person (not yet married, never married or widowed), a single mother with children or a single father with children, and so forth. Dan could learn a significant amount from a good home visit. Just by observing the home environment he could often tell their socio-economic condition, their material priorities, which side of the neat and organized scale they fell on, among other things. At the end of the visit, which normally ran an hour, Dan asked if there were any questions or concerns for him. Then he would read an applicable passage of Scripture, close in prayer, and ask God's blessing upon the person or family.

This evening was a pastoral visit with a middle-aged couple. There he found himself the target of a barrage of criticisms. He was thankful that the church's pastoral intern was with him to witness it. *What! Do I look like I have a bull's eye plastered on my chest?* he yelled in his mind. After addressing their personal problems, he dared to ask, "Do you have any questions or concerns about the state of the church?"

The firing commenced.

"You're making changes you have no right to make!" she pronounced. It was not right that he moved a table to the foyer or that the pastor's office was being remodeled.

"Why are those problems?"

"Because that's the pastor's office!" she replied as if he were stupid.

Dumbfounded, he sputtered, "But, I am the pastor!"

"Hrumph!" she muttered. Apparently it did not matter that the office hadn't been painted in years or that the old desk had not been cleaned out in over twenty-five. "Who gave you permission to change the pastor's office anyway?"

"Well… I am the pastor, you know. The elders said I could paint it and bring in the new furniture."

Still miffed and with her knuckles pressed hard into her sides she shot back, "They didn't talk to me about it! They should have asked the congregation first. How much did all that stuff cost anyway?"

Looking at the furrowed frown on her round face, Dan thought how sad it was for such a pleasant looking woman to turn into something ugly. The woman had naturally rosy cheeks, fair features free from the ravages of teenage hormones, with a medium cut of russet colored hair. Dan's wife, ever the diplomat who had no beef with the woman, described her as "pleasantly plump." "Katrina," he spoke softly and deliberately, "All the furniture in the freshly painted, newly organized office is mine, with the exception of the new desk."

Katrina immediately changed channels. "You don't seem like a pastor. Are you even qualified? Because you are not like any other pastor we've had before." she protested.

"Well, I myself don't like how you preach," Al shot off.

"Why is that?" Dan asked.

"Because you preach like a Baptist!"

"What is that supposed to mean?"

"I don't know; maybe because you show emotion or something. And you keep moving out from behind the pulpit. You're not supposed to do that! All I know is that I don't like it."

After two hours Dan asked the intern to close in prayer, where after the two found their own way out.

"Wow! Some meeting that was," sighed Dan's partner.

"More like a beating," Dan laughed, though his heart ached.

"Are all pastoral visits like that?" the student worried.

"No, not all. But if you are going to be a pastor, an elder, a deacon, or have any official role in the church you better be prepared to have a fair share of these kinds of 'beatings.'" Dan chuckled. "I had five wonderful visits in a row and left pretty encouraged with how those people were doing. But then enter into hostile territory and come out wounded. The battles and scars are the ones you tend to remember."

"And learn from the most?"

"And often learn from the most!"

Wednesday was rewarding as a counseling session went well for one of the members. The evening Bible study was filled with great fellowship and challenging questions. Yet when the Thursday night meeting coasted in, anxiety overtook him. Daniel determined to remain calm but assertive. The meeting opened according to protocol with Scripture reading and prayer. Items on the agenda were systematically addressed as usual. The matter of his preaching was at the end of the meeting.

Undeterred, Bernie reiterated his idea of having Dan submit his sermons for Bernie to edit or rewrite, and to have the elders critique him on a regular basis. At one point, Mr. Dumpleton said "Dan, your preaching is competent, but it is neither good nor great. We want a great preacher in our pulpit." He then blurted rather matter-of-factly, "I don't think you have it in you to be a great preacher!"

Joe, the younger but middle-aged elder, quickly intervened. "What he's saying is that he doesn't know what the Holy Spirit has in store for you." Dan ignored the obvious attempt at softening the blow. "Are you willing to commit to our plan regarding your preaching?"

With his stomach in knots, Dan looked down at the table and paused. "I'll have you know that I have consulted with three other pastors around the country, and at a committee meeting this morning I talked with two additional pastors and an elder. They all advised against submitting to your proposal."

"What! So you won't?" queried a very surprised Joe.

"No. I am not one of your interns and refuse to be treated like one." This took the seven men totally off guard. This plan of theirs was a practice they had established with a couple of their previous pastoral interns, though they had never required this of any previous pastor. "I am not going to preach your sermons. And I will not give messages each and every Sunday knowing they will be graded by men who have never been trained to preach or trained in public speaking for that matter. Do you know how distracting it is to preach to critics? Even friendly ones? Often you end up focusing upon the process, the gestures, the articulation, the phrasing and grammar, the content, or how the judge is going to score. It limits the freedom to preach the Word to the congregation. No, I will not do it that way!"

"That's insubordination!"

"No, it's not. What you are demanding doesn't come from Scripture. It's your *own* rule you are trying to force upon me."

Still somewhat astounded Joe sternly asked, "Are you so proud as to believe you have arrived at the pinnacle of your preaching capabilities?"

Dan, holding his emotions in check, responded, "Do you men know how I long to be a great preacher? Do you really believe I think I have arrived? You don't know how I struggle every day to grow, and not just in my preaching! I will never arrive at the pinnacle no matter how hard I strive. There is not a Sunday where I do not fear going into the pulpit because I am gripped with the burden of responsibility to preach to those souls in front of me. You don't know how often I agonize over this matter, how often I am tempted to throw in the towel! I am well aware that I am not a great preacher. It didn't take Bernie to tell me. But neither am I a bad preacher. Seminary professors gave me A's, my pastor during the internship said I was a strong communicator, and my sermons passed the scrutiny of the ordination exams."

Now in a soft voice Joe responded, "I didn't realize how upset you would be by this." Joe asked forgiveness for being insensitive toward Daniel. He was forgiven.

"I said I will not accept your proposal. However, please consider this one," Dan said as he gave each one of the elders a handout. It was a rigorous one-year plan to improve his preaching. It involved reading at least two books on preaching a month, subscribing to preaching magazines, and submitting one sermon a month to respected pastors around the country for their input. It also gave the elders the occasion, on a quarterly basis, to formally critique a sermon and provide useful suggestions using an objective evaluation form[5] (see Appendix C). Additionally, the plan included a proposal for Dan to return to seminary to take advanced classes in communication and preaching.

Each man studied the plan without comment. Dan continued, "As you see, this plan to improve my preaching involves you elders. However, each elder of this session must also engage in a program for self-improvement." Two of them nodded in agreement. "Each one of you must also read and study the topic of preaching. You cannot be in a position to judge anyone's preaching without a standard for measuring it. You must also commit to more serious, diligent and frequent prayers for the preaching of the Word. Without it, all other attempts at improvement could be futile." Dan was surprised at the willingness of the men to adopt the proposed arrangement. Bernie made no comment.

On a roll he added, "I am already in the process of sending sermon tapes to these other pastors. You will see their responses when I get them. I predict that each will have a different response." Dan admonished the men to find a credible standard against which to assess preaching and to avoid personal preferences. In the past, Bernie had made it clear that Dan needed to become like the previous pastor whom he considered the best preacher alive. A short discussion ensued about the various philosophies of preaching.

"You see," Dan added, "I don't believe we disagree on the philosophy or theology of preaching, but we do on the style and form. What do we do then? How would you determine what style is best? Do you see what I am getting at?" Several nodded in the affirmative. "Isn't the bottom line," Dan summarized, "whether the preacher is faithful to the text and whether the preaching ministry results in changed lives for Christ?"

The elders formally accepted the plan. Joe even admitted the plan was much more thorough than theirs. While things seemed to be resolved, Dan had an uneasy sense that the differences in method of preaching and philosophy of ministry would continue.

At home with his wife, Dan rehearsed some of what happened at the meeting. He went to bed exhausted, but satisfied that the counsel of many was fruitful. Friday morning Dan reported to the other pastors about the meeting. Each was pleased, but warned that Bernie would probably continue to take charge if he wasn't appropriately confronted.

By Friday afternoon Dan was at his computer placing an order for books on preaching by Haddon Robinson and Jay Adams, and subscribing to two magazines. Copies of the previous Sunday's sermon were mailed off to ten different pastors around the country with an explanation and a request for their critique. Dan also retrieved sermon evaluation forms used in seminary and emailed a revision to each of the elders (see Appendix C). He asked them to randomly pick a Sunday each quarter without his knowledge and use the form to assess content, structure, order, flow, presentation, articulation, and so forth. He invited them to put the quarterly assessment on the elders' meeting agenda when they were ready.

On Sunday morning two of the elders appeared relaxed, but Bernie's body language said he was still the antagonist. It was hard for Daniel to ignore Bernie shaking his head, rolling his eyes, and frowning.

Dan's tact was to seek out and serve those in need, in part because that was what he was called to do, and in part because he enjoyed helping others especially if they learned the grace of receiving and began to find resolution in loving, redemptive ministry. He also enjoyed it because he happened to realize that serving others kept him away from pity parties. He learned that among the needy are those where extra grace is required (EGR).

With them he had to increase the volume of kindness, mercy, compassion and wisdom. Those EGRs have a tendency to absorb and take everything from others often without any returns. If a servant is not careful, EGRs can draw him or her down like a black hole. Dan learned the hard way that these folks would consume all the time, energy and even material resources if he let them. All one can do is serve kindly and graciously, but also very wisely. The hard lessons humbled him to where he finally accepted the fact that he is not their savior. So, he deliberately limited the time and energies he expended with the very needy and focused those limited resources on discipling people who wanted change, growth, maturity, and to serve others. That, after all, was the pattern of Jesus.

Dan also learned to surround himself with encouragers and those who were authentic about their own sins and failures as well as their strengths and blessings. He intentionally hooked arms with men and women who served more than were served, who spoke the truth with love, and who knew the joy of Christ and relished life. He fully appreciated and needed the spiritually mature, not merely because of the blessing of mutual benefit, or merely because it bolstered and energized his ministry, but because he knew that one tends to take on the characteristics of those whose company one keeps.

Maturity means thinking less about yourself and more about others. Maturity is about loving God and others at least as much as you love yourself. As he explained to a group of teens at a snow-filled winter camp, "Obviously, babies are the most immature. Nobody is going to argue with that. What is it about them that defines immaturity? Their self-centered absorption. It's all about them! Me-me-me-me-me! As they grow they begin to see that life is not all about them. The more they think about and love others the less self-absorbed and baby-like they are. But what happens when you have a person in a grown up body who chooses to keep the emotional thinking and behavior of a baby? Not a pretty picture. In fact, self-centered immaturity in an adult body is down right ugly! I mean, who likes to see a grown person in a bonnet and dirty diaper throwing a temper tantrum? The more your life is concerned for others the more mature you are. God calls us to become mature like Jesus Christ. What kind of maturity is that? Jesus tells us, when he says, 'Love the Lord your God with all your heart, soul and mind and love your neighbor as you love yourself.'"[6]

Daniel spent his Monday working on household chores but thinking through the months at Grace Church since he accepted the call. Mondays are often down days for pastors, having been drained mentally, emotionally and many times physically the day before. People don't often realize how much energy an average pastor expends each Sunday doing the various works of service. Some studies have reported that the calories burned up through an hour's worth of public communication is comparable to that of an hour's worth of physical exertion, such as playing a rigorous game of football. So when Monday rolls around the minister is usually spent and needs refueling. That is why exhausted Mondays can be days of illness or depression.

Questions began to haunt Dan. He was satisfied the right course of action was taken, and in his heart of hearts he was not spiteful. But were the elders right to say he was being proud by not submitting to them? What is the true nature of elder authority? How is it they could judge his character like they did? Did Bernie have the right to make demands and order the pastor around or tell others in the congregation what to do, even if he was a founding member and the oldest of the elders? At what point does a pastor or elder lord it over others? What pastoral job description were they working from?

Serious doubts smothered Dan once again and he found himself slipping into despair. Maybe Irma, Bernie, Katrina and others like them were correct? Perhaps he wasn't qualified, or if qualified then not competent. Providentially Daniel picked up an article written by Ken Sande of Peacemakers Ministry. In *Strike the Shepherd*, Ken presented more "sobering statistics:

- 23 percent of all current pastors in the United States have been fired or forced to resign in the past.
- 45 percent of the pastors who were fired in one denomination left ministry altogether.
- 34 percent of all pastors presently serve congregations that forced their previous pastor to resign.
- The average pastoral career lasts only fourteen years – less than half of what it was not long ago.
- 24 percent of the churches in one survey reported conflict in the previous five years that was serious enough to have a lasting impact on congregational life.
- 1,500 pastors leave their assignments every month in the United States because of conflict, burnout, or moral failure.

The article went on to state that surveys "reveal that the most common causes for forced exits include:
- The church already being conflicted when the pastor arrives
- A lack of unity and the presence of factions in the church
- Conflicting visions for the church
- A church's resistance to change
- Power and control struggles
- Personality conflicts
- Poor people skills on the part of the pastor
- Conflict over leadership styles
- Dissatisfaction with the pastor's performance
- Theological differences.

All of these reasons for forced exits can be summarized in one word: conflict. When a pastor is forced out of ministry, it is usually because he has been unsuccessful at resolving differences with other people in his church."[7]

Dan seriously wondered if he was going to share the experience of so many other pastors he had known, read or heard about and be forced to leave? At this point his emotions told him to flee, but the good counsel of Jay Adams years before resonated in his head: "Never make a major decision when you are depressed, or if you are a pastor, on Mondays!" Besides, it was not in Daniel's nature to quit.

Though it was hard for him to hide his emotions, he could not reveal to anyone, except perhaps his wife and close friend Kent, that he was this discouraged. It wasn't that long ago at an elders meeting that the elders rebuked him for showing stress. As was their habit they waited until after the agenda had been covered before bringing up a "concern." Dan was beginning to hate that word because the elders used it so often.

Their concern was that not only had they noticed, but the deacons and others had noticed he exhibiting signs of stress. "Leaders don't show stress. You aren't being a good example of a leader if you show you are under stress. What could possibly be so stressful for you?" asked Joe.

"For one, this very meeting is stressful. Accusing me of just one more thing is stressful."

"It's not right that people should be coming to us and asking about your condition."

"No, you are absolutely right. It isn't good for people to come to you and talk to you about me. If they are so concerned, they should be coming directly to me, and you should be instructing them to speak with me about it first."

"Well, it's not good leadership. What are you going to do about it?" Joe pursued.

"You know…" Dan started, pretty exasperated. He took a deep breath and then sighed slowly. He shook his head, looked at each of the elders, then turned to his accuser and said, "You know, you are only adding to the stress or discouragement or depression or whatever you want to call it. Why? Because you come accusing me, rather than coming along side me as fellow brothers in the Lord or fellow elders in the ministry. You could have come privately to me and said, 'Dan, we noticed you're under stress. Is there anything wrong? Is there anything we can do to help you or encourage you?' But no, instead you sit as my judges, make your accusations and then demand I straighten up because you are afraid I am giving off a bad impression of what a leader is. This is disgusting!"

Nothing was resolved at that meeting. The elders never did ask why Dan seemed so discouraged nor did they offer to find ways to encourage him. In fact, they didn't even pray for him.

He wished he had Larry Michael's statement with him at that meeting:

Many Christian leaders become discouraged. The work doesn't go as one imagines, the church doesn't grow as one desires, lay leaders won't cooperate with one's leadership, people are excessively critical, or finances are down. The list goes on and on. Someone said that discouragement is the occupational hazard of the ministry, and Spurgeon was no exception to this rule. As successful as he was, he still experienced discouragement, and, in his case, it often deteriorated into depression. He became so depressed at times that he could barely function. In his lecture on 'The Minister's Fainting Fits,' Spurgeon opened with these words: 'As it is recorded that David, in the heat of battle, waxed faint. So may it be written of all the servants of the Lord. Fits of depression come over the most of us…The strong are not always vigorous, the wise not always ready, the brave not always courageous, and the joyous not always happy.'[8]

It probably would not have made a difference if Dan read them this or not. To them he had failed in presenting a good image of a leader: always up, always happy, always bright, and perhaps always perfect. To them Dan had sinned, because in their opinion stress and depression was clearly sinful. He failed. And that was stressful and depressing!

Once again Daniel found himself on the phone calling his mentor.

A CHALLENGE TO THINK AND DO

What do you think?
1. What main thing(s) did you learn from this chapter?
2. What biblical qualifications are needed for someone to be a pastor of a church?
3. Was Bernie reasonable to demand that he would teach Dan how to preach?
4. What is your response to Dan rejecting Bernie's and the elders' plan to improve his preaching and then submitting his own plan?
5. How would you handle someone like Irma? Katrina? Al?
6. How did you respond to the statistics about pastors?
7. What counsel would you give to Dan regarding his doubts on whether or not he is qualified to be a pastor?

Some things you could do:
1. If you do not already know, find out just how God called your pastor to ministry.
2. Discover what qualifications are needed to be a pastor at your church (and in your denomination).

2

DID GOD REALLY CALL?

—⁓—

Kent could hear the despondency in Dan's voice. Dan was now at the place where he doubted his call as pastor. The elder Kent was good at using questions to cull root problems from his counselee. Training and experience taught him that often times the problem people initially present are not the real issue or at least not the heart of the matter. "How have you come to that conclusion?" he asked Dan.

"The de facto leaders of the first church never received me as a leader, the oversight council of that church questioned my abilities, the elders and others in this church question my competence and do not accept my preaching, the men in our presbytery (the denomination's association of regional pastors and elders) are much smarter than I and seem more gifted than I am…and then the members in the church frequently compare me with previous pastors or celebrity pastors, usually to point out my deficiencies," Dan whined.

There was a long pause. Dan wasn't sure if Kent was distracted or disconnected or thinking. Though his door was shut, Dan could hear in the background his five and three-year-olds fighting and the baby screaming. Obviously Kent could hear it too. "Do you need to rescue your bride?"

"Yeah, 'suppose I should. Can I call you tomorrow?" he asked.

"Try me in the morning around 10:15 at the church office. Take care."

"Thanks, Kent. Call you then."

Dan's pity party quickly turned to frustrated anger with his boys. He yelled at the oldest, the obvious provocateur in the brawl, grabbed him by the arm, and ushered him off to the boys' room. Firmly setting Jake on the bed, he began yelling.

That summoned Mona, baby draped in her arms, to the room. "Dan!" That's all it took to awaken Dan out of his escalating rage.

"Jake, you stay right here. I'll be back." Dan stormed off to the master bedroom.

Dan did not want to get into it with Mona, but Mona insisted on confronting the problem. "You can't take it out on Jake," she started.

"I suppose you are going to say I'm unfit…"

"Don't even go there," she rebuffed with a stern scowl.

The pity party continued in his mind, *Man! If the elders saw me now they'd remove me for being a bad father.*

Husband and wife stared at each other. Dan sat down in the bedroom's wing-backed leather chair. He rested his right cheek in his fleshy palm, elbow dug into the armrest. Mona's deep brown eyes stopped glaring and now sympathetically watched him. Six-month-old Hannah began squirming for attention. She was still hungry. Mona nestled on the queen-sized bed, crumpling their silk comforter. Dan's straight black hair raked his forehead. His cobalt blue eyes punished the carpet. Hannah's rhythmic sucking now humored her parents. Calmed, Dan slowly rose and made his way to the boys' room. Jake was playing airplane with his hand. Dan asked Jake's forgiveness for being sinfully angry with him, and then proceeded to administer appropriate correction.

After Dan and Mona's teamwork successfully rested the children in their beds, Dan went back to his home office to reflect. It was too depressing, so he forced himself to work on Sunday evening's message. During a break he checked his email. Among the six was a short note from Kent: "Go back and review how the Lord has led you to this point in your life. Talk soon." Thankfully Dan had only a little more to do on his sermon. There was still time to stroll memory lane before retiring.

Mona entered the tiny office and wrapped both arms around his chest, while resting her chin on his head. She quickly read the email and decided to register her account of his call. Her thick auburn hair began to drown his face. "Hey! I can't read!" he protested. She grabbed his hand and led him out to the living room couch. There she ignored Dan's impulse to analyze things through theological or philosophical lenses. Instead, she reminded him that since he became a believer in Christ during his freshman year at the community college he was always involved in ministry related things, discipling and teaching. He also became a bookworm. "Oh, excuse me, a bibliophile," she joked, "who can never satiate your hunger for history, theology, and philosophy."

"Maybe I should be a teacher instead?"

"Mmmm, guess it might be much easier. But you wouldn't be happy there either. You like getting involved in people's lives and doing more things than teach. You are a good counselor and teacher, and great at discipling other men," she pronounced.

"Try convincing the grumpies of that!" Dan complained.

"You know what your problem is?" she pressed, as she leaned away from him. Mona had just finished Fitzpatrick's *Idols of the Heart* with a group of mothers of preschoolers and what she learned quite applied in this situation.

"Oh, and now you are going to add to the list?"

"Daniel Scott, your problem is that you've made the grumpies your idol. You are allowing them to be your judges and jury, and you are letting them determine your call and ministry. That's just plain wrong."

He looked at her and started to laugh. She frequently struck him funny when she got angry at him. "Stop that!" she insisted as she slapped his elbow.

"Yes, Madam Counselor," he teased. He knew she was right.

For the next forty minutes Mona did most of the talking as she chronicled a history of his call to pastoral ministry. "Remember what Dr. Adams said to you when you first arrived at seminary? If you want to do or can do anything else other than become a pastor, then do it. You haven't done it all, but you've had enough jobs since high school to know that of all the things you love to do, pastoring is at the top."

It was time for bed. Mona had given him enough mental fuel to burn into the wee hours of the morning.

In the morning he barely had energy to make the prayer breakfast, an event he enjoyed with the company of a few delightful men. He was relieved his eight o'clock appointment canceled, but he still had to prioritize the day's workload. At 8:30 the phone rang. The caller ID warned him it was a Dumpleton. "Grace Presbyterian, this is Pastor Dan, may I help you?"

"Daniel!" barked Ms. Dumpleton. "I'm calling you to tell you Ellie May is in the hospital. When are you going to visit her?" Mona's admonition immediately scrolled across his mind. "Well?" she commanded.

Something came over Dan. He had an unusual poise and presence of mind. *She is not my idol, and she is not my boss*, he reminded himself. "Ms. Dumpleton. I've been kind to you and quite patient with you since I came to this church. I'm not sure what you believe your role is in our church, but I will say this, you are not my boss. I am not accountable to you and what's more, I will no longer tolerate your abusive behavior. Do you understand what I am saying to you?" he commanded.

"No one treats me like this and gets away with it, young man!" She slapped her old phone down.

Dan knew this would not be the last of it, but perhaps it was the beginning of a radical change for him.

At 10:15 in the morning, Dan almost panicked when he realized he did not clarify if it meant Kent's time zone or his. Right on the button Dan dialed his friend. He was grateful for Kent's kindness even though the appointment was in Dan's time zone. After a quick update, Kent reassured Dan that he had rightly chastised Irma with a firm yet gentle diplomacy. The mentor was pressed for time so he got to the point. "I just sent you an email. Open it and follow along." Dan complied. "You are filled with doubt. I believe that wavering and constantly doubting is harmful at best and sinning at worst. Right thinking and right evaluating can help. Do you have the email?" Kent asked.

"It's open."

"Look with me then. I want you to continue working through your own history under God's providential hand that led you to this point. But I also urge you to put together a study for your church intern. Teach him from Scripture what it means to be called by God to pastoral ministry. Before you do, though, send me a copy and if you like, we can review it together."

"Okay," replied Dan.

"Dan, do you know what you are wrestling with?"

"Wrestling with?"

"You have allowed the varying opinions of some controlling people to determine whether or not you are qualified to serve in the office of pastor."

"You sound like my wife."

"A wise woman. Recall the qualifications given to elders in the Old Testament. They had to possess the credentials of godly character. They were to have a spiritual disposition and enablement from the Lord and were to possess an authorized call to office. In the New Testament God requires His offices to be filled by male believer-priests who manifest the right qualities, the right equipment and the right motivation.[1] You with me so far?"

"Yes, I'm reading along with you," Dan uttered.

"Let's see why it's necessary to have the right equipment. You know, even though I'm talking about pastors, this applies to elders as well. To have the right equipment is to say they must have the right gifts for the work. Now, you know God endows men with certain gifts and gives the men to His church. As I see it a pastor must be gifted and able to exhort, to lead, to serve, to share his resources with others, and to show mercy.[2]

"The pastor should also have right qualities. As Kevin Reed points out, 'These qualities focus upon the three important aspects of a man's life: his moral behavior, his knowledge of Christian doctrine, and his family life. An elder continually will be in public view. The respect an officer receives often depends more on his example of good character than from anything else about him'.[3] All godly men should have these qualities, but the man selected for the office of elder or pastor must be measured by these qualities to see if he is ready for the office.[4]

"This is important, Dan. I recall my first pastorate where most of the elders were selected merely because they were prominent leaders in town. Many of us had very serious doubts about whether two of the elders genuinely trusted in Christ as Savior and Lord. Three of them had questionable moral behavior, always living on the edge of biblical propriety. I even recall as a child, when one of my pastors had a major moral problem. However, because he was so verbally abusive and controlling, nobody dared challenge him about his immorality. Based on Biblical norms, not my opinion, none of those men should have been in church office."

Dan remained in a studied silence.

"The third thing a pastor needs is the right motivation. What this means is that he has a definitive inward, subjective call from God. He is responsive to the gifting and the call of the Holy Spirit in his life, and hence he desires the office. Often times this call or desire is so compelling that he cannot do anything else. But it takes other people and wisdom test whether his motives are biblical and Christ-like, or if they are self-serving."[5]

Dan interjected, "What do you mean by that?"

"Some have a desire for attention, or enjoy the idea they have of a pastor played out in the theatre of their minds. Let's quickly look at 1 Peter 5." Kent instructed.

Dan read the first six verses before Kent stopped him. "What are the ways elders, serving as Christ's under-shepherds, *not* to serve?"

Dan read, "…shepherd the flock of God that is among you, exercising oversight, not under compulsion, but willingly, as God would have you, not for shameful gain, but eagerly; not domineering over those in your charge, but being examples to the flock (ESV)."

"So then, other false motives would be one, the man must not be under outward pressure to become an elder or pastor, and two, financial greed should not propel his desire to be pastor. Years ago, while at a Christmas party, I met a young man; Bob was his name. He had just become a Christian. He seemed rather depressed and I figured it was because he was far from family during the special season. But it turned out that even though he was a new Christian his pastor told him he was going to become a preacher. Bob told me he didn't want to be a preacher, but was being forced into it. He felt trapped. We had a long talk about that. Sadly, his pastor had given him unbiblical advice."

"Well, we could exhaust the rest of the day listing false motivations, but hopefully you get the point, which is: one's motivation is important to interpreting the inward call from God." The teacher continued, "However, not only must the pastor have the inward, subjective call of God, but he must have an outward, objective call. This is where it takes others. As you know that call must be recognized as qualified and legitimate by the community of God's people (e.g.: Acts 6). He cannot merely assume that because he may be gifted and has that inner motivation that he can assume the office of elder or pastor. He must also be properly called of God through the appointed means in God's church."[6]

This material was a good review for Dan. Many times good counsel provokes the troubled soul to recollect the good things already learned.

"Hey, Dan, I gotta leave. You know what's next?"

Dan said, "More homework?"

"Yes, but what specifically?"

"Flesh this stuff out?" he queried.

"You've got it. Let me know when you're finished."

"Okay. Thanks so much, dear friend," Dan expressed.

"Hugs to your family. Talk next week!" Kent rejoined.

With his sermons finished, luncheon with a deacon, and a counseling session behind him, Dan was free to dive into his study. The subject of a pastoral call sat at the top of his priority list. He retrieved a few books from his growing library and set the pile on his medium oak desk. The first book was Edmund P. Clowney's *Called to the Ministry*, a short read, but insightful. He wrote down Erwin Lutzer's definition of a call, "God's call is an inner conviction given by the Holy Spirit and confirmed by the Word of God and the body of Christ."[7] He searched through *The Making of a Leader* by Frank Damazio, Patrick Fairbairn's *Pastoral Theology*, Thomas Murphy's *Pastoral Theology*, and read from John Calvin's works. In all, by the end of the afternoon, he had searched or perused through twenty books and several journal articles. Before he left, Dan arranged to meet with the intern. Dan and Bill agreed upon the following Thursday afternoon at 2:00 sharp.

Strangely, on Sunday several people, mostly new folks, approached Pastor to convey how meaningful the message was. Meanwhile, Dan's nemesis glared at him from a distance; he hadn't given up communicating his disapproval through negative body language and gestures. Dan turned away and deliberately sought out those who were graced with the quality of encouragement.

One of the deacons, a gifted encourager, expressed how excited he was to see growth, not only in the church but also in his own life. He was a retired chiropractor and seemed aware of the dynamic between the pastor and the lead elder. He approached and elbowed Dan. "Don't let him get to you. He's been that way as long as I've known him. Seems to have the gift of petulance." He winked and walked toward the exit. Dan had to look up "petulance." At first Dan thought he said pestilence.

Irma Dumpleton was noticeably absent from the day's church services.

Dan disciplined himself to take Monday off and spend it with his family. School let out early for Jake, so Dan picked him up from school, and then took everyone to a park outside of town for a fun picnic. That was Mona's idea. And fun it was, with the boys – Dan included – playing tag and mock football. On a whim they drove over to a petting farm. The boys enjoyed the pony ride, even if it was only six times around post. Jake and Ben had a blast trying to catch piglets. But their favorite part was a comical escapade with two goats. While the boys were having fun feeding the little goats, one of the bigger goats kept ramming their father when he wasn't looking. The most hilarious scene was when another gray, long-bearded goat managed to take a bite out of Dan's rear pocket and tear a substantial chunk out of his pants. Jake kept teasing his dad about his underwear showing. Dan wasn't as appreciative at first, but then saw the humor in it all, all the more so, when he quietly named the goats Bernie and Irma.

Tuesday and Wednesday were relatively uneventful, which gave him time to work on his sermons, Bible study and a Sunday school class. He also found a goodly amount of time to devote to the lesson on the call to pastoral ministry.

Bill knew in advance the subject of Thursday's meeting. He too had been reading and came prepared to bring something of value to the table. As he recently learned, that is one trait of a good leader – always bringing something of value to a meeting. Bill was a like-able personality: bright, assertive, gregarious. His blond hair, square features and chiseled physique leftover from high school gymnastics made him the star of many young ladies' eyes, and to his delight the object of doting mothers. He seemed to be a natural leader. Dan did not let this handsome intern charm him out of the rigors of the training program though. Bill also needed some hard knocks and a good dose of humility before he was really ready to take a pastoral charge. Like Dan, Bill came out of seminary filled with idealism and a great deal of confidence believing he was released to save the world – or a small church.

The pastor opened in prayer and got right to the point, reminding Bill that the subject of the meeting was about a pastoral call. He hoped that Bill brought the fruit of his studies. He was not disappointed. "I've just discovered the works of Charles Spurgeon," Bill boasted. "Have you read Spurgeon?" he asked the pastor.

"Oh yes. I'm familiar with the famous 19th Century Baptist preacher of England. Never met him" Dan said with a straight face.

Bill didn't get the elder man's dry humor, so continued. "Let me read this to you." He opened to a page in *Spurgeon on Leadership*:

How does one know whether he is called? As Spurgeon lectured to his students at the Pastors' College, he stated the following definitive signs for determining one's call to ministry:
1. An intense, all-absorbing desire for the work. There is an overwhelming passion for the ministry that motivates the leader to pursue it.
2. Aptness to teach and some measure of the other qualities needful for a public instructor. 'A man must not consider that he is called to preach until he has proved that he can speak.'
3. He must see a measure of conversion-work going on under his efforts. Specifically related to the role of the pastor, one must see evidence that one's ministry is resulting in the bringing of unsaved persons to Christ.
4. His preaching should be acceptable to the people of God. The people will provide sufficient testimony as to his 'gifts, knowledge and utterance.'[8]

Dan was not familiar with that book, so he asked to look at it for a moment. He read the table of contents, and then flipped through the pages. Bill was a man after his own heart; he marked up his books with various notations. One highlighted section read:

Some Christian leaders battle a lack of confidence in their calling/ministry. Through the trials of their calling, they might have lost confidence in their spiritual leadership. Perhaps they have their eyes on themselves rather than on God.

How can one become more confident? It sounds simple but is profoundly true: have faith in God. Draw closer to Jesus. Believe the promises of His Word! Spurgeon wrote, 'Brothers, if you do not believe in anybody else, believe in God without stint. Believe up to the hilt. Bury yourselves, both as to your weakness and strength, in simple trust in God.'[9]

The young intern also brought a typewritten page of quotes from other books and magazine articles he had been reading. That was a skill he learned from his mentor.

Dan thanked his student for the page and promised to read or interact with it later. The elder then placed a typewritten page on the table for the two to share. It would be Bill's copy. "Bill, since I wrote this, why don't you read it and then we can discuss each point afterward." The young man obliged and began by silently reading it. "Excuse me. I meant to say, 'Read it aloud,'" Dan snickered. Bill also laughed and then read through the page out loud.

"Thanks. Now let's take each point and you can ask questions along the way," Dan instructed. "First point is: if you have that special call to the Gospel ministry as teacher, preacher and Christ's undershepherd you will have an intense, all-consuming desire for the work. Turn with me in your Bible to 1 Timothy 3:1. Where it says, if any one aspires or desires the office of overseer, that word aspires means to stretch yourself in order to obtain it. You really want the office. The second term that says 'he desires a good thing' means that he covets or strongly sets his heart on having it. I recall one evening years ago while employed as a janitor but very active in leadership roles in a church breaking down and crying out to God to let me serve him as pastor. No line of work that I had done before or after that ever satisfied that incredible aspiration."

"But, what if you desire it sometimes and not other times?" Bill asked.

"Then perhaps you should consider seeking out another vocation, but still put your gifts to use in a local church. I did that for a while, but as I said, it was clearly not enough," counseled the pastor. Bill remained quiet and pensive.

"The next point is you should have at least the natural ability to teach. Some would argue that you should have the spiritual gift of teaching. Teaching and preaching are skills that can be learned." Bill was an unquestionably good teacher.

"The third is that you should see some fruitfulness in your evangelism or in discipling others. Not that everyone you present the Gospel to is converted or that all those with whom you work will turn into super Christians. Not even the Lord Jesus experienced that kind of ministry. However, there ought to be some growth in Christ among a few." Bill nodded in agreement and related how a couple high school and college men were growing and changing. Matt was the strongest.

"A fourth area, as we've discussed before, is whether other people see God's calling upon your life. Members in the congregation, deacons, elders, and pastors should be able to bear witness to the call in some degree." Dan went on to teach about the pattern of affirmation in the Scripture. Moses was called by God in Exodus 3. He answered the call saying "Here I am." His call was evident by the power of God working through him to accomplish the purposes of God. Samuel received the call from God according to 1 Sam. 3. Jesus, who had the mighty call of the God upon him, was affirmed by the Father and by John the baptizer. Jesus in turn called his disciples in Matthew 4:18-22. The deacons in Acts 6 were compelled to serve by the Holy Spirit, but they were affirmed as qualified and gifted by God's people. In Acts 9 we learn that Paul's call came at the same time as his miraculous conversion, but disciples had to bear witness to God's work and call upon him to serve as apostle to the Gentiles before he was sent. Timothy was likewise affirmed as an able individual ready to join the apostle Paul in ministry. That's found in Acts 16.

Just because one believes he is called and gifted does not necessarily make it so. The individual could be self-deluded. One important concept in the selection process to church office is that of emergence. In other words, qualified and gifted men will emerge or rise to the fore and be recognized by God's people and leaders (Acts 6; 20:28; 1 Tim. 3:1). God's people have an important role in helping the man recognize God's ministerial call upon him; and they would be of greater service if they understood the biblical requirements for an individual who would be pressed into the service of Christ's church.

Bill asked, "You did not mention family members. What about them?"

"Good question. They can be fickle. Sometimes they are the last to recognize your call, and for many reasons. Think about Jesus. His ministry was not accepted by his home town or even his own family, with perhaps the exception of his mother. That is, not immediately so."[10] Bill was nodding his head in agreement as Dan continued. "In my own experience, my father was very opposed to me becoming a pastor and my mother kept trying to talk me into finding a 'real' job."

Bill combed through his hair with both hands and then leaned forward. "What's the difference between a vocational call and the Gospel call?"

"Good question again," Dan said as he opened up a file drawer and retrieved a folder. Dan pulled out another sheet of paper and placed it on the table between the two of them.

As Dan read the paper, he explained along the way that the first and most important calling is to a personal relationship with Jesus Christ. God calls out to all people through his good news. "A good summary this good news is in Paul's first letter to the Corinthians, chapter fifteen. From other passages we learn that the good news is that Jesus, the eternal God, became man to live God's perfect standard of holiness because we could not as sinners; died upon the Cross to pay for those sins because we could not; removed our guilt;

gave to us His righteousness; and restored the broken relationship with God. He was raised from the dead and is now alive and well, ruling as the perfect God-Man in heaven."

He continued to read that this general calling is a universal one presented to all to whom the Gospel is preached, calling upon them to receive and believe in Jesus Christ and His work of salvation. This is an external call or proclamation (Matt. 22:14; Matt. 28:19; Luke 14:16-24; Acts 13:46; 2 Thess. 1:8; 1 John 5:10). It is a sincere presentation of the Good News in Christ to sinners, exhorting them to turn from their sins and turn to God for the forgiveness of their sins with belief. Theologians call this a universal call since God extends it universally, that is, he does not consider one's gender, nationality, race, or status in life when giving it (Isa. 55:1ff; Joel 2:32; Matt. 11:28; 22:14; John 3:16; Acts 18:9,10; 2 Cor. 5:20; Rev. 22:17).

Hearing no questions from Bill, the pastor continued, teaching that there is also a special saving call from God. This calling is internal. The Holy Spirit brings the Good News message of salvation to the very heart of a person, and that person is able to receive and believe it. Theologians have labeled this God's effectual calling. It is effectual because God's external call through the Gospel is made effective by the work of the Holy Spirit (Acts 13:48; Rom. 1:6-7; 8:29-30; 11:29; 1 Cor. 1:23-26; Eph. 1:18; 1 Thess. 2:12; 2 Thess. 2:14; 2 Tim. 1:9; Heb. 9:15; 2 Pet. 1:10 Rev. 17:14).

"What this means," Daniel remarked, "is that a person who has the inward call from God is responsive to salvation by the work of God's Spirit, such as we see in Acts 16:14 or 20:28. That responsiveness is expressed through one's character and life.[11]

"Then, through the gifting and work of the Holy Spirit in his life, God calls each one in Christ to fulfill his or her own place in the community of believers. All believers in Christ are believer-priests, and all have been given gifts to work out their particular role in the church body.[12]

"In certain cases God gives gifts to men in order to fulfill special roles as official leaders in his Church. Those men are enabled, and given an internal passion for the work. However, they must have the maturity, character, competency of developed skills, and be recognized by others as fit for the position."

The pastor went on to teach Bill that every believer has another calling in life. That would be to fulfill the God-given mandate to live a Christ-like life before the face of God by applying the natural talents and spiritual gifts God has given to him (1 Cor. 7:17; Eph 4:1-4; 1 Thess. 4:7; 2 Tim. 1:9; 2 Pet. 1:10). This is a person's vocation. The term is from the Latin word which means to call. "A vocation is more than a job. It is living out and doing what God has placed within that person to be and do in life," Dan pronounced. "While I am talking about Christians, even non-Christians, in some sense, have a vocation because they have been created in the image of God. Those outside of Christianity might explain this as what a person is destined to do in life. It might be as a doctor, plumber, or musician, a teacher or an artist. God is honored and glorified by this, as much as He is glorified and pleased by those whom He has called to particular kingdom office, such as deacon, elder or pastor. Now let's get back to this special call to Gospel service."

At some points their discussion got pretty heavy. Since Bill became an intern, he began to question if God's ministerial call was upon him. This class exercise was beneficial to both men. Bill said he was going to send a copy of the materials back to the pastoral search committee at his old home church. He thought the study could help them ask some good questions of candidates.

"Good idea, Bill," Dan affirmed. "When men go through the process in our denomination there are several stages to test whether they have the call. I remember meeting with the elders of the church where we were members while in seminary. They had already seen a fellow intern and me in action and were convinced we had what it took. Then, we had to meet with a committee of pastors and ruling elders. That meeting is still a vivid memory. The first thing they asked right after I gave my testimony of faith was, 'Why do you think you are being called to serve as minister of the Word?'" Bill was absorbing it all with a heavy contemplation.

"I told them about the passion to serve, teach and disciple people from the day God saved me. The call was different for me than for some of my seminary peers. Those guys went to seminary thinking they were going to be pastors because they really enjoyed theology. Then there were some like me who enjoyed people and had to learn to like theology. I also told the committee about the various ministry opportunities God opened up for me in churches, at college, on mission trips and the like. There were a number of people all along the way who kept saying I should become a pastor or asked if I was one." The mentor urged Bill to continue to evaluate his call, and then recited "If there is anything else you could do, then do it!"

"Hey, that sounds like what Barnhouse said," he announced energetically.[13] Bill lifted from Dan's desk his page of excerpts and gave it as a gift to his instructor. "Now would be a good time to read this," pointing to the middle paragraph.

Dan complied, "Sure, I'll read out loud:

Unless a man is divinely sent to preach the Word, his ministry will be ineffective to produce faith and life in those to whom he ministers. God must do the sending. I always tell young men who ask me about entering the ministry that they should never become ministers if they can possibly help it. If a man could be satisfied as president of the United States, as president of a band or a college, as a pitcher for a big-league ball team, or in another position of honor of distinction, he has not been called to the ministry. God has not sent him. When God sends a man there is a yearning, churning, burning inside him. Like Paul he must cry ...'Woe is unto me, if I preach not the gospel' (1 Cor. 9:16). This must be the heart feeling of everyone who had been sent with the Gospel.[14]

"I certainly agree with the yearning, churning and burning inside. But like I said, that passionate desire is half the equation. That inward tug toward dedicated service, must be identifiable, and must be confirmed by others, particularly by ordained elders and pastors. This call toward service in God's church is, as they used to say, a holy vocation. The pastoral ministry is not merely just another job or career. As my friend Dominic says, 'A call is what you do in service to others. A career is what you do in service for yourself.' The ultimate confirmation of a man's call is when he is ordained," Dan stated.

"That brings up another question," Bill interjected. "I've been taught that ordination is an Old Testament thing and not a legitimate practice for today."

"I've heard and read that too," Dan affirmed. "I believe there is sufficient evidence in the Bible that once a man has emerged and has had confirmations on his call, existing elders formally recognize him and ordain him to ministry. See 1 Timothy 4:14. The man comes legitimately to the office, not on his own accord, and this is a very important point, but by an official appointment to serve. You see, ordination is an act that sets a man apart to the office. There are unique situations where one is called and ordained by the very hand of God. Jesus, of course was the prime example of this. Abraham was such a man, as was Moses, Elisha, Isaiah, Ezekiel, and Jonah. But those were special circumstances. Jesus called and commissioned his disciples. In the New Testament we see Barnabas being called by God for ministry, along with Saul who became Paul. Paul, like the other apostles, received his call and ordained commission from Jesus. Then, the apostles appointed and ordained elders in various churches. Since then elders ordain qualified men to serve as pastors or elders. Ordination is the church's solemn affirmation of and public witness to the person's qualifications, gifts, and calling. It is also the instrument where the church prays for, supports and sends the man to a particular work."[15]

Dan went through the verses with Bill, then concluded that the church office of elder created by Christ (2 Cor. 3:9; 4:6) must be perpetuated with sound, godly and faithful men who are also gifted, called, and qualified (1 Tim. 1:11; 3:1-7; 4:14). It must be perpetuated through the laying on of hands by ordained elders of the church (Acts 6:6; 13:3; 14:23; 19:6; 1 Tim. 1:5; 2 Tim. 1:6). Think about how the church as a whole could be spared with so much grief when new cults arise. So many, perhaps most, of these cults come about because the leaders are self-appointed men with no confirmation or formal ordination on them.

The interaction wound down as the afternoon drew to a close. Bill walked out of the office and over to his room to close up for the day. Though more informed, he was also more conflicted.

Rolling his chair back behind the desk, Dan picked up the paper Bill had left for him. Bill had a couple of quotes from a book he borrowed from Dan's bulging library; a book that sat on the to-be-read shelf. Several sections of *Staying Power* resonated with him, such as:

At times I have felt that my work in ministry was wasted. At such times I identify with the apparent contradiction described in Isaiah 49:1-4. There God speaks of his high purpose for his people, comparing them to a sharpened sword and a polished arrow for divine use. 'You are my servant, Israel,' the Lord concludes, 'in whom I will display my splendor.' But the servant of the Lord has quite a different feeling. 'I have labored to no purpose,' he replies. 'I have spent my strength in vain and for nothing. Yet what is due me is in the Lord's hand, and my reward is with my God.' In apparent futility, the servant can only console himself with his ultimate reward from God. Most who have ministered in churches for any length of time have known the servant's paradoxical state; a stirring sense of call and a frequent sense of futility. We do the most important work in the world with the greatest resources imaginable, yet we sometimes feel as though we are accomplishing nothing. What gives?[16]

The pastor also meditated on a passage from Lutzer's book:

I don't see how anyone could serve in the ministry if he felt it was just his own choice. Some ministers scarcely have two good days back to back. They are sustained by the knowledge that God has placed them where they are. Ministers without such a conviction often lack courage and carry their resignation letter in their coat pocket. At the slightest hint of difficulty, they're gone.

I'm disturbed by those who preach and teach without a sense of calling. Those who consider the ministry to be one choice among many tend to have horizontal vision. They lack the urgency of Paul, who said, 'Necessity is laid upon me.' John Jowett says, 'If we lose the sense of wonder of our commission, we shall become like common traders in a common market, babbling about common wares.[17]

Dan reflected deeply on the meeting. Everything he and Bill discussed flew in the face of the few naysayers. It also bolstered his confidence; and he was all the more encouraged when he read yet another citation:

I have learned God has not called me to be everything to everyone. He has designed me with a unique personality, gifting, and background, and who I am in Christ will reach some people extremely well, while others not at all. My inability to minister to some people does not mean I am unqualified for ministry. I may be poorly equipped to reach some, but I am tremendously qualified to reach others.[18]

The pastor circled the notation to make sure he ordered that book too.

As he stepped into his home, Dan had an obvious change in his demeanor. The boys were at it again, but Dan's police action was better tempered. After supper and a little wrestling with the boys, came the bedtime routine of bath, story, prayer and kisses. Even the baby was cooperative, so Dan and Mona had time to talk more about Dan's call.

A CHALLENGE TO THINK AND DO

What do you think?
1. What main thing(s) did you learn from this chapter?
2. Have you heard and responded to Jesus Christ's call to receive and believe in him? How do
   you know?
3. What are the different kinds of calls from God?
4. What are the two sides to God's call to the Gospel ministry?
5. What do you think about Pastor Kent's comments that a person must have the right qualities, right equipment and right motivation to be a pastor?
6. What would you say to someone who said that God was calling him to pastoral ministry?
7. How is it some can be deluded in thinking they are called by God to ministry?
8. Do you know what God's call or vocation is for your life?

Some things you could do:
1. Read E. Fitzpatrick's *Idols of the Heart*.
2. Find ways to encourage your pastor in his call.
3. Do things in service to your pastor to give him more time to fulfill his ministerial call.

3

IS HE A CHARACTER OR DOES HE HAVE CHARACTER?

—⟋⟍—

"Just who are qualified to be elders?" asked Brad, as if on cue. Six men had gathered for a Saturday morning breakfast and leadership training at Mo's Café. The young intern had shared with the men his concerns about being qualified for pastoral ministry. Someone had asked if he would become an elder instead. Four of the men looked to Dan for an answer, while Harold was too absorbed by his pancake stack to look up. Mo was famous for cooking the best breakfasts in the area.

"Funny you should ask," chuckled Pastor Dan, "because that is what today's lesson is about." The notes were passed around, along with a fresh carafe of caffeine. Since he and Kent discussed this very thing a few weeks back, Dan decided to put together a class lesson. He hoped it would be useful to preach through a series on church elders, or to give out to church members in advance of nominating elders.

"God stamps a fairly high standard upon the office of elder. And this goes for pastors too since they are teaching elders. God requires the position be filled with believer-priests who have the right call, the right character and the right competencies. I think this is what is implied in Romans 15:14. Bill is going to teach the lesson on having a call from God," he said smiling at his graduate student. The men teased Bill until Dan brought the meeting back to order by pounding the salt shaker on the red and white gingham tablecloth.

Dan began by asking, "What is character?"

"He's sitting at the end of the table with egg on his mouth," ribbed Mike. All eyes were on Harold who was unfazed.

"Nooo; come on now. Be kind! I'm not talking about a character, but the definition of character." It took a while for the laughing to subside. Harold was a retired carpenter and a lovable bear.

Pastor Lee said, "One definition of character is the abilities and features that describe a person. Another definition is a person's moral composite or strength."

Amidst the waiters' discordant percussion a discussion ensued for several minutes about the varying views of character. Pastor Dan pointed them to two important chapters in the New Testament: 1 Timothy 3 and Titus 1.

"Hey! That's just what I've been reading about in the *Disciplines of a Godly Man*," exclaimed Jerry.

"Who is the author?" Bill asked.

"Kent Hughes."

Since Jerry virtually gulped down all his food, he was chosen to read the selected texts from the Bible.

"What can we gather from these passages that Jerry just read?" challenged the teacher.

Brad quickly answered, "He is someone who lives an exemplary life."

"What else?" nudged Pastor.

"The guy has to have a special quality so that others are willing to trust and follow him," responded Bill.

"Good. But there is a key ingredient we haven't identified yet." The silence gave the men time to order up more juice and coffee.

"I'm going to powder my nose," Harold announced as he lumbered off toward the alcove. Rheumatoid arthritis made it hard for him to shuffle through the maze of red vinyl-covered metal chairs. The 1950's decor wasn't chosen to bubble up sentimental memories of good ole times. Mo just never saw the need to change anything from the day she bought the joint. "See, it's back in style!" she would apologize. She'd still park that old '57 Chevy out front if her husband hadn't sold it twenty years ago.

"The character of an elder or pastor is not merely a matter of moral qualities. It's about becoming more like Jesus Christ and being an example of his holiness, his moral purity. It's about Jesus, men!"

The mood became serious as Pastor Dan continued instructing. Christ-like character is a very significant requirement for church office. Their focus was now on the next two pages of the lesson which were arranged thematically. "Let's go over these pages together," Dan said while passing the notes he put together (see Appendix D).

With spatula in her right hand shelved upon her hip, the five-foot five-inch Mo donned with a blue hairnet, white dress, pink and white pinstriped apron, and black and white saddle shoes came out to check on her favorite customers. She said that about all local customers. Although a faithful Roman Catholic, Mo respected the Presbyterian minister in town. She grew up a Presbyterian in Scotland, but became Roman Catholic when she married her American husband of Irish descent. She frequently reminded Dan, whose grandmother was Irish, that she liked the Irish. She always let Dan know that he was out of uniform without the priestly attire. Not aware of any possible impropriety she would call him "Father." It was cute rolling off her Scottish-Brooklyn tongue.

Mo was as sweet as her special syrup. She reminded Harold of the beloved 1960's TV character Hazel in a show by that name. Like a grandmother she egged on each "kid" to clean up his plate. It was almost unpardonable to leave anything on their plates or in their cups. "I'll not be bothered with a bunch of dirty dishes, mind you!" she complained. When everyone assured compliance she was off to the next table.

After covering the outline, Pastor opened up the time for questions. Hands folded and elbows resting on the metal table, Bill led off. "How mature should a person be before he can become an elder?"

"Yeah, doesn't elder mean older?" quipped Harold.

Smiling, Dan replied, "The Bible does not give us an explicit age in terms of years when a man can become an elder. However, here are some things to consider." He retrieved his old Palm Pilot and searched for the information. "Can't go anywhere without my brain," he joked.

"First, in the Old Testament elders were those who ruled God's people. See Exodus 3:16; 24:1, Leviticus 4:15, Numbers 11:16, and Deuteronomy 21:19. Elders were depositories of Israel's traditions and religious knowledge. Heads of clans were elder-chieftains who wielded significant authority. They too, were expected to have a matured skill in life that came from a well-founded knowledge in God's Law-Word."

Not allowing for interruptions, Dan continued. He taught that during the time of Moses, elders were indeed older men who had reputations for wisdom and virtue. The older of the elders were appointed to official positions in the community of Israel to lead, judge, and oversee God's rule in the Promised Land. Later, after the seventy-year Babylonian exile, elders governed local synagogues. The number of elders in each synagogue depended upon the number of people in its local community. These elders in turn became the pool from which men would be chosen to serve in the central government, called the Sanhedrin. The Sanhedrin was a council of seventy elders.

In Hebrew there are different terms for the various age groups.[1] For example there was the lad (*na'ar* or *bahur*), who was between twelve and twenty years of age. The words *ish* and *aner* often referred to males who had qualified for manhood through marriage, managing a family, or by serving in worship or the military. *Ish* or *aner* normally signified a man between the ages of thirty to sixty. A man had to be at least thirty to serve as a priest. It was rare for anyone to serve as elder under the age of thirty, and the standard age was fifty.

The third Hebrew word is *zaqen*. A *zaqen*-man was an elderly man or even an official ruling elder who advised and trained the younger generation of leaders. *Zaqen* men were fifty years and older.

"Oh, so you are saying that elders are no spring chickens?" clowned Blake.

Dan smiled, but did not respond. Due to time constraints he wanted to press on. "Now the meaning invested in the Old Testament word for elder carries over in many ways to the New Testament. I keep talking about elders and pastors. In our denomination there are two main official positions called offices in the Church: the deacon and the elder. Of the office of elder there are two types. One is ruling and the other is teaching. Both are Christ's servants who administer the Word of God and the rule of Christ in a local church. You can write these references down," Dan urged the three who were taking notes: 1 Cor. 4:1 and 12:28; Rom. 12:7-8; Eph. 4:11-16, and 1 Tim. 1:11.

"They are equal in authority, but the emphasis on the ruling elder is to govern the church while the emphasis on the teaching elder is to preach, teach, and administer baptism and the Lord's Supper. Of course there are varying views in the church at large about this. Some independent Bible churches have multiple elders who teach and preach equally. Some Baptist denominations have only one elder who is the pastor. Their other official position or office is the deacon. Then you have the Roman or Orthodox churches that have priests. Some of those priests function primarily in a pastoral capacity. Save all that for a church history class."

This was new material for a couple of the men. Hearing only the clinks and swirls of spoons in refilled mugs, and hushed sips from Brad and Bill, Dan continued his lesson. "Again, in our tradition, we understand that there are three interchangeable terms that refer to the same office of elder. The first is *presbuteros*, which is commonly translated into English as elder.[2] Check out Acts 20:17 and 28. When the Old Testament was translated into Greek, called the Septuagint, they translated the Hebrew *zaqen* into the Greek *presbuteros* over fifty times. Do you recall what age *zaqen*-men were?"

"My age!" grumbled Harold. "So you better respect me, you buncha whipper snappers" he warned as he slugged Blake in the shoulder. They all laughed.

"As it turns out, the term *presbuteros*-elder often has the sense of one who is mature and qualified. See 1 Timothy 5:17. The emphasis in this term is more upon a man endowed with age and wisdom," said Dan.

"Well, you got one out of two, Harold!" Blake taunted Harold, as he jumped quickly out of Harold's reach.

Pastor Dan didn't mind the boyish antics. It built camaraderie. Dan went on, "What denomination is named after this term?"

"Zaqenerian?" joked Blake.

"Man! What'd they put in your coffee?" Bill chastised.

"Presbyterian, of course, which has to do with the form of government we have. Our churches are governed by a plurality of elders. Strictly speaking, that means no single elder has the sole authority. The elders rule jointly. This is true even though a pastor or elder might believe he is has all power and is the only one in charge."

Dan then taught that the two terms, *episkopos* and *poimen*, often referred to the same position. *Episkopos* means overseer (1 Tim. 5:17) and is translated bishop in some English Bibles. It has the sense of one who acts as a guardian. There are several denominations that have a form of government based upon the role of the *episkopos*. They are the hierarchical churches such as the Roman, Orthodox, Anglican or Episcopal, and Methodists. The emphasis with this term is upon the function of an elder. The third word is *poimen* and is translated shepherd or pastor (Acts 20:17, 28; 1 Pet. 5:1-4). "Next question?"

"What does it mean to be above reproach?" questioned nineteen-year-old Nate, scratching his short red beard.

"Blameless," responded Bill.

Dan added that it means an elder's character as revealed in his behavior could withstand scrutiny or false accusations. "This is because his observable conduct is impeccable, and difficult to fault. However, we have to understand that while the Bible is concerned with behavior, it is not concerned with behaviorism. That is, merely outward, contrived or disciplined moral actions which are not rooted in a changed heart. This is also moralism, which was the problem with the Pharisees of Jesus' day. Moralism is hypocritical, and blatant hypocrisy often catches up to people. Good, exemplary behavior is not enough because God desires behavior that exhibits a changed heart, where life and lip matches the redemptive work of Jesus Christ within.

"To be above reproach means that nothing in his life is open to serious rebuke. He has an impeachable integrity consistent with Christ-likeness. Not that the man is sinless, but rather he exhibits the sum total of these godly virtues listed in these passages, and he does so substantially, though not perfectly," the pastor finished.

"Pugnacious sounds like a breed of dog," quipped Nate, reading from the list.

"To be pugnacious is literally, to be a striker. Apparently it was common for teachers in Greek and Roman culture, and rabbis in Jewish culture to slap, hit or punch their students when they did or said something for which the leader did not approve," taught Dan.

"See, Harold? Don't be a striker!" smarted Blake.

"I'm an older, not an elder," Harold threw back.

"In other words he shouldn't be a fighter?" Nate asked while wagging his finger at the two teasers.

"Woodenly put, he should not be a hitter. Now, of course, this is not to say that he could not engage in boxing or the martial arts for sport. It means he is not what we today consider physically abusive. He is not a violent man. He does not delight in fighting or hurting others," responded Dan.

He went on to explain that the godly man aspiring to office or who is already in office should not be contentious. He is patient (1 Tim. 3:3 cp. Gal. 5:22ff) and not pugnacious (Tit. 1:7; 2 Tim. 2:24-26). He has a restrained control and is therefore gentle (2 Sam. 22:36; Ps. 18:35; 1 Tim. 3:2, 3) like Jesus (Matt. 11:29; Acts 24:4; 2 Cor. 10:1; 1 Thess. 2:7). Neither is he argumentative (1 Tim. 3:2, 3; 2 Tim. 2:14), which means he is not a contentious disputer (1 Tim. 6:3-5; 2 Tim. 2:22-26; Tit. 3:9).

Dan gave an illustration of a man he knew who had been an elder in a previous church and wanted to become an elder in the church to which he had moved. He had many leadership qualities, but he also had a bad reputation for being highly competitive and contentious. If you said something was beautiful he would argue that beauty is an illegitimate concept and that nothing can be defined as having beauty, which probably did not go over well with his wife. When he played sports he was often the one who provoked a fight. He hopefully learned his lesson when told he would not be considered for office until he learned and displayed patience, gentleness and humility.

Sitting next to Dan, Bill jumped in with the next question, "Does an elder have to be married?"

"Good one," Dan said while patting his younger friend on the back. "This will be another one of those areas that has been and will be debated for a long time." It was another concern of Bill's. He was not yet married and had recently read a book by a popular author that said pastors and elders must be married.

Dan outlined his answer for them. "First, the text could be read either as 'the husband of one wife,' which most English translations have, or it could be read with a stricter literalism as 'a one-woman man.' Second, there are some who take this to say that an elder must be a married man. And some within that camp also add that he not only must be married, but he must never have had in his entire life any woman other than the one he married. Even if she died, he could never be married again because he is perpetually devoted to one woman. This view is in the minority and does not square with Jesus' own life who was not married, or with Paul whom most scholars say was probably not married, or even the general practice of the Church in its two thousand year history. Third, another group teaches that this verse means if an elder is married, he is devoted only to her and must not have any other wife or woman. This is the more popular position among Christian scholars, theologians and pastors."

"What about divorce?" chimed Harold, whose wife left him sixteen years ago.

"Let's save that for another day, okay?" begged the minister. "Being a one-woman man may have been addressing a cultural practice of the day, which was to have a wife and a concubine. The concubine was a slave. Let me give you a sense of what slaves were like," Dan continued. "Did you ever see the movie *I Robot?*" he asked looking around for any reaction. "Until one particularly special robot was developed who had been given the ability to express emotion and show concern for ethical issues, robots were considered impersonal, sub-human things that were at the complete service of their owner. That's a loose analogy for the way slaves were treated. Slaves were possessions who had to do virtually anything their masters wanted. So, taking the analogy, would it be ethically wrong for a man to engage in some sexual act with an anatomically correct robot that had such a capacity?" he asked the bunch of stunned males.

"I dare say, in our culture, even within some Christian circles, there might be those who would argue that since a robot is not a human it would not be morally wrong to engage in sexual acts with it. So it was with slaves. The general belief of that ancient period was that a man, married or not, could engage in sex with a slave and it would not be considered immoral or wrong. That's because a slave was a possession and non-person.[3] Therefore it is possible that this verse is addressing a common cultural practice."

The elderly couple sitting in the booth across from the little class looked disapprovingly at the pastor and then moved to another booth out of earshot. "The Christian slave owner must keep fidelity with only one woman, his wife, and not with any other," Dan concluded.

The men were speechless. The pastor had just served something fairly provocative, yet insightful.

Again Bill spoke up, "How new or young of a believer would disqualify him? I became a Christian in college and went straight to seminary, so in a sense I'm new."

"Some versions say 'not a recent convert' while others say 'not a novice." Certainly this disqualifies someone who recently converted to Christ. What do you think are some of the reasons for this?" he tutored.

Nate hurried ahead of other possible respondents, "You can't be spiritually mature and spiritually young at the same time."

"Excellent! Another reason?"

"I've seen a lot of big named people supposedly become Christians. Churches get a hold of them, make a big deal about them becoming saved and then put them into all sorts o' leadership positions. Before ya know it they're gone. Lots o' them deny Christ and move on to somethin' else," Harold declared with disgust on his face.

"That is probably the meaning of the phrase following 'not a recent convert' which is 'lest he fall under the condemnation of the devil,'" Dan replied looking into the senior's grey eyes. "It could be that he might fall into the same trap Satan did when he fell from heaven due to pride. It's a risk that the pride of the novice who comes into an honored position might put him into a compromising situation. Spiritually immature people are at higher risk of becoming inflated with a sense of their own importance. That seems to have been the trouble with the false teachers in 1 Timothy 6 or 2 Timothy 3:4. Immature or proud leaders desire approval rather than humility, desire service from other rather than serving others, or desire control rather than grace and freedom."

"There's at least one more reason I can think of. Anyone know?" asserted the minister. No one spoke. "An elder must be able to teach. Teaching in the biblical sense is not merely imparting facts or even merely communicating good, solid stuff. Teaching done by an elder or pastor instructs in sound doctrine in a way that guides God's people along the righteous path of godly virtue. It trains believers to become like Christ. Teaching the truth also has the element of guarding God's people from false teachers or ungodly leaders. Therefore, elders need to log time and grade in doctrine and life in order to be a seasoned and wise, and who can properly shepherd God's sheep. A new convert cannot possibly be skilled in the Scriptures well enough to teach in these ways."

The breakfast club had occupied two tables for nearly two hours. Mo waddled out again, this time with a butcher's knife, "Order lunch or pay rent!" she teased.

The brunch crowd was beginning to saunter in. It really was time to go, so Dan called it a day. Grabbing jackets and hats, each one threw their tips on the table. Nate, slower than the rest, complained, "What a meany beany!" prompting Mo to give him a swift kick on the seat of his faded jeans.

"Getcher self gone, you brat," she rolled with her Scottish brogue while winking.

"Bye, Mo!" they all nearly said in unison.

Waving her weapon she scolded, "You can come any time now, Father, just as long as yeh keep yur boys behavin' themselves."

While the others drove off toward town, Dan and Bill headed toward the hospital in his blue Saturn. Judy was in room 306 with two other patients. Sitting up in bed, she was entertaining her guests when Pastor Dan and the church intern popped in. Judy was recovering from surgery that removed her gall bladder. This sweet, middle-aged woman had more than her fair share of challenges. Two of the three visitors greeted the newcomers. Dan and Bill acknowledged each one with firm handshakes. Wes, however, was visibly perturbed by their presence. On the other hand, Judy's face lit up and she waved them to come over to her bed. Her younger sister just finished "prettying me up" Judy reported. And pretty she looked. So good, in fact, that it was hard to tell she had been through any sort of trauma.

"Stand right here," she directed Dan, "and you stand over on this side, Good Lookin'." The two newcomers complied after giving gentle hugs to the infirm celebrity. "What brings you way out here?" she giggled, as if she didn't know.

"They're supposed to be here. They should've been here to visit you every day," nagged Wes as he turned away toward the door. He was Judy's ex-husband's cousin. Wes, the twin son of the Dumpletons, was a member of the church. He was just as critical as his father. He was exceptionally charming with women, but could be caustic with men. The grapevine said he was going to be nominated for the office of elder. Bill was visibly angry at the snipe, but Dan's disapproving head shake at Bill helped to control his tongue.

Wesley's brother Les moved a thousand miles away years before. He was the proverbial black sheep in that family. Disowned by his father and the heartache of his mother, Les was the kindest of the foursome. The irony was that while growing up he had a reputation in town for Christian virtues, but had faded away from the Faith in which he had been raised. "Too legalistic," he told others. He was a child of the Church, outwardly obedient but inwardly rebellious. "What a nice young man," the eighty-three-year-old Bertha recited every time his name came up, not that his name came up often since he was an embarrassment to the long-time members. Rumor had it he was gay, yet no one knew if that was because the apparently righteous lot needed a reason to shun him or if it were indeed the truth.

Wes, on the other hand, was outwardly rebellious growing up. He, on the other hand, remained in town, stayed with the church, and recently took over his father's contracting business. His mother bragged that Wes was a godly man. There was no question that he was a hard worker, and very actively involved in the church. Once in a rare while Bernie would commend his son to others, though never in Wesley's presence. That would only make him proud, you know. Bernie never talked about his other son. Dan had been pastoring for quite some time before he even knew the Dumpletons had another child.

Dan was very concerned that a significant segment of the church was favorably disposed toward voting for Wes as elder. This group appreciated the Dumpletons for their hard work and deep devotion to the traditional programs at church. Some even boasted that Bernie had rid the church of bad pastors several times. Dan knew that if Wes became an elder he would leave, most likely because the elders would be pressured by the two Dumpletons to push for Dan's resignation. After all, something similar had happened to three previous pastors. This pastor was not concerned because he had already spread his resume across the denominational network.

At this juncture in his life Dan was inclined to find another line of work and be done with the ministry.

However, what distressed Dan more than anything was how seemingly blinded so many of the congregation were to the real Wes. Now, of course, nobody but God knows the inner hearts of men and women, but in Dan's mind Wes was clearly not qualified.

"Oh, he's qualified all right," insisted deacon Walt. Why? Because Wes knew his theology, could recite nearly all of the shorter catechism, was faithful at every work day at church as long as anyone could remember, was a successful businessman, and Bernie's son!

Oh sure, Dan thought skeptically every time he heard an accolade about this supposed angel.

The pastor knew something about the man he opposed, like the time a woman counselor and the minister counseled with Wesley's wife. She had the tell-tale symptoms of abuse, and her husband's behavior was consistent with patterns of abusive people. For example, he could charm one moment and then become explosive the next; he was constantly critical of others, bitingly sarcastic and condescending; he always blamed others for his problems; and he was a very jealous husband who kept his wife on a short tether. It was rare to see her out and about by herself. Those who knew about her plight could not charge Wes with sin or breaking the law, because she refused to call the police or bring charges against him to the elders so they could discipline him (as if that would go anywhere). One week she abruptly quit counseling and retreated all the more from church. Her husband, the pious star, apparently learned more than business from his father.

On another occasion, Dan invited Wes to lunch at Mo's. Midway through the meal Dan suggested Wes join his wife for marriage enrichment sessions. Immediately, Wes morphed into an ugly dragon, spewing a sulfuric tirade that drenched the pastor with verbal venom

– of course without any expletives – and then stormed out. A brief encounter before the explosive meeting was the last time Wes was even remotely civil toward Dan.

In the pastor's first year, during a men's cabin retreat in the hills, Wes had a sentimental moment and divulged an inner demon. Some suspected he was "lightly" drunk, which a few of the men claimed happens with light beer. It was a classic, sentimental, kumbayah event when, sitting in front of the retreating flicker of the last burning log, Wes became emotional, let his guard down, and revealed he was addicted to porn. No defense, but acting slightly shamed, Wes explained how it all started, how often he engaged in it or his fantasies, where he found it, and so forth. It began to sound like he was bragging. The men were stunned. The pastor cut Wes off when his confession turned toward blaming his wife. Always one with the last word, Wes then defended himself as a normal man with hormones and the fact that "all men are addicted to porn." Too bad neither Bernie nor the other elders were there that night.

"Don't let him mistreat you!" Wes ordered Judy as he pushed aside the male nurse entering the room. Wes was looking at Dan when he barked the sick humor.

Judy rolled her rich hazel eyes and was demonstrably relieved when Wes left. "He gives me the creeps," she declared through gritting teeth. "I don't even know why he keeps coming to see me."

"Why don't you tell us how you really feel," laughed Bill.

"Let's not go there," Dan said.

"Yeah, better not. The nurse would have to remove bed pans of the stuff I'm thinking right now. Even if he is my ex-husband's cousin," Judy half joked.

"Judy…!" Dan scolded, even though he could understand her anger.

She could never figure out why any of the Dumpletons, particularly Wes, even cared about her. Judy and her ex-husband graduated high school a year ahead of Wes. They got married two years later and had a baby within ten months. That promising little football player contracted leukemia when he was only four. At first it seemed like the bone marrow treatment was going to take, but the disease came back and when it did, it was relentless. Three weeks before Johnny boy died Judy's husband moved out. In the crisis Judy turned to God while Johnny Sr. turned to drugs. A year to the day of the child's funeral their divorce was finalized.

The remainder of the hospital visit was actually fun. Pastor and intern left Judy in good spirits with wit, humor, reading appropriate Bible verses and prayer.

During the ride home Bill fretted, "What are you going to do? Wes can't become an elder. He's not qualified!" Bill had observed enough of Wes to make such a statement. Since Bill's internship ended the last day of the year and the congregational meeting was traditionally held in January, it would not affect him. Yet Bill had come to care for the people and voiced genuine concern. There was a little more than five months before the big vote.

"Pray!" Dan said with a smile. How he wished he could divulge all his thoughts about the Dumpletons, but he knew that would not be good. Bill rightly perceived that a fourth of the congregation would vote favorably for Wes either because of fear or due to allegiance to the family. Historically, anything the patriarch and his family wanted they got. Bill theorized a positive vote for Wes could split the church, but Dan doubted that would happen. More than half the congregation had a strong allegiance to the church and had tolerated the antics of the dragon family for too long. The rest could not financially support a new church and there weren't too many other churches in town from which to choose. Besides that, there were more biblical ways to address conflict than fighting or fleeing. Since Christians are supposed to be peacemakers, reconciliation should always be the first course of action. Dan urged Bill to read the book on peacemaking by Ken Sande, and then proposed he use the materials by Peacemaker Ministries for the upcoming adult Sunday School quarter.[4]

The pastor then outlined his strategy for addressing this long term problem. First, he would preach a topical series on the qualifications and duties of deacons and elders. The sermon series would be a spin-off of 1 Peter 5, which speaks to elders. Pastor was finishing up 1 Peter 4. The timing was obviously providential. Next, he would supplement his preaching with weekly bulletin inserts, and would place articles on identifying godly deacons and elders in the monthly newsletters. The inserts would come from articles by the congregation's universally respected "great old dead men;" theologians such as Luther, Calvin, Knox, Baxter, Edwards, Whitefield and Spurgeon. Of course, anything of value by contemporary pastors, authors or scholars wouldn't be excluded. Third, Dan would follow through on the elders' commitment to improve upon their lives and roles by taking them through Adam's *Shepherding God's Flock* and Strauch's *Biblical Eldership*. He would also try and dialog with them about recommended books on preaching. Fourth, the leadership breakfasts would turn into bi-weekly classes that would last four months and be open to anyone. He hoped it would provide the forum for deeper discussion and study on the important subject. Fifth, two weeks before the congregational meeting voting members would receive a checklist against which to evaluate their candidate(s) (see Appendix E).

Dan was hopeful the people would override their propensity to vote according to sentiment and instead to think more biblically and objectively. However, the thirty-seven-year-old minister was hit with enough disappointments to teach him that he tended to be idealistic, and that he could be just as stubbornly anchored to his deeply embedded preferences. He had to try. Finally, he would outline the biblical requirements on the nomination ballot itself.

Bill clenched his fists when he declared, "All this stuff just makes me so mad!"

"Nothing *makes* you mad, Bill. No one is forcing you to be angry. You are choosing to be angry," Dan counseled, speaking as much to himself as to Bill.

"You know what I mean."

"Yes, I very much do. Welcome to ministry, Bill."

"I seriously doubt I'm cut out for this stuff. It's disgusting that Christians act this way."

"Perhaps you are not called to ministry? However, I can't tell you how often this stuff wears on me, how often I doubt or want to quit," Dan announced.

"What?" Bill chopped, pressing his back into the passenger door.

"At least once a week," Dan confessed.

"You? Seriously?"

Dan did not want to discourage Bill too much, but he realized that much like himself, Bill had graduated from seminary fairly clueless to the rigors, challenges and all too frequent battles that exist in Christ's Church. It was time for Bill to get a dose of reality, at least enough to knock those romantic spectacles from his face. Dan had done the same with a previous intern. That intern protested by claiming pastors were to think positively about life. The pastor explained that if medical schools put their future doctors through reality checks or the trials of the profession, or if the military put their elite soldiers through excruciatingly difficult training, why should it be any less so for pastors who have in their charge the destiny of eternal souls? "Pastoring is not for pansies. In a sense, the pastor is engaged in spiritual warfare, but in another sense the pastor is the Great Physician's assistant," Dan defended. That intern resented it, went into the pastorate anyway, and abruptly left after three years.

The stun was frozen on Bill's face as Dan revealed the heartbreaking statistics about ministers. "I've said it before: pastoring is not for pansies; or I should say biblical, God-honoring ministry is not for the wimps and the weak! Look, like my professor and friend says about common problems in church, 'It's not a church thing! It's a people thing!'" No sooner did Dan make that declaration than an overwhelming sense of guilt overcame him. *Am I a pansy?*

He went on to instruct Bill how sin is sin, and sinful people express their sinful ways in all relationships, even in the church. There are belligerent, obnoxious and abusive people in families, schools, businesses, government...everywhere. There are power players who are rich and poor, black, brown, yellow and white, among Americans and aborigines, atheists and agnostics, Baptists and Buddhists. Bullies come in all sizes. Some are only capable of controlling a small group while others are able to control entire nations. It's a people thing. What makes it so reprehensible in churches is that Christians are supposed to be like Jesus Christ. That makes us appear like bigger hypocrites than your average run-of-the-mill non-Christian hypocrite, because we become blatant contradictions to the Faith of Christ's truth, justice, righteousness, grace, mercy and love.

Bill stared at the black vinyl dashboard absorbing as much of his mentor's comments as the heat of the reflected sun. Dan continued the lecture giving a few of his own not so wonderful experiences as evidence that the pastorate is not easy. Certainly not the cushy job so many lay people think.

"Like you, Bill, I came out of seminary ready to take on the world with all of the youthful exuberance and a good dose of unrealistic fantasy. Any time I heard about something bad happening in a church or with a pastor, which was pretty rare, I figured it would never happen to me. But if it did, well then I'd be able to handle it the right way. You see, I had a junior messiah complex!"

Now the intern's eyes became fixed upon his leader's face. "That was how I was thinking just a few weeks ago." He meditated during the rest of the drive.

As the Saturn pulled into the cracked driveway lined on both sides with red bricks, Bill said, "But maybe this church is unique? Not all churches can have this many problems."

"Not all churches do. Some seem to do very well and have a marked absence of problem people, while other churches are far worse. There is much written in the past few years about how conditions are different for pastors these days compared to even in the recent past. That's what I've been reading in *The Heart of a Great Pastor*.[5] Nearly everything I've read says that the ministry is far more challenging than it has been. Pastors who have served for forty and fifty years are making that claim. I'm not sure if that's really true, especially when I read about how Jonathan Edward's own congregation treated him and then kicked him out after all those faithful years of service.[6] Or when I read about the rugged treatment Spurgeon received by his fellow peers and from a number within his own church. Maybe we don't read much about the relational conflicts or problems within churches from the good ol' boys back in the good ol' days of the Reformation or the Great Revivals, because none of the pastors and theologians were surprised by the sinful antics of churched sinners. They just dealt with them as such. Or more likely, the pastors and theologians were often too busy engaging hostile factions outside the church to deal with the pettiness that occurs inside the church. One thing is certain, there are many more books written by pastors for pastors addressing the conflicts, challenges and problem people than ever before."

"Like what books?"

"There's *Exposing Spiritual Abuse* by what's his name, Bixby's *Challenging the Church Monster*, *The Wounded Minister* by another whose name I can't recall, and finally the popular book called *Well-Intentioned Dragons* by Marshall Shelley. There are several others, which you can find in my library."

With the car parked and the ignition off, Dan leaned against his door, turned toward his young friend, and looked him squarely in his eyes. "Listen, it took me a while to realize that I am not a junior messiah. I can't save any church. I can't save any person. That's God's job. I have to remind myself of that fact every week, and then have to try to convince some people of that too. From what you've told me you have had it relatively easy through school and seminary. People listen to you, seek you out and follow you because you are bright, articulate, fun-loving, and caring." Bill smiled and blushed. "And it doesn't hurt that God gave you great looks and a strong physique!" Bill snickered and tried to dismiss it.

"C'mon Bill, you know what I'm saying is true. Especially the handsome part. I mean, girls and women are after you like flies on honey!" They both laughed. "But not any of that is going to make a lasting difference when you begin to pastor, or lead for that matter. Even with everything going for you, with godly character, competence, the whole nine yards, there will be those who will find you disappointing or failing. Some are so needy they'll try to suck the life out of you. Some are so selfish they'll try to use or abuse you. Some are so mean they'll try to do you in just because they want to. You can't help everyone. You can't save anyone like Christ can. If you are truly called to serve as God's minister, you can be faithful, you can be loving, and you can be what he wants you to be. The question right now is whether you are called, qualified, and pursuing godly character."

Bill headed for home. Dan walked over to the church office to retrieve a few things. He had a nauseous heart just thinking about Bernie, a couple of the elders and the prospect of Wes becoming an elder. Based upon his prior pastorate he could not collect optimism about this church. *Too many allegiances, too many old habits, too many negative people. Man! They're even affecting me! I wish I knew if my antagonists were going to win out. Maybe I should get more serious about looking for another call?*

A CHALLENGE TO THINK AND DO

What do you think?
1. What did you glean the most from this chapter?
2. What is Christ-like, godly character?
3. In what way(s) are you pursuing Christ-like character?
4. Why does the Bible have more to say about the character of a church officer (deacon, elder and pastor) than about their gifts and talents? In other words, why is character so important for church leadership?
5. Who stands out to you as having godly, Christ-like character? How so?
6. Does your church evaluate the character qualifications of a pastoral candidate, or of a deacon, elder or other church leaders? Why or why not?
7. How would you deal with a church leader (official or unofficial) who obviously does not have many Christ-like character qualities?
8. What would you do if Wes Dumpleton was nominated to be a deacon or elder in your church?

Some things you could do:
1. Evaluate your own character using Appendix F. Ask others to help you.
2. Develop a written plan to improve and grow in godliness (1 Tim. 4:7). Enlisting the help of a wise and godly person is recommended.

4

ONLY A SAINT WILL DO

—⁓—

Three weeks before school started the Lee family took vacation. They determined to spend one full week with Mona's family on the West coast, and then take two weeks to tour Salt Lake City and Yellowstone Park on the way there, and Las Vegas and the Grand Canyon on the way back. It would be a challenge with three little ones, but they were adventurous. Friends and family claimed they were crazy, but the two had planned for years to see those sites and they were as ready as a racehorse at the starting gate.

Most of the time they camped along the way, though they did splurge with gift money and stopped at motels in the two big cities. Cutting short their visit with family by two days helped cram everything into their time allotment. Neither one could say the vacation was restful. However, it was the adventure they wanted. Except for the flat tire on the highway going through the salt flats in Utah, and their three-year old nearly drowning at a Las Vegas pool, God graced them with a safe and smooth excursion. Because they were so preoccupied with their type-A agenda, picture taking, playing with and entertaining their children, and visiting Mona's rather large family, Dan had little reserve in his mind to give to the dynamics at the church. All in all it was a great time away, but Dan was not ready to return.

Someone once said that 98 percent of what you worry about never happens. Now, how anyone could scientifically quantify worry is a mystery. Before they left, Dan said he wasn't worried what might happen when he returned because he already knew what would happen. "So you're a prophet now?" Mona jibed. He defended himself by saying he very, very strongly suspected what awaited him because he knew the people and the patterns of the church. They had been in a changeless mold for more than half a century.

"It's like that one television episode on the original <u>Star Trek</u> where aliens who had the ability to live in a hyper-accelerated time warp invaded the <u>Enterprise</u>. From the crew's perspective time was normal, but something was wrong. From the aliens' perspective, the crew seemed like they were in suspended animation," Dan enlightened his wife.

Mona crooked her mouth and rolled her soft eyes with mocked disgust.

"So, you see, it's just like that. We're going away. To us it will seem like three weeks, but in reality it will be as if we never left. Nothing will have changed."

"Are you finished, Mr. Optimist?" she demanded.

"It's Mr. Realist, I'll have you know."

Mona made him agree not to play the prophet while on their trip. He agreed so long as he could play the king.

Pastor Daniel Scott Lee started out the front door the morning after their return – very, very slowly, that is. Mona watched her husband step out the door in slow motion. It took her a while to catch on, and him a second to catch it when she bounced the dog's stuffed animal against the back of his head. "Cut it out, Danny!" she pleaded. He sauntered with the gait of a bored child while flipping through the pile of mail he brought along. "I'm watching you!" yelled mother Mona from the front door. He stopped. "Get going!" she sang. He stopped indeed, but only because he came across an envelope from Mrs. Wesley Dumpleton with no return address. On the bottom left corner sprawled in nervous scratch were the words: For Pastor's Eyes Only! Abruptly he started moving again, this time almost in a jog.

He unlocked the old, oak, front door of the church building and switched on a few lights. He went to unlock his office, but was startled to discover it was already open. Obviously some of the things on and in his desk had been rifled through. Dan became angry. A wasted energy, for previous complaints about people violating the privacy of his office were met with, "It's our pastor's office!" Translated, "this is everyone-who-is-a-member-of-the-church's office which the pastor has permission to use." That was why the pastor kept all his important files in a sturdy, locked cabinet and why he kept everything else, including his laptop computer in his briefcase with him or at home.

Dan sunk into in his old, brown leather chair and quickly sliced open the envelope. "Dear Pastor Lee," Katherine scrawled in red. "Me and the kids can't take the beatings no more. I took the kids and we're going far away so Wes can't find us. I had to tell you. Thank you for all you done for me. Kate." The postal stamp indicated a delivery date five days old. His scattered thoughts raced to a bottleneck; he could feel a headache coming. Obviously Wes knew, but what was he doing about it? What about his parents? Did others in the church know? Probably, since you can't keep a secret like this in a town this small. Where is the secretary? Who's been rummaging through my things? Was it Wes? In a way this was good news for Kate and the kids. In another way this also was good news for the church. Well, potentially, since this should remove Wes from the list of nominations. Amazing - change had occurred!

The pastor hunted for the telephone number of the local sheriff. In Dan's mind it was the right thing to inform them of this letter. Knowing Wes, Kate was probably being accused of kidnapping. Since the children were involved, he was also legally bound to report any reasonably suspected child abuse. Dan made an appointment with one of the officers for 10:00 A.M. Then he called Melissa.

Melissa did not answer her apartment phone so he tried her cell. "Hello, Pastor," she softly answered.

"Hi, Melissa. Are you okay? You sick?"

"No, um. I can't come in."

"Perhaps tomorrow? Can Mona and I do anything for you?"

"No, um, I'm not the secretary any longer."

"What!" Dan gasped. "Why not? What's going on!" he demanded with a fist to his desk.

Melissa explained that she was fired by the elders two days previously for her supposed complicity in Kate's disappearance. She promised that even though she was an old school friend, Kate never said anything about leaving until she and the children were miles away and had called from her cell phone. The last time she would use it though. The police had come by to question her too. Melissa warned the pastor that he was already being accused of plotting with Kate to get her and her children out of town. The Dumpletons had made it known they believed the timing of pastor's vacation and Kate's departure were just too coincidental. Small town politics, he thought. He felt enraged and disgusted.

After Dan's short meeting at the sheriff's station, he returned to the office and systematically called each elder. A special elders' meeting was called for the next evening to discuss the Wes Dumpleton family and Melissa's termination. He immediately contacted the clerk and moderator of the presbytery to inform them of the recent turn of events and to secure the name of someone to arbitrate the foreseeable dispute. His day was full.

The elders' nightly meeting took place in the musty basement of the old church building. The dark paneling in vogue during the 1960's sucked much of the fluorescent lighting dangling between yellowed asbestos ceiling tiles. "Decorated in early attic," Dan often joked with Mona. The most recent remodel in 1972 added what became the sacred avocado green carpet. They did not invest in commercial grade materials, so the permanently stained and well-worn donation by Widow Bertrand remained an enduring fixture. The ambience enhanced the depressing agenda.

Dan initiated the meeting by saying he wanted to discuss ways the church and, in particular, the elders could help Wes, Katherine and family. He said that the second item on the agenda was the elders' firing the secretary in his absence. Immediately two elders retorted saying that the Wes Dumpleton family was not a church matter, and that the pastor should stay out of it since he already had done enough to contribute to the departure of Katherine and her children.

Predictably, Bernie picked up on what the elders said, switched track and accused the pastor of a number of additional things. In fact, he had come with a stack of papers he said were records of things he had on the pastor. He said that not only was Dan a bad preacher and a terrible leader, but that his character was questionable, because he knew Dan was responsible for Katherine running off with the children. Bernie called it a kidnapping. Dan denied the accusation. Bernie responded that, in the least, Katherine's departure was due to Dan's incompetence as a pastor. Bernie pulled out a few letters written by some of the discontented folks in church. All written, it turns out, at Bernie's request.

This did not rattle Dan. Not too much, that is. He expected something like this would happen. He opened his Bible to 1 Timothy 5:19 and read, "Do not receive an accusation against an elder except from two or three witnesses." Bernie assured everyone that he had plenty of witnesses. Pastor then opened to the appropriate section in their denomination's book of church government and outlined for them the procedures for bringing formal charges. "Men, be honest. If you want me to leave, just say so!" he admonished. "If you are going to accuse me of things, then do it formally." All but Bernie denied that was their intent. He then strongly recommended to them that before they take that step it would be the right thing to have someone mediate the problem and give appropriate counsel. Again, everyone except Bernie formally agreed to the motion that was made and seconded.

As for Melissa, the elders were convinced she had encouraged Katherine to flee. They did not believe Melissa's claim she did not know Katherine was planning to leave. The men insisted she had the responsibility to inform the elders, and especially Wes, of the Kate's plans. Therefore, they concluded that her actions contributed toward disrupting the Dumpletons' "good" family life. They remained unanimous in their decision and informed the pastor they had no intention of bringing her back or providing any other secretary, at least not in the near future.

The elderly Bernie switched gears again and announced that Deacon John, whom Bernie and his gang were hoping to vote in as another elder, was so distraught by the pastor's supposed bad character that he and his family were on the verge of leaving the church. Dan didn't know if that was another of Bernie's manipulative ploys or if it was indeed the truth. The elders agreed to have John meet with them. Dan protested, saying that the more appropriate action would be for John to bring his complaints directly to the pastor first, then if there was no resolution to bring an elder or two into the discussion. In other words Dan was urging them to follow Jesus' procedure for reconciliation found in Matthew 18. After a lengthy debate, Joe pleaded with Dan to allow the meeting for the sake of peace in the church. The pastor reluctantly agreed and the meeting was scheduled for the following Thursday evening.

Dan was surprised to find a retired pastor sitting among the elders next to John that cloudy Thursday evening. "We called Pastor Ray to come and mediate this meeting," Joe declared.

"Nobody informed me," Dan objected as he took his seat at the end of the table. Though he was a few minutes early, it was obvious the rest of the party had been there a while before Dan arrived. This was not good.

"You surely don't object to having him here, do you?" asked Joe.

"It is highly irregular and inconsiderate." The pastor was angry at this apparent ambush.

Ray responded that this was one of those occasions Dan should forgive and let love cover over a multitude of sins. "Can we start with prayer?" the senior pastor inquired, clearly usurping Dan's role as official moderator. Without hesitation the senior began praying for the meeting. With barely a pause after the amen, Pastor Ray proceeded by instructing each of the men to be biblical in their behavior. Everyone but Dan waved their heads to signal agreement. Turning to Dan, the elderly minister pontificated from 1 Peter 2:21-26 about how each man was not to be defensive, but rather to be like Jesus and remain silent before his accusers. Joe followed saying that this was necessary because Dan was hyper-sensitive and had a tendency to be sinfully defensive. Dan was clearly upset, but restrained his impulse to leave the 'beating.'

Ray gave some additional remarks and then turned to the deacon and asked him to present his complaints. John pulled open his briefcase and set a jumbled heap of yellow handwritten and white, typed papers on the table. He systematically, but not logically, accused Dan of many sins of character. He said that Dan was an unloving husband and bad leader in his family. Why so? "Because he takes vacations without his family." That was only partially true. Dan would take three to five days out of his allotted vacation time to get away by himself for prayer, to read, to plan out personal goals, to brainstorm on church matters, and the like. The elders took turns to complain about its being a wretched practice, a bad example to others, and definitely unloving toward his wife on Dan's part. One elder said the reason it was wrong was that he had never heard of anyone, especially a pastor, doing such a thing.

Bernie encouraged his deacon friend to bring up the example of Dan being too independent, uncooperative and insubordinate to the elders. One example he gave was when Dan did not get the elders' permission to help a local parachurch ministry in town. Why that was a personal offense against John was beyond Dan's imagination. And this accusation is an example of gossip, thought the indignant pastor.

John next accused the pastor of not managing his household. The proof was that Dan and Mona had placed their oldest child in the local public school. Dan reflected back to another elders' meeting where he explained to them that the private school was too far a drive and too expensive. At that session the elders told the pastor he should be able to find the money or direct his wife to school the children at home. They then accused Dan of not controlling his wife because she dared to mention to the other elders' wives that she and Dan were considering all options regarding their son's schooling, and one of those options was enrolling him in the public kindergarten. All Mona said was that it was a possibility for them to send Jake to the public school. She only told the wives so they might join her in prayer for wisdom in the difficult decision. When word got back to the elders, they challenged him about the supposed misbehavior of his wife. Mentioning the public school as a schooling option was highly offensive and considered sinful by three of the wives. Now it was also a sinful offense to the elders. The session chastised Dan for allowing his wife to say something so odious. They also commanded him to direct his wife to never bring up such a controversial matter again. Not only that, she was to bring any major matters or decisions to the elders first before saying anything to anyone in the church.

Dan insisted they had no right to violate her conscience like that, and that they had no such authority over him or her. Furthermore, she had done nothing wrong when she asked other women, whom she considered friends, to pray along with her about the issue. Dan further insisted the decision was more of a family matter than it was a church matter. But Joe rebuked the minister for thinking this. Since Dan and his family were public figures who lived in a fishbowl, nothing about their lives was private. "You are not your own, you belong to God and the church!" insisted Joe. The pastor's family is to be careful not to offend others, and also is to be the model of an ideal Christian family.

Dan supposedly violated 1 Thessalonians 5:22 because sending his child to public school was not abstaining from every appearance of evil. He also supposedly violated the exhortation from 1 Timothy 3:2 for elders to be blameless. Because Dan had done something offensive and sinful in the minds of several at the church, his character was therefore not blameless.

Years before. Dan had been of that same conviction as the elders. He had read many books on the subject of Christian education. As usual, Dan consulted with a number of pastors and seminary professors around the country. Most of them personally favored home-schooling, but they all admitted it was a matter of the parents' personal convictions. One of the pastor's friends suggested Dan would be better suited for a congregation which shared the same convictions on these and similar issues. After much study and seeking the counsel of others, he and Mona mutually concluded: a) since Scripture does not explicitly speak to schooling options it therefore does not forbid them from sending their son to public school, b) they would closely monitor what he was taught, c) due to financial and other family dynamics sending him to a school two blocks away was preferable, and (d) this was one opportunity to find ways to get involved in the local community for witness and service. With that, they decided the best option for their family at the time was to send their son to the local school. The elders would hear none of it and told him he and his wife could not do so.

Dan's protest was disregarded. In fact it angered the men all the more because now the pastor was not only a bad husband, but also disrespectful and insubordinate to the elders. They demanded he home-school his children and keep his wife in line. Now, Deacon John brought up the issue up again. It was none of his business.

At one point, Deacon John pulled from his pile a short stack of emails stapled together. They were correspondences between John and an elder from a distant church. Deacon

John and this elder knew each other through their mutual involvement with a parachurch group.

The teachings and practices of this large organization were more than suspect, and considered by many pastors and theologians to be cult-like. Dan's own research and communications with the leader himself convinced Dan that the man was very much like a cult leader and his teaching was out of sync with orthodox, Evangelical doctrines. Deacon John and others who followed this leader proclaimed the leader's praises. They said the man was the godliest person they had ever known.

The pastor in that distant church learned of Dan's extensive research on the man and organization, so he called Dan. The pastor told Dan that he was concerned because an elder and several others in that church were heavily involved with and committed to the cult-like leader. Dan and his pastor friend agreed that people like Deacon John and the elder idolized the leader to the detriment of their relationship with Christ and to the harm of the local churches.

In turn, during several discussions with his elders, the pastor of that distant church voiced serious concerns about the parachurch leader and organization. He told them he was not alone in his concerns, and mentioned Dan's name.

That elder, upset with his pastor and now with Dan, contacted Deacon John to complain about Dan.

The seventy-five-year-old, white haired Pastor Ray asked Dan if the things John read about were indeed true, and ordered him to answer with a simple yes or no.

"May I speak to this issue?" Dan asked.

"At the risk of being sinfully defensive, showing pride and a lack of humility, yes you may respond."

Though he believed he would not be wrong to speak and Ray was manipulating him, Dan chose to keep quiet.

With a modicum of success under his belt, John proceeded to throw more from his arsenal at Dan. Twenty-eight minutes of page-turning allegations apparently was enough for the tired moderator, so he stopped the deacon. "I believe we've heard enough. Is there anything that would be substantial?" John said no. Dan hoped the men would recognize how ludicrous the majority of the accusations were.

The meeting was about to close when Joe spoke up, "Perhaps there might be some things Pastor Dan has against John? Do you Pastor?"

"Actually I do," Dan said, thinking that he would have an opportunity to speak.

"All right. I suggest that you and Deacon John get together privately and work through your grievances," ordered Ray. Joe suggested the same place and time the following week. Dan, the whipping boy, was furious over the injustice of it all. Why was it acceptable for the deacon to bring charges and allegations against the pastor in front of a group of elders when it was the first time the deacon brought up the offenses? It was a violation of Matthew

18. Now, Dan was supposed to go to the deacon in private. Nevertheless, Dan reluctantly submitted to the elders' plan and put the appointment in his Palm Pilot. He left abruptly as the others shook hands and patted one another on their backs.

On the agreed upon date the following week, Dan arrived at the building thirty minutes early. He was prepared, and had put together a list of ways he believed John and his family had sinned against him and his family as well as against others in the church. The deacon arrived right on the hour. They greeted each other, and immediately sat down on khaki green metal chairs at the same folding table where most meetings were held.

Dan opened with prayer and then calmly presented areas he believed John was in error or sin. John wrote rapidly upon his yellow tablet. It took the pastor no more than five minutes to list how John, and even his boys, were sinfully offensive. The minister made it clear that John's devotion to the cult-like leader and his aberrant doctrines contradicted the teachings of the church and caused a number of problems within the church. What's more, John and his family's legalisms and judgmental comments insulted quite a few members and chased away many a visitor.

John stoically asked, "Is that it?"

"That is all. Do you have anything to say?"

"I need to take this home and pray about it before I reply."

"Okay, fair enough."

"When can we meet next?"

"How about the same time, here, next week?" suggested John.

"Very well. Next week it is."

John would not shake Dan's hand, but neither did he appear vindictive or angry. Dan remained behind to write about the episode in his journal, as he had learned to do many years before.

When the next meeting pulled up, Dan was again early and John right on time. John was just as somber as he had been in the previous meetings. "What did you come up with, John?"

"Well, Dan, I have to tell you. I've thought about it and prayed about it, and I have to say that I feel sorry for you."

"Oh?"

"I have to say that I have not sinned in any way at all, and I have a clear conscience about it. I feel very sorry for you Pastor, very sorry. That's all I have to say. Now, where do we go from here?"

Dan was stunned. The facts were clear enough to him that John had adopted doctrinal errors and had sinned in particular, obvious ways against him, his family and others at Grace. "I'm not sure at this point if we can go anywhere from here!"

"Then I guess that's it." With that John got up and left.

Though a week or two later, John's wife called Mona to apologize for offensive things she apparently had done, and John's children wrote letters of apology to Dan's two boys for offending them, nothing came from John except a letter addressed to Pastor Dan and the elders to announce he and his family were withdrawing their membership immediately. They would never have anything to do with the church or denomination, and they were not to be contacted by anyone from the church – ever! The letter was proof in Dan's mind that he was right, but was proof for Bernie and three elders of Dan's incompetence and "inability to get along with anyone."

Over the course of a couple months the pastor and elders met several times with a counselor who tried to address the problems and find biblical solutions. Seemingly the elders were willing to reconcile, but even the counselor pegged it when he said that Bernie had an unreasonable, unwarranted, and sinful hatred for the pastor. He said that the problem was not that Dan failed to measure up to God's character standard, but that it was obvious Bernie, and perhaps others, did not care for Dan's personality. The counselor also said that he could see no warrant for bringing charges against the pastor. Bernie, on the other hand, claimed that his family, another deacon and "many others" were willing to be witnesses against the minister. They had contacted representatives from presbytery saying they wanted to bring charges against Dan. The counselor advised the elders to dismiss the charges and recommended to presbytery they do the same. Further, he heartily recommended the elders bring charges against Bernie for being divisive and disrupting the peace of the church. The elders would not charge Bernie.

Bernie's attempts to put Dan on trial might have panicked the pastor if this crisis had occurred months before, but his thinking had changed. He had nothing to lose. If he left the church that would be great; if he stayed under the changing conditions that would be acceptable too. If there was a church trial, he was sure he would be vindicated. In the presence of the counselor, Dan initiated a bold exercise. He asked the elders to assess their character qualities on the basis of the biblical requirements for elders and pastors. Dan distributed a form he put together for the leadership training and as a tool for members to use when evaluating potential candidates (see Appendix F).

The first of the new leadership classes was held at Mo's Café on the second Saturday in September. Sixteen men, two of the wives, and Melissa attended. Mo was very happy, even if it meant arranging six tables to accommodate the crowd. The mood of the people was not with the usual joviality, because news of the recent elder meetings pulsed through the grapevine.

Dan determined to treat the matter of godly leadership seriously, but with tact and a little humor. "A good leader, particularly in God's church is a godly leader," he started off. "Before we look again at the character of a godly man and elder, let's describe the qualities of an ungodly man. Those of you who still have your handout from the last leadership class can look at your notes and help us by listing opposite traits of godliness."

Bill propped the new grease board and easel in the corner. Mo's grandson finished taking breakfast orders while Dan wrote these verses on the board: Isaiah 2:1ff; Joel 2:28-30; Matthew 15:19; Acts 2:19-23; Ephesians 4:17-32; Colossians 3:5,8,9; 1 Timothy 3:1-12; 4:1-7; 2 Timothy 3:1-4. "You can also look up these references," he strongly hinted.

Harold uncharacteristically started off, "He'd be pugnacious."

Brad nodded with approval and added, "Argumentative and greedy."

The spigot was turned on, and Dan had a time writing quickly enough:

- *Unrestrained control and undisciplined*
- *Given to selfish anger*
- *Given to much wine*
- *Self-willed and proud*
- *Irreverent*
- *Inhospitable*
- *Unjust*
- *Unwise*
- *Not Respectable*
- *Has a bad reputation in the church*
- *Has a bad reputation outside of the church*

"This is quite a list! Anything else? Has anyone searched those verses we have on the board?" They had, so Dan had to erase the first list in order to put up a more extensive one. Most everyone was taking copious notes as he quickly printed:

1. *Lover of self; self-centered; self-seeking – in other words, PROUD!*
2. *Boastful*
3. *Blasphemous*
4. *Disrespectful*
5. *Disobedient to parents and rebellious*
6. *Not trustworthy*
7. *Immoral and lives to satisfy immoral desires*
8. *Not loyal, someone who betrays others*
9. *Not thankful*
10. *Discontented*
11. *Slanders and gossips*
12. *Loves pleasure far more than God*
13. *Not loving toward others*

14. *Self-serving; does not serve others*
15. *Takes or steals instead of gives*
16. *Abusive*
17. *Outwardly religious, but hypocritical with no power for godliness*
18. *Deceived by false doctrines*
19. *Curses others instead of blesses*
20. *Foolish*
21. *Seeks revenge*
22. *Unforgiving*

Dan stopped the flow, stating that they had more than enough to get a picture of an ungodly character. "Would you say that someone who obviously displays a substantial amount of these qualities is ungodly?" he asked.

"Of course," they all agreed.

"What about half? Or a third?" he challenged. "Everyone is a sinner, and everyone is going to have all of these in a lesser or greater degree. Even believers will wrestle with a proclivity toward this sin or that," the minister revealed. Dan went on to explain that holiness is a quality all true believers have in Christ, and godliness is a question of heart, degree and perspective. Godly character comes from the life of Jesus Christ within. The more mature a Christian becomes by the life-changing power of the Holy Spirit and God's Word the godlier that Christian becomes. The character that is required of those who aspire to church office has a preponderance of godly traits, whereas the individual who has a preponderance of ungodly characteristics are definitely disqualified.

"Without a radical change of heart that comes from God and faith in the saving work of Jesus Christ, nobody has power for godliness. Godly character can be faked, but it's hypocritical and powerless." Pastor Dan reviewed the previous lesson and told them that the focus of this lesson was upon true holiness and godliness wrought by radical transformation in Christ. "Godliness is a matter of sanctification, which you all know is when God sets the believer apart to himself and does a special work of holiness in him."

"How many of you are saints?" Dan smiled as he asked the group. Less than half of the students raised their hands.

"Brad raised his hand. Isn't he arrogant to think that he is a saint? How would he, you or I know that he is a saint?"

"'Cause he's sooo gooood!" Blake taunted.

"Seriously. How would he know?"

No one was willing to respond.

"What does the word 'saint' mean?"

"Someone who is holy," called out Harold.

"Right. Who is holy?"

"Someone who is in Christ?" asked Melissa.

"Absolutely! Someone who has trusted and believed in Jesus Christ is holy. But, what does the term 'holy' mean?"

"To be a saint!" Blake proudly answered.

Everyone groaned.

"To be holy is to be set apart. In the biblical sense, it is to be set apart to God. If you are in Christ by faith, you have been set apart to God in him. This is why Paul often addresses his letters 'to the saints.' He is writing to those who are set apart to God in Christ. The basic New Testament word for 'holy' is *hagios*." Dan explained.

"Hey! Does that mean an old hag is an old saint?" Blake clowned. Brad threw a biscuit at him. Dan rolled his eyes.

"When the New Testament was translated from Greek to Latin, the word used for the term 'holy' was *sanctus*. What words we use today are derived from that word?"

"Sanctified," called out one.

"Sanctity!" declared an eager youth.

"Anything else?" Dan inquired. No one answered, so he said, "Saint. The word 'saint' comes from the Latin term for holy. To be a saint is to be sanctified. The process for growing in holiness is called 'sanctification.' If you are holy you will be godly. Am I being clear?" They all nodded affirmatively.

Paraphrasing the Westminster Larger Catechism question 75, he said, "Sanctification is God's work of grace where he takes those whom he has chosen to be holy in eternity and makes them holy through the Holy Spirit's powerful work. That power applies the death and resurrection of Jesus to them, renews their entire being after God's image because he has put seeds of repentance to life and other saving graces into their hearts. Those graces are stirred up and increase more and more to strengthen them so they more and more die to sin and rise into Christ's new life."

The students listened while eating breakfast and without taking time to visit. Pastor took occasional sips of juice or coffee. He did manage to eat his butter-soaked English muffin. He reported that the term for godly in the OT is *hasid* (Deut. 33:8; Ps. 4:3; 12:1; 16:10; 32:6; 52:9; 86:2; Mic. 7:2), is also rendered holy. "*Hasid* literally means 'one who has come under the bond of *hesed*.' The 'one who practices *hesed*,' practices faithfulness, kindness, allegiance and thus devoutness if used of one's relationship to God."[1] It can be translated as pious, holy, faithful servant, or religious.[2]

In the New Testament, the term for godly is *eusebeia* (1 Tim. 4:7; 6:3,5,6,11; Tit. 1:1; 2 Pet. 1:3, 6, 7; 3:11), which also means to be dedicated, religious, pious, and of the true religion (Acts 3:12;1 Tim. 2:2; 2:10; 3:16; 4:7,8; 6:3,5,6,11; 2 Tim. 3:5; Tit. 1:1; 2 Pet. 1:3, 6, 7,11).[3] It's worth noting that a predominant use of the word is found in Paul's letter to Timothy, the pastor and teacher whose assignment was to disciple and ordain godly men as elders in service to the Christ's Church.

The opposite quality, godlessness (Job 8:13; 13:16; 15:34; 17:8; 20:5; 27:8; 34:30; 36:13; Prov. 11:9; Isa. 9:17; 10:6; 33:14) is translated from various contexts of the Bible as hypocrite, proud, ungodly, unjust, profane, and worldly. In the Old Testament a godless man (*hanep*) generally means "one who is alienated from God." In the New Testament, the word (*hebelos*) is understood as someone who is profane or unholy.

The concept attached to the word holiness in the Scriptures has to do with inward character revealed through outward conduct. Holiness or godliness is the result of that orientation. Holy living is the consequence of being set apart to God. What's more, the result of a holy life that loves God is a life that loves people.

"Someone once told me that godliness is a quality which only pastors and other special Christians have. Is that true?" Pastor asked the class.

"I don't think so," responded one of the women.

"You are right. Godliness is not only for pastors or elders or special saints. Of course pastors and elders are to be examples of godliness. It is a quality any of you have who believe in Jesus Christ as Savior and Lord. It is the positive result of God's redemptive work in your life; a work he begins and promises to complete (Phil.1:6). If God has truly saved you, then he has called you to holiness. Mark these verses down," he commanded as he marked them on the board: Deut. 10:12, Hos. 6:6, Mark 12:33, 2 Cor. 7:1, 13:9, Gal. 4:9, Eph. 4:13; 1 Tim. 2:2 and 2 Tim. 3:17.

Dan read 1 Thessalonians 4:3-8 and 2 Peter 1:3-11, two explicit passages that tell us we are to be holy because God calls us to be holy. "But God not only calls each and every Christian to be holy or godly, he also commands it!" Dan said with a little more animation than usual. That got the attention of more than his class.

They took turns reading Matthew 5:48, 2 Corinthians 7:1, Hebrews 12:1 and 14, and 1 Peter 1:16. The minister also pointed out that even though holiness comes by God's Spirit through grace, holiness also requires work and discipline. Dan gave proof for this by having different people take turns reading 1 Corinthians 9:25-27, 1 Timothy 4:7, 1 Peter 1:13, 4:1-2 and 2 Peter 1:3-11 again.

"Holiness or godliness is a conforming work of God's grace that begins at the moment God saves someone. There is a definitive nature and time to our holiness; that is when we become saints. But holiness is also a calling we all have as believers in Christ as well as a command God gives us. At the risk of being redundant, all believers in Jesus Christ are called to be holy or godly! So that means Blake is holy," teased the teacher.

"About as holy as a donut," Melissa cried out.

"Ooooo," sounded a chorus.

"Hey! What's this? Pick on Blake day?" the wounded protested.

A couple of busboys cleared the tables while Mo's grandson and friend refilled mugs and glasses. "Here's another question: is holiness God's work or your work?" Dan asked, looking at Bill. A few answered it was God's work and a couple answered it was the Christian's work.

"Both!" declared one of the women with sweet confidence.

"Right!" Dan rewarded. He had someone read Philippians 2:12.

Brad obliged reading from his worn Bible, "Therefore, my beloved, as you have always obeyed, not as in my presence only, but now much more in my absence, work out your own salvation with fear and trembling."

"That's our responsibility. Some read this verse saying it all falls upon us to do the work of holiness. But now read the next verse, Brad."

"For it is God who works in you both to will and to do for His good pleasure."

"That is God's side of the equation. He is at work in each of you to desire and to perform his good will. What is his will except to be holy as he is holy by conforming to the image of his Son Jesus Christ. The Lord grants you the means by which you can be the godly and holy person he calls and commands you to be. He never asks nor requires of his people anything that he does not also give the grace and the means to accomplish. As I said, the agent of the transformation is God the Holy Spirit who works through the holy Word of God," Dan declared while providing them additional verses to demonstrate his point (1 Cor. 15:10, Eph. 2:4-10, Heb. 2:11; 4:16, 1 Thess. 5:23). He concluded the lesson by explaining how God gives additional means through his grace for his people to become more holy: baptism, the Lord's Supper, church discipleship and discipline, and prayer.

"The point I'm driving hard is all believers are chosen, called and commanded to be godly, but gifted men who serve as deacons, elders or pastors must be models of authentic godliness. Before you leave make sure you get this handout," he urged while passing out the same assessment form he had given the elders (see Appendix F). "Your homework assignment is to grade yourself in terms of developing godly character. Then, there are two additional spaces. If you are brave enough, ask a family member and a friend to grade you too. Obviously, this is not a scientific examination. It's simply a tool to check your own life against Christ-like character. Bring them back with you to our next leadership class. Don't forget to leave a tip!"

Blake pointed at Dan and shrugged his shoulders with a smirk.

"Nooo! The tip is for Mo's crew, not for me, Goofy!" he laughed.

Mo was apparently too busy to usher the gang out as she normally did, but as Dan was about to exit, the sheriff and his deputy entered the café. The threesome greeted each other and Dan introduced the officers to Bill. The sheriff excused the other two and pulled the pastor aside. Again, he wanted Dan's opinion about the charge of abuse Katherine levied against Wes.

For many pastors Sunday skips around too quickly. For some it is with dread, others with delight. Dan had mixed emotions about this Sunday. The barrage of criticisms from people like Bernie, Irma, Al and John extracted the joy and deflated the enthusiasm he once had for ministry. He took pleasure in serving others, teaching classes, discipling new or young believers, brainstorming for events, engaging in hospitality and even liked many of the administrative tasks for ministry. He loved many of the people and worked hard at caring for all of them. On the other hand, he hated the encounters with the critical people who were always the most vocal. That group shared the gift of discouragement and exercised the gift quite well. Their pious judgmentalism underscored by their natural ability to slice and dice their pastor with daggered looks or to murder him by mouth over and over again more than drowned those good things. It was hard for Dan to heed Mona's constant reminder to "think on the good things" when the dragons were perpetually in his face provoking him to think on the bad things.

Never one to quit, Dan persevered, hoping to outlast the goats or the sheep in wolves' clothing. He was able to fulfill his sermon schedule and systematically preach messages on the qualifications and duties of elders and deacons. Though the series was topical, he worked hard to stay faithful to the various applicable texts such as John 21:15-19, Acts 6:1-7, Ephesians 4:1-14, Hebrews 13:7 and 17, 1 Timothy 3:1-13, Titus 1, and of course the text from which he launched the many week series, 1 Peter 5. Midway through he distributed to every member the character assessment and challenged them to use it for their own edification (see Appendix F). At the end of the series, he distributed it again, this time with the other form (see Appendix E) exhorting the members to use the assessment to make a biblically informed decision in nominating someone for the position of deacon or elder.

A fascinating event developed out of the preparation: one of the elders resigned. This retired man now questioned his own qualification as an elder, even though he had held the post for a couple dozen years. He did not and could not teach, wasn't doctrinally astute, and recognized sinful patterns in his own life that he believed were enough to disqualify him from the position of elder. The elders tried to talk him out of it, but the pastor commended him for being honest and advised he retire rather than demit the office. But he retired and resigned from the session any way.

On the first Sunday in the New Year the congregation had a farewell party for their intern. The year sped away too quickly for most of the members, but seemed to drag like a hoe in a field of clay. When Joe publicly asked Bill about his immediate plans, Bill announced that he became engaged New Year's Eve and the two were planning a wedding some time in the fall. His fiancé was graduating with her master's degree the end of May.

What about receiving a call to a church? Bill had done a masterful job deflecting that question until now. Only Dan knew what he had decided. "I've made up my mind to join my father in his business," Bill blurted nervously. He had just dropped a bomb, exploding expectations and predictions with loud gasps followed by the silence of shell shock.

Joe, speechless, stood staring at Bill in disbelief. After an interlude like the length of a turtle's two-mile crawl, Joe ventured, "May we ask why?"

Unhesitatingly, Bill declared "No!" He then smiled, combed his fingers through his drooping hair and sat down. Bill composed himself like a mature and dignified man, and held his tongue from expressing his anger or revealing his reasons for not going into pastoral ministry. This brilliant and beautiful adopted son of the church could not have disappointed them any more than he just did. Not only were mothers and daughters terribly crushed by his announced engagement, but others so fond of him expected that he would soon outshine the best Evangelical preachers. Some even hoped he would replace Pastor Dan.

Bill, who deliberately placed himself next to Dan and Mona in an obvious display of support for his mentor, was embraced by a misty-eyed pastor. Dan knew that Bill wanted to tell them that he no longer believed he was called, especially if it meant taking a church like this one. He was unwilling to endure the kinds of attacks Dan experienced each week, knowing full well his physique, good looks and charm would never be enough capital to shield him from well-intentioned dragons, dogged wolves and rabid sheep. He was a great communicator, but four elders told him he was a lousy preacher. What church needs a lousy preacher? He was a fine teacher, but he could do that as a member or even as a ruling elder at his home church. Dan believed if God placed a call upon Bill, then the young disciple would eventually heed the call and enter the ministry. Bill was of the same opinion, but right now he was too disillusioned and angry to seriously entertain that possibility.

That evening Bill cleared a few remaining items out his studio apartment, packed his blue '97 Honda and drove it over to the Lee's garage. The next morning, filled with ham, eggs, a bran muffin, and a travel mug of sugared coffee in hand, he gave Dan and Mona strong embraces. Mona refused to subdue her tears, and Dan allowed himself to choke up. Bill was both sad to leave, and excited to drive off into the sunrise with happy anticipation of a new chapter in his life.

Two weeks and one day later the dreaded congregational meeting rolled into place. It was normally held near the end of January. Since the fall the church had seen an increase in new members who liked the pastor and his family. Breaking tradition, the meeting counted the largest attendance ever. Yet sweeping the hall with calculating eyes, Dan predicted trouble and a close vote for nominees. The pastor opened with the obligatory prayer, Bible reading and a devotional. The clerk officially reported that a quorum was present, so the official meeting began with the tap of that cherished gavel left behind by the church's first pastor.

Various committees gave their reports. The chair of the deacons gave their report. Joe gave the elders' report, and Dan finished off by presenting his pastoral report which reviewed the past and cast a vision for the upcoming year. The treasurer gave the financial report with enthusiasm. The tall, thin, middle-aged woman of Danish descent explained that the giving had been strong the second half of the year, no doubt due to the influx of new attendees and members. The church was able to invest the $10,000.00 record surplus in various portfolios. When the chair of the deacons took the podium to explain the proposed new budget, Wes quickly raised his hand to question the wisdom of giving the pastor a raise. The budget had initially passed the scrutiny of the deacons with only one objecting, and the scrutiny of the elders with only Bernie objecting. Bernie's family and small entourage began to take control of the discussion. The deacon attempted to bring order, but it took Dan's authoritative voice and position as moderator to calm things down. He insisted the meeting be conducted orderly, according to *Robert's Rules of Order*. Wes and a few of his gaggle grumbled.

The debate about the pastor's salary raged for a strong and long thirty minutes. When arguments seemed to be exhausted, the moderator put the question to a vote. Bernie stood up, hunched over by crippling arthritis. He raised his right index finger toward the ceiling, shook it, stretched his white haired and balding head forward, and began to pontificate: "Brothers and sisters, to have such a man as our pastor is a great disservice to the church of the Lord Jesus Christ. But to give him such a salary of which he is unworthy is to compound that disservice. It is a travesty that we would even consider half the amount he is receiving now, as we all know that any good Christian pastor is content with humble means, believing his reward in Jesus to be sufficient."

As Bernie continued, his face colored like a radish, his halting tempo increased with his volume, and his vitriolic diatribe slanderously chopped up the pastor and his family. When Bernie's fervor, egged on by his cheerleaders, particularly his son and sister, let slip an expletive through spitting pursed lips, Harold pulled his broad frame up and boomed, "Mr. Moderator! Point of order! No – point of personal privilege."

Everyone was stunned by this bold act of a normally reserved man. It stunned Bernie into silence as well. Harold was not that familiar with *Robert's Rules of Order*, but that did not stop him. "I don't know what you call it, but I have something to say!" Turning away from the moderator, he called to Bernie who was to Harold's front and left. Bernie turned around, wiping his handkerchief from the brow to the underside of his chin and the same again on the other side. "Are you a Christian, Bernie?" Harold scolded.

"What? What? Of course I am," Bernie squawked.

"Then behave like one! Enough already. Sit down!"

The majority of the audience clapped. The embarrassed elder submitted, sat hard upon his steel chair, folded his arms and scowled his ugly frown.

The vote was taken and it passed by more than a three-fourths majority. Pastor Dan was astonished. His calculations were quite wrong.

The next and last item was a call for nominations for the office of elder. Four names were verbally proposed and speeches were given in favor of each candidate. As anticipated, Wes' name was put forth by none other than his aunt, Irma.

Melissa raised her hand and then stood when acknowledged by the moderator. "I don't know if this is proper. People are giving speeches in favor of these men, but I have to say something against one candidate. I do not believe Wes is qualified for two big reasons: first, he is certainly not above reproach. He has a terrible reputation with many women in this church and a large number of people in town. Talk about a travesty!" she blasted at Bernie. "To have him represent us as a church and rule us as an elder would be a major travesty. Second, everyone knows he does not have his own home in order. The Bible is clear, if a man cannot manage his own house how can he manage the church? I beg you all to vote against his nomination," she pleaded with puddled eyes. Judy, sitting next to her, clapped.

Irma was now unraveling. She rose briskly, knocking over her chair, in order to give a defense of her nephew. She did not wait to be formally acknowledged by the moderator and began by attacking Melissa's character.

Harold, now quite angry, stood again, leaned forward, and pointed his knobby finger at the old matriarch. Like a dog whisperer in the role of alpha male, his demeanor and stance silently overpowered the woman. She ceased her speech as if an angel had magically removed her vocal chords, then slowly sat upon the chair that had been restored to her.

The ushers passed out the new ballots with information written on them to remind the voters of the qualities they should be looking for in a candidate (see Appendix G).

When the secret ballots were counted, Wes did receive seven votes, a significantly smaller count than could have been. Dan was relieved. He knew Wes would not be able to survive the training or a future vote of affirmation.

Seven or even ten votes could not overcome a simple majority. Wes, humiliated by the turn of events, stood and declared he was removing his name from the list of candidates and stormed out.

A number of people congratulated Dan for a successful meeting. The wearied pastor felt agony in the pit of his gut. At home he explained to Mona that most would see the meeting as a victory for him and those who stood by him, but it was terrible that the conflict continued without resolution. The Dumpletons and a handful of others were unwilling to reconcile. Victory? Yes, but at what cost? Changed lives or hearts? Perhaps.

Mona, as usual, saw things differently. Dan's strategy was effective. People voted wisely and more biblically. They looked at the character requirements of Scripture, measured various men against them and found only three able to pass the test. Four months prior to the meeting the grapevine reported that there was going to be at least eight nominees. Four of them were strongly opposed to change, to new people, and to the pastor. Yet only three men were firmly nominated, and those three were men of godly integrity. What would Bernie, Wes, Irma and the others do now? It didn't matter this evening. Dan went to bed a bit more assured.

A CHALLENGE TO THINK AND DO

What do you think?
1. Are you a saint? How do you know?
2. How saintly does a pastor have to be? A deacon? An elder?
3. Is it really true that the results of a holy life that loves God is a life that loves people?
4. Were the elders justified in firing Melissa, the secretary?
5. What advice would you give the elders about whether or not to discuss the recent developments between Wes and Katrina?
6. Was it right for the elders to insist that Pastor Dan meet with Deacon John to hear the deacon's accusations against him in the presence of the elders? Why or why not?
7. Deacon John accused the pastor of sin and bad character. Were his accusations biblically legitimate? Why or why not.
8. Is it wrong or sinful to defend yourself against the accusations of others?

Some things you could do:
1. Follow through on Pastor Dan's lesson on holiness, and study more on the subject.
2. If you have not already done so, read Jerry Bridges' *The Pursuit of Holiness* and/or *The Practice of Godliness*. Better yet, read and study it with others.
3. Read and discuss with others Appendix E's *How to Identify a Potential Church Officer*.

5

A WISE GUY

—⁓—

Matt poked his head in the door of the office and knocked twice. "Hey, Matt! C'mon in!" Dan responded. "What's going on?" Matthew, a freshman and sports jock at the community college had become a Christian four years earlier at a youth camp sponsored by the association of the denomination's regional churches to which Grace Church belonged.

"Two of my classes were canceled so I thought I'd come and check on you."

"Check on me? Well, you caught me. I confess, here I am working away, "Dan teased. "How'd you get here?"

"A friend dropped me off. Do you have time to talk? I know you keep busy, but I've got a question."

"There's someone who is meeting me here in fifteen minutes. Is it something I can answer quickly?"

"Well, no. Not really."

"What's it about?"

"It's about temptation. Like, how do you handle all these temptations?"

"Life is filled with temptations, Matt." Though the pastor suspected what Matt was alluding to, he asked, "What kinds of temptation? Temptation in general or temptation toward a specific sin?"

"Uhhh, with stuff like girls, and sex and all. How do you handle it? Pictures, and porn and girls who are aggressive and, well, uh, I don't know what to do."

"Look, that's a topic that will take more than what we have right now. Can it wait until tonight?"

"No. Can't tonight, I've gotta work."

"How about tomorrow? What's your schedule like?"

"Tomorrow? Let's see. After three is okay."

Dan checked his calendar and confirmed he had an hour open for Matt.

"Cool. Thanks, Man. I also have another question for you, which maybe we can talk about on Friday? What would you say is the one main thing a pastor should have in order to handle all the stuff a pastor does?"

"Just one main thing? It wish it were that easy," Dan replied. "But, okay, I'll give it some thought and we'll talk about it Friday."

Dan drove by the college the next afternoon and took Matt to the church office. Matt's main concern was whether it was a sin to be tempted. His second concern was how to deal with temptations that come his way, especially sexual ones. They first talked about lust and love, dating and marriage, and sex. Then the pastor turned to James 1:12-20. "What does this passage tell us we need in the face of the temptations we have?"

"Wisdom."

"Right. What is true, biblical, godly wisdom?"

"Having common sense?" Matt questioned timidly.

"That's part of it. Biblical wisdom is the spiritual skill of thinking and applying God's thoughts to life's issues. As a believer in the Lord Jesus Christ tests and trials give you opportunities to demonstrate and confirm what you know and believe, and how you live out what you know and believe. The question to ask is, Am I thinking and living like Jesus Christ in this trial or temptation? If not, what do I need to know and what skill must I learn?"

Matt sat and contemplated what Dan said.

"In the Bible and certainly in James, the true test of wisdom is not so much the quantity of your knowledge, but rather the quality of your thinking and conduct, especially in the midst of trials and temptations. Where do we get wisdom, according to James?"

"From God," Matt said.

"Therefore, since you need wisdom you need to get it from the only source available - God! But, take note: this is not a suggestion, it is a command! You are commanded to pray, and to pray for wisdom. Look at verse five and tell me what promise do we have when we pray for wisdom?"

"That God will give it in generous amounts."

"Yes! And the sense of this verse is that we keep on asking God. It's not a one-time request. What implications does this have for your quandary?"

"To pray when I find myself tempted. To ask God for wisdom."

"Exactly. We obtain wisdom by asking for it from the Lord.[1] Now, according to verses 6-8, in what way do we pray?"

"Let's see… without doubting, and… that's all. Without doubts," Matt answered.

"Take a moment and read the whole chapter. Then tell me what the subject of this chapter is. I'll be back," Dan said.

Dan returned a few minutes later. Matt was ready. "Trials."

"Is that all?"

"Oh. Uh, trials and temptations."

"Good. Wisdom is to be applied to trials and to temptations. What's the difference between the two?"

"That's what I was going to ask you!"

"Well, a trial is a test. The particular word used here is unusual in that it is not often used outside of the biblical texts. It was what doctors did to try out medicines. It was the word used to describe the test whether someone or something was genuine. The Bible uses this term twenty-one times, but never of unbelievers! Only believers are tested to see if they are genuine, if they have genuine faith in Christ. So what does that say about your trials?"

"My trials test my faith? My trials test whether I have genuine faith?"

"Right! So, a test or a trial is pressure brought about by the Lord to develop your faith. His aim is for your good and your ultimate triumph in the faith." Dan had Matt write down these verses: Roman 8:28-30, 1 Peter 1:3-9, 2 Peter 1:3-11, and James 1:2-4, 12.

"Then, how do you define temptation?" Matt asked.

"Temptation is the pressure and solicitation to sin. However, God never tempts you to sin, so says verse thirteen. Sources for temptation are the world, the flesh and the devil. Temptation is not just a feeling, not some emotional impulse over which you have no control. It is, first of all, how you think. That is why thinking rightly about God and thinking God's thoughts about life is so important. This is where wisdom comes to play."

Dan further explained that wisdom is needed to replace wrong thinking. Wrong thinking often happens when tempted, such as "I really need to have this thing", or "I deserve better than this," or "I can't control myself." Jesus had right thinking, even in his temptations. When Satan tempted Jesus in the wilderness, he had the thoughts of those temptations in his mind. He was genuinely tempted (Matt. 4:1-11; Heb. 2:18; 4:15). How did Jesus reject each temptation? Jesus Christ rejected each temptation by citing a biblical reason for the temptation and why it should be rejected. By thinking God's thoughts he resisted sin. So, how do we resist temptation? By knowing and bringing to mind the thoughts and will of God.

"The problem with those temptations to which we easily give in is that we often just respond without consciously thinking first. We act impulsively. The way we resist temptation is to stop reacting out of impulse, to think rightly, then to take right action."

"So, do I take it that temptation is not a sin?"

"Correct. Jesus was tempted in ways just like you and I are tempted. But he did not sin. It is when you give in to your temptation that it becomes a sin."[2]

"Okay, how do I deal with sexual temptation?" Matt posed.

"First, fill your mind with what God says about men and women, marriage and sex. Learn what God teaches, commands and forbids, so when you are tempted you are able to bring to mind God's thoughts. Second, when you are tempted, refuse to give into the notion that you need to have sex now, or that you are entitled to it, or any of the other ideas

85

that counter God's Word. Third, replace your tempting thought with something else, such as praying for the woman you are lusting after, or reciting a memorized Bible verse, or so forth."

Dan and Matt were interrupted by a light knock on the office door. The pastor's counseling appointment had arrived. Matt thanked his pastor and excused himself. He would walk the mile or so to his house.

The conversation with Matt provoked thinking and conviction. Dan was obviously going through trials. No doubt his faith in Christ was being tested, much like when Dan was in school, where exams were given to check his knowledge and skill level. Unlike his teachers, God did not need to know the level of Dan's knowledge and skill. God is omniscient, yet Dan needed to know. And Dan needed to grow. In some things he fared well; in other things he was failing miserably.

Along with trials there were also temptations. Dan was being provoked or pressured to sin. How so? He was tempted to sinfully respond in multiple ways to the words and actions of his antagonists or enemies. He was tempted to feel sorry for himself, to fight back, to harbor bitterness, to hide from conflict, and so forth. He recognized this, became convicted and then prayed for the grace of repentance to change.

He took a couple hours to do a self-evaluation. Dan asked, "How have I grown in the following areas of my life this past year? How have I grown spiritually, in my knowledge of and relationship to God? With prayer, worship, and devotion? To my knowledge, am I pleasing God? Do I enjoy the Lord? Is my character becoming more like Christ's? Am I more disciplined and self-controlled? Am I bolder? More loving? Is the fruit of the Spirit manifested through me? How's my knowledge and comprehension of God and his Word? Of myself, my calling and my work? Am I growing more knowledgeable in general? Am I growing more competent in life skills? In pastoral skills? How about growth in my natural talents? Spiritual giftedness? In communication skills? Am I better skilled with various kinds of relationships than I was a year ago? As a husband and father? "

Self-evaluations are never objective and almost always tough because one either thinks too highly of oneself, or too lowly. Dan was able to acknowledge areas in which he had grown as well as areas in which he needed growth. He prayed that God would grant his promised wisdom.

Matt ordered two fish sandwiches, two cheeseburgers, a large serving of fries and a strawberry shake. He blamed his wrestling practices and body workouts for his hunger. Dan only smiled and ordered a small burger and coffee. They found a two-seater table in the middle of the fast food place. The restaurant was packed with college and high school students. It seemed as if Matt knew every customer who came in.

"So, Pastor Dan, were you able to give any thought to my other question about the most important thing a pastor needs in order to deal with everything as a minister?"

"Yep. How about you? What do you think?"

"After our conversation the other day, I'd say it would have to be wisdom. Right?"

"That's what I would answer. A pastor needs to know and love the Lord Jesus Christ, authentically love others, have God's call upon his life, be gifted and trained, have a Christ-like character, and all that, but as far as the most important thing he needs in order to do his work, it would have to be godly wisdom."

A couple of Matt's teammates sitting two tables away kept pointing at him and laughing. He thought they were just trying to be funny. Dan turned around to see what the commotion was and noticed two of the wrestlers pointing at Matt and cackling. He then turned back and paid greater attention to Matt. The young man had not shaved for several days so whenever he wiped the tartar sauce off his mouth and chin, he painted his upper lip and chin with flakes of napkin. Dan revealed why they found him funny, which prompted the clown to rub his entire face with napkins. It earned laughs from several tables.

"A fool for Christ," the young man said.

"Don't think that's quite what the Bible is referring to, you fool," Dan joked. "You know a fool is the opposite of a wise person?"

Matt looked at his pastor with a sheepish grin. "Yeah, I know." He took off for the restroom to clean his face. Several minutes later he returned with a small pie.

"So tell me, O Wise One, what is it to be wise?" Matt winked.

"First, Grasshopper, a wise person is humble. Do not be wise in your own eyes, Proverbs 3 says. Paraphrasing Proverbs 11:2, 'where there is pride there is dishonor, but wisdom is with the humble person.'" Dan pulled a napkin out of the table container and started to write. "You can look at these verses later." He wrote down Proverbs 8:12-13 and 26:12.

"A wise one is like Jesus Christ. Christ, the almighty God, humbled himself when he obeyed the Father, became a creature to serve us, and then died a gruesome death upon the cross. That is the quintessential example of humble wisdom. God tells us to humble ourselves before God." He wrote down James 4:10.

"How does a Christian become wise?" Matt wondered. He took a bite out of four fries and then slurped his shake.

"Wisdom is for anyone who really wants it from the heart. Even fools are invited to feast upon wisdom," Dan instructed, writing down Proverbs 9:4 and 16. "Training in wisdom is hard, and costly. God reserves wisdom for those who are morally upright."[3]

"Proverbs 23:23 tells us to buy the truth, and obtain wisdom, instruction and understanding. That means a person seeking wisdom values the Lord and his truth enough to pay the price to have it. The first chapter of Proverbs tells us that wisdom comes by instruction. But it also comes by way of correction and reproof."[4]

Matt busied himself with his food and drink. His dessert was waiting.

Dan went on to say that a wise person is knowledgeable and learned. He knows the Lord (Prov. 2:5, 3:6) and fears him (Prov. 1:7). A reverent fear of God is the starting place for becoming wise. God reveals knowledge to a wise person (Prov. 2:6, Jas. 3:17). It's not all about having intelligence or a cranium filled with facts, but about having a soul filled with faith and God's Word. James 3:17 says that the quality of a God kind of wisdom is pure, peaceable, gentle, reasonable, full of mercy, fruitful, unwavering and unhypocritical.

"Who's the wisest person of all time?" Dan asked Matt.

"Solomon, right?" Matt said with a mouth full of fries.

"Good answer, but who is wiser than Solomon?"

"Oh, well, Jesus of course."

"Did you know that the wisdom personified in Proverbs chapter eight is most likely referring to Jesus Christ, in whom, Colossians says, is all the treasure of wisdom and knowledge?"[5]

"Oh, yeah…sure…" Matt replied sarcastically.

"Isaiah predicted that the Messiah would have the Spirit of God resting upon him with all wisdom and understanding. He would have the spirit of counsel and strength, of knowledge and of the fear of the Lord. When Jesus went to his home town and taught in the synagogue, the people were amazed and wondered where he got his wisdom and power. If we want to understand wisdom or if we want to see what wisdom looks like in action, we need to look at Jesus."[6]

"How do you get to be wise?" Dan asked his hungry friend.

"Humbly pray for it. That's what the first chapter of James says."

"After you pray for wisdom, how to you get it?"

"I'm not sure. Read and study the Bible?"

"There are many who have read and studied the Bible but never became wise. God grants us wisdom through faith. He gives believers the mind of Christ. Therefore, this special wisdom is given by the Spirit of God through the Word of God by faith. This kind of spiritual wisdom pertains to the skill of Christ-like living."[7]

The jock crumpled all his containers and placed them on his tray, then set it on another table. He excused himself to get hot chocolate. On the way back he stopped by the table of his comrades to give them a hard time. A few playful slaps on the back of a couple heads, sitting on the chest of another, and kicking their feet was punishment enough for giving him a hard time. He left happy. His revenge was sweet. They only laughed and called him names. He flipped up the collar of his brown leather jacket and strutted away.

With his drink in his left hand, he slid into the chair and asked, "Can unbelievers have wisdom?"

"God grants a certain kind of wisdom to unbelievers. Like the wisdom to use their talents, or various kinds of wisdom for the good of humanity. But this particular sort of wisdom about which the Proverbs and the rest of the Bible speaks is a moral and righteous wisdom. The natural person without Christ rejects this wisdom of God because he rejects God. Everyone needs a change of heart to turn from this natural, sinful condition, and from his or her cherished independence. Every person must turn to the Light of true wisdom."[8]

"So we pray for wisdom and seek it out? But you said it comes by faith."

"True wisdom does come through faith, but once God grants it, you seek it out. Proverbs tells us that we should seek it with everything we have. We should also become devoted disciples of wisdom, who treasure it to the end."[9]

"It all sounds kinda generic, so in what way does wisdom help you as a pastor?"

With raised eyebrows and a hint of a smile, Dan patiently answered his friend. "That's what godly wisdom is, skillfully applying the mind of Christ to all areas of life. Its most important aspect is spiritual and moral. Wisdom gives you understanding about things and insight into life. Wisdom has the ability to discern between right and wrong, good and evil. Is there any calling or line of work that isn't covered under what I've just mentioned?"[10]

"Hmmm. No. Well, none that I can think of."

"Let me list them as I can remember them. If not I'll have to pull my brain out of my pocket and turn it on," he snickered. "First, such a person deals wisely with others. This kind of wisdom is what we would classify as success. Second, a wise person does the morally good and right thing. Along with these verses I'm writing down for you, look up Hosea 14:9."[11]

"Okay."

"He is like Jesus Christ who walks in the way of righteousness and the path of justice. Jesus taught that we are to hunger and thirst after righteousness. This righteousness is not only moral and religious but also very practical. Tell me, who doesn't want to be treated fairly?

"Third, a wise person is both shrewd and discreet. What pastor doesn't need to be astute and circumspect?"[12]

"They all need to be," Matt agreed. "Just what does that all mean?"

"A shrewd and discreet person takes the trouble to learn his way around and plan out a realistic course. This course could be short-term goals or major life plans. You need to be shrewd and discreet at school, dealing with friends, and girls, and your dad, and in making plans for the future. See how that works?"

"Yeah."

"A shrewd and discreet person shuns naiveté. He thoughtfully considers what he's doing and the steps he is taking down a particular path."

"That's my problem. My dad says that I'm too naïve."

"I don't know you well enough to comment. Perhaps he's right. If so, what are you going to do about it?"

"Pray for and seek out wisdom."

"See! There you go. Off to a good start! A shrewd and discreet person learns the ropes of life. He becomes a skilled craftsman in the art of life. He's streetwise, but not immoral" he said, referring to Proverbs 1:1-7.

"Can't wait to get there," Matt moaned.

"Hey, I know what you mean. To some people I'm a raving idiot. To a few others I'm quite the wise man. However, when I talk with my friend and mentor, Kent, he seems much wiser than I am. It can be both discouraging and motivating. I just press on. Okay, so can you see how all these qualities of a wise person are important for you as a person?"

"Totally."

"And for a pastor?"

"Absolutely."

"With wisdom God gives you good sense and discernment. A wise person has a certain, godly rationality, an orderliness about his ways, and sensible answers to various matters and situations of life. A wise person has sound judgment. The biggest thing, I would say, is that a wise person is able to bring to bear what God is revealing and teaching to the small and the big concerns in life, and…and…he trusts in God's direction and will for his life. Why would that be important? Because we have a difficult time wrapping our heads around things that happen in our own lives, let alone what's beyond us. Even when we can't get it, whatever it is, we can trust that the Lord is ever directing our steps because he has ordained those steps according to his wonderful plan."[13]

"I'm not sure I understand what you just said."

"Let me try it this way: a wise and godly person seeks the will of God and lives accordingly.

Right?"

"Uh huh."

"But can a wise man possibly know everything or be prepared for all of life's contingencies?"

"No way."

"So then the best a wise person can do is to live as wisely as he can, and also trust that the Lord is in control of his life and will continue to direct him. He trusts that God is sovereign and such a mastermind that he will use good and evil, good decisions and disobedient ones, for the ultimate good of those who love him and are called according to his purposes."[14]

"Sweet. That's way cool! Sorta takes the worry out of life, huh?"

"Man, it's getting late. Let's head to the car and I'll finish on the way home."

They got up, cleaned off their table, and headed out to the car. A strong wind snapped the flag out front and flapped Matt's open jacket. They were shoved several times toward the car.

On the way home, Dan talked about two more important qualities of a wise person. He is someone who knows how to control his tongue. He says the right thing at the right time (Prov. 10:13, 31-32; 11:9, 12; 15:2, 7; 17:27; 18:4; 20:12; Jas. 1:26; 3:5-8). This is not merely a vital quality for a pastor, but for every believer. Secondly, he has a good reputation (Prov. 12:8). God says that a person's good name is better than great riches (Prov. 22:1). The deacons in Acts 6 were chosen because they each had a good reputation, and were filled with God's Spirit and wisdom. If that was the case for deacons then, how much more it should be for pastors now.

Dan pulled up to the curb in front of Matt's house. Matt's father was just driving away. He waved at his son. Matt stood on the grass and steadied the door against the gusts. He leaned in and said, "How does a person make wise decisions?"

"Do ya have another hour?"

"What? Now?"

"No, not now. My evening is booked. Say, I'll email you some notes I've put together about making decisions. They are also taken from Proverbs. I used the time during one of my get-aways to investigate what Proverbs said about making wise decisions. My wife and I had a few very serious decisions to make, so the exercise was quite useful. I'll send it to you and we can talk about it the next time we meet. Do you have anything important in mind?"

"Actually, yes. I have an opportunity to go to Europe on a short term missions trip. I also have a thing going with this girl, but… well, ya know."

"We can talk about both of those things if you want. It's been fun meeting with you."

"Hey, me too. I really appreciate you. Thanks for everything. Catcha later, man."

As promised, Dan went to his home computer and sent the attachment (see Appendix H). In the email Dan wrote, "Look over these attached notes, write down your questions and comments, and we'll talk about this soon. In the meantime, a good book you should get is *Decisions, Decisions* by Dave Swavely. You can borrow mine if needed. Take care, Dan."

At supper Jake and Ben begged their father to watch an old Lassie movie with them after they ate. Dan apologized and told them that he already had a church meeting at 7:00 P.M., but he would get his calendar out and pencil in a time when they could.

"You won't forget to do it, will you?" asked a very disappointed Jake.

"Jakester, I'll get my PDA right now." And he did. "How about Saturday night after supper?"

"But Daaaady, that's way, way far from now!" protested Ben.

"It's the soonest we can do it, Mr. Ben." Dan sympathized and questioned the wisdom of being so busy at the expense of his family.

Ben sat slumped in his chair. He quit eating.

"Don't pout, Ben. It's how it is, and it really won't be a long time from now."

"Can we watch the movie tonight with Mommy?" Jake compromised.

"What? Without your dear old, movie watching Dad?" Mona's eyes approved of Jake's suggestion.

"Please, pretty please, Daddy," pleaded the little blonde Ben.

"Oh…I suppose so. If you can handle a night without Dad and his famous popcorn."

Jake rolled his eyes and sighed, "Oh Dad, it's just that microwave stuff."

"Oh yeah, it is, isn't it?"

After supper, Dan rushed off to another meeting. Nearly every evening was filled with some activity. He kept telling himself to cut back on the activities, but he just could not find time to fit everything in. Not a wise thing, he admitted. Something had to give.

It was after the children were tucked away and Mona was nearly asleep on the couch when Dan got home. He and Mona talked about the day. The evening meeting went well. The movie night with the boys went well, for about half of the movie. Hannah got fussy, and Ben fell asleep. Jake was bored. He also did not appreciate watching a black and white movie.

Dan and Mona prayed before Mona went off to bed. She couldn't stay awake any longer. Her husband would join her as soon as he finished checking his emails. He had a reply from his young disciple. Matt thanked Dan for the meeting, but said his notes brought more questions to mind. The student also asked for clarification on the character of a wise person. He wrote, "I think I'm getting it. Wisdom isn't only about making decisions or only about how we think. Wisdom is both of those and also how we live out our lives before God. Right? You said wisdom had a moral dimension to it. Well, I was thinking, if that is true, then a wise person will also have moral qualities. What do you think?"

"Hi, Matt," the worn-out pastor wrote back. "You listened well. Yes, a wise person is able to make sound decisions, think God's thoughts, and be skilled at life. Because he knows the Lord and therefore lives morally, justly and righteously, he exhibits godly virtues. Think about Jesus, the epitome of wisdom. If you go back and read over Proverbs a few times, you can find virtuous qualities of a wise person. Compare Scripture with Scripture too and see what you come up with. We can talk about it when we meet again. Later."

After the morning worship service on Sunday, Matt, followed by two friends, rushed over to the pastor. He had a piece of paper in hand. "I did it."

"Well, congratulations! I'm so proud of you!" He paused a bit and then asked, "What did you do?"

"Huh? Oh, I did what you assigned me and looked up traits of a wise person. Here's the list," giving Dan a college ruled paper with a list in a crooked cursive.

"Yo, dude! You could be a doctor with that scribble," a friend jabbed.

Matt punched his left arm. "Go away."

Dan took the paper and read the list: "Meek, morally pure, peace-loving, considerate, delights in mercy, justice and faithfulness, submissive and obedient, full of mercy, full of good fruit, impartial and fair, authentic."[15]

"Good list. Now, do you know what these things mean?"

"Most of them."

"What does it mean to be meek?"

"Well…uhhh…that's one I don't know."

His friends laughed at him. "Hey! Do you know, jerks?" They stopped laughing.

"To be meek is to have a controlled, disciplined energy," Dan taught. "So these are the moral characteristics of a wise person according to Proverbs and other verses?"

"Yep."

"Very good. Now, here's your next assignment: define what they mean, write out five applications for each, and try to think of a person who models that quality. Got it?"

"Huh? Write out applications?"

"A wise person is morally pure. What does it mean for you to be pure? Pure in thoughts? Pure in your behavior, especially toward women? Like that. Got it?"

"Oh, okay. Yeah, I got it."

"And you clowns can help him," Dan said, patting both of Matt's friends on the back.

Marcus, Phil and Neil, the new elder candidates, had a preliminary meeting with the pastor to schedule the training sessions. Dan gave each a syllabus that included the topics and homework assignments. It took all of thirty minutes, but Neil had a question, "I sat in on one of the elders' meetings. It looks to me like they had a hard time coming to an agreement on a couple of things. Is that how it always goes?"

"Not always, but we have some very strongly opinionated elders. It makes for a lively discussion."

"That's putting it diplomatically. You'd be a good politician," Neil responded.

"Takes wisdom and insight," Marcus commented.

"Funny you should say that. I met with one of our college kids this week and talked about wisdom. So, how do we make a corporate decision? I'll propose to you what I believe ought to happen in an ideal world," Dan told them.

Phil approved. "Okay."

Dan walked over to his file cabinet and pulled out a handout (see Appendix I). He went into the secretary's office and ran off some copies. Each of the men received a copy, and Dan sat down. "This is something I put together about three years ago. Frankly, I hate contentious arguments, especially with others who relish them. This is a handout I gave to our elders in one of our first meetings together."

"Didn't work, eh?" Neil observed.

"Wisdom is skillfully applying God's truth. The key is applying what we know is truth. If you men are confirmed by the congregation, then it would be great if we operated within these parameters, or something similar."

"That's fine by me," Marcus asserted.

"We agreed that this meeting would be short, so I suggest we table this for a future class. Take the handout home, read it over, and come prepared to discuss it. Write down the tough questions, make notes or additions, anything to make our time more profitable. Then we can also talk about how to apply this in various scenarios of life."

"Sounds good to me," Neil said.

The other men also approved of the plan. They left looking forward to the training sessions. Dan was excited to have three, solid, quality men in training. He prayed God would bring them on the elder board.

A CHALLENGE TO THINK AND DO

What do you think?

1. Define wisdom.
2. According to Scripture, how do you become wise?
3. Who do you know is a model of godly wisdom?
4. How do you know when you are making a wise decision?
5. What do you think of Dan's advice about making decisions?
6. How does your church's governing board make decisions? A church's committee?
7. What is temptation? Is temptation a sin?
8. How do you handle temptation?
9. What is your opinion on what Pastor Dan said about trials and temptations?

Some things you could do:

1. Do the homework Pastor Dan assigned to Matt and his friends: define the biblical meaning for meek, morally pure, peace loving, considerate, merciful, just, faithfulness, submissive, and fruitful. Write out tangibles ways to be meek, morally pure, peace loving, etc.
2. Read over Appendix H (Gaining Advice and Making Plans).
3. As you read through the Bible, keep a record of what the Bible says regarding making good or foolish decisions, and what the Bible gives as examples of good or foolish decisions..
4. Read Appendix I (How to Make a Corporate Decision). How can these suggestions be applied in your life? How can they be improved upon?
5. Read Dave Swavely's *Decisions, Decisions*.

6

IF BOOKS COULD SKILL

—⁓—

It was ironic the young seminary graduate thought of himself competent for pastoral ministry but questioned his character qualifications. In contrast, the pastor with seven years experience continued to pass the tests of a call and of godly character, yet continued to question his competency. If one hears the same thing from enough people enough times he probably will believe it. And it doesn't matter if it is good and positive or bad and negative. Dan believed the negative.

Dan was not alone. According to London and Wiseman, "While recent surveys of pastoral satisfaction seem to be up, 4 in 10 pastors across the country say they doubt their call; 3 in 10 say they think about leaving the ministry; 10 percent say they're depressed some or all of the time; 40 percent report being depressed or worn out some of the time; and 76 percent say they're either overweight or obese."[1]

For more than half of the previous year the pastor dealt with the issue of his character qualifications for pastoral ministry. Counseling with his mentor Kent and consulting with a few additional pastors, counselors and seminary professors was very helpful. Teaching leadership classes, preaching topically on deacon and elder qualifications, and applying it to real life issues was even more helpful.

Do I have the right call and motivation? Yes, Dan reminded himself. Do I possess the right character? This was the difficult question since he had both his low self-confidence and his antagonists questioning him regularly. He knew his heart well enough to know he fell short so often because he still grappled with residual sin. If I were to measure up to all the biblical requirements, not merely the ones outlined on the checklist, and had to have an A+ score, then I do not qualify, he often reminded himself. That was the perfectionist in him. However, Dan would counter with what he had been teaching others, which is he had to demonstrate godly qualities substantially and obviously, but not perfectly.

Reading biographies and autobiographies of well-known Christian leaders and pastors throughout church history assured him that he was not alone in this personal conflict. All of those men faced doubts and questioned their call or character or ability from time to time. Since true humility is an essential requirement, one who believes he has arrived or is flawless has not been humbled before the very presence of God. Perhaps he never came humbly to the foot of Christ's rugged cross.

When it came down to it, his doubts were provoked by the Dumpletons, the elders, and people like them who questioned Dan's call, character and competence. Who knows, but God, where they came up with their standards for judgment? What was quite apparent is that they were not using God's objective standard to make proper evaluations.

One time Bernie's old friend Mr. Strenk, in an unannounced office visit, told the pastor that he was not above reproach. Dan challenged him to explain his comment. He accused Dan of wearing colored shirts instead of white shirts to church services, and rarely wearing a tie during the week, owning a foreign car, allowing people to call him Pastor Dan instead of Reverend Lee, and having dinner at a restaurant that served alcoholic beverages. When Dan pulled open his file drawer and gave the character assessment form to Mr. Strenk, the man claimed he had previously read it, but curtly told Dan not to get theological on him (see Appendix E). Dan then pulled Swavely's book off a shelf and gave it to him. "What's this? *Who Are You to Judge?* I don't need this!" the man complained, tossing the book on the desk. That promptly ended the meeting.

Personal preferences are frequently used to evaluate a candidate for the office of deacon, elder or pastor. For example, most of the church members were convinced the intern was well suited for the ministry. He was a tall, great looking, physically fit, intelligent young man with charm, a charismatic personality and many talents. Apparently that was all he needed. It was the same criteria Israel made when they evaluated Saul as their king (1 Samuel 8-10). Thankfully Bill knew better.

Decades ago the local church had used other personal preferences when they elected three of their elders. For example, if a man was a business owner or community leader, actively involved in the life of the church, commanded attention or took charge, and was willing to be a deacon or elder, then he was qualified. Of course, it was an added bonus if he knew the doctrines of the church. It was an exceptional bonus if he could teach. The issue of character requirements was strangely new to most of the members of the church.

Although Dan could justify his calling and character, he arrived at another fork in his ministerial road. Was he truly competent to serve as elder-pastor-teacher or was he the bumbling incompetent his critics claimed? This was a more difficult question as far as he was concerned. How do you measure the many different skills a pastor needs to be proficient in his calling? Like other vocations, being a servant-shepherd is a skill and an art, a talent and a gift. The man might have some natural talent, but not be spiritually gifted. He might learn solid doctrine and even learn about teaching, and yet not be able to teach effectively. He might thoroughly enjoy theology, but not be able to relate with people. He may be trained in counseling, but be inept in social relationships.

"All you are saying is true, Dan. But you must remember that you are ordained and that should be enough proof," said one of his pastor friends. *That's not helpful*, Dan thought.

What Bernie and others were doing is a story that has been repeated often in local churches. Frequently it isn't pretty, as Gilmore describes in *Pastoral Politics*:

> Take a poll sometime of the ministers you know who have been terminated at some pastorate during their lifetimes. I've talked with many in this category. Some have written by snail mail, others by email. I have saved their correspondence. I got to the point where the duplications were too sad to explore anymore. The similarities of experience and exasperation are astonishingly uncanny even though the denominational affiliations are different. You would be surprised how many have – in frustration – had their 'brains fried,' their sensitivities numbed, their hopes dashed, their wills thwarted, their ambitions poisoned, their dreams zapped, their ideas trashed, their souls scarred, their skills diminished, their families ridiculed, their reputations questioned and their achievements belittled. Some pastors — beaten so badly in monthly meetings — felt if they ever got Christmas bonuses, they should look upon them as hazard pay rather than incentives to stay.[2]

Kent was unavailable at this time. He was on a month's sabbatical studying in London, Amsterdam, and Geneva. But Dan knew what Kent would advise, so he set about doing it: reviewing his personal journals, considering his training, and reflecting on the grueling process of becoming a pastor in his denomination. He would also read a few books on the subject of pastoral training, talk to a number of individuals, and research what the Bible says on the subject.

The timing couldn't be better, given that Matt had asked Dan to disciple him in preparation for the ministry. He was a buff, nineteen-year old with average looks and ruddy cheeks. The teen dressed cleanly but wasn't style conscience, or so judged the cool girls. He liked to keep his thick, light brown hair in a tail. The freckled five-foot nine-inch stock wore clear contacts over his emerald eyes.

During the year he was the church's intern, Bill made a strong impression on his younger friend Matthew. Matt and Bill had several things in common: both enjoyed sports and were weight lifters. Matt, involved in gymnastics and wrestling at his high school, was gregarious like Bill, and an honors student. They both hungered after the things of Christ.

Matt lived with his father from the time of his parents' divorce, which happened during his sixth grade. His older sister lived with his mother. As a latchkey kid of a free-spirited, very permissive father Matt found himself living on the edge. He might have spent time in juvenile hall had he been caught, and he would have been involved in drugs were it not for his serious commitment to health and school sports. Drinking, however, was a problem for him. Then he believed in Jesus Christ. He became a seriously devoted follower of Christ.

His orientation to life changed. Bad habits and addictions pealed away like Eustace's dragon scales. He had purpose and a destiny.

Since Matt's conversion, he found a surrogate father in Bill. More like an older brother, the man helped Matt become less of a free-spirited rebel and more of a self-disciplined zealot. The rebel now had a cause and his life was radically altered. Matt's father dismissed it as another phase his son would soon get over.

Matt was dead serious about becoming a missionary, youth pastor, or pastor and he wanted his minister's help now that Bill was gone. In many ways the college kid reminded Dan of his own younger days.

Dan catered to Matt's fondness for fast food, so arranged to pick up the young athlete at the community college after wrestling practice each Thursday and conduct training at a nearby fast food restaurant. Normally the two men would start off chatting about life in Matt's world. At least the young man had grown beyond the proverbial teen responses of "uh-huh, uh-uh and I don't know" to have serious interchanges. This supposedly average dude had quite a bit going for him, such as his large appetite for wisdom and spiritual things, and a quick, funny wit. Matt's habit was to wash down two of the largest burgers, a large order of onion rings and a dessert with a chocolate milkshake. It was enough to tide him over until supper.

As the sun was being pulled closer to the nightlife Matt's question for the day was about what it took to become a pastor. "In our denomination and for most other evangelical groups the first and foremost thing is that you have a vital, saving faith in Jesus Christ. Then you should sense God's call in your life with a passionate desire to devote a significant portion of your labors toward the ministry of God's Word. In a narrow sense that means teaching, preaching, evangelizing, counseling, and so forth. In the broad sense it means doing works of mercy and compassion, working out your talents and gifts, and so forth. People should be able to see the hand of God's call upon your life as you live it out. That inner call should also be verified through the witness of God's people and elders." Dan watched his young friend vigorously chew while juggling his dripping burger, napkin and shake.

The next most important thing is that the one who seeks to serve as a pastor must possess the right character. "Like what?" Matt muffled through his mashed onion rings.

Pastor reminded him of the handouts members received prior to the congregational meeting and of the sermons he preached. "It's not merely having knowledge of Bible doctrine. God places a significant emphasis upon godly character, moral behavior, family life, and relationships. That's what we see in the letters to Timothy, Titus and in First Peter."

"Yeah, but what about the men God called in the Old Testament? Most of them didn't live exemplary lives. Think about Gideon, or worse, Samson! They were called by God but you can't say they had upstanding morals, good theology or great family lives! Not even David would measure up, but they were all called."

"True enough. But the focus of their call in God's plan of redemptive history was to serve as types of the future, promised Savior-King , who would rescue and redeem God's people. Their calls had to do with rescuing and redeeming. They were unique and extraordinary in that way. But God didn't let immorality or violations of his law to go unpunished. And don't forget that priests were called to be especially holy. Their duty was to guard God's holy things and God's holy people. Prophets were also called, and they were supposed to live consistently with the words of a holy God. When you get to the New Testament, there is only one true Savior-King who rescues, redeems and renews God's people. In the New, all believers are made holy and called to be holy, and those who handle the Word of our holy God are called to live consistently with its message of grace, truth and love in Christ."

Matt played with the cup of milkshake while his slurping rattled away every last drop. Dan waited until the recital was over. With his face practically buried in the container, Matt paused and raised his eyes to check on his teacher. The two of them broke out into a laughing spell, and Matt apologized for his poor manners. "Then what?" he probed.

"If you intend to pursue the ministry, you also need to be competent. If God is leading you in that direction he would have endowed you with the needed natural abilities, but more than that God will provide you with spiritual abilities and gifts."

While Matt worked on finishing his greasy rings, Dan sipped black coffee and continued to instruct. There is no Bible chapter that explicitly spells out the gifts a pastor is given, but it is clear that the pastors and elders who were protégés of the apostles were specially gifted (Mark 16:15-18; Luke 21:15; 24:49; Acts 1:8; 1 Tim. 3:1-7; 5:22; Tit. 1:7). Most were spiritually gifted:

- to exhort (Acts 20:12; 1 Cor. 14:3; 2 Cor. 1:4-6; 1 Thess. 2:11, 12),
- to lead and rule (Acts 20:28, Rom. 12:8; 1 Cor. 12:28; 1 Thess. 5:12, 13; 1 Tim. 3:4-5; 5:17; Heb. 13:7,17) ,
- to preach God's Word (Acts 28:31; 2 Tim. 4:2),
- to serve (Acts 20:24f; Rom. 15:26-33),
- to share resources with others (Acts 4; Eph. 4:28),
- to show mercy (Matt. 25; Rom. 12:8; 1 Cor. 12:28; Jas. 3:17),
- and to teach (Matt. 28:18-20; Acts 20; Rom. 12:7; 1 Tim. 3:2; 4:11; 6:2; 2 Tim. 2:1-2; 2:24; Jas. 3:1).

Dan paused to sip more coffee and reflect on more statistics in an article he had recently read. The article stated that:

More than nine in ten pastors (92 percent) have taken a spiritual gifts assessment and have had their spiritual gifts confirmed by others. This type of feedback was helpful since our survey gave pastors the opportunity to assign to themselves up to five of the nine spiritual gifts. On average, pastors recognized 2.9 spiritual gifts in themselves, while congregants recognized an average of 2.5 gifts in their pastors."[3]

The graphic showed that 80 percent of pastors believed they had the spiritual gift of teaching, while 70 percent of the congregants believed that. Then 62 percent of the pastors believed they were gifted to shepherd but only 49 percent of the congregants thought that. A bigger disparity was with exhortation, with 42 percent of the pastors thinking they had the gift of exhortation, but only 23 percent of the congregants held to that.[4]

"So a pastor has to have a gift of leadership?" Matt posed.

"Many would argue he must, but we need to qualify what we mean by leadership. Pastors inevitably lead in some capacity. They govern, administrate and oversee the affairs of the local church under the authority of Christ. But their leadership is of a quality not exactly like secular leadership found in politics or business. George Barna, the Christian pollster who writes much on the church and leadership, defines a leader as '[O]ne who mobilizes; one whose focus is influencing people; a person who is goal driven; someone who has an orientation in common with those who rely upon him for leadership; and someone who has people willing to follow them' In that book he lists twenty-three competencies a Christian leader should have, such as motivating people, decision making, team building, instigating evaluation, etc.[5] Those are qualities or competencies, as he put it, that both a Christian and non-Christian leader need to possess. However, the leadership in God's church about which the New Testament speaks is somewhat different."

"How so?" Matt asked, tossing the last fried onion in his mouth.

"We can get into that more later, but suffice it to say that the New Testament doesn't refer to God's ministers as leaders. This has led some to believe that pastors do not have to be leaders. As I mentioned, they might possess the gift to lead or govern, but God speaks of them as servants and shepherds, not as leaders. The reason, David Fitch points out, is that the New Testament authors were careful not to use terms of leadership because they were often synonymous with abusive leaders of the day.[6] Wagner in his book even charts the difference between leaders and shepherds.[7] It's a pretty revealing comparison. J. Oswald Sanders does the same things in his *Spiritual Leadership*, a classic book on the subject. The pastor, who is a shepherd, leads by the authority of God's Word in humble service, as a model of Christ and through various methods of communication. It seems to me that the pastor has certain leadership traits, but again somewhat different than secular characteristics. For example, pastors should be at the head of the line when it comes to serving God's people. That's not a trait you will always read about in management books. Like natural leadership he should be a problem solver, but as a pastor he should be wise, thinking God's thoughts after God and bringing them to bear upon problems."

"Oh – I get it! Exactly like a leader but different!" joked Matt.

"Okay, whatever," chuckled Dan.

"I'm not leading anyone in either sense," Matt complained.

"Pastoring is a gift. Leadership is a skill you can learn. Learn to be a good servant and you may grow into the kind of man who can lead. My brother in the Army often tells me that great leaders first learned to be great followers and servants."

"That's all?"

"Well, no. You can take classes, attend seminars, read books on leadership. I've made it a habit to read at least one leadership book each month. Read biographies about leaders. Watch and observe, hang around or become friends with those who are leaders. In other words, become a student of leadership especially of the biblical kind."

"I'm not a good teacher either," Matt whined.

"Do you enjoy speaking in public?"

"Yes, even though I get very nervous."

"So. Who doesn't? Do you enjoy explaining things to people, or like to inform or challenge them?"

"Yes."

"Do you enjoy studying to find answers to questions and problems so you can inform or explain things to others?"

"Yes."

"Have you done any teaching?"

"Very, very little," Matt said.

"It sounds to me like you may have a heart for teaching. The way to find out is to try teaching. If you do have the gift, you can grow and develop that gift. When I was your age I was given the job of substituting for my friend in an adult Sunday school class. I wanted to take it, but was scared out of my skin. He pressured me to take the class and gave me some tips and materials. I studied my brains out, ended up having way too much material, stumbled through the lesson and at the end figured I messed things up badly. But surprise of surprises, the people said they got a lot out of it and I was asked to teach again. I then took classes and read books on how to teach by men such as Hendricks and Wilkerson. You should try teaching to see if you have the gift in you. If you have it, nurture it to competency."

On the way home Dan inquired of Matt's home life. Matt's role at home was more like a roommate than a son — pretty independent. Too sensitive a topic to talk about Matt switched to asking advice about a girl he liked at college, which guzzled up the rest of their fifteen minute drive. As he pulled up in front of Matt's house Dan made sure his young disciple understood that he was always welcome to call any time of day or night. Matt was surprised by the offer, so just nodded approvingly.

Pastor parked the car outside his garage. No sooner had he opened his door than he was tackled by his two little men. Snow or no snow, Dan had to wrestle them down to the ground, whereupon the three engaged in snow warfare.

"Hey! Boys! What are you doing?" yelled Mona with baby saddled on her right hip, just in time to see Jake's snowball smack his father in the back of the head. The three stopped and looked toward their queen as though stiffened by an ice wizard. "Dan! They don't even have their coats on and look, you're getting them all wet," she scolded. He proceeded to act as if he was going to paddle them for being so naughty but instead chased them up the steps into the foyer.

"Well? Uhh…you can't fault me for wanting to play, can you?" Dan asked as if he were the biggest kid of the trio.

After dinner the three went back outside, this time properly attired, to build a monster snowman. Even though they set about their project by the light of the porch lamp, they managed to put up a fairly gruesome looking creature. It was christened "bomibal" by the three-year-old.

When the children were wrapped away under their comforters, Mona brought Dan the mail. She waited for her husband to sort through bills and the unusually high stack of junk before extending her right forearm from the couch toward him in his recliner. She kept a grip on the letter, her head tilted, chin slightly tucked in with eyebrows elevated. Her eyes peered through the tip of her bangs. "What's this?" Dan said with a frown, fearing another bad letter from Katherine.

"It's from one of the churches out West. Looks like a letter."

Dan, relieved, opened it up and read aloud a letter from a church in Oregon. They wanted Dan to fill out an additional questionnaire and have an initial phone interview with the pastoral search committee.

"What are you going to do?"

"What do you think we should do?" he volleyed back.

Needless to say, it drew them into a heavy discussion for the next couple of hours. Things seemed to be improving at Grace, and Mona hated the very idea of moving again. Yet, she was from Oregon and they would be much closer to family. They concluded that it would not hurt to see where it all led. The church might end up rejecting him or he them. In the meantime the Lees would continue on as if they were staying for the next ten years.

Dan couldn't sleep. He tried to read, but just sat in bed thinking about the letter and about his time with Matt. Was he competent to take another call? *Let's see*, he bantered in his mind. *I am competent to teach. Mona and I both have a heart of mercy, and love hospitality. I'm a good, hard working, diligent servant, even though some would disagree. But that's because I don't serve the way they want. I am competent to shepherd, and a good administrator. Exhortation? No problem there. Hmmm. It's really not an issue of competency as it is about conflict with certain people and conflicts over my role, vision and mission for the church.* The last time he glanced at the clock it was after 1:00 A.M., and though he continued to sit up with the light on, his thoughts drew him down into slumber.

The boys played trampoline in between the sluggish adults. Their frolic wasn't as welcome to Dan this morning as it normally was. He patiently allowed them to tug on his left arm in a futile effort to pull him to the floor. Coffee could not come soon enough. He was so tired he wanted to dunk his whole head into the caffeine. After breakfast, Dan agreed to walk Jake to school. He figured the walk there and a return in the other direction to the office would stimulate his circulation, and perhaps arouse his numb brain.

This particular Friday had a light load and promised to be quiet, but a pastor must always be ready for the unexpected. At ten o'clock he received a call from Matt who wanted to come over and talk for about an hour. "Sure, how about right before lunch? You could join the family and me for a bite to eat?" Dan proposed. Sounded good to the lad.

When Matt arrived he was panting hard. He had jogged the two miles over. "Coffee?"

"Do you have hot chocolate?" asked the sweet tooth.

"Yep. Here's a mug. The rest is in the kitchen. Use the microwave, it's faster."

Settled with steaming mugs in their hands, the two sat across from each other in the office. Nothing was urgent, but Matt wanted to know more about what it took to be a pastor or a missionary, and how to become competent at it.

"First, there are things you can be doing right now while you are going to school."

"Yeah, I had a question about that. Should I go to Bible college or do I even need to go to college? I have a friend who is in another church and their missionaries don't need to go to school."

"Some groups believe that. But they end up getting trained somewhere and somehow. You can go to a Bible college. If you wish to pursue a ministerial calling in our denomination you would also need to go through seminary. But let's first back up and talk about what you can do now."

"Cool." Matt agreed compliantly. He perched his wet shoes on the small coffee table.

"You should explore your life to see what gifts you might have. We can have you teaching the teens, or even the sixth through eighth grade classes. Volunteer at church for different service activities or ministries, such as working with the group that goes downtown to feed the homeless or become an usher or greeter on Sundays. Get a breadth of experience in things you have permission to do in order to explore your likes, dislikes and abilities." The two made their way back to the kitchen for refills.

Dan made a commitment that as long as he was the pastor and Matt was around they would continue their weekly discipleship meetings. Matt was urged to get involved in all of the church's leadership classes. "I'll also begin to work with you to help you develop some good communication skills, teaching skills and above all, relationship skills. Those will be needed and useful no matter what vocation God leads you in, but they will especially help to equip you as a minister."

"If I have to go through college and then seminary it'll be years before I will be able to serve as a missionary or youth pastor!" Matt panicked.

"Not really, Matt," the pastor said while going after another cup of coffee. Matt followed him into the kitchen. "If you want to work with youth, then you can work with our youth under the oversight of the elders. I doubt they would pay you, but under my tutelage and watchful eye there are things you can do that youth pastors do."

Matt got excited. Cleaning up the chocolate powder from the counter he asked, "Like what?"

"Evangelize kids at your old high school or at the college you attend. Teach a study or take a couple of the youngsters and have Bible studies with them on a regular basis. Mentor them like I am mentoring you!"

"Really? I can do that?"

"Why not? Volunteer to work with a few adults, recruit a few adults even, to set up activities for the youth. There are lots of things you can do. It would be a great service for the church, a blessing to the kids, and a good exercise for you. Just follow Bill's lead."

"And missionary work?"

"Matt, there are many different short term missionary opportunities in our denomination alone. That's not to say anything about the dozens of other opportunities outside of our denomination."

"What kinds of things does our denomination do?"

"Work with Native Americans in their various needs. They build houses and conduct vacation Bible schools down in Mexico. Join medical missionaries for short term work in places like Kenya, Egypt or Central America. Lots of possibilities! What great ways to serve and to check if you really cut out to be a missionary. And you can do that during your school breaks in the winter, spring or summer."

Matt was excited. Dan proceeded to explain how many pastors major in subjects like the social sciences, philosophy or history before going on to seminary; however some are pre-medical or mechanical engineer students. "The first and foremost thing you need to develop and train yourself in is Christ-like character. That's what Paul told Timothy in his first letter and fourth chapter, and what Peter alludes to in his second letter, first chapter. Train yourself in godliness and those life skills we talked about earlier. Do well in school, and if you are still convinced of God's hand upon your life for a lifetime of pastoral ministry then go on to seminary."

"What kind of training is needed at seminary to become a pastor or missionary?"

"Speaking for the school I went to, you would take courses in the ancient languages of the Bible, Bible interpretation, theology, church polity, church history, pastoral ministry, counseling, and studies of the books of the Bible."

"What ancient languages? You mean like Latin?" Matt wondered.

"The ancient Hebrew for the Old Testament and the Koine Greek for the New Testament."

"Ohhh. Tough stuff? I have a hard enough time with Spanish."

"Yep. Can be tough. But it's worth the study. Competency in the languages frees you from becoming dependent upon commentaries or even enslaved to linguistic scholars and Bible translators."

"Once I'm done with seminary... what is that, four years?"

"Generally three years for a Masters in Divinity. Depends on the school."

"Then what?" Matt wondered.

They moved from the kitchen back to the warm office. "Toward the end of your time at seminary, provided you are an active member in a local church of our denomination or one like ours, you can come under the care of the elders and pastors of the regional church. We call that the presbytery. They can monitor your progress. They will later test you in order to license you to preach."

"What kind of testing is that?"

"Your testimony and how you know you have a call from God for Gospel ministry. They'll ask about your devotional life and your daily walk with Christ. Then they will test you in Bible knowledge, Bible doctrine, and a foundational knowledge of our church government. They will also have you present a short sermon."

"Then I can serve after that?"

"In an official capacity? It's limited. You can preach in certain circumstances under the watchcare of pastors and elders. But to serve in the way you are talking about requires formal ordination," Dan piled on.

Matt nodded his head indicating he wanted to hear more.

"We like for our men to go through an internship before being ordained. Some do that while they are in seminary. Others spread the training out in summer months, while still others intern for a year after seminary."

"Like Bill?"

"Yes, like Bill and the man before him."

"Once the internship is completed, you will be tested again by presbytery for ordination. They want to observe men during that time period to see if they have what it takes to build up and rule the church. The ordination exams are like the licensure exams, just more comprehensive. Your tests will be written and oral, and you will be examined by committees and then in front of an entire presbytery of elders and pastors. Once you have passed all that and receive a call to a definite work, whether here in our nation or overseas, then you become ordained to that calling."

"Man! I don't know if I can handle all of that."

"If God is leading you in that direction, then you will handle it. It's worth it. If God has called you to the great and lofty vocation of Gospel ministry being well equipped will only well serve to make you a real blessing to others. Without good solid training it is very hard to develop the competency needed to do all that a pastor is called to do!"

"I suppose you're right."

"A few years ago I had an opportunity to take a call to an independent church. I had college but no seminary. At first it seemed like I could do it. I mean, technically I could in many areas. Yet after a short while I realized that I wasn't really equipped in theology or counseling or for basic pastoral challenges. I was not competent, especially theologically, and to get up to speed and serve the church fully and really well I realized I would still have to get training somewhere and sometime. So, though it was a great ego booster, the decision to head for seminary was made."

The two easily consumed the hour, and Mona was now calling to verify if lunch was still on. Ben said he was starving and couldn't wait to eat. Dan and Matt hurried over to the house, managing to avoid the hazards of crunching through frozen snow and sliding on the iced walkway.

After lunch Matt took off for home. Dan went back to the office. He was quite happy for the providential opportunity to talk with Matt on the very subject about which he had been most recently conflicted. While looking at the different diplomas and certificates hanging on his wall, he once again rehearsed the process through which he had gone. The wall mountings were symbols of his various and diversified experiences and training. He was assured again that, contrary to the dragons, he was fit to the task. He was more competent than anyone else in his church for the task as elder-pastor-teacher. What is more, he passed the rigorous tests of seminary and the scrutiny of his peers. He was competent in theology, church government, church history. He was competent to show mercy and hospitality, to evangelize and disciple, to offer biblical counsel, and to administrate, to teach and even to preach. He knew he would continue to grow and to learn new skills in the areas of communication and leadership, as well as in areas where he was weak, such as dealing with needy, difficult or demanding personalities.

The question now was not so much about his competency, but about his fit in this church. Perhaps he would be better suited for another church. "There's only one way to find out, and that's to call Oregon," he declared to himself with a rested resolve.

CHALLENGE TO THINK AND DO

What do you think?
1. Before you read this chapter what did you believe was required to be a competent pastor?
2. What are your personal expectations about the skills your pastor should have?
3. Do you think formal ministerial training (Bible college or seminary) is beneficial for a pastor? Why or why not?
4. What talents, skills and spiritual gifts do you have? For what ministry are they useful in your church? Are you applying them?
5. How would you have dealt with Mr. Strenk if you were Pastor Dan?
6. What advice would you have given Matt regarding his desire to become a youth pastor, missionary or pastor?

Some things you could do:
1. Compare your personal expectations about the skills your pastor should have with Scripture and with what Dan presented in this chapter.
2. If you are not already aware, find out what training and skills your pastor has in order to fulfill his duties and responsibilities.
3. Find out what expectations the pastor has of you.
4. Read Dave Swavely's *Who Are You To Judge?*

7

ALL IN A DAY'S WORK

—w—

Winter was exhausting itself in futile attempts to suppress the emerging spring. This March witnessed a rigorous battle of the seasons, but the brilliant hues of the newborn spring won out like a persistent hatchling. It was Mona's favorite time of year.

One Sunday afternoon a month the Lee family hosted a luncheon for the new visitors and members. The night before, Melissa, a naturally talented decorator, charmed the usually plain living room with a full bloom of spring. Mona was elated, but had to work hard to keep her little brood from spreading spring color and cheer all over the place. Sunday school could not come soon enough.

Warming temperatures and cheerful buds most likely contributed to an especially pleasurable morning. It seemed everything went well and overall things at church were upbeat. Two new members were formally received. By now the grumpy bunch made it a habit of leaving almost immediately after the service, sometimes before. A couple of the elderly ladies set their watches to ring right at noon. "Since good preaching should take no more than fifteen minutes," they expected Dan to be finished by noon. If he wasn't, then too bad – they would just stand up, shuffle to the aisle and leave. Thankfully they sat in the back row. They missed the reception after church for the new members and a special cake afterward to celebrate the new union.

Because the new members brought their friends, and Matt brought a few of his new college mates, the Lees' living room was filled. After prayer everyone circled their way around the dining room buffet. Mona's expertise was cooking so she was used to hearing admonitions to open a catering business or restaurant. With brightly colored plastic plates balanced precariously on laps, people sat on the couch, dining room chairs and even on the floor. In the background one could watch Melissa helping Mona feed the children and ready them for their naps.

The format was simple: enjoy the food, get to know each other, and ask the tough questions. Dan enjoyed the tough or theological questions, but nine out of ten times questions were of a more mundane nature. Crystal washed the bite of hoagie down with punch before she spoke up. "I have a question," she declared almost apologetically and kept her hand raised until Dan acknowledged her. The stylish twenty-something was a regular visitor and friend of one of the new members.

"Go ahead, ask away."

"Like, don't get upset or anything. I'm not sure I should even ask this."

"Don't apologize; just ask the question," Dan kindly pressed.

"Uhm, what do you do? I mean, as a pastor. Like, I know you are busy on Sunday but what do you do the rest of the week?"

With a very serious face Dan teased, "Sunday is the only day I work. It's a great job."

Most laughed, but Crystal wasn't sure how to take him.

"He's just giving you a hard time with his bad humor," Mona apologized, coming down the stairs. "Dan, shame on you!"

"That really is a good question and I'm glad you asked. I get that quite often. Sometimes people actually believe the pastor only works on Sundays. Maybe there are pastors who only work that day. After all, one could be extremely lazy or a workaholic and get away with it. In some ways it is like being self-employed. You have to be fairly self-motivated and organized to get things done unless you are in a church that dictates what will be done."

"My old pastor, and he was really old — older than you, Pastor Lee — used to say that his job was to study all morning, eat lunch and then knock on neighborhood doors in the afternoons, teach classes and preach on Sunday," proclaimed a serious college kid.

"I didn't know thirty-seven was old, Brian. Yeah, what you are talking about was one popular school of thought. A few even hold to that today. So, what do you think I do?"

"I know for a fact that you disciple people one-on-one," Matt defended.

"Do you do counseling?" asked another.

"Sometimes I offer counsel. Yes."

"Obviously you have to prepare for sermons and class lessons," said Matt.

"He teaches then," surmised Crystal's other friend looking at Matt.

"Yep. Keep going…" Dan encouraged.

Melissa spoke up. "I know he reads a lot. You should see that library of his! And he visits people in the hospital."

Scott volunteered, "He also visits people in their home for a spiritual checkup. That's what my cousin told me."

"True. Anything else?"

No one offered anything more than the clatter of forks on plates. In the pause three of the young men went back to reload their plates.

"All these things would take up at least two days. Now, what else do I do with the rest of my time?" Dan questioned with a leer.

Mona jumped in right away. "Well, whatever it is, it keeps you busy day and night, practically the entire week." Turning to Crystal she added, "I know he's consumed by the work twenty-four-seven. It's even hard for him to take one day off!" She was a little defensive since she had on too many occasions been the recipient of people's complaints that her husband did not do enough.

"I really appreciated that page you had in the membership class that showed your average weekly schedule. It was revealing. You really do work ten hours a day?" asked one of the new members.

"Thanks. Yes, ten hours is normal, but sometimes it is eight and sometimes it is sixteen. Depends on the day's demands. Jane Rubietta says that 'Most pastors work in excess of 70 hours a week. Seventy percent don't take a week of vacation during the year, and sixty percent don't get a full day off during the week.'[1] I'm glad I have vacation time that is somewhat mandated by our denomination's tradition. All right, I have a question for you," Dan proposed, scanning the circle of guests. "What do you think a pastor should do? And I want you to be honest."

Again, for a while the only sound was the symphony of the feast. Matt broke the silence with a dribble of mustard on his chin, "Weddings!" Everyone broke out laughing. "What? What's so funny about that?"

"Got someone in mind, Matt?" one chided. He threw a pillow at his challenger.

"Funerals!" spoke another which provoked more laughter as they all looked at Matt's target.

"I know you run meetings. What's that called?" Tom queried.

"Moderating," Dan taught.

"Do you do the finances too?" Rose asked in her Argentinean accent.

"I suppose some pastors do the finances, but it's not a practice in our church. Our churches normally have treasurers. In some churches the treasurer is a deacon. The only part I have with finances is when the elders review the budget each month and at the end of the year, and prepare a new one for the next year."

"Are you the janitor for the building?" Maria asked seriously.

"No. Okay, it's time to let you in on a secret: pastors do many, many different things and wear many different hats. Because of the varieties of churches and philosophies of ministry you could not formulate one job description for all churches based upon the wide range of views out there. People expect the pastor to do everything from being the church's CEO to working as its maintenance engineer. Some expect him to be the great communicator, a building architect, the master problem solver, and all around jack of all trades. Excuse me, I'm gonna get something," he said while whisking off to his home office.

Mona and Melissa were just returning from the kitchen with trays of sliced pies and a large ice cream container. They took count of who wanted dessert or dessert a la mode. Rose and Maria offered to serve the plates around. Dan returned with some papers in hand.

"A friend of mine once said that many think the Bible says a pastor must be all things for all people, but the Bible says that Paul worked to be all things to all people. My friend made that comment because of the unspoken expectations by a host of self-appointed bosses. Those of us who are people of God's book must look to what God says he wants his pastor to do, and downplay the rest," Dan intoned.

He added, "I remember the time one unhappy man came up to me after I gave a sermon on the roles of a pastor. He said, 'Two things: pastors are supposed to be everything we're supposed to be but aren't, and pastors are here to serve us. That means you serve me!' Writers London and Wiseman said, 'Churchgoers expect their pastor to juggle an average of sixteen major tasks.'[2] On a lighter side, let me read you an email that circulated years ago; the author is unknown:

Results of a computerized survey show that the perfect pastor...
- Preaches exactly 15 minutes, condemns sin, but never upsets anyone.
- He works from 8:00 AM until midnight and is also the janitor.
- He makes $60 per week, wears good clothes, buys good books, drives a good car...and gives about $50 per week to the poor.
- He is twenty-eight years old and has been preaching for thirty years.
- He is wonderfully gentle and handsome.
- He has a burning desire to work with teenagers and spends all his spare time with senior citizens.
- The perfect pastor smiles all the time with a straight face because he has a sense of humor that keeps him seriously dedicated to his work.
- He makes fifteen calls a day on church families, shut-ins and hospitalized;
- Spends all his time evangelizing the "unchurched" and is always in his office when needed.

If your pastor does not measure up, simply send this letter to six other churches that are tired of their pastor, too. Then bundle up your pastor and send him to the church at the top of the list. In one year, you will receive 1,643 pastors and one of them should be perfect. WARNING!! Keep this letter going! One church broke the chain and got its old pastor back in less than three months!

The small group roared. Matt's laughing knocked over Scott's coffee.

"You asked a very good question, dear one. Jane Rubietta wrote that 'Expectations are the reason 33 percent of clergy leave their pastorate. Pastors are 'one of the most frustrated occupational groups in our country...the reason may have much to do with their inability to live up to the expectations placed upon them.'[3] I would add that it's not the expectations so much as the wrong expectations people have, and the undue pressure they place on pastors to fulfill those wrong expectations. Another author wrote:

The pastoral role now includes an unfocused and expanded range of duties. The congregation expects the pastor to be in charge of nearly everything (except activities that the powerbrokers want to control). Being 'in charge' here means not only seeing that the activities get done, but also that everyone interested in them is happy with them. From doing the bulletin, to repairing the furnace, to increasing the pledges and enhancing the congregation's image in the community, the pastor must see that everything is taken care of.[4]

"This is some heavy stuff, but it is something we cover in the membership classes. Just what is a good job description for a pastor?" Dan asked rhetorically. "The pastor's job description is derived from his priority to serve Jesus Christ as he serves God's people in the ways God sets forth. What people often do is set up their own job description of a pastor, usually unspoken, based on one of three models: a slave, a genie or a junior messiah. That is what London and Wiseman are referring to when they say:

Most ministers have too many bosses and wear too many hats. In many cases, congregations expect their pastors to do whatever task anyone dreams up; after all, no one knows exactly what a pastor's real job is. This may be the primary reason many churches stand still and stagnant – the pastors are overwhelmed with trivia and have no time left for what matters most.[5]

A fair percentage of denominations outline in a general way what their pastors are expected to do. Ours does. But it is difficult to put down everything a pastor does because it varies according to the God-ordained roles he fulfills and the needs he addresses."
Dan read another excerpt. This time from *The Cross and the Christian Ministry*:

Those who follow Christian leaders must recognize that leaders are called to please the Lord Christ – and therefore they must refrain from standing in judgment over them. In other words, if it is important for the leaders to see themselves as servants of Christ entrusted with a magnificent commission, it is also important for the rest of the church to see them as ultimately accountable to the Lord Christ, and therefore to avoid judging them as if the church itself were the ultimate arbiter of ministerial success.[6]

"What does this church's denomination have as your job description?" asked one of the college kids.
"I don't have our *Book of Church Order* with me, but I can get you a copy later. Let me see if I can recall: watch over the lives of God's people in his care with regard to their doctrinal beliefs and morals. Exercise church discipline, visit people in their homes, especially the sick. Teach, comfort, nourish and guard the children. Be a model of Christ.

Evangelize and disciple. Our book says that these things are done in concert with the other elders. The pastor also ministers the Word of God through preaching, baptizing, and serving the Lord's Supper."

"What roles are you talking about?" Matt asked, still sponging clean his spill.

"What does the word pastor mean?" Dan asked.

"Shepherd?" Scott replied hesitantly.

"Exactly! Think of all the things attached to the role of a shepherd. What are they?"

"Feed sheep," remarked Michael.

"Guide," added Scott.

"Protect," said Maria.

"See, you've got it. Now, can we write up an exact job description that details how the pastor shepherds God's sheep? Even in a day's work?"

"No," sounded a chorus.

"Another very important role, perhaps even more important than the role of the pastor, is that of a servant. Again, he serves the Lord first and foremost, and then serves people according to God's directives. Just like Jesus did. Like other believers he is a priest who intercedes, and like other believers he is a peacemaker or reconciler. Paul says he is like a father and a mother, an athlete, soldier and farmer. He is also a professor or teacher, a preacher, a mentor or disciple maker, a model and an evangelist. Now, imagine all the work involved in each of those roles."

"Wow! That's a huge list," exclaimed Melissa. "No wonder you were going all of the time."

"Still is!" Mona added.

"I'm really glad you asked this question. It is so important for God's people to understand and encourage their pastor in the roles and duties God has for him and not to add superfluous, extra-biblical requirements. It is most important that God's people not expect their pastor to be their personal slave, genie or junior messiah. It is also very helpful to your pastor to correct false assumptions, views and expectations by fellow members."

Melissa started clearing away the table. Others got up to lend a hand. Some of the young men went back to finish off the dessert or refill their mugs. After thirty minutes, the living and dining rooms were cleaned. Crystal and Rose washed the serving platters, while Matt took out the garbage. He was still embarrassed for spilling coffee on the braided rug.

Dan invited people to stay and relax. He pointed to the cabinet of games. Jake, awake from his nap, was six steps from the landing when he yelled for Scott to play a game with him. Some expressed heart-felt gratitude for the time and left, but a few people took up the offer to stay while Dan excused himself to take his short Sunday nap.

Later that evening Dan and Mona related to each other how encouraging the day had been. "Wish the Dumpletons and some of the others were here this afternoon," begrudged Mona.

"Wouldn't have changed a thing. Might have angered them. They want what they want and they want control. John Maxwell is right when he says that people with big problems often cause problems. In some ways they are to be pitied."

Hearing the baby crying, Mona hiked the stairs to check on her. Meanwhile, Dan went into His office to journal the day's events and reflect on the matter of his duties. He had a file folder on the subject of a pastor's job description. In his heart of hearts he knew he was fulfilling the vocation to which he had been called. He identified with London and Wiseman's comment as pastors that "Our legitimate discontent centers around playing church, coddling emotional infants, worrying about personal security, preaching arid doctrinal scholasticism, baby-sitting trivia, being controlled by spiritual pygmies and living by savage schedules that leave no time for prayer, study or outreach."[7] (1994, p. 201).

It was a hard challenge for one who hated conflict and hated confronting others even more. Dan kept a plaque by his desk that read

"Five Reasons to Glory:
1. God has entrusted you with the pastorate.
2. You have the high privilege of being identified as an undershepherd of the Chief Shepherd.
3. Sheep respond to a shepherd.
4. You are privileged to watch God's sheep be born, grow, and mature.
5. You experience unspeakable joy unknown to anyone else."[8]

In his more sour moments he would add, "and experience unspeakable pain and discouragement unknown to most." "Whether real or assumed, expectations choke the vitality out of a pastor's spirit. Then what others think or what they want tortures him with worst-case scenarios of what might happen. As a result, disquieting fears nag every expression of ministry, and pastors become so spooked that they can't see the difference between a pesky mosquito and a ferocious lion."[9] (London and Wiseman, 1993, p. 72). For Dan those fears came true in his previous pastorate. Those were pesky lions buzzing around after all! The question Dan could not get a handle on now was, "What do I do with people like Irma and Mr. Strenk, and especially with Bernie and the elders?"

Dan knew he often feared and treated the antagonists like idols in his life. He was constantly repenting of that. He also recognized that he tended toward an over-inflated sense of his importance, caught up from time to time in the self-expectant role of junior messiah, much like what Leighton Ford wrote: "Sometimes we think that God's work depends so much on us that we become feverish, compulsive and overly involved – workaholics of the kingdom rather than disciples of the King. This kind of hyperactivism does not come from the obedience of faith but from the anxiety of unbelief."[10]

London and Wiseman again nailed it with their diagnosis:

Pastors are facing a juggling act as they deal with mushrooming expectations the congregation, denomination, community, spouse, children or even self. In the Church, for example, members sometimes say straightforwardly, 'Pastor, you are paid to do the church work, so you unravel the problems and care for the details.' Even emotionally robust pastors find it takes energy and patience to cope with whining traditionalists, demanding visionaries and lethargic church members all at the same time.

To confuse the issues even more, the expectations often conflict with each other at church, at home and in the greater community. As a result, dehumanizing fatigue becomes a way of life for pastors, so even the strongest feel their stamina wearing thin…As a solution, he suggests, 'Expectations, like cataracts, must be removed because there is no way around them.'[11]

The authors also provided a prescription:

A miraculous cure for unrealistic expectations is to provide distinguished ministry especially in highly visible areas such as preaching, worship or pastoral care. Word then gets around that you do your work as well as or better than any previous pastor. Excellence means doing the work God has given His Church well and in an exciting, interesting manner.

Such an excellent expression of ministry can give you a line of credibility that you might need to weather tougher times. Many congregations overlook a pastor's faults when they know he serves competently in other important phases of ministry.[12]

Dan's lust for approbation tended to ooze a self-destructive poison in his soul. He learned he too easily catered to others' wants and wishes. Jesus never did that because he was always about his Father's business (Luke 22:29; John 5:17-47; 9:4; 10:35-38). Neither his father, mother (Luke 2:48-49) nor brothers could dictate the agenda God set for him (John 2; John 7:1-10). The pressure of the great crowds always calling him to do what they wanted was not enough for him to cater to their desires. Even in their excitement when Christ miraculously supplied a meal of bread and fish for thousands and they wanted to make him a king, he did not give in (John 6:1-15). His disciples pressured him to rescue his dying friend Lazarus, but he only went when the time was right (John 11). They were constantly trying to persuade him to do their bidding. Then there is the time when Peter was harshly rebuked as being Satan when he tried to pressure Jesus to circumvent God's redemptive plan through the cross (Matt. 16:20-28). And of course the Pharisees, Scribes and Sadducees were persistently trying to impose their Spirit-less, legalistic program on Jesus. His rebuffs and righteous rebukes contributed to their growing hostility toward Him. The man who would never bend or conform to their image of a good teacher paid for it with his life. Dan knew he had not suffered like that.

He was just as London and Wiseman described:

> One pastor opens windows of grace for others while criticizing himself: 'To a great extent, I'm a victim of expectations, my own and others. Many of us who preach grace as a way of life do not practice it in a relationship to our ministerial tasks. We're more eager to please the people than we are to rest in the fact that God wants to use us the way we are. We preach grace, but we practice a theology of works.[13]

Pastor Dan's conundrum was placed before his pastor-friends, as well as his mentor, Kent. He emailed with a very explicit question: How do I handle the pressure of unrealistic or unbiblical expectations from people in this church, especially the elders?

Dan deliberately avoided his email on Monday, so he was not aware that some solutions were waiting for him. He spent the morning on honey-do chores, including cleaning up winter's mess in their backyard. When Jake got home from school, Dan decided to take the boys to a matinee while Mona and Hannah attended a baby shower. After the movie the boys played freeze tag in the park across from the theatre. The playground equipment got a good workout too. The park was located in a large roundabout. The theatre anchored the north side, an old fashioned drugstore complete with a soda fountain was posted on the eastern entrance, the Dumpleton hardware store secured the south, and a row of small shops, including Ben's favorite reptile store, gated the western side of the street.

It was while swinging the boys on the swing set that Dan noticed Irma glaring at him through her sign littered window. Dan's first reaction was to feel a knot in his stomach, but then he stopped and asked God's forgiveness for fearing man (Prov. 29:25; Matt. 10:22-26), well, in this case a woman. *What can she do to me?* he applied Hebrews 13:6. After much study and meditation, Dan came to believe that fearing others was due to a lack of a proper fear-revere of God, and such a wrongful fear caused him to abdicate his responsibilities as an authentic, loving pastor. It contributed to his discouragement, defeats, depression and unwillingness to take calculated, Scripture-inspired risks. He had to think long and hard on what John wrote in 1 John 4:18 - that perfect love casts away fear. Doing the righteous thing before a fearsome God out of love for others is the power and antidote to fearing others.

Now, Dan wondered, how am I going to do the righteous and loving thing for this miserable woman? His first proactive step was to stop, face her and wave with a smile. Even though she quickly turned away, he showed an undeserved kindness. The second thing he did after the boys were clearly tired of the park, was to walk over to the store and track down the woman. Directed to her office upstairs, holding his boys hands, he walked into the open office. "Good afternoon, Ms. Dumpleton. Business going well for you today?" She was obviously startled and tried to brush off her unexpected guests.

"Who's dat?" Ben asked of the woman smartly dressed in a grey suit.

"That is Ms. Dumpleton and she owns this store. She's made this business very successful, you know. Practically every contractor in this county comes to her for supplies and tools." Dan could literally see the winter thawing from her. "Do you have time to give the boys a tour of your place?" Dan asked.

"I'm too busy. I can have Max help you."

Not to be put off, Dan decided to press his good fortune, as it were, and insist she show the trio around. She tried to protest. "Aren't you supposed to be at your office, Mr. Lee?"

"This is my singular day to recharge so I can go hard at it the rest of the week. I like to spend it with my family. Surely you know that, don't you?"

She scowled. A hard, self-driven perfectionist herself, she rivaled Mr. Scrooge's work ethic. Surprisingly she relented. "Oh, all right. I only have a couple minutes, but I can show you what we have here."

The tour lasted twenty-five minutes as she provided the history of the store, especially from the moment she inherited it. She explained the various departments, ways she made her clients happy, and the challenge of keeping just the right inventory. When she began to digress on the minutia of invoicing the big contractors, Dan had to excuse himself and his boys. They were getting pretty restless, and Dan's warning that the little one was having a hard time keeping his hands to himself was enough for Irma to grant them leave. She had Max show them to the door, and dismissed them with no more than a proper "Good day."

Dan pitied her all the more and determined to pray daily for her, especially as an enemy (Luke 6:28). He also determined to find ways to bless her and thereby heap hot fiery coals on her head (Rom. 12:19-20). It was a commitment to do the loving thing, a very difficult commitment.

At home, the boys told their mother about their afternoon venture. Mona was very surprised to hear about the escapade at the Dumpleton store. Dan had to explain his change of heart and tact. He told her that he wasn't going to hold his breath for change, but still prayed for change to come. Instead he was going to do what God called him to do. That was in his job description.

Dan had already outlined a pastor's job description in the class materials for new members (see Appendix J). However, what would he do to communicate that description to long term members with personal and preconceived notions about what he should do? They were not about to go through another membership class. And what of the elders who should know better but also had their own ideas? It was time to seek the wisdom of his mentor and other pastoral friends. But Dan would force himself to wait until Tuesday. That night he and Mona decided to go out for a movie. They were in the mood for a comedy. Melissa volunteered to baby-sit.

Early the next morning, he switched on the pot of coffee, and then checked his email. Dan had twenty-three messages. First, he deleted the spam and junk, quickly checked the five humorous ones his cousin sent, read through emails by the elders about church issues, and finally got to the posts he sought. He went back to the kitchen for his first cup of coffee. Back in front of the computer he opened and read the relatively short emails. None of them offered anything surprisingly insightful or gave advice he had not already considered. Still, it was good for Dan to receive confirmations that he was on the right track.

The energized father coached his boys to finish the oatmeal and toast Mona had prepared. Ben wouldn't eat it without lots of syrup. Hannah had no trouble with the porridge at all; in fact she had lifted the pink plastic bowl and buried her face in it, licking as much of the sweet cereal as she could. It was an uproarious scene of grunts and slurps followed by the display of an oatmeal-framed head. This was one of those Kodak moments, so Dan snapped a picture. Mona was not as amused since it meant a morning bath and shampoo. Perhaps Hannah conspired for the bath, an event she relished?

Jake left for school, Ben played in his room, and Hannah headed for the bath tub. Dan took his time getting ready, but was in his office by 9:00 A.M. Usually, Tuesdays were a little more difficult because he had to assume the secretarial duties Melissa once did. That meant sixteen additional hours a week of clerical work that robbed him of essential tasks. Dan's protests and pleadings to the elders went unheeded since they argued that for more than forty years the church went without a secretary and previous pastors did all the clerical work. It wasn't an issue of finances, for the little church was now in a position to hire a full time office worker. Dan argued that while tradition might explain why some things are done, tradition alone does not mean some things should be done. Dan also pointed out that he would have to cut back on other things or just let the administrative things suffer. "Giving me more non-essential things to do robs me of the time I need for studying, counseling, and discipling." They countered with a charge that he would be derelict in his duties and that he had more than enough time to fulfill their demands. Dan seriously wondered if this was a ploy to pressure him into leaving or if they were that ignorant of his tasks.

Because Dan was unable to put together the monthly newsletter, that only provoked Bernie and two other elders. Here was the occasion Dan was looking for to discuss his job description. This would be one part in his overall strategy to broadcast the job description he had formulated from Scripture and from a mound of books and articles. Along with presenting the study on the responsibilities and duties of a pastor to the elders, he would teach the subject at both the leadership class and the officers' training. When the time was right he would also interject a topical sermon series on the various Scriptural roles for a pastor, which incidentally applied to elders too. At that time, sermon notes or supplemental materials could be inserted into the bulletins as he worked through each of the main themes, and the outline would be posted on the church bulletin board. Time or not, Dan determined to work hard to have a series of newsletters speak to the subject. At least now the newsletter would have a more focused purpose than merely fulfilling tradition.

"This paper is well and good, but you are not limited to doing only these things," announced elder Frank at the elders' session. Dan usually placed a study or hot topic for discussion at the bottom of the agenda in order to accomplish normal business items first. Often times the discussions were unfinished because Dan believed 10:00 P.M. was a bewitching hour, a time when tired minds and bodies were ill-suited for a wise discussion, and ripe for irritability. Therefore, he would stop the meetings at 10:00 P.M. and put the unfinished discussion as old business on the next agenda.

Quite surprisingly, Bernie agreed with Dan's job description. "I have no problem with this paper. But, these are only the basic things a pastor does."

"I might underscore again that these are also biblical responsibilities and duties for all elders, not merely for the one dubbed pastor," Dan challenged. "Obviously the Bible doesn't spell out in specific detail how we are supposed to accomplish these things, but it gives us God's mandate and priorities for service."

"I don't agree. That's your opinion. These are things you are being paid to do," Bernie fired back.

"So you are going to argue with the clear teaching of the Bible on this subject? And argue with dozens of pastors, biblical theologians and scholars too?"

"You can make the Bible say anything you want it to!" Bernie snapped back.

"Then you also disagree with our Confession of Faith and our denomination's Book of Church Order about what the minister of God's Word does?"

"No. I think all they do is give a skeleton for what a pastor's duties are. There is nothing that says the elders can't formulate their own job description for a pastor, and nothing that says we can't add to other lists. Besides, so much of that is outdated and doesn't even touch on things the pastor should do in this day." Bernie pronounced. This was a surprising contradiction to Bernie's previously stated position.

"Bernie, are you arguing against the Bible, our Confession, and Book of Church Order on the grounds that they are out of date? But you are the one who advocates for the tradition! What – a tradition that dates back only forty or fifty years? Come on!"

"What is your point in all of this?" Joe interjected.

"To bring clarity and some objective standard to my work as elder-pastor in this church; and to prioritize my work load." Dan replied.

"Are you confused about what you should be doing? Because if you are, we can draft a job description for you," commented another elder.

"That's a good idea!" declared Bernie.

"I agree," added Frank.

"No. The point is that the very priorities for ministry found in Scripture should determine what I do and what all of us as elders should do. Other things such as planning youth activities or doing clerical work or mowing the lawn are secondary, even tertiary, to the very essential ministries I am called to do. My recommendation is that you adopt this outline as this church's job description. In fact, I so move," Dan said. Though nobody seconded the motion, Dan explained that it was very problematic for any pastor to try to fulfill all of the spoken and unspoken demands and expectations of members, including the elders. "On many occasions, you men have made it clear that what I do around here is either not enough or not good enough! What is also clear is that I am not doing much of what God says I should do because our priorities are wrong."

"Whose fault is that?" Bernie snapped.

After a ten-minute debate, the vote was cast against adopting Dan's outline. It supposedly limited elders from asking or requiring other tasks of the pastor. Dan told them that he planned on teaching this material and preaching on the Biblical roles of pastors and elders. The elders told him he could not preach on the subject, but if he wanted to he could teach it in classes, and warned him that if he did preach on the subject he would be charged with insubordination, refusing to submit to the will of the elder board.

They also decided to put together a committee of three elders to draft a job description for the pastor. Obviously the meeting did not go as well as Dan had hoped.

"So what do I do now?" he asked Kent the next morning.

"Look, here's the thing: you are not what they want in a pastor. No matter what you do, unless you conform to their paradigm for a preacher and pastor, they will never accept you."

"But Pastor Rick said that I should put up a good fight; take the men to the presbytery and all that."

"That's one way to approach it, but let me ask you a few questions: Do you believe you are ever going to change their minds?"

"Doesn't look like it. They haven't changed so far."

"Do you believe you can push this issue and gain support from the vast majority of the church? Or would it cause a split?"

"There would definitely be some sort of a split."

"So what are your options?"

"Stay and deal with it or leave."

"If you stay, you should know that it would likely take a long time to see the kind of changes necessary to bring your church into a greater conformity to Scripture. The other option is to conform to their paradigm for ministry. To see change you will not only have to outlast the antagonists, but you will also need to build up a new and strong base of people who agree with a biblical vision and mission for the church. It could happen, but you'll need to commit yourself for the long haul, ten to fifteen years perhaps," Kent advised. "Two books that might be helpful to you…"

"Okay, I'm always ready to read more."

"The first is *Red Light Green Light* by John Cionca. It's basically a book to help you decide with some objectivity whether to stay where you are or to leave. The other is Craig Larson's *Staying Power*, which argues for staying and making a difference. If you can get them in time you could read them during your trip to Oregon."

A CHALLENGE TO THINK AND DO

What do you think?
1. Name at least one main thing you learned from this chapter.
2. According to the Bible, what job description does God have for a pastor?
3. If you were at the meeting that Dan presented a biblical job description to the elders, what advice would you give?
4. What does your pastor do in a given week?
5. Does your pastor have a formal job description? If so, is your local church aware of it?
6. What is your response to Dan's statement when he said, "A friend of mine once said that many think the Bible says a pastor must be all things for all people, but the Bible says that Paul worked to be all things to all people. My friend made that comment because of the unspoken expectations by a host of self-appointed bosses. Those of us who are people of God's book must look to what God says he wants his pastor to do, and downplay the rest,"
7. How should your pastor handle the pressure of unrealistic or unbiblical expectations from people in the church?

Some things you could do:
1. Study the Bible and list the things God expects a pastor to do (refer to Appendix J). How would you prioritize these things?
2. Write down your personal expectations of the things the pastor should do. Compare them with the Biblical list. Why would your expectations be more important than anyone else's?

8

AT YOUR SERVICE, MASTER

—⟋⟍⟍—

The ringing was coming from some distant and remote place. It was persistent and grew louder, until he realized it was the phone on the nightstand. With his mind muddled from deep sleep he picked up the phone more out of habit than cognition. "Hello," Dan said weakly.

"She's only got an hour or so to live. Please come. Our family needs you here," he vaguely heard.

Without even thinking he agreed. "I'll be over as soon as I can." He forced himself to sit up, rubbed his face with his hands, and tried to crawl out of his dreams. Grabbing his robe, he practically stumbled down the creaky stairs and into the kitchen. The mug came off the rack and was placed under the running faucet. Dan shuffled over to the microwave and zapped the container for two minutes. He threw a slice of bread in the toaster and then made his way back to the sink to wash his face with cold water. The mental mist was beginning to dissipate when the microwave beeped.

He took two caffeinated coffee bags, dropped them into the bubbling water and added a touch of sugar. Leaving the coffee to steep he practically jogged up the steps. It took him five minutes to dress and make it back downstairs. A scribbled note was promptly stuck to the white fridge. Dan then snatched the unbuttered toast and braced it between his teeth while grabbing his mug on the way out the kitchen door. The stove's clock read 2:34.

He stepped out into the warm sultry air from his air conditioned house. It was oppressive, yet fit the occasion. Intermittent dollops of fog especially thick where the four-lane road cut through meadows put a drag on his time. The snail's pace gave him time to inhale his toast and guzzle the black ink. Parking near the three-story building was easy. Dan double-timed his way around to the emergency room entrance. No one stopped him as he charged through the closing elevator doors. The ride up two stories seemed to take as long as his drive out.

When the noisy old doors pulled open, he turned immediately left and fled down the corridor to the fourth room on the left directly across the hall from the nurses' station. With the door nearly shut, he gently knocked and entered a dimly lit room. The stuffy room with the scent of the hospital's medicinal potpourri was overpowered by a putrid urea. The haunting melody and rhythmic beat of clicks, hisses and beeps from the various machines pulsated in the background. Wires and tubes draped here and there monitored her breathing, pulse, and blood pressure and regulated drips of morphine and sedatives to ease the pain and panic.

Marilou's tall husband tearfully shook Dan's hand and thanked him for coming. The two daughters stood to the right of their mother. Jane, the oldest child held holding her mother's right hand. Lydia was backed up against the large window, her husband seated to her right. Jane had obvious command of the situation from day one. It helped that she was a nursing supervisor at her hometown hospital. Even this night she was well put together, dressed in a silver halter top blouse, charcoal grey slacks and dressy black sandals, which coordinated with her salt-and-pepper hair. Tears had washed her navy blue mascara and most of her rose-tinted blush away.

Jane acknowledged Dan and explained that her mother had lapsed into a coma around 1:00 A.M. Although the doctor gave her several more hours, Jane had a confident sense that it was a matter of minutes. Jane recounted for him the previous day's events and the last words her mother uttered in the early afternoon.

Marilou's breathing was as weak as her skin's grayish-yellow undertone. As did Jane, Dan sensed the sixty-seven-year-old rested on the precipice of another world. From the day the doctors confirmed their diagnosis, Marilou fought the breast cancer courageously but the beast had come upon her with a treacherous swiftness. She refused to surrender to her beast until three weeks ago; and she refused to return to the hospital until she could no longer bear it. On his regular visits Dan could literally see both cancer's daily possession and death drawing the life from her. He gently encouraged her to give in to heaven's call and assured her that her husband, daughters and grandchildren were in good hands.

Marilou had made a profession of faith at Grace and was baptized shortly after her first round of chemotherapy. Although Dan was willing, he had never been trained for this kind of ministry. At seminary he and his classmates received an hour's worth of lectures on various mercy ministries.

Jane asked Dan to lead the little group in prayer. He agreed and kindly ordered everyone to gather around the bed. Mack held his wife's left, cold, limp hand. Dan stood at the foot of the bed in between the sons-in-law and reached for their hands. "Let's pray," he softly commanded. He could hear Marilou take three short gasps each followed by three long pauses. The very moment he said "Amen" she gasped one last deep breath through her parched and peeling lips and then exhaled her last.

A machine's hushed beep of her erratic pulse now softly whined. Mack and Lydia broke down. Jane and the men remained silent. Two nurses quickly entered the room to check on their patient. One immediately left the room and summoned the doctor on call. In five minutes he arrived and officially pronounced her deceased. The attending nurse wrote down 3:24 A.M. as the official time of death, and then shut off all the machines. She told the pastor she would give the family as long as they needed before returning.

After tearful reminiscences, around 4:15, the family decided it was time to leave their beloved wife and mother. Mack stopped at the nurses' station to sign a few forms before joining his family in the vacant cafeteria. Jane did most of the talking, explaining the funeral plans and other essentials to Dan. When exhaustion caught up to the family they hugged and promised to gather the next day at Dad's. They thanked Dan profusely for his service. Dan committed himself to be available whenever they needed him, and with that, he walked out into Saturday's rising sun.

This was one of the most difficult weeks in Dan's life. The previous Sunday started quite well, with the blessing of a baby's baptism. The infant girl's parents were relatively new members at the church, having given a credible profession of their faith in Jesus Christ about the time their child was conceived. They understood that the baptism did not confer a guaranteed salvation upon Madison's soul, but rather it was a sign and seal that pointed to the sacrificial death of Christ for sin. Her parents vowed to love and nurture her and to call upon her to apply a saving faith to the meaning of her baptism, trusting in Jesus Christ as Savior from her sin, guilt and God's wrath. That afternoon was spent celebrating the baptism with the parents and their extended family at the baby's new home. Dan and Mona left their two sons at home with a babysitter, but brought their own little newborn with them.

He was unable to take his normal Monday off because of another crisis: a middle-aged woman made a surprise visit to the Lees' home to talk with the pastor about leaving her husband. The thirty-seven-year-old minister and his sweet wife listened to the frantic woman's story of neglect, verbal, and emotional abuse. The meeting lasted over two hours. Dan was able to get her to commit to counseling, but she said she could not ask her husband to come for counseling because he would explode in a rage and that would only make things worse for her and the children. She was a member of the church, but her husband never professed faith in Christ. The story was uncannily familiar.

That afternoon at the hospital, he extended his visit with Marilou. His evening supper was interrupted with a frantic phone call from one of the long-term members. She was crying so hard that at first he understood her to say that her husband had died. Dan's heart sank. He immediately took off for her home only to discover her husband standing with her at the door and to find that it was her husband's father who had passed away. Obviously the two were grieved and quite upset. For Dan it was a big relief on the one hand seeing her husband alive, but also sad to share their grief.

Dan also discovered mid-week that a deacon and several families had been meeting privately to discuss "the issue with the pastor." When the pastor asked the deacon about it he admitted there was a gathering, but said it was an informal fellowship that had nothing to do with the pastor. Knowing full well this deacon's friendship with the Dumpletons and Deacon John who had left the church, Dan urged the man to follow Matthew 18 - to talk with him directly about concerns or Dan's apparent sins before talking with others. He also warned him that if the rumors were true and he was involved in gossip or slander or divisiveness, Dan would have to proceed with formal discipline against him. The deacon acted as if there was nothing wrong and assured the pastor he would come to the pastor if he had any grievances.

Wednesday afternoon Ellie May's family asked him to visit her in the nursing home. She was an eighty-one-year-old member with Alzheimer's disease whose health was also failing. She did not recognize him or remember his visits, but the family appreciated them. Irma was always quick to remind him it was his duty to check on her, and Bernie would scold him if he missed a week.

These were unexpected events that fought for Dan's normal schedule of the regular Tuesday morning Bible study, a pastoral visit that night, a luncheon appointment Wednesday, a care group meeting on Wednesday night, the bi-weekly prayer meeting in the church's basement on Thursday night, the Friday morning prayer gathering with some of the elders and deacons, Friday afternoon discipling with Matthew, Friday night youth activities, and the Saturday morning breakfast and leadership training after the hospital ministry. Dan was finding it very difficult to finish his sermon and the Sunday bulletin. The pastor had to get the hymns to the pianist and finish the bulletin in time to run it over to the printers. He also had to prepare for Saturday afternoon's presbytery committee meeting to investigate charges against one of the pastors in the region for supposed abuse. He hadn't finished his assigned homework on that either.

Then very early Saturday morning he received the dreaded summons to the hospital. No one, not even his mother, told him there would be weeks like this. Nevertheless, as his military brother would remind him, this is what he signed up for. It was. He was called to serve. From the moment he became a committed Christian, and got involved in the life of a church all the way through seminary, he had a romantic vision of serving as a pastor. The school of life often has a habit of teaching masterful lessons through strong doses of reality.

It took Dan more than four years of pastoral service before he understood that his priority was to serve the Lord before serving others (Acts 20:19; Gal. 1:10; 1 Thess. 2:4; Eph. 6:6-7; Col. 3:22-24), and to serve the Lord by serving others. It also took that long for him to catch on that he was to serve the Lord's agenda, but not any other agenda that deviated from his most vital mission. Not until he learned that hard won lesson did he run across Brian Dodd's statement: "Bob Schaper, a seminary professor of mine, taught me a motto that has helped me keep the balance between obedience to Christ and a servant-like posture towards people: I am your servant, but you are not my master."[1] Dan had a friend take the professor's statement and make a framed calligraphic wall hanging for his office, not so much for visitors to the office but for him to keep this cogent and balanced truth always before his eyes.

Various opinions abound about the nature of pastoral service, just as there are about his roles and duties. Even scholars, theologians and pastors differ on the subject. Some say the primary role of a pastor is as a priest and worship leader. That was a predominant view of the medieval church and is a pronounced feature in certain hierarchical churches. Others declare that the primary role of a pastor is as preacher. The Reformation period emphasized this role, and various traditions still hold this position. In the Reformed tradition the pastor is preacher, declaring the will of God to sinners and saints. In some Baptist or other like churches the pastor is preacher who preaches an evangelistic message of salvation to the sinners sitting in the pews. Certain independent Bible churches see the role of the pastor as teacher whose purpose is to teach the church solid doctrine whenever it gathers. Such churches were quite popular in the 1960s to late 1980s, though several exist today. Their model for church is taken from the classroom. In the era of megachurches pastors are perceived as chief executive officers who oversee a large staff who, in turn, direct and run the many programs. Recently there have been many books calling for churches and pastors to see the pastoral role as primarily that of a biblical shepherd, which, of course, is the meaning of the term pastor.

However, the overarching model in Scripture for a pastor which ties all other roles and duties together is that of servant, just like Jesus the grand Servant. Christ declared that anyone who desired to be great in his kingdom must be a servant, just as he had come not to be served but to serve, even to the point of sacrificial death (Matt. 20:26-28). That was God's mission for him – the eternal Son of God came to be a man, and in a radical reversal of human proclivities became a lowly slave in order to accomplish the high purposes of God (Phil. 2:7; Heb. 12:1-2). He was and is the perfect prophet, priest and king, the wonderful shepherd, teacher, healer, and savior, but he executed all those roles through God-ordained, God-directed service. Jesus was and is the consummate humble servant (Isa. 49:5; Luke 22:27; Heb. 3:1-6), the One who was self-sacrificing (John 10:11, 15; cp. Luke 10:34, 35).

Jesus made it clear that the manner in which his disciples were to function, rule, lead, and shepherd the citizens of God's kingdom was in the form of a willing servant and a humble slave. That was the object lesson the Master taught in Luke 22 when he said that while he sat as the premier one at the table he really sat as servant. Then, when he wanted to summarily demonstrate what he had been teaching all the while about the nature of his disciples' role and position in the Kingdom, he dressed down and acted just like a common slave washing his disciples' feet (John 13:1-17). This living parable was punctuated by Christ's own teaching: "You call me Teacher and Lord, and you are right, for so I am" (Jn. 13:13 ESV). In other words, they were right to address and treat him as dignified royalty. Yet though this King of kings and Lord of Lords had every right to claim his place and title he does something dramatically profound, once again a reversal to humanity's sinful nature – he declares himself an honorable servant: "If I then, your Lord and Teacher, have washed your feet, you also ought to wash one another's feet" (John 13:14)! And should his disciples be as dense as many of us, he explains exactly why he said and did what he said and did: "For I have given you an example that you also should do just as I have done to you. Truly, truly, I say to you, a servant is not greater than his master, nor is a messenger greater than the one who sent him. If you know these things, blessed are you if you do them" (John 13:15-17). "[S]ervant leadership must be humble because proud people serve only for what they get out of it. Humble people serve for the sake of those being served, not for their own sake."[2] Christ's people are servants, and leaders in Christ's church are servants of servants. A reversal from the natural world.

That's the nature of Christ's kingdom – a topsy turvy world as John Gilmore tells it:

Hans King writes: 'For those who supported law and order, he turned out to be a provocateur, dangerous to the system. He disappointed the activist revolutionaries by his nonviolent love of peace. On the other hand, he offended the passive world-forsaking ascetics by his uninhibited worldliness. And for the devout who adapted themselves to the world, he was uncompromising. For the silent majority he was too noisy, and for the noisy majority he was too quiet, too gentle for the strict and too strict for the gentle.'[3]

To understand how radical and also how degrading was Christ's self-imposed position and the servant place of his disciples we must understand the nature of the ancient slave. There were several Greek terms for servant or slave.[4] The first, more common word was *doulos* which identified the person as being on the opposite side of the class spectrum of freeman or citizen master-owner. A *doulos*-slave was owned either by the government or by a personal master. The public *doulos*-servant had no rights, but could control a city's treasury and, as such, wield considerable influence. The *doulos*-slave owned by a personal master was the more common type of servant. As a non-person he or she had absolutely no rights: no right to marriage, to children, or to protection as a slave, but merely protection as the master's property. The slave existed for the master's purposes. The will and desires of the master were to be obeyed and fulfilled. Anything the master wanted of the slave he got – anything![5]

The Romans had over a dozen different terms which defined the nature of the slave's duties: a cook, farmer, footman, gardener, messenger, prostitute, steward, storekeeper, etc. In other words there could be specialist slaves and those might include the role of teacher or physician. A *doulos*-slave could be given the responsibility to oversee the finances and run the household, in which case he was a household steward who had control over the master's other slaves (Matt. 8:9).

There was the *pais* or *paidos*, which described someone of a child's status (Matt. 2:16; Luke 8:51). When these terms referenced an adult it was to identify a servant or slave who would most likely always remain in that status of a "boy" unless some gracious circumstance emancipated him and brought him to the legal status of a man.

Another type of servant was a *diakonos* who rendered service, help or aid to another, many times voluntarily. Usually the tasks were of a necessary, but mundane or menial, nature. The very term itself did not necessarily mean he or she was a slave; but he or she served or ministered in some capacity. The individual could be a waiter at a special function or a household servant. The *diakonos*-servant may or may not have been paid. Those godly men specially gifted and filled with the Spirit of God whom God called to serve alongside the apostles in order for the apostles to dedicate themselves to the tasks God had ordained for them were called deacons (*diakonos*) (Acts 6).

One other Greek term the Bible uses is the *huperetes*-servant. This was an assistant or helper who was given the task of carrying out the expressed will and explicit orders of another. He could be a court officer (Matt. 5:25), an officer in the Jewish Sanhedrin (Matt. 26:58), a king's attendant (John 18:36) or an attendant in a synagogue (Luke 4:20).

Of all those above the most contemptible, despicable position of that day was that of a *doulos*-slave. Yet, it is that very classification Jesus, Lord of the universe, took upon himself (Phil. 2:6-8). Jesus, was God's master servant who came to serve and not be served (Mark 10:45; Luke 22:27). He is the glorified *paida*-servant of God (Acts 3:13; 3:26; 4:27, 30). Jesus fulfilled the model of *doulos*-slaves Moses (Deut. 34:5; Ps. 105:26; Mal. 4:4; Rev. 15:3), Joshua (Josh. 24:29) and King David (2 Sam. 3:18; Ps. 78:70; Luke1:69; Acts 4:25) exemplified in the Old Testament. Jesus came not only as God's slave but came to be a *diakonos*-servant to Israel (Rom. 15:8). Like a perfect slave, Jesus put his life subordinate to the cause of the Father's will.

As the steward-slave, Jesus was and is the overseer of God's other servants or slaves. He told the disciples that if anyone would serve him that person must follow him, and wherever Jesus would go his servant would also be there. But not only that, those who serve the Christ-Servant will be honored by the Master-Father (John 12:24-26). Later Jesus identified another position disciples have, and that is as his friends (John 15:15-27). His point was not that they were emancipated from serving their Father-God, or Christ, or one another, but that they were now privy to understand the will of the Master in a way similar to Jesus. But the specific will they were to understand was the inevitability of being persecuted and suffering just as their fellow *doulos*-servant Jesus (John 15:20). All true disciples of Jesus Christ are *doulos*-slaves of their Master. And therefore all disciples hold that same level status with all the other *doulos*-slaves of God.

Jesus, the master servant, orders his subordinate servants to minister just like him (Matt. 20:25-28; 23:11-12; Mark 10:43, 44; Luke 22:26-27; John 13:1-20). That means Christ's disciples, who would be given the Spirit, be empowered as apostles to lay the foundation for the New Testament people of God, who had Christ's delegated mandate and authority, were to administer their positions first and foremost as servants (1 Cor. 4:1-2; Tit. 1:7). After Christ's death and resurrection this rag tag group of class-inferior men was elevated to a remarkably high and lofty position in the eternal body of Christ. Nevertheless, they and all those who immediately followed in their footsteps had the mind of Christ in them. That is, since Jesus set aside his rightful place as God and lived for others as the Servant of servants (Phil. 2:3-7) they did too. If he did, and they did, so should we.

In the New Testament the term that most frequently classifies one in the role of oversight and administrative rule in church government, is not "pastor." For that noun is used only once, in Ephesians 4:11 and the verbal form "to pastor" or "to shepherd" is used in Acts 20:28 and 1 Peter 5:2. The overwhelmingly most popular terms are the *doulos*-slave or *diakonos*-servant. The person in this position is a serving minister. However, today the word minister tends to pack baggage that escapes the lowly, humble service role of a slave. Perhaps the pastor should be labeled slave or steward-slave? Yet again, he is a slave to Christ and of God, who sacrificially serves others (John 10:11, 15; cp. Luke 10:34, 35). Other slave-disciples are not masters, even over the specially called and ordained minister.

The identities given to the apostles, elders and pastors in the New Testament fully illustrates this. They are all identified as *doulos*-slaves or *diakonos*-servants that do specific ministries (acts of service) (Acts 6:4; 2 Cor. 3:3). Peter, James, John, Jude are *doulos*-slaves of God and the Lord Jesus Christ (2 Pet. 1:1; James 1:1; Rev. 1:1; Jude 1:1). Paul uses *doulos*-slave and *diakonos*-servant at least as often as the title apostle. This is because more than anything else he is called to serve God, the saints (Rom. 15:25; 2 Cor. 8:19), and even Gentile unbelievers. He is a *doulos*-slave in Rom. 1:1; Gal. 1:10, Phil. 1:1; Ti. 1:1, and a *diakonos*-servant in Eph. 3:7; Col. 1:23, 25. At his conversion, God abruptly called and appointed Paul to be God's *huperete*-servant (attendant, assistant who carries out the explicit orders of his master) of the Gospel of Christ to the Gentiles (Acts 26:16-18). Paul labels what he does service or ministry in Acts 20:24, Rom. 11:13, 2 Cor. 3:1-6; 4:1-2, and 1 Tim. 1:12. Luke later says that he received his information for the Gospel record he wrote from the eyewitnesses and *huperete*-servants of God's Word (Luke 1:1-2).

These apostles were not the only slaves or servants. Paul's young protégé and fellow-servant Mark, author of the Gospel, was useful for *diakonos*-service (2 Tim. 4:11), as was Paul's son in the faith, Timothy (1 Tim. 4:6; 2 Tim. 4:5). Phoebe, a godly woman and friend of Paul's was it (Rom. 16:1-2). Other men, often recognized as church planters or pastors were *diakonos*-servants, translated *ministers*: Archippus (Col. 4:17), Epaphras (Col. 1:7), and Tychicus (Eph. 6:21; Col. 4:7).

The ways in which God's servants minister vary. As noted already, they are to serve as slaves to God (2 Cor. 6:4; Tit. 1:1, 7) and of Christ (Phil. 1:1; 2 Tim. 2:24). These ministers must understand, along with others, that their lives and ministries are living sacrifices to God (2 Sam. 24:24; Acts 20:24; 21:13; Phil 2:7; 3;7-8; 2 Tim. 4:6). Through love they also serve one another like a *doulos*-slave (Gal. 5:13), using whatever gift(s) God gives in order to *doulos*-serve one another (1 Pet. 4:10). The Corinthian church, fellow servants of Paul, is an example when they ministered to the saints in Jerusalem through their financial gifts (2 Cor. 9:1, 2, 11, 12).

All believers in Christ are equal as humble slaves (Acts 2:18; 1 Cor. 7:22; Eph. 6:6; Col. 4:12; 2 Tim. 2:24). They are called to do God's bidding, serve Christ, and minister to one another. Yet, as we have seen, some of these slaves have been called, gifted, trained and ordained to be steward-slaves in a special office ordained by Christ (2 Cor. 3:9; 4:6; Eph. 4:11ff). These stewards administrate and oversee God's household by means of God's Word through love (Matt. 28:18-20; Mark 6:34; Acts 20:20; 1 Cor. 12:28, 31; Col. 1:28; 1 Tim. 1:3; 3:2, 16; 4:11-12; 6:2-5; Jas. 3:1 Rev. 7:17), and they serve in the mysteries of God (1 Cor. 4:1). Performing service in Christ for God's people (2 Cor. 4:5), ministers must do so with diligence (Rom. 12:8; 1 Thess. 5:12; 1 Tim. 5:17; 2 Tim. 2:15).

These servants, placed in their respective roles and particular offices, are answerable to God. They are to live for Christ, never be ashamed of him (2 Tim. 1:8-11; 2:11-13), always be focused upon him (Gal. 2:20; Phil. 1:21; 2 Tim. 2:8-13) and always ready to suffer for him (Luke 21:19; 2 Tim. 2:3-7; 3:10-12).

Therefore, the pastor and elder are called to train and discipline their lives for godliness (1 Tim. 4:7-11) so as to become and serve more and more like Jesus the perfect servant (Matt. 20:25-28; 23:11-12; Mark 10:43, 44; Luke 22:26-27; John 13:1-20; 2 Cor. 3:10; 1 Tim. 4:14-15; 6:11; Tit. 2:12; 2 Pet. 1:4). After all, the pastor and elder are to incarnate and model Christ (2 Cor. 12:18; 1 Thess. 2:10-12; 1 Tim. 4:12; 1 Pet. 5:3). The pastor and elder are also to put to use the good gifts the Lord has placed upon them. Indeed, they are called upon to fan the flame of God's gifts in his life (1 Tim. 4:14; 2 Tim. 1:6).

These ministers are to serve God's people as Christ's stewards. Their aim is neither to cater to people, to please people (Gal. 1:10), nor to fear people (Deut. 10:12; Eccl. 12:13; Ps. 118:6; Isa. 12:2; 2 Tim. 1:7; 1 Pet. 1:17; 2:17). At the same time, no judgment is to be leveled against them by fellow servants of Christ based upon their personal preferences or desires (Matt. 20:20-28; Rom. 14:1-4).

While the slave or steward is the all-encompassing paradigm for those who have been gifted, called, tested and ordained to the office of pastor or elder, they minister primarily through God's Word (Mk. 6:34b; Jn. 21:15ff; Col. 1:28; 1 Thess. 5:12; 1 Tim. 5:17; 1 Pet. 5:1ff; Jas. 3:1). What's more, they serve through the various roles identified by God in his Word. The roles a minister is given includes serving as a shepherd (Jer. 3:15; John 21:15ff; Acts 20:28; 1 Pet. 5:12), a professor-teacher, a preacher, parent, a peacemaker, a mentor and model, and as an evangelist. The servant-minister is also described with roles like an athlete (1 Cor. 9:24-25; Phil. 3:14; 2 Tim. 2:5; 4:7-8; Heb. 12:1), a farmer (2 Tim. 2:6), a messenger (2 Cor. 8:23), a soldier (Phil. 2:25; 2 Tim. 2:3-4), and a good worker (2 Cor. 6:1; Phil. 2:25).

Ultimately, Jesus' ministry provides the model for all his ministers. London and Wiseman report:

The life of Jesus provides a wonderful pattern. He modeled spontaneity of service. Wherever He went, He had time for the person in front of Him. I can't remember one time in Scripture where He told a needy person to take a number or make an appointment. When we don't make room for margins, the person in front of us is an obstacle we have to get around to get to our next appointment. But what if the person in front of us is the exact expression of ministry God has planned for us next? Jesus provided a model of caring for the need of the person in front of you.[6]

Marilou and her family were at the front of the line. The abused wife was there too. Other incidentals at the top of Irma's and Bernie's and the deacon's lists were of lesser importance, and in the grand scheme of eternity insignificant. They had no right to dictate their preferences or command their desires to Daniel. No fellow disciple-servant does.

God's providential work was exerting a transforming pressure upon Pastor Dan to teach him in a mild sense what Paul had to learn in a tortuous way:

But we have this treasure in earthen vessels that the excellence of the power may be of God and not of us. We are hard pressed on every side, yet not crushed; we are perplexed, but not in despair; persecuted, but not forsaken; struck down, but not destroyed — always carrying about in the body the dying of the Lord Jesus, that the life of Jesus also may be manifested in our body. For we who live are always delivered to death for Jesus' sake, that the life of Jesus also may be manifested in our mortal flesh. So then death is working in us, but life in you. And since we have the same spirit of faith, according to what is written, 'I believed and therefore I spoke,' we also believe and therefore speak, knowing that He who raised up the Lord Jesus will also raise us up with Jesus, and will present us with you. For all things are for your sakes, that grace, having spread through the many, may cause thanksgiving to abound to the glory of God. Therefore we do not lose heart. Even though our outward man is perishing, yet the inward man is being renewed day by day. For our light affliction, which is but for a moment, is working for us a far more exceeding and eternal weight of glory, while we do not look at the things which are seen, but at the things which are not seen. For the things which are seen are temporary, but the things which are not seen are eternal (2 Cor 4:7-18).

While the pastor had gone through the most challenging week in his pastoral ministry, he did not come close to Paul's "light afflictions:"

From the Jews five times I received forty stripes minus one. Three times I was beaten with rods; once I was stoned; three times I was shipwrecked; a night and a day I have been in the deep; in journeys often, in perils of waters, in perils of robbers, in perils of my own countrymen, in perils of the Gentiles, in perils in the city, in perils in the wilderness, in perils in the sea, in perils among false brethren; in weariness and toil, in sleeplessness often, in hunger and thirst, in fastings often, in cold and nakedness – besides the other things, what comes upon me daily: my deep concern for all the churches (2 Cor. 11:24-28).

Everything Paul did after his conversion, call and commission was in the service of Christ to serve Christ's Church. Moreover, Paul was living out biblical servitude as described in Isaiah 50:4-6 and 53:7, for he endured beatings, mockeries, and spittings without retreating in fear or retaliating in fury. Dan was certainly humbled when he read these verses during his morning devotions. Some of the pressure he had been feeling was self-imposed. He was allowing intruders to stress him out. So what if he did not finish the bulletin or completely resolve people's problems or lead the studies perfectly or unintentionally offend demanding, self-absorbed, self-appointed masters? What mattered was that he was to serve with Christ's priorities by grace, mercy and love. As John Frye says, "Compassion, Christ's activated love, received and given away to harassed and helpless people, is the heart of empowered pastoral ministry."[7]

At the top of the list in need of Christ's compassion were Marilou and her family. So too was the woman in crisis. Yet also preparing Sunday's message from God was a top priority. All else could be done another time. If the critics did not like it, then so be it. Neither Paul nor the rest of the apostles would cater to the selfish preferences and whims of the emotionally and spiritually immature. Why should Dan, or any other minister?

Paul made it clear that his ministry was empowered by God through the Gospel treasure in his own body (2 Cor. 4:7). He went through great trials as he bore the cross of Jesus for others. In Christ Paul took up his own cross, dying to his wants and ways so that the redemptive, reconciling life of Jesus would be brought about in others. That is the nature of true Christ-like, pastoral ministry. In fact, that is the core value of all true church ministries. Paul was often down, but never out. He later defended the ministry of the Cross which he and his co-workers were engaged in against the many different accusations hurled at them:

We give no offense in anything, that our ministry may not be blamed. But in all things we commend ourselves as ministers of God: in much patience, in tribulations, in needs, in distresses, in stripes, in imprisonments, in tumults, in labors, in sleeplessness, in fastings; by purity, by knowledge, by longsuffering, by kindness, by the Holy Spirit, by sincere love, by the word of truth, by the power of God, by the armor of righteousness on the right hand and on the left, by honor and dishonor, by evil report and good report; as deceivers, and yet true; as unknown, and yet well known; as dying, and behold we live; as chastened, and yet not killed; as sorrowful, yet always rejoicing; as poor, yet making many rich; as having nothing, and yet possessing all things (2 Cor. 6:3-10).

Pastor Dan was learning more lessons in humility and seeing some things from a heavenly perspective. Pastoring was indeed hard and challenging, but nothing compared to what he might be called to do for Christ. His ministry in Christ was difficult but relatively easy compared to Paul's and others like Paul who gave all their lives for Jesus in service to his Church.

Paul, in 2 Corinthians 6:3, was not claiming that the antagonists (and he had many) were not offended. They chose to take offense, unreasonably and sinfully so. What Paul was saying was that no matter what his enemies were saying, he had a clear conscience because from God's assessment of things his ministry was not offensive. From this passage Daniel was beginning to really grasp the nature, the core of a true servant's ministry. A far cry from what so many want of a pastor's ministry!

Lest any Christian conclude that only Jesus and his ordained pastors are servants who humbly serve, this call to Cross-centered, Gospel-possessed ministry applies to all true believers. Many within the church seek power, position or praise. The ones who seek to obtain it the most are the ones who are the least in Christ's estimate (Mark 10:43, 44). These also tend to be the most obnoxious and abusive. It is time God's people recognize such arrogant evil for what it is and call for genuine repentance or for excommunication.

All of God's people, regardless of their position in life or in the church are called to serve God for his glory (Exod. 7:15; 8:1; 9:1, 13, 23:25; Deut. 10:12; Josh. 24:14; 1 Chron. 28:9; 2 Chron. 34:33; Rom. 7:6; 12:11; 1 Cor. 15:58; Eph. 6:7). We are all called to serve God:

- in love with all our hearts and all our souls (Deut. 10:12)
- with sincerity and truth (Josh. 24:14)
- with fear and trembling (Ps. 2:11)
- with gladness and singing (Ps. 100:2)
- with goodwill toward others (Eph. 6:7)
- acceptably with reverence and godly fear (Heb. 12:28)
- with humility (Matt. 10:42; 25:23, 37, 47; Mark 9:41; John 12:3; Acts 20:18-19)
- and with joy (Ps. 40:8; Ps. 100:2; Luke 10:17)

In Christ we are also called to use the liberty we have to serve others (Gal. 5:13). In fact, if we are truly the Lord's then we will serve others (John 13:14; 2 Cor. 4:5; Gal. 5:13; Phil. 2:3-8). Pastor Dan recognized the importance of self-sacrificial service for the good of the Body of Christ and therefore taught new members how biblical service is manifested through the New Testament's one-another commands:

1. God's people serve by praying for others in the church. Indeed God commands it of his servants (Acts 13:1-3; Jas. 5:15, 16; Eph. 6:18-19; I Tim. 2:1-4). We see examples in Jesus' prayer for his own (John 17) as well as Paul's prayers for believers (Eph. 1:15-23; 3:14-19; Phil. 1:3-11; Col. 1:9-12; 2:2-3; I Thess. 3:10-13; 2 Thess. 1:11-12).
2. God's people serve by sharing the Truth of God's Word with one another
    a. By edifying or building up one another (Acts 20:32; Rom. 14:19; 15:2; 1 Cor. 14:26; Eph. 4:12-13; 1 Thess. 5:11)
    b. By exhorting and encouraging one another in Christ (Heb. 3:13; 10:24-25; 1 Thess. 4:18; 5:11)
    c. By teaching one another in God's Word (Deut. 6:4-9; Col. 3:16; Heb. 5:11-14)
    d. By admonishing one another. To admonish means to train by word through reproof. (Rom. 15:14; 1 Cor. 10:11; Eph. 6:4; Col. 1:28; 3:16; 1 Thess. 5:12, 14; 2 Thess.3:15; Tit. 3:10)
3. God's people serve when they demonstrate true love and Christian community with one another (John 13:34-35; 15:12; 1 Thess. 3:12; 4:9-10; 1 Pet. 1:22; 3:8; 4:8; 1 John 3:11, 23; 4:7, 11; 2 John 1:5). They do this when they
    a. Seek the good welfare of others (Rom. 15:2), for this is a self-giving, sacrificial demonstration of the goodness and grace of God
    b. Refuse to have ill will toward anyone (Rom. 13:8-10)
    c. Seek to do good to all people, but especially toward those that are of the household of the faith (Gal. 6:10 cp. 1 Cor. 13; Col. 3:12-17)
    d. Show authentic affection to one another (Rom. 12:10ff; 16:16; 1 Cor. 13; 16:20; 2 Cor.13:12; 1 Pet. 5:14)
4. God's people serve because they have Christ's servant's attitude (Rom. 12:10; Eph.5:21; 1 Pet. 5:5).
5. Servants will practice hospitality toward one another (Rom. 15:7; I Pet. 4:9).
6. Christ-like servants will care about the needs of others (1 Cor. 12:25; Gal. 6:2).
7. God's servants will exercise spiritual gifts for the benefit of others (Rom. 12; 1 Cor. 12; Eph. 4:11ff; 1 Pet. 4:10).
8. Believers will serve each others with humility, gentleness, patience, and bear with one another in love (Eph. 4:2).
9. Christ's people will submit to one another in the fear of the Lord (Eph. 5:21; 1 Pet. 5:5).
10. God's servants will build each other up (1 Thess.5:11).
11. His servants will forgive each other in Christ (Col. 3:13).

12. God's people will serve by finding ways to stir each other up to love and do good works (Heb. 10:24).
13. Servants of Christ, among other things, will be careful
    a. Not to condemn others in Christ about matters of personal conscience (Rom. 14:13)
    b. Not to destroy the character of others (Gal. 5:14, 15, 26), nor speak evil against others (Jas. 4:11-5:9)
    c. Not to lie to one another (Eph. 4:25; Col. 3:9)
    d. Not to allow bitterness, wrath, anger, angry shouting, blasphemy or slander and malice to be expressed toward one another (Eph. 4:31)
    e. Not to sue one another in a secular court of law (1 Cor. 6:7)

The things God put Dan through to teach him that he was first and foremost God's servant, were potent and difficult lessons. Nevertheless, he was grateful to the Lord for them. As he drove home from the hospital that sultry morning he was able to ruminate upon the week's crises, but more importantly, upon God's tutorials. Wearied physically and emotionally, it did not stifle that sense of liberty that was welling up within him – a true liberty to serve God's people in God's way.

The question that loomed over him was whether this particular church was willing to change according to a more biblical model of servanthood or if not, should he exert his energies in another church.

A CHALLENGE TO THINK AND DO

What do you think?
1. What have you learned from this chapter?
2. What do you think it would have been like if you were a slave in Jesus' day?
3. Who does your pastor serve?
4. The pastor's "priority is to serve the Lord before serving others, and to serve the Lord by serving others." What does this mean?
5. What is your response to, "In the New Testament the term that most frequently classifies one in the role of oversight and administrative rule in church government, is not 'pastor'... The overwhelmingly most popular terms are the *doulos*-slave or *diakonos*-servant."
6. Interact with the statement seminary professor Bob Schaper made: "I am your servant, but you are not my master." Is that biblical? In what practical ways would that be played out in your church?
7. Consider the many ways believers are commanded by God to serve others in the church. What kind of a servant are you, and how well do you serve?
8. In what tangible ways are you serving others in your church? Serving your pastor?
9. "Many within the church seek power, position or praise. The ones who seek to obtain it the most are the ones who are the least in Christ's estimate (Mark 10:43, 44)." How does this comment affect you?

Some things you could do:
1. Write down the tangible ways you are serving the Lord.
2. Write out the tangible ways you are serving others in your church. How does it compare with the ways God wants you to serve?
3. Write out the tangible ways you are serving your pastor (and elders).

9

SHEEP HERDING 101

—ᴍ—

Summer's heat was established by late March with intermittent bouts of cool and colorful spring. Dan and Mona decided to take advantage of the school's break which followed Easter to visit a friend in Montana. This friend was a pastor who offered strategic counsel to Dan from time to time. As it turned out, he and his family owned a ranch with a small flock of sheep. Rick wanted to immerse himself in the place of a shepherd to understand the dynamics of the biblical metaphor for God, king and leader of God's people. He also wanted to experience firsthand what it meant to handle sheep. It was time for Dan to take advantage of his friend's invitation. He too wanted to learn as much as he could about the subject, and this was also a wonderful learning adventure for the children.

It had taken the Lees a few years to save enough money for this trip, and now the time had arrived. The eight hours it took to travel from house to airport, fly with two layovers, and then driving thirty-minutes to the ranch wearied the family. Nevertheless, the trial for the children was worth it when they finally realized where they would be staying for the next five days. Rick and his dear wife promised the boys a tour of the barn and ranch after supper.

With the help of her three teenaged girls, Sheila prepared a delicious feast of lamb, baked potatoes, corn on the cob, carrots, freshly baked rolls and muffins, served with sparkling apple cider. The boys dutifully ate a few bites of the lamb, but devoured the corn, rolls and drinks. Ben turned his nose up at eating one of Pastor Rick's pets, and Jake did not like the taste or the texture of the meat. Mona, on the other hand, thoroughly enjoyed the lamb with mint jelly. To everyone's delight dessert was strawberry shortcake with real whipped cream.

As promised, Pastor Rick took the boys and Dan for a tour. Mona stayed behind to put the very tired and cranky baby down for the night. Rick and Sheila's daughters performed their normal after supper kitchen routine while Sheila put on some coffee and tea for the evening's visit.

Rick and Sheila purchased the old ranch originally founded in 1922, complete with the stereotypical white house and red barn. Since they knew they were not going to work a large ranch for very many years, they sold off parcels to a contractor, much to the consternation of their long-established neighbors. From the sale they purchased sheep and all the accoutrements necessary for shepherding. They also repaired the barn and remodeled the kitchen, bathrooms and added a new master bedroom with its own bath. That gave each of their daughters their own rooms and a bathroom to share upstairs.

Rick put on his boots and offered Dan the extra pair. Mona, already apprised by Sheila about what to expect at the ranch, brought along coveralls and rubber boots for the boys. Good thing too, since the region had been splashed by a late afternoon shower. Jake and Ben's first impulse was to run outside into what they perceived as boundless fields bordered by patches of forest. After allowing them to run wild on the front lawn, Dan corralled his little lambs.

With their energy expended, Rick summoned them to the barn. It was not altogether spectacular, more of a workshop and storage building than anything else, but the boys liked playing hide and seek in the old stalls. They were especially interested in the winged boarder who had perched its nest near the upper floor's door. The eighteen-inch tall barn owl took notice of the young boys. Its light colored, heart-shaped face tilted slightly to study the visitors with its brown eyes. The shadows made it difficult to see its rust color with brown spots. Rick explained that barn owls usually nested this time of year.

"Will it lay eggs?" Jake asked.

"Probably so. That's why it's building a nest there."

With that the owl leaped forward and flew out the window. The foursome went to the front door to watch it flap and glide to a distant pine. As they turned back into the structure, an unfamiliar sound blew upon their ears, "Shrreeeee, shrreeee!"

"What's that?" asked a wide-eyed Benjamin.

"That was probably the owl," explained the rancher.

"No. Owls say 'whooo, whooo!" declared a confident Ben.

"Well, that's the language these owls speak up here in Montana."

"Ohhhh," replied the little man. Somewhat frightened by what he considered a large bird and its surprising screech, Ben then asked, "Can it eat people?"

"Will it eat lambs?" joined Jake.

"This kind of owl likes to eat rodents like mice and rats. That is why we enjoy having here as our guest in this barn."

Walking through the back of the building the foursome could now easily observe a few chickens and a rooster erratically dancing around in their large screened enclosure. Ben rushed ahead and clawed his fingers through the wire mesh, while Jake tried to mimic the boast of a rooster. They were promised many opportunities to collect fresh eggs during their stay.

To the right, located several yards behind the house was Sheila's garden, surrounded by a makeshift fence. Rick explained to his tourists that the foil ribbons located throughout the garden were intended to frighten the blackbirds, and old soup and fruit cans dangling here and there were to help fend off unwelcome deer. "Sheila has even used lion dung to scare off the pretty but pesky creatures," Rick declared.

"Gross me out!" announced an animated Jake.

"Me too!" chirped his little shadow. "Daddy, what's dung?"

"Poop."

Benny with a scrunched up face and wrinkled nose, exclaimed, "Yucky!"

Dan now could see where Rick was leading them – to a small hill, upon which stood two sheep. He assumed correctly that the little flock was grazing on the other side. When they arrived at the large gate Rick called out toward the hill. The boys echoed, but were soon startled to see a couple dozen dirty sheep running over the hill toward them. Ben immediately ran to hide behind his father's legs.

Rick and his family purchased a few Finn sheep, which they could sheer for its soft and shiny wool or sell for meat. The flock had a mix of white, black, black and white, and spotted ewes, lambs and a ram. Rick explained that the sheep often produced twins, and not wanting a large ranch they would frequently sell the sheep, especially the rams. Ben liked the lamb with markings reminiscent of Holstein cows. Jake preferred the pure black lamb. Dan didn't care for any of them. They stank.

The gang, as Ben called the lot of them, slowed their pace to a stop when they noticed unfamiliar faces. "They have an uncanny ability to recognize the voice and face of their master," Rick taught. "Some studies suggest they can recognize up to fifty different faces of sheep."

"What's the gang doing?" Ben asked.

"The gang," Rick chuckled, "is banding together. They'll do that because they like to be social…they like to be close to their friends. For some reason, they have to see four or five other sheep near them to be comfortable. Otherwise they will get very upset. They'll huddle together too when threatened by an enemy such as a wolf. What they will do is run away from the enemy and then come together as a herd and face him. Sheep that get left behind or separated from the flock are usually the ones who get hurt or eaten. They've slowed down because they probably aren't sure of you three. Did you know they can spot you, a dog or a wolf as far away as 1500 yards?"

"My teacher said sheep are dumb, but turkeys are worse," Jake said, trying to demonstrate how knowledgeable he was about the wooly creatures.

"Yeah, what about that?" asked Dan.

"They can be pretty dumb sometimes, but not as dumb as people tend to believe. They can learn and remember, for as long as six weeks. Somehow they can even figure out what plants to eat to make them feel better or which ones are toxic. They are very friendly, and will keep a few other sheep as friends for a couple weeks at a time. Sheep have a flocking instinct too, so that you can put together two or three flocks and each flock will recognize their own as well as their shepherd. It's been documented among some breeds that they can figure out how to cross a cattle guard by rolling over the pipes rather than walking over them. Leadersheep in Iceland are supposedly quite intelligent."

"That doesn't sound too dumb," Dan concurred while Ben was plucking grass and trying to throw it at the sheep some distance away.

Rick then added, "Where they show stupidity is when a single sheep will wander aimlessly away, sometimes even into dangerous situations, and the flock will naturally follow along. They have a strong instinct to follow the leader."

"Sounds like a sermon illustration I could use," Dan mused.

Rick turned to lead his guests back to the house. Ben yelled, "Baaah, baaah. I said bye-bye to my little lamb." Jake laughed.

After a quick warm bath, the boys were tucked into the eldest daughter's double-sized bed. The girls volunteered to sleep together in the basement. After prayer, Ben insisted that his daddy tell a story about a lamb. Not a collector of lamb stories Dan had to wing it. Thankfully his little ranchers found sleep shortly after "once upon a time."

Downstairs the adults lounged comfortably in the living room, sipping coffee and tea and nibbling butter cookies. The hours passed quickly as they had much catching up to do. Rick and his wife decided to retire when the clock chimed eleven, but invited their friends to enjoy the log fire as long as they wanted. Dan turned off all the lights and cuddled his wife on the couch in front of the stone fireplace. It was peaceful – and incredibly quiet save a few snaps and cracks from a fresh log. They relished the solitude and peace. Their home and church seemed a galaxy away.

Were it not for little Hannah crying for attention at 7:17 A.M., Dan and Mona would have slept longer. The boys had already dressed themselves, though Ben clumsily so. Sheila planned to cook eggs and pancakes, so she sent the boys off with the youngest daughter to collect the eggs. It was a great adventure for them. Hot, black coffee, brewed from dark roasted beans, aroused the sleep out of Dan. Mona was more of a tea drinker. Rick, already out and about the ranch, soon joined them. He needed to get to the church office by 9:00, and it was a thirty-minute drive.

The Lee family found it easy to get into a sweet and leisurely routine. Rick and his family, fantastic models of hospitality, offered the Lees as much rest and encouragement as they wanted. They knew well the challenges and pressures of pastoral life (in more ways than does the average shepherd). Dan suggested they open up a bed and breakfast.

After breakfast the boys found entertainment on the tree swing and otherwise occupied their curiosities and expended their boundless energies in the garden and field by the house. It was all under the mothers' four watchful eyes.

Dan stole away down the street toward a forest. Montana's cool, fresh morning was invigorating, but not as invigorating as the beauty of God's evergreen creation. Whiffs of pine spiced the sweet aroma from the nearby meadow. Thankfully he was spared the smell of sheep. The well-pronounced path indicated that these woods were not strangers to guests, just like Dan's hosts. The path kindly pulled him into abundant shade splashed here and there with brilliant strokes of light. The forest embraced him; it smiled upon him and whispered songs through needles and leaves in a harmony with song birds. A woodpecker provided echoes of occasional percussion. *Heavenly! So heavenly! Father, thank you so much for this*! The pastor now joined the praises of creation in worship and awe.

Dan sat upon an old dead log into which, providentially, a small cross had been carved on the fragile bark. Not with human hands; perhaps by a worm? Irregular, wavy, but a cross nevertheless. Dan was so appreciative and happy at this moment, that he found himself caught up in verbal praises. This peaceful ecstasy easily absorbed an hour. Reluctantly, he meandered back to the ranch, but while in Montana, he would make this his haven every morning.

Rick allowed Dan the freedom to talk shop when he was ready. By the third day Dan was ready. The first item for discussion was Dan's decision to pursue the interview at a church in Oregon. Rick replied, "If you start looking for another call then you are as good as gone from your current ministry." What he meant was Dan had already mentally begun to leave. Most pastors who start in that direction do leave. He also knew that people often believe they have been betrayed if they discover their pastor is seeking another call on his own initiative.

"I'm not a quitter by nature, but the elders and I are not only on opposite ends of the philosophy of ministry, but on the opposite ends in a philosophy of life! Plus they don't trust me, so they won't follow me. Then there is the conflict with Bernie and his clutch," Dan protested.

"You need to stay and fight. Have Bernie and all other trouble makers disciplined right out of the church!" Rick was a no-nonsense fighter. He too had been confronted by people like Bernie, his sister, Katrina, and Deacon John, and often disciplined them. Rarely did they stay and repent.

"Easier said than done. There would be no support from the elders; we've already been down that road."

"You need to take your rod and staff and be their shepherd."

"That's why I am here – to learn more about being a good shepherd."

"Your Bernie has been that flock's self-appointed shepherd. For him it is all about being a big fish in a little pond. It's a power trip for manipulative controllers like him. C'mon, follow me."

Dan walked with Rick toward the grassy knoll. They were going to watch sheep. "Remember that sheep are consummate followers. Their trouble is that they follow pretty much any sheep who will take the lead, especially if the shepherd is not around."

No sooner had Rick said that than a large black ewe began to wander off toward the forest. It did not take long for several others to follow. Rick was not too worried since his property was fenced.

"There's your Bernie or Irma. They don't know what they're doing or where they are going. They are oblivious to danger. Unlike people, that old sheep over there did not intentionally lead the rest of the herd. But sheep can lead other sheep astray. A shepherd is one who assumes leadership over a group of sheep. And as you know, there are good shepherds and bad shepherds. What God's people need are good shepherds."

"So what have you learned about being a good shepherd?" Dan asked.

"What I've learned has given me a more comprehensive understanding of the biblical image. The shepherd is in a humble position. He is a sheep herder who feeds, leads, guides, and protects his sheep. A good shepherd cares for his sheep that can be stubborn and stupid and stink. Their extreme curiosity often causes them to wander. Sheep are fairly helpless without a shepherd. They'll leave the good pasture to graze in areas where the food is sparse and in an area where they become vulnerable and unable to protect themselves."

"Lots of analogies there."

"A good shepherd must know more than the basics about his sheep. For example, there are lots of different kinds of sheep, so I had to research which type we wanted. I understand shepherds in Third World countries will name their sheep and are able to recognize each one by the markings, color, behavior and flaws. It takes work. Not quite the round-the-clock work of dairy farmers, but still, it takes work. Much of it is routine, mundane, and at times pretty trivial. Shepherds who take their flock out into the wild pastures will spend days with them and end up on duty twenty-four hours a day."

"Man! So much like pastoring a church!"

"A good shepherd who knows his sheep rather intimately is absolutely committed to them. It takes real compassion to care for them, courage to protect them and patience to put up with them."

Hmm, am I that good of a shepherd to those people? Dan continued to listen to the different duties of Rick and his family to care for the sheep. He enjoyed the anecdotes, some of which were funny, while others were sad.

After the long walk and talk, the men drove off in the pickup for the church office. Rick and Dan discussed applicable lessons to Dan's current pastorate.

"You need to wear the shepherd's hat and be more assertive," Rick admonished.

"The problem is that we have several shepherds who don't agree. While I believe the church ought to graze over in this pasture, the others want to keep the flock in the same old used up pasture. Bernie has his own flock, and the previous shepherds left behind their different flocks that won't recognize my voice or follow my lead."

"Then maybe you should gain their respect and trust and let the belligerent leave or die off. I still say you should be much more proactive in disciplining the problem sheep."

As he and his family helped around the ranch, Dan got a better sense of shepherding. Their time at the ranch was not only educational, but also very restful and refreshing. Their visit passed too quickly, and before they knew it the Lees were making the long trip back home. When he stepped into the pulpit that Sunday morning, Dan had a slightly different perspective about God's little flock.

As a perpetual student, Dan began to research the subject before the trip and continued to study shepherding for a couple of weeks after he returned. He already knew that God gifted certain men to be pastors (Eph. 4:11). Shepherding is one of the services that God's servants render. They are to oversee and shepherd the flock of God (Acts 20:28; 1 Pet. 5:2).

The one gifted and called to the office of servant-shepherd is to faithfully conduct the work as Christ's under-shepherd. The pastor is a steward who cares for God's flock, for Jesus is the master Shepherd (Heb. 13:20). God the Shepherd-King pastored his flock in the Old Testament (Gen. 48:15; 49:24; Ps. 23, 80:1). While there are many metaphors for God, such as the rock, a refuge, etc., the metaphor of a shepherd is given primarily in God's relationship to his covenant people (Ps. 95:7; 100:3; Isa. 40:11; Ez. 34:11-16). First used by Jacob in Genesis 48:15, and then by Moses in Deuteronomy 32:6-12 this image depicted the Lord as the ultimate provision for life, and God's safe leading and gentle care over his people. The picture portrays God's gracious, intimate and strong character so that one who trusts in him can say with King David, "the Lord – my Shepherd!"

God, the Good Shepherd, took his flock out of Egypt and safely guided them through the wilderness to that holy pasture (Ps. 78:52-54). Ezekiel 34 provides a beautiful image of our great Shepherd. He searches and rescues his stray sheep (Ezek. 34:10-12, 16). He brings them back to his own territory to feed, to water and to protect (Ezek. 34:13-15). He binds the injured and strengthens the weak (Ezek. 34:16). This loving Shepherd tends to his flock gathering in his strong arms the little lambs and leading the ewes with their young (Isa. 40:11).

Jesus, the eternal God, is the Great Shepherd. He said so in John 10. This good Shepherd (John 10:11), knows and loves his own who in turn know and love him (John 10:14). He said this in contrast to the false shepherds who were hired hands with no loving interest in God's flock (John 10:12). Christ's sheep recognize his voice and respond to his call. Subsequently they follow him. Jesus puts his life in the entrance of the corral so that those who are his will enter through him, and receive protection from thieves, robbers and wolves (John 10:12). Once they have entered through him he gives his sheep and lambs a wonderfully full life (John 10:7-10). This Shepherd leads his people to great pastures and keeps them from being scattered.

Old Testament kings of Israel were to shepherd God's people (2 Sam. 5:2; Jer. 3:15; 10:21). They were to do so according to the integrity of their hearts, and to guide God's covenant people by the skillfulness of their hands (Ps. 78:72). Likewise today, God's good undershepherd is to be like his master Jesus (Ps. 23; 77:20; John 10:1-19; Acts 20:28; 1 Pet. 2:25; 5:4) whose life and work is contrasted with hirelings, strangers, robbers and thieves. They care nothing for God's sheep. Indeed they use, abuse, steal and kill them. Jesus sacrificially loved his sheep (John 10:15 cp. Neh. 5:17ff; Phil. 2:17; 3:7-8). He even proved his love by dying upon the cross for them. This is what his Father, the owner of all the sheep, wants in a true shepherd (John 10:16-18).

The hirelings, strangers, robbers and thieves have always been around. God warned, condemned and punished them. He punished shepherds who were pastors in name only. Why? Because, as Ezekiel 34 also tells us, those men called to serve as under-shepherds failed miserably. They fed their own lives but not the sheep (Ezek. 34:2). The hirelings took wool from the sheep to clothe themselves, but they did not strengthen the weak, heal the sick, repair the injured, rescue the stray, or seek after the lost (Ezek. 34:1-4). These pastors neglected God's flock (Ezek. 34:5), and because of their harsh and abusive rule the sheep scattered only to become food for the wild beasts (Ezek. 34:4-5).

Glenn Wagner applies this well:

In contemporary terms, when God's people are led by pastors who lack a shepherd's heart, at least three things tend to happen: (1) People splinter into cliques and never develop the kind of congregational fellowship designed by God; (2) they become much more susceptible to the blandishments both of cultic groups and of charlatans out to plunder them; and (3) they tend to leave behind sound doctrine and a vibrant relationship with God in search of more and more aberrant teachings that promise some kind of spiritual "buzz."[1]

The root of the problem with false shepherds, whether they are ordained pastors or elders, or self-appointed leaders, is that they have no true love for the Great Shepherd or love for the sheep. Again, from Mr. Wagner:

Problem: The heart of a shepherd never beat in these leaders' chests.
Result: The people were led astray and turned away from God. It wasn't that these leaders lacked a vision for the future or that they failed to inspire confidence. It was not that they abandoned good management principles or disregarded sound leadership theory or even that they neglected to hear what their constituents were telling them. The kindling that fueled the conflagration to come was that they didn't care for the sheep. That, God says, is what lit the match that burned down the ancient Jewish nation… In other words, it isn't service that guards leaders against

ineffectiveness and abuse of power, but love; not technique, but concern; not keen insight, but genuine caring – which is exactly the characteristic at the top of a shepherd's job description![2]

God does not take lightly the failure and abusive actions of neglectful or false shepherds. Jeremiah's words are a prophetic indictment where God executes a lawsuit against them. As the perfectly righteous and just judge, God tries their actions and hearts, finds them guilty and discharges the punishment for their evil. In the Old Testament they sinned against the Lord (Jer. 2:8), so God promised to give his sheep shepherds after God's own heart to lead and feed (Jer. 3:15). The trouble with bad shepherds is that they stupidly do not seek out God's will (Jer. 10:21), they trample God's vineyard (Jer. 12:10), and they ultimately scatter and destroy the sheep (Jer. 23:1-4).

What was God's condemnation and punishment? The answer:

Wail, you shepherds and cry out, and roll in ashes, you lords of the flock, for the days of your slaughter and dispersion have come, and you shall fall like a choice vessel. No refuge will remain for the shepherds, nor escape for the lords of the flock. A voice - the cry of the shepherds and the wail of the lords of the flock! For the LORD is laying waste their pasture, and the peaceful folds are devastated because of the fierce anger of the LORD. Like a lion he has left his lair, for their land has become a waste because of the sword of the oppressor, and because of his fierce anger (Jer. 25:34-38 ESV).

Dan's analytical mind kicked in. *If Wagner is right, am I a good undershepherd? Do I really love God's sheep? On the one hand, we have cliques and seem to lack a vibrant relationship with the Lord. On the other hand, I know I do not love all of the sheep like Christ loves them. I am too fearful and selfish.* But then he continued to reflect on the dynamics and history of the little church. They developed cliques because of their allegiances to previous pastors who served short terms and left. The prominent and consistent leaders have been Bernie and his sister.

I don't know their hearts, God. You do. But it seems to me that they don't quite fit the profile of the false shepherds...or do they? Bernie is the only official elder-shepherd of the power players in the church. The others are self-serving, though sometimes well-intentioned, who have no business even trying to act like leaders or shepherds. All Dan had for an assessment of Bernie was observable behavior and fruit. Does the little man truly provide for the sheep at Grace? Does he spend time with them to strengthen and encourage? Does he seek to come to the aid of the sick; or merely see to it that the pastor does all the work of mercy? Does he at any point rescue the stray, such as his own daughter-in-law or seek out the lost? Is he a genuine leader who guides God's little ones or is he just a gatekeeper of traditions that he and his lot have established? Dan could only make an assessment based upon the relatively little time he had been at Grace, but thus far the answers were in the negative. If Bernie was an elder-shepherd in name only, no matter how strong his influence, he had no business being in that position.

At the same time the pastor contemplated how he himself failed God's sheep.

With this new insight Dan decided to put together a lesson for the three men who were being trained for the office of elder. Demonstrating the differences between true and false shepherds, Dan went on to teach what shepherds do. His starting point was 1 Peter 5:1-4:

> So I exhort the elders among you, as a fellow elder and a witness of the sufferings of Christ, as well as a partaker in the glory that is going to be revealed: shepherd the flock of God that is among you, exercising oversight, not under compulsion, but willingly, as God would have you; not for shameful gain, but eagerly; not domineering over those in your charge, but being examples to the flock. And when the chief Shepherd appears, you will receive the unfading crown of glory (ESV).

"We saw in our last lesson," he told the men, "that an elder serves in many ways, especially as a guide of sinners to heaven, as a guardian of the household of God and as a gatekeeper of the corral of God's sheep. The undershepherd is to sacrificially serve the sheep, faithfully feed them, lovingly lead them, and deliberately defend them.

"Peter, the apostle, identifies himself as a fellow elder who witnessed Christ suffer but also had a taste with James and John of the glory to come. One of the main points of Peter's letter is that we follow the same path of Jesus – first the cross and then the crown; first the suffering and then the glory."

Dan taught them that Peter's exhortation was probably the lesson he had learned after the resurrection of Christ. John gives us the account in chapter twenty-one. In his resurrected body, Jesus, the Great Shepherd, was having breakfast with his disciples. He turned to Peter and asked in three different ways if Peter truly loved him. Each time the disciple claimed he did; the third time he became pretty distressed. The lesson Jesus was driving home was that Peter's primary way to demonstrate his love for Christ was not through mere sentiment or even a passionate emotion. The primary way for undershepherds to lovingly serve Christ is to faithfully and lovingly feed and care for Christ's flock!

When Peter wrote his letter, he admonished fellow elders to do what he was called to do: shepherd Christ's sheep. How? By exercising caring oversight. In what way? Specifically, without external pressure to be an elder or pastor, but rather deliberately or intentionally because this is what God wants. The elder or pastor is not to shepherd the flock out of greed or a lust for financial gain, but willingly. They are also not to exercise oversight by domineering. Instead the elder and pastor shepherds by example.

About the same time the pastor and his family arrived at Grace Church, the six-foot one-inch Marcus was hired on as a shift manager at a local factory. The thirty-three year old, big-boned black man married the very feminine and petite Sheree. They had two little boys about the same ages as Dan and Melissa's children. Marcus grew up Baptist, but became a conservative Presbyterian through a university ministry, where he also met his wife. He received his degree in business management. She pursued architectural design. Marcus served as a deacon in their previous church and came to Grace with strong endorsements from them, for he was a serious student of Scripture.

Marcus and Dan were becoming friends. He and Sheree had already encountered Irma and a few of her women friends. Two of the women made it clear with Marcus and Sheree that they did not appreciate that the new pastor was attracting people of color, which included everyone who was not of European-Caucasian descent. Dan and Mona pleaded with their new friends to stay the course and ride out the storm with them. Thankfully they agreed, and the fact that Marcus was nominated by a clear majority indicated that the church was changing for the better.

As a student of management and leadership, Marcus asked Dan to clarify his comment that spiritual, church leadership was somewhat different than secular leadership. "What does it mean to be an elder-shepherd who *leads* God's people?"

"Shepherds lead, hence they are leaders, yet in the New Testament, the common cultural term for leader was never used of God's undershepherds. In the Greco-Roman culture of the New Testament era, respectable leaders were proud, domineering, commanding and powerfully authoritative. Jesus was despicable in their eyes because as a humble teacher he was the opposite of their stereotype of a true, manly leader," Dan explained.

"Marcus has a point," inserted the forty-eight-year-old Neil. "Leadership today isn't like that of the Greco-Roman leader."

Dan answered, "Much of what is being taught today about leadership comes from Christian men or is highly influenced by Biblical principles. Old paradigms for leadership and current models for leadership in many countries outside of the United States are rooted in philosophies not unlike the Greco-Roman ideas. My point is that leaders in God's church are of a quality and lead in a style somewhat different than secular leaders."

The pastor went to the white board to write down significant points. "Our word 'leader' is expressed by the Hebrew terms:

1. *captain (Isa. 9:16; 2 Sam. 5:2; 2 Kings. 20:5; 2 Chron. 11:11)*
2. *governor (1 Chron. 29:22; 2 Chron. 28:7; Jer. 20)1)*
3. *prince (1 Kings 17:7; Job. 3:15; 12:19, 21; 29:10; Ps. 76:12; Prov. 28:16; Ezek. 28:2)*
4. *ruler (1 Sam. 25:30; 2 Sam. 6:21; 1 Chron. 5:2; 2 Chron. 6:5)*[3] (Damazio, 1988, p. 18).

"What is important to note is that the root meaning of one Old Testament term for leader, *nagiyd*, is servant. As we have seen before God's leaders in the Old Testament were described as servants. At the same time it has the idea of someone who is at the front leading followers. In the New Testament Greek the words pioneer, ruler, founder, captain, chief or chief speaker are sometimes translated leader."[4]

Dan told them that virtually no ancient or Greco-Roman concept for leadership would be equated with biblical servitude. However, Jesus Christ, the King of all kings and Master of all masters is the epitome of this model. That is one of the significant differences between the two, which J. Oswald Sanders corroborates:

> Leadership is often viewed as the product of natural endowments and traits of personality – intellectual capacity, force of will, enthusiasm. That such talents and scholastic attainments do greatly enhance leadership is beyond question, but these are not the factors of paramount importance in the spiritual leader…Not the number of one's servants but the number whom one serves, is the heavenly criterion of greatness and the real preparation for leadership. Greatness of exaltation is in proportion to greatness of service humbly rendered.[5]

"I'm beginning to see a difference between the biblical and non-biblical models, but in the Old Testament wasn't God a domineering leader?" Phil posed.

"Do you know what the primary analogy or word picture God uses to describe his leaders in the Old Testament?" the pastor asked.

Silence.

"Shepherd! Do you know what the common symbol was for a king in many Ancient Near Eastern cultures?"

"A crown?" asked Neil.

"Guess again."

The men offered no other suggestions.

"A shepherd's tall staff. Kings were shepherds of people, but true godly kings who followed the Lord were *benevolent* kings like God. He was and is the benevolent ruler-king who loves and serves his people for their ultimate good. That's what the Twenty-third Psalm is about."

Phil responded, "I am having a hard time seeing how someone can be a leader and a servant at the same time."

"Understandable." Dan confirmed. "Growing up, was your dad the leader in the home?"

"Yes, of course. He was the only parent in our home."

"Did your father also serve you?"

"Hmmm…I suppose so."

"Sure he did!" Dan replied. "He served you when he cooked for you, when you were ill, when you needed help with homework, when he drove you to Little League or came alongside of you in the Scouts. Yet none of that negated or made his leadership any less did it?"

"No," answered Phil pensively.

"Like we've talked about before, one can serve you without you being the master, and you can serve others who are not your masters. God served his people like a shepherd and father, but his people were never God's masters!"

The discussion progressed and mental lights turned on. They learned that God told Israel in Deuteronomy 17 what kind of shepherd-king they were to have. Unlike with other nations, Israel's king was supposed to lovingly fear and obey God (Deut. 17:14-20). This was in order to guide God's people along righteous paths, to guard and protect them, and to serve them through the means of God's Word for their good welfare. Incidentally, this is exactly how God's elders are to shepherd the Church today: through the means of God's Word (Mark 6:34; John 21:15ff; Col. 1:28; 1 Thess. 5:12; 1 Tim. 5:17; Rev. 7:17). The books of the Chronicles and Kings evaluated Israel's kings by their faithfulness to God's Word or to God's worship.

The Old Testament Hebrew term *ra<ah* means to care for or tend. When it is used in the noun form it is normally translated "shepherd."[6] Another Hebrew word *paqad* can mean either "bestow care" or "bestow punishment." Wagner stated thus:

> One authority explains, 'The basic meaning [of this word] is to exercise oversight over a subordinate, either in the form of inspecting or of taking action to cause a considerable change in the circumstances of the subordinate, either for the better or for the worse.' Jeremiah used the word in both its positive and negative senses...
> The prophet employs a frightful wordplay to announce to the foolish shepherds that because they did not 'bestow care on' (paqad) the sheep, God would 'bestow punishment on' (paqad) them.[7]

Dan reflected on the lessons he picked up at the ranch. "Shepherding-leaders are humble servants who care for the sheep and do what is in the best interest of those sheep. Contrast that with domineering leaders. We will explore this later, but for now let's just outline some ways leaders can be sinfully domineering."

"Most domineering leaders I know are selfish, proud and lack compassion for others," said Marcus.

"I'd say too," Phil added, "that they love taking charge and insisting on their own way no matter if they are right or wrong."

Neil contributed, "I'm not sure if this is always true. I don't want to get into psycho-babble, but I've known bad leaders who set up an environment where they not only manipulate, but also where people end up having to depend on them. Like a co-dependent kind of situation."

"It happens. It's a danger even for me," Dan confessed. "I want people to need me, but that's not why I am a pastor. I am a pastor in order to serve others for their ultimate good. It's a real fight trying to avoid manipulation and this lust for wanting others to need me."

"Selfish leaders usually manipulate through controlling influences like rules and regulations and policies. They relate to others with an air of superiority," Marcus added.

Phil agreed. "Lots of times they think of themselves as superior because of their position and therefore think and act as if their subordinates are inferior people."

"Isn't that the truth!" joined Neil.

"We could probably continue all day on this, but I think we all get the point," Dan said as they all nodded in agreement.

"You are not saying there are no similarities between spiritual-church leaders and secular leaders are you?" asked Marcus.

"No, not at all! Neither am I saying that secular leadership is always domineering. All true leaders, it seems, are direction setters or visionaries, coaches, lead communicators, and often agents of change. As visionaries they tend to see the big picture and look toward the horizon. As coaches they know how to train the people to become a coordinated team working toward a common goal or for a common purpose. They are generally the ones who are motivated to take the initiative. They are decisive and determined. Unique and strong leaders are agents of change, though as John Maxwell has frequently said, leaders are just as inclined to oppose changing anything they've established. These dynamic leaders are able to recognize a problem that requires change and then set out to help people to understand the reason for the change. These are the kinds of things we see with secular *and* spiritual leadership."

"So then, where is the difference? I still don't see it," Marcus admitted.

"Well, again I refer you to Sander's *Spiritual Leadership*. He outlines a comparative chart between the two," Dan said as he searched for his notes to place upon the board. "Here," said Dan as he wrote some of the list:

Natural Leadership	*Spiritual Leadership*
Self-confident	*Confidence place in God*
Knows men	*Also knows God*
Makes his own decisions	*Seeks God's will in decisions*
Enjoys commanding others	*Delights in obeying God*
Motivated by personal considerations	*Motivated by love for God and others*
Independent	*God-dependent*[8]

"Sanders' comparisons are helpful at one level, but perhaps it might be more useful to compare or contrast the two types of leadership this way." Dan drew two overlapping circles on the board making three sections. Over the left section he wrote "spiritual", over the middle oval he place "shared" and over the right section he wrote "secular."

"Look, we've briefly covered these three areas. But here are some things we all need to get: First, when it comes to leadership within God's church, we must be careful to define and determine our principles for leadership from Scripture. That is our starting point. This middle oval with shared leadership traits and roles is neither our starting point, nor our significant paradigm. All of this stuff in here is secondary to this stuff over here to the left. You with me?"

The men were very much engaged.

"The biblical paradigm and model for leadership informs who we are as elders and pastors as well as what we do. Our methods and philosophy of ministry should then flow from this biblical base," he said as he tapped the left section.

Phil asked, "What about the popular idea that pastors today can be compared to a chief executive officer, or what about all these Christian leadership seminars and books? Is this a bad thing?"

"Some would say it is. But, as that old proverb says, 'Don't throw the baby out with the bath water.' Let's answer your question this way – where would the CEO paradigm fit?" Dan asked while pointing to the circles.

"In the right," the three replied in unison.

"Yes. Are there some aspects of a CEO similar to shepherding? Can we say that some features of a CEO overlap with features of a shepherd?"

"Sure," said Phil.

"Are there aspects about CEO leadership that are dissimilar or that should never be used by elders or pastors within God's church?"

"Of course!" declared Marcus.

"You see, we can go down the line and evaluate contemporary models and ideas for leadership and put them in the same category. Even though God used models fitting to an ancient or an agricultural society does not mean that God's models are antiquated, irrelevant or wrong. The definitions and principles for leadership from Scripture are very relevant for us today. God's church is still more like a flock of sheep than a factory of workers. CEO's do not have to love or necessarily care for their staff or employees to achieve productive success. God's shepherds must love and care for God's people, always having their best interest at heart and seeking their greatest welfare. I would say that the models and principles from this spiritual side of the chart should inform the principles, philosophies and practices of the other two categories. In fact, as we've already discussed, in many ways they have!"

"We've talked about what shepherds are, but what do they do? Well, let me put it this way: what does the Bible say they're supposed to do?" Neil inquired.

"Hold that thought, for, well, how about until we meet again? Since we only have a few more minutes, I want us to summarize what we've learned and then bring it home to our own lives. According to the Bible, what is the chief paradigm for church leadership?"

"The shepherd," Marcus responded.

"How do we know it's the shepherd?"

"Because God is portrayed as the shepherd in the Old Testament, and all kings were to be shepherds like God." Marcus continued, "And because Jesus' own identity as a leader was that of a good shepherd."

"Exactly. As a result all elders are to shepherd God's flock under their care. We saw this in 1 Peter 5 and John 21. That is how undershepherds lead. What do we say about using secular models for leadership in the church?"

"They can be helpful, but they must be evaluated by Scripture," Neil stated.

"Certain things about secular leadership should never be used in the church," Phil added.

"What responsibilities do God's undershepherds have in his church?"

"To feed, oversee, guide and protect," Marcus quickly responded.

"What is the primary means for undershepherds to feed, to oversee, to guide and to protect?"

After several seconds, Marcus said, "Through the Word of God."

"What characterizes a bad shepherd?"

Phil declared, "Arrogance. Working with God's people for selfish reasons."

"And we must never forget that. As I learned from Pastor Rick, bad shepherds use, abuse, steal or kill off the sheep. God punishes bad shepherds, sometimes quite severely. Now, what characterizes a good undershepherd?"

Marcus answered, "Humility."

"And…?" prodded Dan.

"Love," Phil said.

"Aaannnddd…?"

There was a hesitation, then Marcus supplied, "Loving sacrifice."

"Bingo! Humble godliness with a loving sacrifice! Here's something that pierces right to my heart: Do I sacrificially love God's sheep? Am I willing to put my life on the line for them?"

"Ouch," Phil said.

"Yeah, ouch."

The questions weighed heavily upon the men. Dan broke the silence and said with tears, "Men, when I seriously consider these questions, I…" he choked up. "I admit that I fail every day. Some sheep are easier to love than others. There are some for which I would give my life." Dan took a deep breath. "But to sacrificially love all God's sheep in this church the way Jesus did? I'm a total failure. Thank God we have Christ as our perfect and good shepherd!"

The pastor looked at his watch, then stated, "Let me close with this: God calls and anoints men to become undershepherds. The shepherd is our main model for leadership in God's church. God's undershepherds can only successfully accomplish God's purposes by the Spirit and His Word, and God's undershepherds must be willing, in fact strive, to sacrificially love the sheep. If you or I are unwilling to do so, then we have no business serving as elders."

Even though there was much yet to cover, he asked Neil to close in prayer.

A CHALLENGE TO THINK AND DO

What do you think?
1. What main thing(s) did you learn from reading this chapter?
2. How is Jesus Christ your Good Shepherd?
3. What characterizes a good undershepherd of Christ?
4. What are the main responsibilities God's undershepherd(s) have in your church?
5. Give some examples of godly, caring oversight in the church.
6. What characterizes a false or bad shepherd?
7. What is abusive or domineering oversight in the church?

Some things you could do:
1. Make a chart of three columns. In the left column list the qualities and roles of a biblical undershepherd. In the right column list the qualities and roles of secular leadership. In the middle column indicate the overlapping similarities between church shepherding and secular leadership. How would you apply this to godly leaders in Christ's church?
2. Read Psalm 23 and John 10. Write down the similarities about the Good Shepherd between the two chapters.

10

THE ROLES WE PLAY IN CHURCH

—⁓—

One of the elders and Dan were driving home from a specially called presbytery meeting. The elders often took turns going to these meetings with the pastor who was required to attend. By the time the Lees had arrived at Grace Church, Herman had been an elder for seven years. He was tall with an average build, still with a full head of black hair, nearly black eyes, and sharp facial features. Herman was intelligent and very knowledgeable in bible doctrine. He was endowed with an overdose of confidence. Herman was opinionated, argumentative and contrary, According to him rarely ever wrong. At the same time the man tried to live by principles and tried not to cater to one side or another in the struggle between Dan and Bernie, though he usually agreed with the majority of the elders about issues. The elder often held the same viewpoint on many things with Bernie. Yet he wasn't necessarily a friend, nor catered to Bernie merely because the domineering Bernie wanted something.

Herman, who occasionally brought up things that bothered him about Dan, saw the long drive as an opportunity to bring up another issue. He wasn't necessarily trying to be critical; he just had the freedom to express his opinions though almost always without sensitivity. Herman wanted to talk about the vision statement Dan presented at the congregational meeting in January. "Where did you come up with that vision statement?"

"You and a couple of the elders kept pushing me to develop a vision statement. So I read books on developing a vision and mission statement, went on-line to read what different churches had written, and decided to search the Scriptures to see what kind of a vision for a church God has in mind. One of the duties a pastor has is to cast a biblical vision to God's people, to set the direction. Of course, pastors should do so in consultation with the elders."

"You never consulted with me."

"That's not true," Dan said with a little irritation. "I gave rough drafts to all of you elders for input. No one responded. Emails were sent and the matter was on the agenda three times. Nobody provided any recommendations. So I took the initiative and wrote a final draft and presented it to the people" (see Appendix K).

"That was the wrong thing to do! You should have gotten the blessing of the elders first, instead of springing it on everyone. All of you pastors are alike! You think you are in charge, always trying to be independent and pressure everyone to do things your way." He went on to talk about the problems with a couple of previous pastors who had a habit of implementing changes without consulting with the elders. It was obvious the elders still resented what had happened. *Perhaps this is why there is little trust with me?* Dan thought.

"I didn't spring it on everyone. But, yes you are right, I did not obtain the formal blessing of the elders and should have. But we need to move forward. We need to paint a picture of a possible future that God wants for Grace."

"Yes...I did the right thing...but? What kind of apology is that?" Herman chastised. The more excited he got, the faster the car sped along.

"Okay, okay. I agree with you that I was impatient and did not seek the agreement or blessing of fellow elders. I'll do the right thing and confess it and ask forgiveness at our next meeting," Dan said with a stinging reluctance. "In the meantime, why was it that neither you nor the others got back to me with ideas? You had plenty of time, you know."

"I don't know. Busy I guess?"

Yeah, we're all busy. Any apology coming from you? "Did I offend you personally? Did I sin against you?" Dan asked.

"Uhhh. Naw, I guess not."

"If I did, I want to be able to ask you to forgive me."

"It's no big deal."

"Do you have any thoughts about the vision statement?"

"Lots! It's too long, and nobody will buy into it unless they've had the opportunity to present their ideas. People will only take ownership of a vision statement if they have a part in putting it together."

That is not true, Dan thought.

"What – do you mean everybody as in all the elders? Or everybody as in everyone at church?"

"Everyone at church!"

Forming a vision and mission statement based upon eighty-four adult opinions? Dan had to think that one through. Leadership, including spiritual leadership does not take its directives or establish its direction based upon majority opinion. That's American pollsterism. "So what if you get three different perspectives on what the vision of the church should be? How will you resolve that? How will you get the minority groups to buy into the vision established by a slight majority?"

"Majority rules. That's the way it is," Herman declared.

"Where do you get that from Scripture? And what if the majority comes up with a vision statement that has little resemblance to Biblical mandate and directives?"

Herman didn't answer.

Herman did propose making changes to the statement, changes Dan was uncomfortable with. Herman was enamored by different groups who have published books and websites that advocate for a family-oriented church. Philosophically it meant returning to a kind of patriarchy, in a way reminiscent of ancient cultures. Practically that meant no segregated Sunday school, no youth group or activities; all programs structured with families in mind. The men would be able to gather together for studies or social events, but not the women or the children. Dan knew that there were variations on this patriarchal and family-centered theme. Some of it was appealing, and some of the arguments appeared grounded in the Bible. That is, until Dan started investigating and asking the tough questions. At least Dan wasn't trying to lead the church through this sort of radical change. Perhaps three or four families might buy into this vision, but none of the other elders would support it.

"Herman, I've studied that philosophy of church life long and hard and I just cannot see where the Bible requires that we organize or structure the church that way. Christ never did with his disciples. There are too many problems with it. Now, if there was a group who wanted to establish a church after this model, then you probably would be better off there. If the majority of Grace wanted to go in that direction, then so be it. I, for one, am not of that conviction," Dan stated. "Is there anything else about the statement that you find objectionable other than it is too long and isn't family centered?"

"No."

The drive home gave Dan important insight into Herman's mindset. It revealed again that Dan was out of sync with yet another elder. It also revealed that Herman was not thinking like a Presbyterian, meaning the elders, and not the majority, govern the church. It was time to talk with Kent again.

"Glad to hear you are training three good men, Dan!" Kent said, after the preliminary chit chat.

"So far it looks like they'll be great as elders. However, the training and testing is not over. We will see what happens in the next several months."

"Train them well. So what's the challenge this time?" Kent asked, having been fore-warned in an email that Dan had another matter to ask about. Dan told him about the conversation with Herman regarding the church's vision and mission.

"Does the Bible tell you that your church should have a vision or mission statement?" asked Dan's wise friend.

"No. Neither does it forbid it. I know that the whole vision and mission thing comes from business schools and corporate America. But listen to this quote I got from the book *Grace-Full Leadership*:

> Without vision, leadership is little more than simple perpetuation of the past instead of predication on the future. A proper vision builds on the past by allowing room for new ideas and thoughts. Leaders hold in their minds pictures and ideals of what can be."[1]

"What? You just happened to have that quote around?"

"There are all sorts of quotes floating on my desk. I've been studying more on putting together a vision and mission statement. I just think that it is a good idea to present to people a potential foreseeable future, one that is based not upon growth charts or product development, but upon what God expects of us as a local church. In other words, present the Biblical ideal from Scripture and aim for that," Dan argued. "Isn't that what Paul did, especially in Ephesians and Colossians?"

"Fair enough. So what is wrong with Herman's vision for Grace?"

"It is a vision I do not believe is altogether biblical."

"Yet, he believes that it is the biblical way."

"Yes. I know…I know; there is the matter of personal conscience, Romans 14 and all that. But where do we go from here?"

"Take it to the elders and have them make a determination. Have Herman present his case and you bring a counter argument. Remember, historically Presbyterians have been a deliberative body. Then push for a decision from the elders and record it in the minutes."

"Sounds fair enough. Will do."

"Can you anticipate what might happen once the elders make their decision? Let's say they agree with your perspective and not with Herman's. Then what?"

"I can see Herman and the families who hold the same position trying to recruit others to their convictions."

"Probably. So what can you do about that?"

Dan thought a while. Kent gave him time. Finally he answered, "I should also ask the elders to instruct Herman not to make this his soapbox to convince others that Grace should adopt a family-centered church."

"Good. But won't you be restricting his freedom of conscience?"

"Uhhm, in one sense, yes. But all church leadership decisions do that to one degree or another. He can hold to his views. He can even talk about them, but he should not do so in a way that could divide the church. Further, when he does talk about his views, he ought to also express the formal decision of the elders and make it clear that he is promoting something the elders do not agree with. If he becomes divisive then he should be disciplined."

Kent paused for a bit. Dan waited in the silence for him to speak up again. "Have you ever had a round table discussion or a forum at Grace?"

"I know what a forum is, but not sure Grace has ever done that. Certainly not since we've been here. What do you have in mind?" Dan inquired.

"If you think you can moderate a good debate, perhaps you can open it up to the congregation. What we've done with hot topic issues that come up from time to time is encourage people to brown bag a lunch and stay after the morning worship. We have up to three people presenting the pros and up to three people presenting the cons, a point and counterpoint arrangement. The moderator then opens it up for questions from the audience, or even allows them to give their opinion. If it is a large group then each person is given two minutes. Summary statements are presented when it looks like the discussion is winding down and the moderator gives a few closing remarks. It's been a very useful exercise for us here."

"Hey, that's a good idea! Sounds like it would be fun. I'll propose it to the elders," Dan said enthusiastically.

"Now, what about Herman's statement about getting everyone's opinion for the church's vision?" Kent inquired.

"Good leaders don't lead by polls or even consensus from the majority."

"So you disregard people's opinions out of hand?"

"No…"

"Then how do you resolve the problem?"

Again Dan thought about it. In fact, he had been thinking about it and wasn't sure what to do.

"Let me read an excerpt from George Barna's book *Leaders on Leadership*:

A hard pill for some followers to swallow is that God conveys His vision to leaders without asking His followers for their input! As a leader, you may wish to ask for people's input; but remember that the ultimate definition of the vision is from God, not your peers. They may play a role in helping to shape your thinking or perhaps the way you ultimately articulate or position the vision. Vision, however, is not determined by a two-thirds vote; it is not the result of consensus among a group of interested parties; and vision is not identified through a committee-based process. If God has called you to lead, perhaps the most vital and significant function you will fill is that of being the projector and the protector of the vision. The goal is not to become the people's most popular leader, but to become God's most trustworthy leader.[2]

"Well put!" Dan responded.

"Dan, what do you think was behind your fellow elder's statement about getting a buy-in from people?"

"It seems to me now that what he was really saying is that I was supposed to get *his* opinion and buy in. I did solicit his opinion, but he never responded."

"Do you have any idea why that is?"

"Fear, I suppose. I suspect he knew I would not agree with his vision for Grace."

"Do you think he would argue for a majority consensus if it had to do with his vision for the church?"

"Don't know, but highly doubt it."

"What do you suppose would be a wise way to address this? Could it be that church members might have some good insights or worthy suggestions?" Kent wondered.

"Okay, I see where you are going with this. I suppose it would not be a bad thing to solicit ideas and suggestions from them."

"It might even prove to be a good thing. You could learn something from them. You might even develop a better sense of trust. Getting people's opinions does not mean that you have to develop a philosophy of ministry or a program from them. Some ideas can be pretty crazy while others can be downright sinful. Still, you might be pleasantly surprised by what you might find just by asking people for their input. What we do here at our church is to have two informal congregational meetings a year. The people know that we are going to ask two questions: What are some positive things about our church and what can we improve upon? Nobody is allowed to complain or grumble. So far we've had only good come of the meetings these past several years."

"Good idea! Maybe the elders will buy into that too."

"So...why did you call me?" Kent asked.

Dan laughed. "I just wanted to make you feel that you were still needed."

"Oh sure!" Kent snorted.

"You are a good friend, Kent. Thanks so much for your help and advice," Dan said appreciatively.

With the most recent dilemma somewhat resolved, the two caught up on the latest news from both families. Dan was admittedly jealous for the excellent time Kent and his wife spent in Europe. Kent was happy to hear about the trip to the ranch, and that things appeared to be going well at Grace. Dan said the good things were often countered with the on-going friction with Bernie, Irma and others. "God must have them there to keep you humble and to teach you some good lessons," Kent suggested.

A blistering summer parked over the town, actually over the whole region. Dan and Mona planned another vacation trip to Oregon. Dan had recently returned from Oregon for a series of interviews with the elders and pastoral search committee of a small church.

He went to Oregon with many questions in mind, such as, will the church in Oregon be a better pasture or were there some serious problems lurking below the surface? Or if there were no serious problems, would Dan with his gifts and abilities be a good fit for them? At minimum he wanted to get a sense of what the church was like, even though his decision to take the call would be bathed in much prayer and with a reliance upon the providential leading of God. The initial letters, emails and phone calls gave Dan the impression that it would be a good fit. His friend Dominic would often joke, "It's always greener over the septic tank," so Dan went cautiously. He brought with him the questionnaire he put together to help him in the decision-making process (see Appendix A).

When Dan flew into a rainy Portland, one of the elders was waiting with his old maroon pickup to taxi the candidate back to town. Ironically, the small church in Oregon, while within an hour's drive of Mona's parents, was just the kind of place Herman would relish.

The people were friendly, but Dan noticed the composite of the church was young families with many children. There were only two elderly couples and one single woman.

For Sunday School each family sat together at their own separate tables. The elder who taught aimed his lesson at the fathers who were supposed to go home and teach their children the same. Why were the children even present? Dan asked. They were there to learn the discipline of sitting still and how to conduct themselves respectfully in the company of adults. Since all member families were expected to homeschool, it was assumed the children would be getting Bible lessons at home. There was no youth group and would never be a youth director.

The church had two weekly Bible studies which included adults and children. How are the adults supposed to discuss adult issues when children are present? Dan inquired. No issue should be discussed in any group setting that would be inappropriate for young ears. If there was a problem the husband or father would ask the elders in private.

Women's Bible studies? No, because supposedly they were often a source of gossip and slander. The elders found that they could not control what went on there. However, it was possible to have a women's study if the pastor taught it, though the ideal was for each husband to teach his wife doctrinal truths.

It seemed to Dan that this particular church was trying to resurrect a model for church from some seventeenth century European, Protestant church. The two elders told Dan there were a number of churches around the country who have successfully implemented this philosophy of ministry, so they were getting counsel from those churches on ways to develop a family-oriented church.

Quite a number of the people expressed how much they got out of the morning sermon. That was very encouraging to Dan. The families were friendly enough, and the children all appeared to get along well. Yet, after the Sunday evening service, Dan kindly informed the elders that there was no need to continue the candidating process. There was no need to sit with the elders or the search committee on Monday. He wasn't in agreement with their particular vision for the local church or their philosophy of ministry. Dan knew that he could not lead and guide them in a direction that, in his opinion, was centered upon the natural, human, albeit Christian family more than it was upon Jesus Christ and his New Covenant family. Thankfully he was able to change his flight and fly home early Monday morning. Mona was disappointed it did not work out.

The monthly breakfast and leadership classes continued through July. The three elder candidates and two young, childless couples joined the group. Mo was ecstatic to have such a large and regular clientele.

In the meantime Dan continued working with the potential elders. Each class focused on the doctrines and polity of the church. At the next class Dan picked up where they left off – on the tasks of a biblical, godly shepherd. "The shepherd-leader goes at the front of the flock and guides them," he declared as he wrote in blue the following verses on the white board: Matthew 2:6; Acts 7:10, 14; Hebrews 3:7, 17, 24.

"Unlike cattle drivers who prod the creatures, a good shepherd draws them along. Guiding is a necessary and crucial part of leadership. Shepherds, in accordance with God's counsel, set the spiritual direction for the local flock."

"What direction would that be? I mean, how can we know the explicit course we are to take?" Marcus asked.

"I'm not talking about getting God's verbal counsel for every goal or on every detail. The Lord expects us to think his thoughts after him and bring those thoughts to bear upon life. That's the way of wisdom. The godly undershepherd is supposed to use wisdom to guide God's people toward the grand objective. Shepherds lead the local community of God's people toward his intended purposes for that group. Let me read what Brian Dodd wrote about the ultimate goal:

> Many Christian leaders tend to think about leadership in terms of achievement of goals or production of a program that is measured in terms of the number of people who came or the amount of money that was raised and spent. The focus of life-giving leadership is quite different. It is not about production of a product but about reproducing the life of Christ in individuals and the congregation. Reproduction of the life of the Spirit is the focus."[3]

Dan told the men that elders and pastors must always keep before them the ultimate goal of their God-ordained ministry: to equip the saints to do the work of ministry (Eph. 4:11-12) through the faithful exercise of their gifts (Rom. 12; 1 Cor. 12) in order to form Jesus Christ in the local community of God's people through love (Eph. 1:15-23; 3:14-21; 4:13; Col. 1:22-29; 1 Thess. 3:11-13; 1 Tim. 1:5). The objective is to form Jesus Christ in the local church so that the body becomes one new and mature man who lives in the unity of the faith (Eph. 4:13), in an intimate full-knowledge of Jesus that fosters a deep love for and full imitation of Christ (Eph. 4:13), and who lives in the truth that is spoken and expressed through love (Eph. 4:15). "Becoming a Christ-formed community through the redemptive and reconciling work of Jesus will manifest itself in the three important areas of a local church: consecration, community, and Jesus' great commission. All other goals are subsumed under this primary objective. Further, all true goals will bring the church closer and closer to this ideal," Dan concluded.

The pastor wrote *feed* on the board as he spoke. "The second thing Christ's under-shepherd does is feed the flock. Turn to John 21. Phil, read out loud verses fifteen through seventeen for us." Phil complied.

"Two significant commandments Jesus gives to his disciples after his resurrection and before his departure into heaven. Where is the first commandment found?" Dan asked.

Marcus quickly responded, "In Matthew 28:18-20."

"Would you read that for us?"

He read from his new Bible:

And Jesus came and said to them, 'All authority in heaven and on earth has been given to me. Go therefore and make disciples of all nations, baptizing them in the name of the Father and of the Son and of the Holy Spirit, teaching them to observe all that I have commanded you. And behold, I am with you always, to the end of the age (ESV, 2001).

"So then, what is the first commandment Christ gives his apostles?"

"Obviously, to seek out others and form disciples." Neil replied.

"What do we call that process today?" Dan asked.

"Evangelism," Neil answered again.

"Not merely evangelism, but discipleship. That includes all dimensions of making disciples such as, preaching the Gospel, engaging in apologetics or contending for the Faith, establishing new churches, and the like. Now, what is the commandment Christ gives in John's gospel?"

"To shepherd by feeding and caring for God's sheep," answered Marcus.

"Right! And the analogy refers to what?"

"To teaching God's Word," answered Neil.

Dan went on to tell the trainees how very important it was for God's undershepherds to immerse themselves in God's Word in order to handle it well (1 Tim. 5:17; 2 Tim. 3:14-16). They are always to be growing in God's grace and truth (2 Pet. 3:18), holding fast and being nourished by his Word (1 Tim. 4:6; 2 Tim. 1:13; 3:14-17; Tit. 1:9). Shepherding is done through the gracious means of God's Word. Shepherds teach it boldly (Mark 6:34; Acts 20:20; 1 Cor. 12:28, 31; Col. 1:28; 1 Tim. 1:3; 3:2, 16; 4:11-12). They feed the apostolic truth to God's flock (1 Pet. 5:2; 2 Tim. 2:2) in order that individual lambs and sheep become strong and healthy sheep, but also that the entire flock is well cared for and nourished (2 Cor. 13:10-11; Eph. 4:11-16).

Through the ministry of the Word, God's undershepherds should bring loving comfort to the sheep (1 Cor. 14:3, 31; 2 Cor. 1:4-6; 1 Thess. 4:18). At the same time the wayward are called to give up their sin and return to the fold (Gal. 6:1; 1 Tim. 5:1-2) by rebuking them (2 Tim. 4:1-2; Tit. 1:13; 2:15) and warning them of the dire consequences for their errant ways (Acts 20:31). Shepherds know that the service of the Word will convict contrary sheep (2 Tim. 2:25; Ti. 1:9) and confront wolves head on (Eph. 4:15; 2 Tim. 2:24-26).

"We must always remember, though, that as Christ's undershepherds, we must not use the Bible to brow beat or manipulate God's people. We serve the Word in truth *through* love so that they will be built up individually and corporately in truth and grace. We must always be careful to nurture and nourish by means of the Word of God's Gospel. Our ministry is a redemptive and a reconciling one, so the center of the work from which all Christian life flows is the merciful and gracious person and work of Jesus. The Cross of Christ is the hub and heart of God's flock," Dan exhorted.

"But what about God's Law, sin and repentance? Won't emphasizing grace and love corrupt what should be the whole counsel of God? I've seen lots of churches focus exclusively on love and grace so that church life is about sentimentalism where no one offends or corrects or disciplines," Neil wondered.

"In a way you are talking about the alleged tension between love and truth," added Marcus.

"What do you mean by that?" Neil asked.

"There is a common belief, almost a mantra in Christian circles that says something like 'doctrine or truth divides but love unites.' The Scriptures never speak that way. Real love flows from God's genuine truth. All you have to do is read John's first two letters in the New Testament. I understand what people are trying to get at. Truth without love can be cold and harsh. Isn't that the jist of 1 Corinthians 13 or the warning Christ gave to the church of Ephesus in Revelation, chapter two? Without love we are noisy gongs and clanging cymbals. Fact is, we cannot love rightly without God's truth."

Dan continued. "We see the supposed tension resolved in Jesus Christ. He not only spoke truth but he said in John 14 he embodied truth! Yet, how did he minister the truth? With grace, mercy and love."

"But Jesus came down hard on the Scribes, Pharisees and Sadducees, right? That wasn't very loving," Melissa objected.

"In what way was Jesus *not* loving?" Dan challenged.

"His actions sure didn't appear loving."

"You are confusing love with a sweet, sentimental gentility. That is not how God defines love. When he dealt with those people, whom he identified as hirelings and wolves, Jesus demonstrated love by confronting them with the truth. It would have been unloving not to forcefully address their arrogant deceit. At the same time he was showing love for the lost sheep that had been used and abused by those bad leaders. Notice what Jesus and subsequently his apostles did: he dealt firmly and harshly with the proud while showing great grace and mercy to the humble sinners. The Gospels are replete with occasions where Jesus, the perfect Shepherd, ministered truth to the lost lambs and sheep. Remember, his was a ministry of redemption and reconciliation. You don't see him coming down with hell-fire and brimstone against even the lowliest dregs of society. Nor did he do that with those who rejected his ministry, even though his disciples wanted to. We must take our primary cue for ministry from Christ, not from the world, our perceptions, or even from admirable historical figures of Christian history."

"So, what about Law, sin and repentance? In the book of Acts Peter calls upon people to repent and believe," Neil retorted.

"Jesus did the same. Nearly all who favorably received Christ with faith were those who already knew their sinful condition. When they didn't, Jesus graciously, yet profoundly, made them see their true condition. For example, how did Jesus treat the Samaritan woman at the well? Did he look upon her with contempt and disgust knowing the kind of person she was? Or did he gently confront her with the truth about who she was? It was at the moment she admitted the reality of her sinful condition that she understood the truth about Jesus. That is an example of repentance and faith, isn't it?" Dan asked.

The men agreed. Neil got up to get some coffee, which prompted the others to take a break.

With a refilled cup of stale coffee in hand, Marcus started up the conversation. "I was just thinking. I realized that Jesus did call upon people to repent, like the woman caught in sin. Jesus told her to sin no more. That is repentance, isn't it?"

"Sure it is," Dan affirmed.

"One of the previous pastors used to say that ministry and preaching was incomplete if it did not always include a call to repentance from sin. He also emphasized the Law of God to expose our sins and tell us how to be holy," Neil added.

"I would agree with that – to a degree," answered Dan. "The Law is given to reflect and teach mankind the perfect, pure, holy and righteous character of God. We haven't gotten to the lesson on sin yet. Do you know what our Westminster Shorter Catechism says about sin?"

No one could remember.

"It says: 'What is sin? Sin is any want of conformity unto, or transgression of, the law of God.' We will be working on a lesson on the Law at another time, but for now just understand that the Law is given to underscore the reality that we are sinners in need of God's forgiveness. Without the Law we would really see no reason to come to Christ. The Law demonstrates we could never measure up to God's perfect standard; in fact we have crossed over the line and are therefore guilty. So we need to do an about face in mind, will, emotion, body... in our whole being. That's what repentance is all about – turning away from sin and toward God. When we face God we are to come to him by faith. The good news message of Jesus is that he lived the Law of God perfectly because we could not, then died upon the cross to pay for our sin and remove God's declaration of our guilt, and then was raised up again with a new and living body."

"Then you agree with my previous pastor?" Neil asked.

"When it comes to making the Gospel or good news of Jesus clear, yes. Where I would disagree, I suppose, is that in the New Testament the stress is not upon law, sin and repentance but upon the grace, mercy and love of God who sent Jesus Christ to redeem us from the curse of the Law and therefore to reconcile us to him.

"Certainly, as Christians we are time and again called upon to repent. It is a daily thing even after our initial repentance and faith in Jesus Christ. Peter says to repent and believe, so does the author of Hebrews. Paul says we are to put off sin and put on the new life of Christ. In his first letter John says we are to 'confess our sins because God is faithful and just to forgive our sins and to cleanse us from unrighteousness.'"

"I still don't see how you differ," Neil retorted.

"It has to do with emphasis. There are pastors who never preach about the need for repentance *and* believing. For them it is all about faith or sometimes about doing the moral law. You know, living moral lives. But that misses the fullness of the truth of Jesus. What people take from those messages is that we are all fine and okay and perhaps with a little help from Jesus, our lives will be better and we should live better. That is a sad distortion of the biblical Gospel.

"Then there are other pastors who preach Law with a focus against sin, immorality and vice, always calling people to repent. Their emphasis is upon how guilty or sinful or bad or wicked or evil people are. Yet sadly, they rarely ever highlight the fact that Christ's work dealt justly with our sin. What people take from those messages is that we believers are hopelessly left in our sinfully decrepit condition and we should constantly beat ourselves up or feel terribly guilty for our badness. Under that kind of ministry we tend to see ourselves without reference to the radically saving and transforming work of Jesus Christ. But the truth is this: as believers we are by nature sinners, but we are now forgiven and declared righteous *in* Christ!

"That is why we call unbelievers to *repent* of their sin *and* also come to Christ by *faith*. We also urge believers to regularly repent of the remnant of sin in them and live *in Christ* by faith. Believers in the pew need a biblically balanced understanding of Law and grace, sin and salvation, repentance and faith. Our ministry as shepherds is not to direct the eyes of God's people to focus only upon sin or faith, but rather upon Jesus who paid for our sins and who lives in and through us by faith. We do not disregard sin or law, but rather the weight of our ministry and message should be upon living Christ's life of love by grace through faith. You with me?"

"Yeah, I get it," Neil replied. "But shouldn't we emphasize God's Law to show us how to be holy?"

"Here is something to remember, Neil: God's Law is the measure of holiness, not the means to holiness; it is the model, not the method for holiness!"

The foursome continued to discuss the topic, but Dan cut it short by encouraging them to review the previous lesson on holiness or sanctification, which is also by grace through faith in Christ.

"While we haven't gotten into a comprehensive study of all the things a shepherd does, we will close now with the last main thing that he does. Which is what? Do you recall?" Dan asked.

"You told us before: it is to protect the flock of God," answered Phil.

"Right. In what ways do shepherds protect the flock?"

Blake said, "From themselves. They sure can get themselves into a lot of trouble!"

"Good. What else?"

"From wild animals," Matt replied.

"Yes. Another?"

"From hirelings or false shepherds," Marcus contributed.

"Yeah, you're right. We could divide the protection of sheep into a couple of categories: from inner enemies who could harm or lead sheep astray, and from outer enemies who could harm, kill, or steal sheep away," Dan said as he went back and scribbled on the white board:

A true, loving shepherd will protect God's flock (John 10:12; Acts 20:28-30; Eph.4:14; Tit. 1:9; 2:1; 1 Pet. 5:8 and 1 Jn. 4:1-3) from:
  1. *Enemies within (2 Tim. 2:16-18; Jude 12-13)*
  2. *Enemies without (Matt. 13:24-25; 2 Cor. 11:12-15)*[4]

"Let's define some of the enemies within the church. What or who would they be?"

Marcus made his quick reply, "Goats who might look and act like sheep, but lead the sheep down a sinful or immoral path."

"Like we said, false shepherds or hirelings," inserted Neil.

"Neil, read this paragraph from *Reforming Pastoral Ministry*," Pastor directed as he gave Neil the book:

Note that Jesus said that such a neglectful leader is really no shepherd at all ('The hired hand is not the shepherd'). Since the word pastor is literally the word shepherd, we must assume that what we are seeing in so many of our churches is a 'pastor' who is not a pastor. He may be concerned for truth; he may be concerned for preaching; he may be concerned for growth; he may be concerned for evangelism. But if he is not concerned about the sheep, he is only a hireling.[5]

"Thanks, Neil. How about enemies without?"

Matt volunteered first, "Wolves, whether or not they are in sheep's clothing."

"True. Recall that Jesus had no tolerance for wolves. With good shepherds there is no dancing with wolves! And good shepherds will not run away when a wolf snarls or snaps," Dan said.

"Thieves," Phil rejoined.

"I've got a question," Judy blurted. "Who are wolves and thieves?"

"Anyone want to answer her question?" the pastor challenged.

Marcus volunteered. "A wolf would be someone who would seek out a Christian and work to convince him or her that orthodox Christianity is false or who would lead toward a corruption of biblical virtues. An example of a thief could be someone who tried to steal a believer away from the historic Christian faith or church, and bring that person into a cult group."

"Okay, good. Any other questions? No? Let's take a break and then we'll come back and close our time by outlining the roles sheep have, including the responsibilities of sheep to shepherds." Several people stopped and looked at Dan with puzzlement. "Oh. So you didn't know members of the local church have responsibilities toward their God-ordained leaders?" Dan responded with a smile.

After the break Dan had them turn to two passages in Hebrews chapter thirteen. Harold read verses seven and seventeen. Dan then had them turn to the handout he provided and follow along.

"We will focus on three main ways God's sheep are to relate to God's undershepherds. The first is that God's people should follow their example. The second is that God's people should respect their position, and the third is God's people should obey their biblical rule. This is a teaser, because we will be looking more closely at these areas as we continue our training.

Let's go back to the first point: God's people are to follow the shepherd's example. Phil, read 2 Thessalonians 3:7-9."

He flipped open to the New Testament section and read aloud:

For you yourselves know how you ought to follow us, for we were not disorderly among you; nor did we eat anyone's bread free of charge, but worked with labor and toil night and day, that we might not be a burden to any of you, not because we do not have authority, but to make ourselves an example of how you should follow us.

"Neil, would you turn to Philippians 3:17 and read that verse for us?"

From his old Bible he said, "Brethren, join in following my example, and note those who so walk, as you have us for a pattern."

"So what do we learn from these verses?"

"God's shepherds must have the character of Christ and God's people must follow or imitate that example," Marcus taught.

"Yes, an example of Christ, not perfectly, nor completely, nor sinlessly, but in a way that appropriately and sufficiently reflects Jesus. It is the shepherd's Christ-like character which sheep are to imitate. As we will see some time in the future, God's people are to imitate or follow the undershepherds God has placed over them in other ways as well. Hebrews thirteen and verse seven calls sheep to follow their pastor's or elders' faith. Other ways would be by living in the Spirit producing the fruit of the Spirit, following in God's

Word, following as a serious disciple of the Lord, and so forth. What was the next way members relate to God's undershepherds?" asked Dan.

"Respect their position," offered Matt.

"Yes, and there are three ways to respect their position. The English Standard Version of 1 Thessalonians 5:12 says: 'We ask you, brothers, to respect those who labor among you and are over you in the Lord and admonish you.' The term 'to respect' is translated as to recognize, to know or to appreciate. In other words, God's people are to give God's ordained servants who are called to the role of shepherd the recognition, respect or appreciation their office deserves. The opposite would be to disrespect or despise. Look with me at your notes. Paul commands the church in Corinth, 'When Timothy comes, see that you put him at ease among you, for he is doing the work of the Lord, as I am. So let no one despise him. Help him on his way in peace that he may return to me, for I am expecting him with the brothers.'"[6]

Following his notes Dan explained that the way God's people respect their pastor or elders is to esteem them. This is what 1 Thessalonians 5:13 tells us. To esteem is to hold them in high regard, and the particular way to do so is very highly and in love. God gives the reason for esteeming them highly. "Because of their work" the verse says. In other words because of their work in God's Word, and also that their ministry through God's Word would be effective. Sometimes the reason why believers or churches are not benefiting from the ministry of God's Word is that they have little to no respect for the undershepherds God has given them.

Another way to respect the pastor and elders is revealed in 1 Timothy 5:17 and 18: "Let the elders who rule well be considered worthy of double honor, especially those who labor in preaching and teaching. For the Scripture says, 'You shall not muzzle an ox when it treads out the grain,' and, 'The laborer deserves his wages'" (ESV). In the Old Testament, the idea behind the verb 'to honor' comes from the root term which meant 'heavy or weighty.' It came to convey weightiness in the sense of being noteworthy or impressive. From that came other words such as glorious, to glorify, to be honorable. So the word honor comes to mean giving glory to someone who is deserving of respect, attention or obedience. The New Testament term for honor carries with it the idea of something of great value or price. In other words, God's people are to look upon the office of elder or pastor as a position of high value and well worthy of respect.

Dan told them that the Bible shows us how honor is exercised or demonstrated. The first is to fear, revere and respect. Only the Lord is honored in the sense of a trembling but reverent fear (Matt. 10:35ff; Mark 10:29f). Christians are not to fear man, and no pastor or elder may demand that people fear him. If members in a church fear their pastor or elders, then there is a strong indication of unbiblical or even abusive leadership. Another example of honor is when parents are given respect. The opposite would be to curse them (Exod. 21:17; Lev. 20:9; Prov. 20:20; 30:11) or despise them (Prov. 23:22).

Another aspect of honor is submission. Submission involves humility and obedience. This is why believers are commanded to obey those who rule over them, as we will see shortly.

A third aspect of honoring someone is to give them a provision of time or financial support. For example, God's people honor God with their first fruits (Mal. 1:6; 3:8), and they honor ministers with an equitable, remunerative support (1 Tim. 5:4, 8, 17).

"The third or final way sheep relate to God's ordained undershepherds is by obeying their rule. Our text is from Hebrews 13:17. It says, 'Obey your leaders and submit to them, for they are keeping watch over your souls, as those who will have to give an account. Let them do this with joy and not with groaning, for that would be of no advantage to you.'" Dan instructed, standing by the white board.

"To obey is to submit. It is difficult to take, but this requires an active obedience. God's Word says that we actively obey those whom God has placed over us when they command us to do that which God clearly expects and commands. We submit even when we do not personally like the one who has legitimate authority over us so long as what he requires is right as clearly defined by the principles of Scripture."[7]

He told them that many Christians, particularly in the United States, are fearful of the abuse of power by those who are in positions of authority. Abuse of power would be discussed later. However, statistically, a very small percentage of elders or pastors are abusive. God has more to say about abusive people, abusive mobs or uncontrolled sheep than he does about abusive rulers. In fact, if the research is to be believed the abuse of pastors and elders today is at epidemic proportions! Lest one might be tempted to think that the pastor or elders have authority and power without responsibility and accountability it must be remembered that theirs is a greater, more stringent responsibility and account-ability. They have a more severe discipline for the very reason they are servants in God's ordained offices. Not only are they *not* exempted from general church discipline, but they will be held to a higher account before the throne of God for how they conducted them-selves in the office of undershepherd!

The New Testament gives us several examples for how the Lord's people follow Christ's undershepherds through obedience, but three will suffice for now. The first example is found in 1 Corinthians 16:13-16: "Be watchful, stand firm in the faith, act like men, be strong. Let all that you do be done in love. Now I urge you, brothers — you know that the household of Stephanas were the first converts in Achaia, and that they have devoted themselves to the service of the saints — be subject to such as these, and to every fellow worker and laborer" (ESV). Christ's followers were commanded to submit to those who had ministered to them.

Another example is found in Titus 2:11-15. God's grace teaches that we should deny ungodliness and worldly lusts in us and in our midst, and should also live "self-controlled, upright and godly lives in the present age" (ESV). As Christians, we have the means to do these things because of the hope and sacrificial work of Jesus Christ. Jesus is the one who redeemed us out of that old, lawless and sinful life in order to be holy and to do good works. Yet the other reason why the Lord's people were to obey Pastor Titus is because he taught, spoke, exhorted and rebuked them with full authority of God's Word (Tit. 2:15)! The same reason applies to believers today.

A third example comes from the next chapter in Titus where Paul tells undershepherd Titus to "Remind them *to be submissive* to rulers and authorities, *to be obedient,* to be ready for every good work, to speak evil of no one, to avoid quarreling, to be gentle, and to show perfect courtesy toward all people. For we ourselves were once foolish, disobedient, led astray, slaves to various passions and pleasures, passing our days in malice and envy, hated by others and hating one another" (ESV; emphasis added).

Dan concluded by saying, "God's people follow his undershepherds in various ways. They are subject to the authority of elders and pastors and are to be obeyed so long as they are not led into sin or in anything that would violate God's Word or violate a good conscience that comes from God's clear teachings. When do God's sheep obey the under-shepherds? Whenever their instruction, rule, admonition, rebuke, reproof comes from the plain teachings of God's Word."

"Let me give you a personal example," requested the pastor. "Some years ago I was counseling a young couple. The husband admitted he was having an affair with another woman. To make matters even worse, the other woman was married and not even a believer. Of course this devastated his wife. Though he was not a member of our church he was a member of another church. So I told him that he was sinning and needed to give up the adulterous relationship. Do you know what his response was? He said that no one had any right to tell him what to do. More than that, he said God was leading him to this other woman! You see, I and then his elders, had not only the delegated right but also the duty to command him to quit his sin and do the lovingly righteous thing in Christ – return to and love his wife. This right and duty was not invested in me as a counselor, nor in the fact that it was injurious to his bride, but came from God's unambiguous Word ministered through the office of pastor and elder."

A stack of papers were pulled from his briefcase. He asked Matt and Brad to pass a set of notes to each person or couple (see Appendix J). "What I'm passing out are notes on the responsibilities and duties of a pastor. However, these also apply to church elders. So," Dan concluded while looking at the candidates for eldership, "You sure you want to become elders?" They all smiled without comment.

A CHALLENGE TO THINK AND DO

What do you think?

1. Identify a concept or two that challenged you. Why was it challenging?
2. Jesus is the one true Shepherd. However, he has assigned certain roles, and delegated responsibilities and authority to undershepherds in his church. What does that mean and how does that work?
3. What biblical roles and responsibilities do a pastor and/or elder have in Christ's church?
4. The work of God's undershepherd is through the ministry of God's Word. How do pastors and elders minister God's Word in the local church?
5. What goal or destination is the pastor (and elders) supposed to lead God's local church?
6. What does the Law of God have to do with the Gospel of Christ? What's the relationship between the two?
7. What does Pastor Dan mean by "God's Law is the measure of holiness, not the means to holiness; it is the model, not the method for holiness!"
8. What are the three main ways listed in this chapter that God's people relate to God's pastor (and elders)?
9. The Bible is clear about how Christians demonstrate genuine respect for their pastor (and elders). What are they?

Some things you could do:

1. As thorough and detailed as possible, write down what kind of a vision you have for your church. In other words, what do you expect the local church to be like now? In one year? Five years? Then, compare it with God's vision for the church. This will take quite a bit of Scripture reading. How did the two compare?
2. Read Appendix K, *A Proposed Biblical Vision for the Local Church*. Highlight, circle or underline the qualities you believe your church has. What are the good things about your local church? What are some things that could be improved upon?

11

MORE THAN LIP SERVICE

—◠◠◠—

It had been more than a year since Bernie and the elders confronted the pastor about his preaching, though occasionally someone would refer to their favorite preacher and remark, "He's a really great preacher!" Dan could not escape the comparisons.

Dan had been faithful to his commitment to do what he could to improve. He took classes, subscribed to relevant magazines, had his sermons evaluated by various pastors and seminary professors around the country, read at least two books a month on the subject, and gave a report to the elders as to his progress at the regularly stated meetings. From time to time he would give the elders a copy of the sermon evaluation form (see Appendix C), but no one took advantage of it.

It was August; time to spend another week in advanced seminary classes. This time the class was on preaching. Dan was pensive about going. Frankly he was more than tired of the subject. He had read so much that his new books were repeating the same ideas as other books. He was also gun-shy about putting himself under the scrutiny of a professor and a class. Seminary was painful enough, and the mental beating he had received from the unmerciful element at Grace deflated any sense of confidence or joy in preaching. He had come to the point where he dreaded stepping into the pulpit. On a typical Sunday morning Bernie sat to his right squirming and wiggling disapprovingly. To his left was another who frowned through much of the sermon before falling asleep. In the back sat yet another disapproving elder who often remained expressionless, and nearby was a negative deacon. About a third of the congregation at one point or another criticized his preaching style or content. Even an occasional out-of-town visitor took it as his or her duty to criticize. And there they all were, Sunday after Sunday, each sitting like Simon the judge on TV's American Idol, daring the pastor to impress them.

The elders had their regular monthly meeting the week before Dan left for seminary. He reminded the men he was taking vacation time to take the preaching course, and was again fulfilling his commitment to improve. "Don't think it will do much good! You don't have what it takes to be a great preacher," Bernie said with a studied grimace. Joe uttered a slight giggle and then told Bernie his comment was inappropriate. Dan remained silent, keeping his temper in check.

Dan decided to drive since the school was only a few states away. It took slightly longer than the eight hours, his on-line directions said, but that was okay. The drive gave Dan plenty of time to contemplate life as a preacher, and to rehearse his sermon for class. Each student was expected to come prepared to preach a fifteen-minute message at the beginning of the seminary's week. Then at the end of the week each would be given a passage and one evening to prepare a message. Dan arrived in the early evening, and checked into a local hotel with a kitchenette. It was a refreshingly cool and dry evening, so Dan took advantage of it and walked around the nearby neighborhood.

Classes on the small campus began at eight o'clock A.M. Being a short-term class with ten men they met in one of the brightly lit, well-equipped and most comfortable rooms upstairs. The professor was a pastor who also had a consulting business as a professional communicator. He was a very gracious and encouraging person who could correct or instruct communicators and preachers without the venomous barbs Dan was used to. As with all the short courses, each student received a syllabus in advance with reading and preaching assignments. When it came time for a student to preach, he would give his manuscript or outline to the teacher, then read the text and preach until the professor stopped him fifteen or so minutes later. Thereafter the teacher would solicit critiques and then positive comments from the class before giving his evaluation.

On the first day of the class as the teacher and students were getting to know one another, the leader asked each one why they were taking the class. Without divulging too much, Dan explained that his preaching was a matter of contention with a number of his parishioners and all of his elders. Dan recited for them some of the negative comments that were often made or hooked fast in his mind.

When Dan got up to preach, the room was very quiet. He finished preaching before the end of his time period. The room remained quiet for what seemed a long time. *Oh great, what have I done now?*

"Anyone want to start off?" asked the professor.

"Wow. Wow! That was the best sermon I've ever heard," declared a fellow student and pastor.

"What in the world are they complaining about at your church?" exclaimed another.

Dan fought back the tears. It seemed unbelievable to have this kind of a positive response after such a long time in negativity. The professor added, "The message was excellent. I have nothing to add or suggest. You need to go back encouraged and know that you do preach well!" He continued by giving a little pep-talk aimed at Dan's heart, trying to encourage him. He volunteered to be available if the elders at Grace wanted to question him about Dan's preaching, or to write a letter of recommendation.

Dan knew then that the supposed problem he had with preaching was not all his. However, instead of feeling sorry for himself, he became angered and thereafter had to fight resentment toward his antagonists.

"Sounds to me like you need some encouragement from the folks back home?" asked the instructor.

"Who doesn't need encouragement?" Dan replied.

"But leaders can't expect encouragement from followers," proposed one of the students. "Or shepherds shouldn't expect it from sheep!"

"Yeah, like one retired military guy at my church has told me a number of times, 'Expect you are doing well. If not, people will tell you,'" said Spencer.

"I would disagree with both those statements," countered Dr. Williams folding his arms and looking over the top of his eye glasses. "Here's why: while we do not have a right to demand or expect encouragements or accolades from others, especially in a fallen world, we should expect mercy, grace and kindness from our fellow believers. It seems to me that too many church folks act as if pastors are super human people who have the emotional, mental and social strength of a god. Even God demands praise and glory.

"Now, obviously he is worthy of it in ways we would never be as his creatures. But God also gives praise and rewards good servants. He does things providentially to encourage his servants, and we have the promises that faithfulness in the end will be rewarded with crowns and a 'well done good and faithful servant!'"

"So what do we do? Tell our churches to encourage us?" asked another with an insincere laugh.

"Why not?" Williams posed while shrugging his broad shoulders with his hands up in the air. "Why not? There are so many imperatives in the New Testament that tell us how we are to conduct ourselves as family members in Christ. We have a social code – kingdom etiquette if you will – for how we treat and live with one another. It's not all negative, is it? There are so many places that tell us to build up one another, speak only that which edifies, encourage one another, rejoice with those who rejoice and weep with those who weep, be kind to one another, speak the truth in love, and so forth. Right?"

Most of the students nodded in agreement.

"Well, there is pastor appreciation month in October, you know." Carey said.

"Well and good, but is that the only time pastors should be encouraged? No! Of course not. As pastors your responsibility is to instruct God's people in the way of Christ-like love, telling and showing them how to bring the thoughts and will of God to bear upon life, especially in the context of the church."

"So you've done this?" Dan asked.

"Sure! I do this in my teaching, preaching, counseling, one-on-one interactions. I also incorporate a brief lesson in the membership classes. From time to time I put out a page in our monthly church newsletters. It's also on our web site under resources.

"What does your lesson say?" John inquired.

"Give me a moment to set up my laptop and I'll project it on the screen. Carey, can you pull down the screen for me? Let's take a five minute break while I do this."

Most of the students got up. Some left the room. John turned around and set his elbows on the table behind him to engage in a conversation with two fellow students.

Dan visited with a man sitting next to him. Carey fixed the screen and then ran out of the room to retrieve a diet soft-drink. It took about ten minutes for Williams and a student to set up the computer to the projector. "Now this is what I have used to show people how they can encourage me and our pastoral staff in preaching," he noted as he turned on the projector and opened the file to flash his notes on the screen.

You can positively encourage the preacher in his task in these ways:[1]
1. Be attentive.
2. Have good eye contact.
3. Concentrate on the message.
4. Provide appropriate positive non-verbal feedback (smiling, nodding in agreement staying alert, etc.).
5. Tell the preacher how you are being convicted, challenged, comforted or taught.
6. Apply the Word and then report back to the pastor or elders on your spiritual progress and how the preaching of the Bible is impacting you.
7. Share what you are learning with others. This is best done immediately after the sermon while fellowshipping with other Christians, or sharing with your family members.

"This is the first part. As you can see I list seven explicit ways church members can encourage their preacher. Obviously there are many other ways, and you could certainly think of more. But remember to keep it simple."

The computer froze so it took several more minutes to bring everything back on line and onto the screen again. "Okay, here is the second portion for ways not to discourage a preacher:"

Don't discourage the one who is ministering God's Word to you by: [2]
1. Having poor eye contact with the speaker.
2. A wandering mind, or negative responses expressed in negative body language (bored, dead-pan face, negative look, etc.).
3. Sleeping during the preaching of the Word.
4. Criticizing the preaching or the message. An honest critique is fine.
5. Comparing the preacher with other preachers.
6. Being fruitless with little or no change in your life.

7. Being chronically late, leaving in the middle of the service, or before the message is finished.

"Do you have other pages to show how members can encourage their pastors?" Carey wanted to know.

"Sure, but you can go on our church web site to retrieve them later. We want to focus on preaching in this class," replied the professor.

Dr. Williams' method was to lecture and then have a time of interaction. He reminded his seasoned pastoral students that preaching God's Word is one of the main instruments through which God imparts His grace by the Spirit.

"I've never heard that before," said Brian.

"You'll run across a fuller explanation in the study notes and readings about the matter. However, let me say this: the Bible is rather clear that the means of grace or the way God imparts greater grace to you for life and godliness is by the Holy Spirit working through the reading and the preaching of God's Word. One passage worthy of study is Second Peter chapter one, verses one through eleven. Scripture is also clear that the way God speaks to your heart and mind is through preaching. By his Spirit his voice comes through his written Word through his human agent. In fact, the graces obtained by personal reading are dependent upon the grace of the preached Word of God. Take these verses as a starting point," he said as he placed Luke 24:25-27, Acts 8:32-40 and 1 Peter 1:25 on the board.

The instructor went on, "Think about the nature of the declaration of God's Word. God's proclaimed word comes first in the order of all things! Think back to Genesis one and two – God declared his Word and out of nothing creation came into being. God speaks and things happen. God's Word later comes to be written down but when people heard it read and then explained, things happened. God would encounter patriarchs or prophets, and give his word to them. In turn, they would act on God's word and things would happen. His people were set free, for example. In worshipful events led by Ezra or Nehemiah, God's Word was read, then explained, then the Spirit moved through the Word, and revival happened!" He brought home the point that God's Word is God's work. What the Lord spoke through his ordained mouthpieces set into action what he was doing. Several passages such as Isaiah 55:10-11, Jeremiah 1:9; 23:16, 28, 27:14-16 and 2 Peter 1:21 establish the fact.

The teacher outlined for them several important facts about preaching and God's Word:

1. The coming of God's Spirit is the coming of God's Word (Gen. 1:1ff; Num. 11:29; Num. 24:2ff; 2 Sam 23:2; 2 Chron. 24:20; Neh. 9:30; Ezek. 11:4; Luke 1:67-79; John 14:16-17; 16:26; 16:13).

2. The coming of God's kingdom is by the power of God's Word (Acts 1:4-5, 8; 2:14-18).

   a. The preached word of Christ revealed his power over Satan, demons and evil (Matt. 11:12; 12:22-32; Mark 1:24; 3:20-30; Luke 4:35-39).

   b. Christ's preached word was evidence of his kingdom power (Matt. 11:15; 13:16, 17; Luke 4:16ff; 16:16).

   c. The primary way God uses to bring people into and to extend his kingdom is by the preaching of his Word (Luke 2:29ff; 24:46-49; Acts 2; 8:4, 12ff, 32-40; 10:36ff; 11:1ff; 13:5; 15:35; 19:18; 28:23ff).

3. The growing of God's church is by the growth of God's Word (Acts 1:7-8)

   a. Salvation in Jesus Christ comes through the preaching of God's word (Rom. 10:14-15).

   b. The apostles were sent for the purpose of preaching God's Word (1 Tim. 2:7; 2 Tim. 1:11).

   c. As the Word grows so grows the church (Acts 2:41; 4:4; 6:7; 8:14ff; 10:36ff; 12:24; 13:49; 19:20).[3]

4. The preaching of God's Word is therefore the priority of God Church (Acts 2:42-27; 5:42; 17:11; 1 Pet. 1:25; Rom. 1:14ff; 1 Pet. 2:2; 2 Pet. 1:3ff; 3:18; 1 John 2:5).

In that sunlit, air conditioned room the ten men took copious notes. The good professor reminded them that the preached Word is the very power of God. Upon the gray chalkboard he scribbled:

1. *1 Cor. 1:20ff – preaching is foolishness to natural man, but the power to save.*
2. *Matt 11:12; Mark 3:20ff – the preached Word is power over Satan's kingdom!*
3. *Matt. 4:23; 9:35 – the preached Word either brought forth miracles and signs, or was confirmed by miracles and signs. It was and is life changing.*
4. *Matt. 11:15; Lk 16:16; Isa. 40:9 – the preached Word is the power that brings down the gates of Hell and is the power through which God's kingdom grows.*
5. *Acts - Many illustrations for how God's Word goes forth and his church grows.*

The men took a lunch break and walked to a local franchised restaurant. Each ordered different plates from the menu and dialoged about as many different subjects. Theology was mixed with personal matters. The latest philosophical question or theological debate had to be chewed upon before each one divulged their own ministerial blessings or challenges. Everyone had some problems, but the vote was in and Dan's situation seemed to be the worst. Bob had someone like Bernie, but that was all. Gerald had a few people leave because of his preaching. George had a few strange families. Kurt had his version of Irma. Bryan seemed to have a ministry most dream of. Nobody had all of the problems or as many antagonists as did Dan. He didn't know if that was a commentary on his life or ministry. *Maybe I attract people like that or am attracted to folks like that*, he wondered. *Is there such a thing as a pastor-church co-dependent relationship?*

The walk back to the school in the heat drew most of the men to the soda machine before climbing the stairs to the classroom. The prof brought in a large cup of iced tea smartly purchased at the restaurant. "Let's get going again. If we move along well we might be able to get out of here before five o'clock. All right, where were we? Oh yes, we were answering the question, what is preaching? How would you define it?"

Dan quickly responded, "The authoritative declaration of King Jesus through his official herald."

"Very good. But where do you get that from?"

"When we take the many different terms in the Old and New Testaments," said Kirk, "we can conclude that they all are found in the contexts of God officially speaking his will to his people, most of the time through a prophet, priest, apostle, and so forth."

"Here, write this down," the teacher commanded. "Biblical preaching is God's redemptive, life-saving, grace-giving, mystical, Spirit-endowed work …because it is the official proclamation of King Jesus about His will to His people and the world about His justice (law and hell) and mercy (grace)!"

"That's a pretty radical statement, considering all we hear today about preaching. For many preaching is an antiquated form of communication or a condescending lecture," Jeff inserted.

"Right. In fact, if you were to take a survey in your churches what words would people use to define the word preaching?" asked Williams.

"A lecture," said one.

"An entertaining or motivational talk," added another.

"Some dry speech," said Dan.

"A chat or talk," said Robert.

Bryan called out, "A scolding!"

"What an evangelist does at large rallies," James suggested.

"What about a sermon?" asked the teacher.

"Sure. Isn't that what it is?" inquired Ken.

"Not merely a sermon, because true preaching biblically defined is a powerful message from God spoken through his human voicebox."

Dr. Williams pointed them to page twelve in their syllabus. "Someone read 2 Timothy 4, verses one and two."

Jerry read from his well-used *New American Standard Bible*, "I charge you in the presence of God and of Christ Jesus, who is to judge the living and the dead, and by his appearing and his kingdom: preach the word; be ready in season and out of season; reprove, rebuke, and exhort, with complete patience and teaching."

"As many of you know the verb 'preach' is from the Greek *kerux* family of words.[4] *Kerux* means to herald; *kerrusso* is the act of proclaiming, and *kerygma* is what?"

"It's the result or the product of preaching. What you get from *kerux*," Anthony answered.

"Yes. *Kerux* in the extra-biblical literature was often found in the contexts of a god's or king's messenger declaring an official message or decree to others. This is what Hermes did for Zeus in Greek mythology. This is what the Stoic philosopher-preachers did. Sometimes the representative negotiators of warring kings would *kerux*. Any questions?"

Anthony blurted out, "What about the Hebrew Old Testament?"

"You mean, what words are used?"

"Yeah."

"The word *kerux* has no direct Hebrew equivalent. But, *kerruso* is the Greek word chosen to translate the Hebrew in the Septuagint describing official religious or royal proclamations, such as in Exodus 36:6 or 2 Chronicles 36:22. It is used in Genesis 41:43 for the work of a court herald. Here are a few other verses for you," he said while putting them on the far right side of the now frosted board:

Jonah 1:2; 3:2, 4 – preach
Exod. 32:5; Zeph. 3:14; Zech. 9:9 – proclaim

"I encourage you to go back home and do more homework. You will find how frequently the Hebrew word translated using the *kerux* family of terms has to do with a public verbal proclamation of an official decree."

"In the New Testament we see the word in Luke twelve, verse three translated something like 'to publish.' It has many synonyms in the English," he announced as he erased the board. The air conditioning vent swirled a cloud of chalk dust about the room. "I'll write them up here for you," he said as he scribbled again in relatively legible writing:

1. *To herald (Rom. 10:14-15; 1 Cor. 2:21; 2:4; 1 Tim. 2:7; 2 Tim. 1:1; 2 Pet. 2:5)*
2. *To exhort (2 Tim. 4:2)*
3. *To witness (Acts 26:5; 23:11)*
4. *To announce (Luke 9:60; Acts 20:20; 1 Pet. 1:12; 1 John 1:3)*
5. *To teach (Acts 4:2; 5:25; 13:12; 2 John 9)*
6. *To evangelize (Luke 16:16; Acts 21:8; Gal. 1:11; 2 Tim. 4:5)*

"There are twenty-seven other terms synonymous with our word for preaching. Any questions? Thoughts?"[5]

It must have been the heavy lunch most of the students ate, for they were all trying to break through the drowsy mental fog. Seeing no response he added, "Okay, let's take a break."

Everyone got up and stretched. Some headed for the coffee room looking for a low sugar caffeine jolt. Others chose to walk around the building. A few stayed behind to talk shop. It took fifteen minutes for everyone to meander back into class. "Any questions before we continue?" Dr. Williams asked.

"Where are we going with all this?" Mark queried.

"We are moving full circle to prove the point Dan and Kirk made at the beginning of the hour. Preaching is the authoritative proclamation from a king." He shuffled to the left of the wall-to-wall blackboard and printed:

1. *Gen. 41:43, Dan. 3:4 – an official order from a ruler or king*
2. *Exod. 36:6; 2 Chron. 36:22; Jon. 3:2, 4 – the official word of God declared through a human agent*
3. *Exod. 32:5; Zeph. 3:14; Zech. 9:9 –a religious proclamation*

"You see, these are just a few illustrations to underscore the authoritative force of the word *kerux*. Without spending more detailed time in our syllabus, let me conclude what I've been emphasizing - that the word is used to translate the some Hebrew Old Testament terms to refer to the official herald of a king, a state or a religion.[6] Again, let me stress, in nearly all the cases it is an official, public, verbal proclamation of a decree. So this is the term Paul and other New Testament writers used to describe preaching. Can you sense the weight behind it? Preaching in the biblical sense is not merely giving a talk! It is a unique form of proclamation! Your homework for tonight is to answer this question: is just anyone able or authorized to preach in this sense? Class dismissed."

It was four o'clock. Everyone had plans so Dan drove his car to the motel room and changed into more casual clothes. He flipped on the television to catch the latest news flipping from the local station to Fox News to CNN. He decided to call home and check on Mona and the children.

"Hi, Sweetie! How are the classes going?" Mona asked, excited to hear her man's voice.

"Lots of review, some new stuff, but very, very encouraging," Dan replied. He went on to tell her of the responses to his sermonette from the professor and peers. "And he's a professional communicator as well as a pastor. I'll take his word above a grumpy old Bernie anytime."

"Honey, be nice. Oh, speaking of Bernie, he came by today around lunch time."

"What?! He's never come to our place. What did he want?" Dan said with aggravation.

"I don't know."

"What do you mean you don't know? What did he tell you? What did he say?"

"When I answered the door he asked if you were home. I reminded him you were out of town taking a preaching class at seminary. He didn't say anything to that but was perturbed you weren't home."

"That was it?" Dan asked rather disgusted.

"He didn't say anything after that. He just stormed off," Mona replied.

"Well, I'm sure if he really needed to get in touch with me he would call my cell phone. I gave all the elders my number and where I would be staying. I don't know what he's up to, but it bugs me!"

"It's okay. It's probably no big deal, Honey."

"Everything is a big deal with Bernie," spouted an angry man. "If he comes back you call me immediately."

"That won't be…"

"No! You call me immediately! Got it?" he commanded.

"All right, all right. Calm down. The boys are fine. They miss their daddy. You want to talk with them?" Mona asked, hoping to calm Dan and to encourage the boys.

Dan talked with Jake and then with Ben for fifteen minutes. Ben had a long story about the dog getting into trouble. "What trouble, Ben?"

"He ate the water things outside," Ben proudly announced. Dan could hear his mother scolding, "Ben, I told you not to say anything to Daddy!"

"Benny boy, what are you talking about?"

"And the hose is chewed all the way gone," the little man said almost gleefully, ignoring his mother's wishes. Mona took the phone from him.

Dan urged, "Ben, let me talk with Mommy."

"I'm here. I didn't want the boys to say anything because I wanted you to have a restful week at school."

"So what's the problem with the dog?"

"Well….he dug up and ate three sprinkler heads and the new hose you bought. The backyard flooded when the sprinklers came on this morning, but I've turned them off."

"Oh man! What is it about husbands going away and things fall apart?"

"It's not that big of a crisis. You'll handle it when you get back," Mona reminded him.

"Just one more thing on a growing list of things to do," Dan pouted. The rest of the short conversation went well. Dan even cooed and talked baby talk with their toddler-to-be. She preferred putting the phone in her mouth and banging it on her high chair than talking with her father. When Mona retrieved the drool soaked phone she thanked Dan for calling and assured him all was well. He promised to call every day about the same time.

After a short nap Dan drove over to Yummy Buffet. The quality of the food did not quite match the name, but the price was great. From there he was able to find a mall with a theatre with the latest movies. He was in the mood for a sci-fi.

An unexpected cool front washed over the state that next morning. The class did not need the air conditioning since an open window provided a comfortable atmosphere, but it was somewhat of a challenge trying to hear over the nearby traffic. The good doctor greeted his students and started right in where he left off. "We saw that the Old Testament term for preaching was a herald's official proclamation from a king, emperor, state or religion. It usually declared the decree of a king or pronouncement from the god of the people. In the New Testament we see that Jesus is the true Word according to John 1 and he is true preaching according to Hebrews 1:1-2."

The lesson continued, and revealed the important fact that salvation comes through true biblical preaching. According to Romans 10:14-15, Christ's voice speaks through the one God sends, and it is Jesus who is heard. The apostles were sent out as heralds or ambassadors to preach (*kerux*) and to teach God's Word (Matt. 10:5-7, 40: 1 Tim. 2:7; 2 Tim. 1:11). Paul tells Timothy as a faithful pastor to preach (*kerux*) God's Word. The important force of the word is clear. Timothy is not merely giving a talk, or even merely sharing the Gospel through a loud voice, but he is coming to others as God's official spokesman declaring the mighty will of God.

The point being hammered again and again is that the work these student-pastors were doing in the pulpit was of the highest importance. They were standing in the place as God's heralds announcing God's will for the life of the local church as well as for the lives of each listener.

"Let's be clear about something," Mr. Williams ordered. "Just because a preacher gets up and speaks does not mean that he is delivering the authoritative Word from God. The authority is not invested in his person or even merely in his office. It comes from the very Word of God itself. But more than that, true preaching is Spirit-filled preaching and Spirit-filled preaching is not only preaching in a supernatural, God-empowered way, but Spirit-filled preaching can elevate and glorify the very person from whom it comes! In Romans 10:14 we have Christ preaching through the one whom he has sent, while the rest of the Scriptures tell us that Jesus Christ should be the central subject of the preached message!" he propounded, again scribbling verses upon his well-marked board: Acts 3:15; 5:42; 8:5, 12, 35; 9:20; 11:20; 17:2-3.

"Paul made it obvious that he preached Jesus Christ and him crucified (1 Cor. 1:23; 2:2; Gal. 3:1, 6:14). True Spirit-filled preaching is the true and selfless offer of the person and work of Jesus Christ! Arturo Azurdia on page nineteen of his book says that Spirit-filled preaching is the 'instantaneous, sudden and sovereign operation of the Holy Spirit of God coming upon a man so that his proclamation of Jesus Christ might be attended by holy power.'[7] May God grant his church with Spirit-empowered preachers!"

Dr. Williams rounded out the morning by making the case that God has always spoken through specially called and selected individuals. His official word did not merely come through anyone (Matt. 10:7; Mark 3:14; Luke 9:2). God called, gifted and ordained apostles to be his official spokesmen (Matt. 10:5-7, 40; 1 Tim. 2:7; 2 Tim. 1:11). The ordained evangelist or elder-pastor is God's official herald according to Romans 10:14-15, 1 Timothy 5:17 and 2 Timothy 4:5. "Here is some homework for tonight. Read these verses and see who was called to preach the Good News or the Word of God," he said while writing out the lists:

1. *Mark 1:14; John 1:1ff; Heb. 1:1-2 –*
2. *Mark 3:14; 1 Tim. 2:7; 2 Tim. 1:11; 2 Pet. 2:5 –*
3. *Acts 14:14; Rom. 15:20, 16:7; 2 Cor. 8:23 –*
4. *Eph. 4:11-12 and 2 Tim. 4:5 –*
5. *Acts 13:1; 1 Cor. 12:28; Eph. 4:11 and Jas. 3:1 –*
6. *Mark 1:45 –*

"Take a closer look at Mark 1:45 and see what happens when God does not commission someone to preach but who takes it upon himself to do so anyway," he said as he finished his scribbling.

The cool breeze turned into a more forceful wind. The smell of rain painted the air. It started getting dark outside. Two of the students rushed to close the westerly windows. The professor quickly reviewed the materials in the syllabus showing who and how certain individuals are commissioned to the role of official herald (1 Tim. 4:14; 2 Tim. 2:16; 4:2). He reminded the students what they knew about the inner and outer call from God, and the official commission they receive through ordination. "How should you perceive your call as servant-preachers?" he asked. "Yes, Jeff!"

Jeff answered, "I don't think I've ever learned this. If I did it slipped my mind. But it puts a whole new light on what role I play and what I do. I'm not just some communicator giving a good talk. This really changes things!"

"It scares me thinking what my job is as a pastor-preacher and what I say on Sunday mornings," Carey added.

"The Reformers captured this during the age of the Reformation. That's one of the reasons why they emphasized preaching from the Bible. In fact, one of the Reformed confessions, the Second Helvetic Confession of 1566 declares that preaching the Word of God is the word of God," the professor spoke.

"What do you mean by that?" questioned Bill.

Dan was fast to respond. "What they were saying was that if the preacher is speaking from the text of Scripture, that word empowered by the Holy Spirit is God speaking to his people. At that time many evangelical people went to hear the preached Word because they expected to hear God speaking through the sermon to them."

Kirk added, "Yep, and why they also believed that personal reading, devotions and Bible study was very important, but only a supplement and second in importance to the official proclamation of God's Word. It's too bad that we've lost that concept today. We tend to think that the only way God speaks to us today is one-on-one, personally, by a still small voice, or audibly, or by some prompting."

Trying to be funny, Andrew pronounced, "We just need to go back and tell our congregations that when we preach it is God speaking through us…Thus says the Lord!" With that a brilliant flash and loud snap with an immediate peal of thunder shook the building and shook up the students. Everyone laughed. A few of them ran to the windows to check the trees, cars and buildings nearby for damage.

The remainder of the week was spent taking turns preaching and evaluating one another's sermons. The students had turned in their reading homework and were required to finish another assignment to get credit for this course. They had to go home and preach or teach about what they learned, and then had to research what constitutes a good or great sermon.

The teacher determined that they covered enough of the material and everyone had opportunities to have two sermons evaluated, so he dismissed the class before lunch on Friday. Dan had already checked out of the hotel. He flipped open his silver cell phone to call Mona. Nobody answered, so he left a voicemail message.

He drove through a fast food restaurant to pick up plenty of food and drink for the trip, and then went across the street to fill up the gas tank. By 11:10 A.M. he was headed down the highway for the long trip home. At least he would be getting in home at a decent hour. He was thankful for that. He had eight hours to meditate on all he learned, soak in all of the encouragement he received, and to try to prepare himself for a sure confrontation with Bernie when he returned.

A CHALLENGE TO THINK AND DO

What do you think?
1. What are you able to take from this chapter?
2. How would you define preaching according to the Bible? How important and valuable is it?
3. What does it mean to preach Christ?
4. What does it mean that God's Word is God's work?
5. Do you go to worship expecting to hear God through the preaching of the Word of God? Why or why not?
6. Do you regularly pray for your pastor and the messages he prepares and delivers? If so, what exactly do you pray for?
7. Do you encourage or discourage your preacher in the important task of preaching the Word?

Some things you could do:
1. Go back through the chapter and review the suggestions on how to encourage your pastor. Put them into practice.
2. Make a list of things you may be doing to discourage your pastor when he preaches. Then resolve to stop doing those things.
3. Put Appendix N to practice. Let your pastor know you are committed to praying for him.

12

WHAT A GREAT MESSAGE!

—ᗢ—

Jake and Ben came running from around the back of the house when their Dad pulled up. The sky was barely lit with a blue-gray fluorescence. The evening was warm and muggy. They were so excited to see their Daddy that they ignored the mud on their almost naked bodies and nearly succeeded in tackling him to the pavement. "Whoa! Boys! What have we here?" Dan cried out. It was too late, but thankfully Dan was not in his dress attire.

"Daddy's home! Daddy's home, Mommy! Maaaaaahmmyyy! Daddy – is – home!" Ben shouted toward the kitchen window.

"We missed you, Daddy!" said Jake wrapped around Dan's right leg.

"I missed ya'll too. What are you boys up to?"

"Playing in the pond," Ben grinned proudly.

"Pond? What pond?" Dan asked with a little trepidation. The boys then grabbed their dad's fingers on both hands and led him down the driveway, turning right and around the back of the house into the yard. Sure enough, there was a pond of sorts: an approximately four-foot round pool of settled water in a depression toward the back fence. It used to be the dog's hole, its resting place during hot days. Obviously, the water was not shut off all the way.

Just as they brought him to show off their new pond, Mona popped out the back door with Hannah. Ben was telling their dad they could put fish in it. Jake wanted it bigger.

"Hi, Honey! I see you found our pool?" she half grinned.

"Yeah. Thought you turned the water off?"

"Thought so too, but water keeps filling it up," she apologized.

A pastor's life isn't altogether different than everyone else's. In the home or in other places the pastor is usually like every other person. In the excitement Dan left his car door open. As he was toying around with the automatic controls for the sprinkler system, talking with Mona and making baby noises for his little girl, Ben, ever the precocious child jumped into the driver's seat, mud and all.

Normally Dan was pretty handy around the house, but he could not determine the cause of the leak. Darkness was blanketing the evening, so he put off the project for another time. When he went back to retrieve his briefcase and laptop, he discovered Ben in the car.

"Look at me, Daddy! I'm big like you! I can drive," he exclaimed as he pulled the stiff steering wheel from side to side.

Mona was afraid Dan might explode, so she rushed to pull the unlicensed driver out of the car. Jake proudly yelled at his brother, "Ooooo, you're in truh-uh-ble!"

"Jake," Dad commanded, "You go inside and get ready for a bath. Now!"

In her left arm Mona carried Hannah, and in her right hand she held Ben's left arm.

"I'll handle this," Dan said. He took both of Ben's arms in his hands, squatted down and looked at him squarely in the eyes. Ben kept looking away. "Ben, look right at me."

With his muddy head down and big eyes up, the little nymph sheepishly asked, "Are you preaching me now?"

Dan laughed. "No, son. What I'm going to do is not preach at you."

He grabbed his middle child and embraced him. Dan's right cheek rested upon the child's wet and dirty hair. Ben smelled like mud, sweat and dog, but Dan loved his son beyond his filth. He scooped him up and carried him into the house while giving Ben a firm, but gentle talk about what he had done wrong. As a consequence, Ben would help his father clean the inside of the car the next day. After rinsing him off in the master bathroom's shower, he plopped him into the bubble bath with Jake. The two enjoyed a lengthy stay under the bubbles.

"Preach at me? Where did he get that from?" he asked Mona as he cleared out his briefcase and put away the laptop.

"Probably from Jake. Jake often pretends to be you. Ben and the stuffed animals are the church. You know Ben – he can't sit still very long. So Jake will yell at him and tell him to behave, that he needs to preach at him."

Dan exploded in a howl and belly laugh. It was a good and productive time away at school, Dan shared with his wife, but it was far better being home.

Dan helped Mona put the boys down and then rocked his little princess to sleep as he and Mona talked about the things he learned at seminary. Mona didn't have much to share since she had already apprised him of the daily events. Dan then raided the refrigerator for leftover meatloaf – he loved meatloaf sandwiches with plenty of ketchup.

After breakfast early Saturday morning, Dan and the boys went out to the yard in their bathing suits. Working out regularly gave Dan a fairly good physique, but he was still hesitant to be seen by unappreciative members who would take offense at his relative nudity. That was why the threesome tackled the exterior of the car first, to get it over with quickly. By the end of the wash all of them were drenched in a cocktail of dirty, soapy, hose water. Just as Dan was about to retrieve one of the few dry towels, Bernie and his sister unexpectedly pulled into the Lee's driveway.

Too late - all Dan could do was hang the medium sized, old towel around his neck. "Boys, run inside now and get some snacks. I'll get you when I am ready."

As they ran off, Ben stopped, turned and asked, "Daddy? They going to preach at you?"

"Benny, go see Mom!"

Irma got out first. She glared at Dan's water plastered black hair on his head and chest. After a struggle, Bernie was able to extract himself from his sister's brand new Lexus.

"You're indecent, Mr. Lee!" were the first words Bernie blurted.

"Mister Dumpleton. Miss Dumpleton. What's the occasion of this visit?" Dan said as he rested against the trunk of his car. "Need a car wash? The boys and I can offer you a great deal," he said with a smirk spread across face.

"Don't get funny with me, young man!" Bernie scolded.

That was enough, and Dan finished being mister nice guy. "Mr. Dumpleton, your abrasive and arrogant manner will not be tolerated. I'll not have you treat me with contempt!"

"Mr. Lee – where have you been this past week?" Irma interrogated.

"You should have known. Your brother, the elders, and deacons and anyone who read the announcements knew I was off to seminary to take an advanced preaching class. Bernie was there at the elders' meeting and approved my absence."

"Ellie May died Monday, Mr. Lee," Bernie chopped through his thin lips. Irma began to sniffle.

"I'm sorry to hear that. I didn't know. Why wasn't I called?"

"You should have known. You should have been here for her. You knew she was dying, but you selfishly took off on some pleasure trip. I'll have your job for this! This is the last straw." Bernie threatened.

Dan bent over and picked up the nozzle of the hose. "Bernie, you are one rude and abusive man. This conversation is over. Leave now!" he countered as he pointed the hose in their direction. The temptation was resisted, but the thought was pleasurable.

The two Dumpletons turned and shuffled back toward the car doors. Irma, the first to find the driver's seat, kept yelling at her brother to hurry up. Even before Bernie slammed the navy blue door Irma was squealing out the driveway and down the narrow street like some hot teenager.

Are they mental? Lord, what is their problem?

Mona was a stealth figure behind the front screen door. She observed everything and for the first time witnessed how abusive the Dumpletons acted toward her husband. She began to cry. Sympathetic little Hannah began to cry too.

Dan turned toward his girls. He could not see them very well, but could hear their sobs.

"Hey, they were just upset I wasn't wearing a tie!" he announced.

"Dan! Stop that," Mona chided. She opened the black metal screen door. Hannah tried to toddle out onto the cement landing.

"Courage and levity, my Dear!" Dan quipped as if unfazed by the incident. In fact, he was amazed at his self-control and lack of anger. *Thank you, God, for the fruit of your Spirit!*

The issue no doubt would again rear its beastly head soon enough. Dan decided to spend his Saturday with his family and allow the crisis to develop without his involvement.

Before Sunday School the next morning, he learned that Ellie May's family had held the funeral the previous Wednesday. They did not see any reason to contact Dan since her son decided to have the funeral in the family's old hometown where most of Ellie May's family and old friends lived. So what in the world were the Dumpletons so tweaked about?

During the Sunday morning announcements, Dan told the congregation of his plan for a new series of messages on the subject of preaching, as per the seminary requirements. He finished the chapter of the book through which he had been preaching and promised to pick up where he left off at a later date.

The same grumpies and judges were in their reserved seats waiting for Dan to impress them. It didn't matter now. He had his fellow classmates' and a professional communicator's words of encouragement ringing in his ears.

For the first time Dan recognized that even though a majority of the members who had been at Grace before Dan arrived were negative toward his preaching, he would occasionally receive expressions of appreciation from a small number of the long-term members, including two of the nominated men for office of elder. Another was a deacon who was very encouraging and often told Dan of his personal growth because of the messages. Music to a pastor's ears!

Then there were the few, who predictably said, "Nice message, Pastor," as they shook his hand on the way out the front door. Frankly, Dan hated that, for it was meaningless and trivial. He could understand that they were trying to be nice, but they were not really being kind. It's just something people get into the habit of saying, kind of like the rhetorical greeting, "How are you?" So Dan began to respond to such comments with something like, "Thank you for your feedback. What did you get out of the message today?" It put most of them on the spot not knowing how to answer him. That was not what he wanted to do. He wanted to challenge people to think – to think about the message, to think about the possibility the message could be relevant to their lives, to think about what they were really doing. The platitudes quickly ceased and, instead, the parishioners responded with remarks such as, "Good to see you today, Pastor," or "Isn't the weather lovely?"

None of the elders ever commended Dan for his preaching. Dan did not expect any changes from them even after he took the classes. As for preaching issues, Bernie had significantly backed off since the original confrontation. He no longer shuffled to the entrance of the church after the service to say things like, "Unacceptable!" or "That was a miserable message!" or "You're not cutting it!" All the verbal lashing ceased, but not the negative body language. It was so distracting that Dan quit looking in Bernie's direction when he preached. Dan's pastor friend in Montana would have the guts to stop the message and verbally chastise Bernie for his belligerence. Dan was not as bold.

Occasionally one elder or another would let the pastor know that he did not like the way he moved out from behind the massive oak pulpit, or ended his sentences with a preposition, or read while looking down at the Bible, or looked at his sermon notes. They wanted Dan to memorize his sermons. At the same time they criticized him for being too conversational with the audience. They also wanted Dan to speak with better articulation and eloquence. He was told he was dumbing down the messages because he no longer used those grand theological terms or multi-syllable words. He argued that profound truth can be articulated simply. Jesus did that, and that was what he was trying to do. They would have been happy with a lecture from a brilliant seminary professor. In fact, that is what Bernie had told him one time – he wanted a brilliant preacher to attract the college professors and white collar professionals. Such an expectation never came up during the candidating process.

Bernie and a couple of the elders believed that criticism and nagging was the most effective method for provoking the pastor to improve. But criticism, nagging or other negativities are never as effective as nurturing, teaching, encouraging, or rewarding. It's as Don MacNair said, "Criticism can also inhibit preaching. If a pastor feels threatened by possible criticism from a segment of his congregation, his ministry of the Word will be hampered, and the presence and power of the living Lord will in that measure be restricted."[1]

At one elders' meeting Dan asked, "Just what is it you are looking for? You still haven't defined what a good sermon or good preaching is. If you can't do that, then just give me names of men or samples of their sermons, so I can get a sense of what you think is good." However, no one offered a definition, and only Bernie could remind Pastor Dan that a previous pastor was the best preacher of all time.

Okay, so Dan rummaged through the old boxes of recorded cassettes and found several by Bernie's idol. He listened to about a dozen of them. While the content was good and the sermons were biblical, the rather expressionless delivery put Dan to sleep. The man wasn't even eloquent, though he had a rich vocabulary. His style was somewhat reminiscent of the sermons Dan had read by certain preachers of the English Victorian era. It was high brow with thick theology that spoke about a subject, but never to the people. The messages did not resonate with Dan.

Dan was very uncomfortable about evaluating the pastor's sermons, though. Just because the man's style did not resonate with him did not mean that he was a bad preacher, or even a great one as Bernie claimed. As Dan was known to do, he gathered all of his books on preaching and systematically put together his findings into a written report. He had been keeping a running file of notes, clipping, articles and excerpts from books, so the process would not take too long. The two main questions he wanted to answer were: What does God say about preaching? and How does God qualify good preaching? Now, providentially, these were questions he had to answer for his class assignment.

Preaching is a funny thing. Like most issues, everyone has an opinion about it. During his previous seminary training the three professors who taught homiletics agreed that preaching is the official and authoritative message from King Jesus proclaimed through his official herald. However, the three of them did not agree on the method for preaching. The first instructor insisted that you never preach topically but always from the theme derived from a segment of a book, which could be a paragraph or a whole chapter in the Bible. The ideas from the passage should be arranged so as to present three main points. Every point was presented in the declarative, just like his lectures. A poem or quote or portion of a hymn could dress the sermon up. No application was to be given since that is the prerogative of the Holy Spirit. The other professor did not have such a restrictive view, while the third teacher was heavy on application.

Even the pastors and professors to whom Dan sent his sermons for evaluation responded with conflicting reports. While one message was rich and well-presented according to one man, it sounded too condescending according to another. One message did not flow, said a third pastor, but to a different minister across the country the same message was too logical and didactic. Another fellow preacher called it "a good message," another labeled it as "adequate," while a seminary professor said, "Yeah, you aren't a good or great preacher, but neither am I."

Dan noticed a contrast between the disfavor of his preaching in the eyes of most of the long-time members, and the profit and enjoyment of the messages by the new members. Most of the new people said that Dan's preaching was a primary reason for staying at the church. Nevertheless, no matter how often the new people commended or encouraged Dan, he still had to fight the sting of the vocal critics. "Trying to please people will get you nowhere!" his dear wife would often remind him. He just had to face the fact that no matter what he did he could not please everyone. Dan could not preach like any of the previous pastors, nor did he have a desire to do so. If he did he would be a phony, and some would be dissatisfied anyway.

It was much easier preaching at the previous church. At least there the only challenges he had were from two men and a family. The two men had strong but opposing perspectives about preaching, and Dan didn't fit either view. It was humorous because the one claimed Dan's preaching was too applicatory or moralistic while the other man said Dan did not stress application or holy living enough.

The family was a different case. Dan noticed anytime he would say something that apparently offended the father the man would bow his head and look into his lap. As if on cue, his wife and children did the same. When it was apparently safe for them to listen again the father would look up, as would his family. It was distracting, but humorous; almost like marionettes with a puppeteer controlling them. Dan was too cowardly to ask husband and father why they did that.

The father never criticized the pastor, but did tell Dan that his children were not permitted to ask the pastor any questions because it was his responsibility to teach his children. He did not want the pastor to usurp his role as a father. Also, the pastor was not permitted to directly counsel or teach the children anything. Dan respected that, even if he strongly disagreed. But then he began to be confronted by the oldest son who believed he had the freedom and duty to correct or rebuke Dan for making comments in sermons the young teen believed were wrong. Pastor put a stop to that.

Dan was painfully learning that the pastor's duty is to please God not people. Relying upon God's Spirit, faithful to God's Word and with much work to develop effective communication skills, the messages should be good. In the meantime, Dan realized that his supposedly bad preaching was an obstacle to developing a good relationship with the elders. As he found out later on Dan would never be acceptable to these elders. One elder said he never got anything from the messages, because they never did anything for him. The other elder said he learned something a couple of times. Other than that he was ambivalent toward Dan's preaching. Nevertheless, the advanced training at this seminary was changing the pastor's perspective on the issue.

An even larger group had come to the breakfast training session at Mo's. The little air conditioner didn't pack much of a punch in her café. Not many ordered coffee, but plenty of iced water and juice kept coming to the table. Dan was now teaching on the subject of preaching. The best way to learn is to teach. It was time to apply the fruit of his labors and schooling. When Mo came over to check on her "good customers" Dan turned to her and asked, "Mo, does your priest give a sermon at your worship?"

"You mean a homily?" she asked in her brogue.

"Yes, a homily."

"Oh sure, every Sunday."

"How long is the message?"

"The Father takes ten or fifteen minutes, God bless him."

"Is that a good or a bad thing?"

"I'm supposin' it's a good thing, but he could do without it."

Everyone laughed.

"Why say anythin' at all when you don't have anythin' to say?" she added.

The crowd roared.

"Good point. Don't you get anything out of the homily?"

"Oh sure, sure I do. I get a good nap!"

Now the group was hysterical.

"Well, Mo, don't you think it's possible you could get something out of his messages if you listened?"

"Deary, after fifteen years of hearin' the same man drone on and on about the same old yarns, there's not much to hear."

"Oh, that's too bad," Dan said trying to sympathize with her.

"No, lad, it's not. A good shnooze is good for your heart, you know?"

"What keeps you at the church then?" Dan inquired.

"Now that's a funny question. You don't think we go to hear the man speak do you? No, Sonny. We go for the Mass. And for a good fill of tea and sweets afterward. Most of us have friends there too."

"So the preaching isn't the main thing for you? Does it affect the way you or others think about your priest?"

"Oh hel…heck no! We all love the father for his kindness and the wonderful things he does. Just like everyone loves you, Father Dan."

The crowd around the table chorused a resounding, "Ahhhhh."

Dan blushed. *I wish that were true.*

"I learned this in seminary recently," he said as he wrote on the right side of the board:

Types of Sermons:
- *Book study*
- *Expository sermon*
- *Informational – usually thematic or theological and doctrinal*
- *Instructional*
- *Occasional sermon – such as in a crisis situation*
- *Topical – theme based sermon or series*

"Preaching the Word of God can come through any one of these types of sermons."

From his research Dan organized a handout he gave out at this Saturday class and

intended to later present to the elders. He also put together some bulletin inserts to supplement his short series on what the Bible says about preachers and preaching. "Turn with me to Acts 20. While you are doing that, here's a question: 'What constitutes good preaching?'"

There was a lull as people wrestled their minds for an answer. "Good preaching is what speaks to me," offered Melissa.

"What speaks to you, Melissa?"

"Good preaching," she bounced back, somewhat embarrassed. "I don't really know."

"But you think you know it when you hear it?"

"Right! What is the purpose of good preaching?" directed Dan.

"Good preaching teaches me something," joined Blake.

"It talks to my head and heart," declared Harold.

"You mean it teaches you and is directed at your will?" asked Dan.

"Exactly."

The group volleyed the questions and answers around for another ten minutes or so. Some people took the opportunity to visit the restrooms, or refill their drinks, or order more food.

Harold volunteered to read Acts 20:17-27. When he finished, Dan asked, "What are some things this text tells us about Paul and his ministry of the Word of God?"

"He didn't keep anything from them," Phil, one of the elder candidates said.

"Paul taught them, and gave them what was helpful to them," Neil, another candidate volunteered.

Dan was writing these things on the white board.

"He called for repentance and faith!" Blake noted.

Melissa spoke out, "Paul says that his life and ministry testifies to the Gospel of Christ."

"Anything else," the pastor asked.

"He preached the kingdom of God," Harold contributed.

"And he taught the whole counsel of God," spoke Dan's favorite deacon.

"Wonderful responses. Now, let's go back and use these points to inform us as to what good preaching is. First, Paul did not hold back any truth from his hearers. This is Biblical doctrine applied to life. Second, Paul taught them and gave them what was helpful. Good preaching is proclaiming from God's Word anything that would be instructive and helpful in Christ. A parallel verse would be 2 Timothy 3:17."

"The third thing about good preaching, and we assume it is good because God spoke it through his messenger Paul, is that it calls for people to repent and believe in Christ. Melissa, you made a good point, that his life was consistent with the message. This is certainly very important, isn't it? The fourth thing is good preaching involves preaching the kingdom of God and also preaching the whole counsel of God, which is the message of Christ from the Old and New Testaments."

"Explain what you just said about 'the message of Christ'?" Blake asked.

"Our sermons must be centered upon and flow from the person and work of Jesus Christ. Good preaching is not centered upon us as people and what we do. Instead, good preaching centers upon Christ as the God-Man and what he did and does for us. To summarize Greidanus from his *Modern Preacher and the Ancient Text*,[2] good preaching is biblical when it imparts a Bible-shaped word in a Bible-like way. The Bible must govern the content of the sermon, while the function of the sermon must come out of the very Scripture itself. Being Bible-centered means being Christ-centered, since the central theme and message of Scripture is Jesus Christ. Listen to what D. A. Carson brings out in *The Cross and Christian Ministry*:

> But rhetoric brings with it many dangers. Those who pursue eloquence and high-sounding insight with precious little content are often doing little more than

preening their own feathers. Such oratory made Paul nervous. It affords far too many   temptations to pride to be safe for anyone interested in preaching the Gospel of the crucified Messiah.[3]

"Carson later says about First Corinthians:

In light of 1:18-2:5, this is the power of the gospel, the power to forgive, to transform, to call men and women out of darkness and into the kingdom of God's dear Son. Mere talk will not change people; the gospel will. So Paul is going to ask for their credentials: What people has your eloquence genuinely transformed by bringing them into a personal knowledge of the crucified Messiah? He is going to expose them for the empty, religious windbags that they are."[4]

"But what if you have all that in your sermons and people don't think it is good preaching?" asked Michael.

"Okay, excellent question. What of that?"

Harold was quick to offer an answer, "Doesn't the Bible say something about itching ears?"

"Right on the money, Harold. Turn to 2 Timothy 4:1, and read to verse four."

Melissa said, "I've got it:

I charge you therefore before God and the Lord Jesus Christ, who will judge the living and the dead at His appearing and His kingdom: Preach the word! Be ready in season and out of season. Convince, rebuke, exhort, with all longsuffering and teaching. For the time will come when they will not endure sound doctrine, but according to their own desires, because they have itching ears, they will heap up for themselves teachers; and they will turn their ears away from the truth, and be turned aside to fables."

"Remember what I said about this word 'preach,' that it is an official proclamation from a king's herald. In the context of telling Timothy to preach with that kind of authority, Paul also warns that there will be those who will reject good preaching and instead will want what?"

Harold answered again, "Not good teaching, but anything that will suit their own desires."

"Yeah, but Paul was a good preacher. Who would have rejected him?" the deacon asked.

"Yes, he was a great preacher. Nevertheless, there were many times he was considered to be a poor speaker or not-so-good preacher. Take these verses home with you and look them up," Dan ordered as he copied some of his notes to the board: 1 Cor. 2:1, 4; 1 Cor. 1:17; 2 Cor. 10:10 and 11:6.

Most of the class was astounded to hear that Paul was rejected as a good preacher. Dan got a certain satisfaction from that fact, but he had to remind himself that he would never be a Paul.

"Hey, what if a preacher has all these qualities in his sermons but comes across really, really bad. Is that still good preaching?" Sam wondered.

"I've heard from many different homiletics professors and pastors that it is a sin to give good content but fail to communicate. One man said it's a sin to bore people because one could conceivably bore them right into hell. Now, I wouldn't agree with that, but it is sad when there is little to no passion when it comes to preaching or even teaching God's Word." Dan told them about the quote from the famous preacher Charles Spurgeon who said, "I believe that many 'deep' preachers are simply so because they are like dry wells with nothing whatever in them, except decaying leaves, a few stones, and perhaps a dead cat or two."[5] Spurgeon also said that dull preachers "…make good martyrs. They are so dry they burn well."[6]

"At the same time, some of the old Puritan preachers read their sermons," Dan taught. "Jonathan Edwards's most famous sermon, *Sinners in the Hands of an Angry God,* was apparently read with little emotion or expression. Some say he did that for fear of manipulating people through expressive communication. Others say it typified his stoic personality. But there are at least two things to consider: his sermon was written and presented with great force of argument. The other thing was the role of the Holy Spirit. The Spirit can use any message from the Word to speak to hearts. Listen to what Arnold Dallimore says about Edwards in his biography about the preacher-evangelist George Whitefield:

One who knew him, being asked whether Mr. Edwards was an eloquent preacher replied: 'If you men, by eloquence, what is usually intended by it in our cities, he made no pretensions to it. He had no studied varieties of the voice and made no strong emphasis. He scarcely gestured or even moved; and he made no attempt by the elegance of his style, or the beauty of his pictures, to gratify the taste, and fascinate the imagination. But if you mean by eloquence the power of presenting an important truth before an audience with overwhelming weight of argument, and with such intenseness of feeling that the whole soul of the speaker is thrown into every part of the conception and delivery, so that the solemn attention of the whole audience is riveted from the beginning to the close, and impressions are left that cannot be effaced, Mr. Edwards was the most eloquent man I ever heard speak."[7]

"I hate to say this, but some pastors just can't preach their way out of a wet paper bag," complained Harold. Laughter erupted at the table.

"Look, it's a tough issue to sort through. We live in the age of communication, and as pastors, we have to compete," Dan said marking quotation marks with his fingers in the air, "'with specialists.' There are so many TV anchormen and women, actors, radio hosts, and talk show hosts who just have a natural talent for communicating while others are expertly trained. People go to church expecting their servant-preacher to be of the same caliber. Then you have the big church personalities who by virtue of their God-given natural endowments go on TV, radio or streaming video and attract huge crowds. Some are great communicators who are faithful to God's Word and others are dynamite speakers who handle God's Word terribly. People are often attracted to the presentation more than the content."

As Mo scooted from table to table, the pastor turned to his class and asked, "What styles of preaching can we find in Western churches these days?" Dan read off a list of the various styles he had been told constituted good or great preaching, "practical, ethereal, highly doctrinal or causally soft in teaching, light and upbeat or heavy and morbid, pietistic, moralistic, expositional, exhortational, strongly evangelistic, eloquent with perfected speech, vulgar, passionate or unemotional… You see, the list can be rather endless when you think about it" (see Appendix O).

Marcus spoke up, "It's always been that way. I've been reading about the time in which Peter, John, James and Paul lived. Eloquence and rhetoric was a popular and very important part of society then. But look at what Paul said in First Corinthians two starting with verse one," he urged, while turning to the reference in his *Thompson Chain Reference Bible*:

> And I, brethren, when I came to you, did not come with excellence of speech or of wisdom declaring to you the testimony of God. For I determined not to know anything among you except Jesus Christ and Him crucified. I was with you in weakness, in fear, and in much trembling. And my speech and my preaching were not with persuasive words of human wisdom, but in demonstration of the Spirit and power, that your faith should not be in the wisdom of men but in the power of God."[8]

Marcus paused a minute and then added, "Paul did not preach by human standards or methods, because he wanted full credit to go to the powerful work of God's Spirit!" Marcus was right. D. A. Carson points this out in *The Cross and Christian Ministry*:

> Fascinated by the rhetoric of learned scholars of their day, the Corinthians were sometimes more impressed by form and show than by content and truth. They loved 'words of human wisdom' – literally, 'wisdom of word,' the wit and eloquence that neatly packaged more than one school of thought in first-century Greece."[9]

"Thanks, Marcus!" Dan said very appreciatively. "Having said that, it is not an excuse for those who are called to serve in preaching to be lazy or boring or poor communicators." The table was interrupted when the attendants started clearing away the dishes. Mo's grandson refilled glasses, cups and mugs.

"You know what else?" Marcus interjected.

"What's that?" Dan asked.

"According to the book of Acts the disciples were considered unlearned, unsophisticated, earthy and raw, and yet based upon the results of their Spirit-filled preaching they were great preachers. The Jewish government was so upset by their success that they told them to shut up! Now that is great preaching." he said slapping his large, fleshy hand on his Bible.

"Well, I still don't know how we can determine good preaching. It all sounds too relative," complained Blake.

"To be good is to have a superior quality or excellence. We've already seen that there is some standard for evaluating good content. The question comes down to what constitutes a good presentation. In a sense, that is relative. Years ago a liberal Lutheran set about to study what constituted a good or great sermon according to listeners. He wanted to quantify objectively. Hans van der Geest was his name."[10]

"Sounds Dutch. Hey, you're Dutch aren't you Harold?" Blake asked his elderly friend across the table.

"I'm German. And don't you forget it!" he shot back waving his fork at the young teaser.

"Anyway, Hans said that good or great sermons had all three of the following elements," Pastor said while writing again on the white board. "The first is *geborgenheit*, not easily translated into English, which has to do with the sermon's appeal to the emotions. Like was it gripping or moving, did it give a sense of trust or assurance? Did people respond with a greater trust or peace? Does it touch the love relationship with God? The second thing is whether or not a sermon has *befreiung*."

"Bee frying?" joked Blake.

"Behave, kid!" snapped a smiling Harold.

"This second dimension has to do with a sense of liberation and freedom. Does the message touch my life, awaken wonder, or offer hope by underscoring the victory of God's kingdom in my life today? Did the preacher preach in a surprising way?"

Dan took a few gulps of orange juice. Seeing no questions or comments he continued, "The third dimension is what he called *erkennen*."

"Air cannon?" Blake joked again.

"Go home, kid!" Harold scolded.

"Did the sermon teach, and did the listener learn? Did it address faith, knowledge and growing in truth? What do I know now that I may not have known before?"

"So, mind, will and emotions?" Sherry asked for approval.

"Kind of like that. The point of his work was that after evaluating dozens of sermons by different pastors and many responses from various audiences, these three characteristics were consistently found in messages that people said were good or great," Dan concluded.

"What is a great preacher, then?" asked Marcus.

"The word great means remarkable, markedly superior. One pastor friend said that he believed great preaching was a message from God's Word that was consistent with the purpose God had for that portion of the Word and presented by a special unction of the Holy Spirit. A great preacher is someone who preaches consistently good sermons over a long period of time," Dan provided.

The group was getting restless having sat in the uncomfortable red vinyl, padded chairs for nearly two hours, and the pastor was aware of it, so he decided to bring the meeting to a close.

"I've got three more things to say and then we'll be dismissed. First, the New Testament does not say that the purpose of preaching is to preach well! Many students, preachers or church members have this as the goal. This confuses the means with the ends. Preaching is not the end, it is one means for a God-transformed life. Make sure you get my handout on how to grow through the preaching of God's Word (see Appendix L). The thing we all should ask, especially the pastor who preaches, is not 'Have I preached well?' but 'Have I served God in Christ and have I served the people by being faithful to the meaning and in the delivery of God's Word?'

"Second, God makes it clear that we are not to compare preachers with other preachers. It's wrong and sinful. Just look at Acts 18:24 and compare that with the context of First Corinthians one, starting with verse twelve. Another place to study is 2 Corinthians 10:12 where Paul said we do not compare ourselves with others. It is a study worth digging into. Pastors are wrong to compare and God's people are wrong to do it too.

"Finally, my last point is a preface to this handout (see Appendix M). It's about how to listen to the preached Word. Are you aware that the emphasis in Scripture is far more heavily placed upon the hearer of the Word of God than upon the preacher's method of preaching the Word of God? In fact, you will be hard pressed to find God coming down hard on the prophets, apostles, teachers, pastors for how they preached. God is concerned with what they preached – were they faithful to God's Word? The Bible makes it very clear that the burden of responsibility is more upon the listener of the Word of God than upon the one proclaiming it!"

This statement stunned more than a few of the students. "You'll be seeing this again one Sunday, along with a couple other handouts or inserts," he warned.

"I have one more thing to say as I give you one last handout," Dan called out.

"That's four things in closing then, Pastor," Blake yelled over the commotion.

"Yep, you're right. And I can see you know how to count," Dan ribbed back. "If you want a good preacher with great sermons, then you need to pray with me that I would be a good preacher with great sermons. Dr. Eby in his book has some suggestions for how God's people can pray for that, and I've added a few additional things to his list," he admonished as he passed around another sheet (see Appendix N).[11] "Not only should you pray for me as your servant-preacher, but there are things you can do to encourage me or any other pastor for that matter. Take this lesson home and review it well," Dan commanded, giving out the notes from Dr. Williams.

Dan had been keeping a running list of preaching resources that pastors, professors, authors, elders and church members claimed to be good or great preaching (see Appendix O). The list could have gone on for scores of pages, but it was clear that preaching, like many other things, is a conflicted issue. Reviewing the list one evening in his office Dan played the role of a church member, "Pastor Dan, if you circled all the answers I like then I will consider you to be a good preacher worth listening to. If you circled most of the answers I like then I will listen to you, but will expect you to change to what I want. If you circled half or less of the right answers I won't listen to you, at least not often. Of course, if that's the case I have only three options: do everything I can for you to get you to preach the right way, or do what I can to see that you leave my church, or I will leave and go where there is a good preacher!"

"Well, Mr. Picky," Dan talked back to himself, "Those don't have to be the only three options you know. You could pray for me, encourage me, endure with me as I endure with you, and you could learn to be a better listener." *Oh yeah, Dan. That would go over like a lead balloon,* he thought. *I need to say it anyway*!

A CHALLENGE TO THINK AND DO

What do you think?
1. What stood out, provoked you or taught you something from this chapter?
2. How would you have handled Bernie and Irma's surprise visit at Dan's house?
3. In your opinion, what makes a good message or sermon? What makes a bad message or sermon?
4. What does the Bible say preaching is? Does the Bible give any direction as to what the minister should preach?
5. What does the Bible say is a good message or sermon? Do you share the same standard of evaluating messages or sermons in church?
6. What do you think about Hans van der Geest's research about what makes a good message or sermon?
7. On a scale of 1 to 10, 1 being not critical and 10 being very critical, how critical are you of the preaching at your church? Why?
8. Is it right to compare your preacher with others? Why or why not? Do you make comparisons?
9. How can a church help a minister who is considered a poor preacher?
10. What do you make of Pastor Dan's comment that "The Bible makes it very clear that the burden of responsibility is more upon the listener of the Word of God than upon the one proclaiming it!"

Some things you could do:
1. Look over Appendix O, *Comparative Views of Preaching*. Circle or underline the items you believe are required for a good sermon or good preaching. Why are your views more important or valuable than other views?
2. Read through Appendix L. Commit to a plan to grow through Biblical preaching.
3. Read through Appendix M on *How to Be an Effective Hearer of God's Word*. Write down other ways that you can become a better listener to Biblical preaching and practice them.

13

YES, BUT CAN HE TEACH?

—∿∿—

Twenty-two-year-old Matthew recently returned from a short-term mission trip to the Czech Republic. The money he was able to set aside from odd jobs and from those who contributed to the scholarship fund was enough to keep him there for a month. He was very grateful for everyone's prayer and financial support, especially for the high school kids who put on several bake sales, car washes and a spaghetti dinner to raise support.

Matt's father was glad his son could go to Europe. He had done the same thing when he was in college, but it was a six-week backpacking, party event with his friend. However, as to the reason for his son's trip, Matt's father was not happy.

The college man came back thinner, with longer hair, and with an ability to imitate a Czech accent. He also came back all the more fired up for the things of Christ and all the more convinced that God was calling him to pastoral or missional ministry. At lunch time Friday afternoon, Dan picked him up from the college campus. The two of them missed their weekly meetings, and were excited to start back up again just as school was beginning its fall semester.

"Yo, scruffy!" Dan taunted his young disciple as Matthew slid into the passenger's seat.

"Hi P.D.!" the college kid cried back as he embraced the pastor with a big hug. Only some of the folks at church affectionately called Pastor Dan, P.D. The elders told him it was too disrespectful and he should not allow it. Dan said the Bible put no such prohibition on it, so he would allow it.

"Do - you – speakah – Englishah?" Dan asked in a loud voice mimicking people who think you have to speak loudly to foreigners.

"My – name – Matthew," the kid joked back. The two laughed at each other.

Pastor and disciple headed away from their normal fast food joint and for a change, went to Mo's. Dan discovered while Matt was away that on Fridays Mo had specials on her huge burgers. He knew Matt would enjoy the almost home-cooked meal. Matthew could hardly contain himself and unloaded the highlights of his adventure like a DVD on fast forward. Thankfully, Dan could hear at the speed of fast forward.

Though the parking lot was pretty crowded, they found a place to park around the side of the café, which was a good thing because Pastor was able to pull into one of the few shady spots under an old oak tree. Or is this an elm? he wondered. As they walked to the front doors, Dan hooked Matt around the neck with his right elbow, gave him a kiss on the head and ruffled his hair. "So great to have you back again! You're looking well."

"Good to be home and with you too," he replied giving a quick embrace around Dan's back with his left arm. "Can't wait to see everyone at church again, and tell them all about the trip."

Opening the door for his young protégé, the two stepped into a cooler, but noisier environment. Mo waved her metal spatula at them and called out with more of a Brooklyn than a Scottish accent, "How ahh yah?" Matthew answered something back in Czech, but only Dan and those near the door could hear the foreign-speak. They made their way to an empty booth, even though the table had not yet been bussed. "This kind of reminds me of Prague," the student declared.

"Oh? How's that?"

"It's old and quaint. But in Prague they don't have a 1950s American style café."

A young girl, assumed to be a relative of Mo's, bussed the table while Mo's grandson brought them water and menus.

"Do you live here, Sport?" Dan asked Mo's grandson.

"Practically. Gotta keep an eye on Grandma. Besides, somebody's gotta run the place."

Dan already knew what he wanted, but it took college boy a few seconds to eye the super sonic burger, a triple pattied, triple bun, monster of a meal with plenty of secret sauce, dill pickles, red onions, large slices of tomato, and layers of deep green lettuce, all held together by five toothpicks. Of course it came with a large serving of fries in its own red plastic basket and a choice of shake. Matt ordered a sweet chocolate malt. Dan had the same.

"Where did you stay?" Dan asked, as he scooted back against the window with his right arm resting up on the back of the booth.

Elbows on the table, leaning forward and playing with his straw, he answered, "Several places. First with a missionary and his family. Then at a dorm. Then with different families. It all depended on where we were and what we were doing."

"What were you doing?"

"I ended up doing a lot of teaching. Not sure why they put me in that role but they did."

"Did you like it? Who did you teach?"

"Oh man! It was so cool! The first week I taught kids. The church was having a vacation Bible school program. In the afternoons, Ted, the missionary, teamed me up with five teen boys. They were eager learners and from what I could understand were fairly new Christians."

"How could you teach them? Did they speak English?"

"Only a couple of them could. I ended up teaching them English using the Bible. They used their Bibles and tried to follow along with my English version. Somehow we understood each other but, man, it was tiring. We had interpreters, which was a totally strange experience."

Mo brought the huge platter with two twelve inch saucers that barely embraced the burgers. She had to pay her respects to Father Dan and meet the handsome laddy. Her grandson followed right behind her with the fries, malted shakes and water glasses. Everything smelled so delicious.

After Matt prayed for the food, he enthusiastically answered the interrogation until he had pretty much exhausted the highlights and favorite events in Europe. Dan encouraged him to put his pictures into a power point presentation to show folks at church. He gave Matthew three weeks to have it all ready. Matt would make his presentation after the monthly fellowship luncheon on a Sunday afternoon.

"So you were pretty jazzed about teaching?"

"Almost the best part about the whole trip!"

"Really?"

"Well, it was the teaching, and taking charge of different activities where I had to teach. Man, it was so exciting to disciple those five guys. They kept asking questions, trying to use English, but mostly about the Bible."

"What were their names?"

"Let's see, Adam, Konrad, Ivan, Jan and Lukas."

"Sounds English to me."

"You have to pronounce them in Czech, and that's not always easy to do."

"What's your name in Czech?"

"Matěj."

"Ohh-kaaay. That's unique."

The two of them attacked their beastly burgers like cavemen. "Can I ask you something?" Matt said with a huge lump of food stuffed in his right cheek and sauce running down his chin.

"That's why we meet, isn't it?"

"What's the difference between preaching and teaching? I mean, if I become a pastor I'll have to preach. But what if all I want to do is teach and disciple? And I met another missionary who is from an independent church who said that you preach the Gospel, not doctrine, but you teach doctrine and not the Gospel."

"True Christian ministry is Gospel ministry. The pastor will teach and preach the redemptive work of Jesus Christ. A good preacher will teach through his preaching. The Bible tells us preaching is the authoritative proclamation of an ordained herald proclaiming the will and decree of King Jesus. I've also heard the statement that you preach evangelistically to non-believers but you teach believers the Bible. It sounds great until you see in the Scriptures that the Gospel and the Bible are taught and preached to believers and unbelievers alike. So the difference would be of importance and method."

"Huh?" Matt said with his head bowed over the plate trying to hold onto a pickle with his teeth.

"Teaching is usually thought of as imparting knowledge and information to others so as to help them understand and comprehend. Wilkerson has a good book you should study, called *The 7 Laws of the Learner*. He says real teaching 'means to busy oneself eagerly with the student's learning'[1] (1992, p. 26). When you teach Scripture as a minister, the authority comes first from the fact that you are handling God's Word, and secondly from the fact that you are a gifted and ordained teacher. However, when you preach, you are standing in Christ's stead as his mouthpiece with his authority. You preach Christ proclaiming his message of salvation while teaching, reproving, rebuking, exhorting, encouraging and so forth. Teaching is an aspect of preaching, but preaching is rarely an aspect of teaching. Here's an example: in the book of Acts Aquila and Priscilla taught Apollos and others. The apostles preached and taught."

"If you are a pastor, do you have to preach?"

"In our circles we believe that is the case. Today there are huge churches that have teaching pastors, but also administrative pastors, counseling pastors, family pastors and so forth who never preach."

The two paused to watch an elderly couple arguing outside their window. "Remember our lesson on elders' duties that said elders are supposed to be able to teach?" Dan asked trying to steer away from the distraction.

"Oh yeah, right."

"According to 1 Timothy 3:2, a pastor is supposed to be able to teach. Timothy, the young pastor, was told by Paul in chapter four, verse eleven, to command and teach others. Then in the second letter to Timothy, two, verse fifteen he tells the young pastor to do his best to present himself to God as one who is approved as a worker, who can unashamedly and correctly divide the Word of truth."

Dan got up and moved around to sit next to Matt. "Move over Skinny," he taunted, shoving Matt toward the window with his hip. He pulled out his pocket PC and scrolled around to find his notes. The young man was licking his ketchup painted fingers. "Here, look at this, but keep your food off my brain," Dan warned.

Matt smiled with one eyebrow raised, as if to say, "Don't tempt me."

"Teaching has always been a vital and integral part of God's program for his people. Here, look with me," he said, showing Matt the notes on his screen. "Why must God's pastor or elder teach? For one, God commanded him to do so:"

- Exodus 4:12 – God will teach Moses' what to say to God's people.
- Leviticus 10:11 – Aaron was to teach the people of Israel the whole Law.

- Deuteronomy 6 – Fathers were to teach their children God's Law-Word.
- Deuteronomy 17 -God's king was to be faithful in teaching and applying God's Word.
- Proverbs and Ecclesiastes – Wise men of Israel were to teach in the open air, at the city gates, at main intersections, in the courts.
- Prophets – They were to teach only what God gave them to teach.
- Ezra 7:10 – The priest Ezra set his heart to study and apply God's Law-Word and then teach it to Israel.
- Nehemiah – The priests taught and explained God's Law-Word so that God's people would believe and do what God said.
- Gospels – Jesus taught and preached God's will.
- Matthew 28:19-20 – Jesus commanded his disciples to make disciples, teaching and baptizing them in the one name of the Father, Son and Holy Spirit.

Matt was chewing away at his fries and slurping his shake, but attentively taking in what his mentor was teaching him.

"Another reason why pastors and elders must be able to teach is that our faith presupposes that the Holy Spirit working through God's Word raises up and trains people to be like Christ. Elders also teach so that the doctrines of God's Word will be faithfully passed on from generation to generation. This is according to Second Timothy chapter two. Look here at two other verses," he said pointing to the screen:

> NKJV Col. 1:28 Him we preach, warning every man and teaching every man in all wisdom, that we may present every man perfect in Christ Jesus. 29 to this end I also labor, striving according to His working which works in me mightily.
>
> NKJV 1 Thess. 2:13 For this reason we also thank God without ceasing, because when you received the word of God which you heard from us, you welcomed it not as the word of men, but as it is in truth, the word of God, which also effectively works in you who believe.

"So everything that I was doing in Europe is what the Bible is talking about?" Matt asked before finishing off his shake.

"Not everything. You taught what?"

"The Bible, English, helped some kids with their schooling, helped the missionary and a few men teach carpentry skills."

"So the kind of teaching you did was more comprehensive, which is good because God desires us to be skilled in life. But the focus of Biblical teaching is that which comes from God's Word. This is why God says in Deuteronomy 4:2, Proverbs 30:6, and Revelation 22:19 that we are not to add or take anything away from his Word. Paul says in 1 Timothy

1:3 that we teach no other doctrine, and warns us in 2 Thessalonians 3:6 to stay away from those who are out of accord with the true tradition of doctrine received from Christ. That means we teach what is consistent with all of God's Word and the Gospel of Jesus Christ."

Matt ordered another milk shake, this time French vanilla. Dan wanted coffee, sugar, no cream. The young lady cleared away the dishes after Dan placed his half-eaten burger in a Styrofoam box.

"What's the objective for pastors and church teachers with their teaching?" Dan challenged his young friend.

"To know more about Jesus?"

"Is that all? Would it serve you much to know about George Washington or to know about our president today?"

"Yes, but that's not what you're looking for is it? What are you saying?"

"Is there a difference in knowing about Jesus and knowing Jesus?"

"Oh…yeah. Oh, I get it! We teach so that people would know Jesus!"

"Exactly! Some think, like I used to, that teaching is to fill our minds with good doctrine. But that's not enough. The objective of all that knowledge is to intimately know the Lord Jesus Christ and then to become like him. Remember what the verse in Colossians said?"

"Yeah, to present everyone mature in Christ."

"You got it! Now, read what I have here in Ephesians 4:11-16. Then let's list the goals for these gifted men God gives to his church."

Matt read silently and then started listing as Dan instructed him to do while Dan jotted the list down on a napkin:

- *To equip the saints for the works of service*
- *To build up the body of Christ*
- *To attain to the unity of the Faith and of the knowledge of Jesus*
- *For the church to become a mature man of Christ*
- *So that we would not be children, tossed around by every wind of teaching, and so forth.*
- *To speak the truth in love, to grow up in every way like Jesus Christ.*

When Matt finished the list, Dan emphasized, "That's the ultimate goal of biblical teaching! That's why we teach, and preach too. Out of that should flow something else. Second Timothy 3:17 says that God's Word is profitable for all sorts of things so that we would become complete, thoroughly equipped in order to do the good works of God!"

"In Prague, there was another guy from a different group. That group met with us for fun events. We got to talking one night and I was telling him about how much I liked to teach. He's my age, but had lots of goofy ideas. He said that teaching happens in church either behind the pulpit or at some official podium. He was so sure of himself. But that's not true, is it?"

Dan laughed. "Where's my pulpit? What have I been doing this past hour?"

"Teaching."

"Who knows where people come up with these things? If that statement were true then Jesus never taught. Either that or God forgot to tell us about it in the Gospels. Look, the methods vary. First, pastors preach publicly and teach privately. Elders can also teach publicly but some scholars say that the Bible makes no requirement for them to teach publicly. Elders who co-rule the church with the pastor-elder must be knowledgeable in the Word enough to teach others God's doctrines."

"So teaching can happen anywhere, right?"

"Sure! Think about Jesus' own ministry. Almost anything gave him an opportunity to teach: events, disputes, from comments, in formal settings, during worship, when he was challenged… many different ways. Think about Jesus' methods and then Peter's and Paul's. How many can you come up with?"

"Through dialog," Matt responded rapidly. "At meals. With their testimonies."

"We're so used to the lecture method for teaching. What other ways of teaching were used Biblical times?"

"Stories."

"Good. What else?"

"Oh …parables and riddles."

"More?"

"Not sure."

"The prophets used drama. God teaches through history. Paul taught through his personal story and application when he wrote his second letter to Corinth. There was the Socratic method, using questions and answers."

Another waitress cleared the table and then gave Dan the bill. He pulled out a few bills and gave them to her. They finished their drinks while she rang up the bill and brought the change back. Dan thanked her, and the men slowly crawled out of their seats. The pastor turned around to drop a generous tip on the table along with the church's business card.

Since Matt needed to get back for afternoon classes, Dan dropped him off at the college. They bid each other farewell and made promises to see each other on Sunday. Dan drove off with a satisfaction that only one who loves to disciple and teach can understand. He enjoyed teaching, but as with some of the others he discipled he loved Matt like a son.

I wish I could do this more often with more people, Lord! Dan prayed. Teaching, discipling or mentoring was one of the very reasons he believed he was called to the pastoral ministry. Not only is it an important role a pastor is called to do, but it was the role he enjoyed most. It was enriching, challenging, rewarding, and delightful.

The pastor got home a little before Jake did. It was Jake's first week back to school. When Sarah and Ben's daddy walked into the back door, Ben jumped off the kitchen chair and ran over to greet him – popsicle and all. "Hey there, little man! Let's put this down in your dish and wash your hands before sliming my new slacks with orange stuff," he declared with a funny grimace. Ben laughed.

After wiping off the slime and sticky, Dan gave him a big hug and then sat him on his lap. "Whatcha been do-in'?"

"Nothin'!"

"What? You've just been sitting there alllll day doin' nothin'? How do you do that?"

"Daddy, you're silly! I'm eating!" he expressed with a squeal.

Just then Mona entered with toddler Hanna in her arms. She had just woken from her nap. She had a sippy cup plugged into her mouth and her blankie tucked under her right arm. Hannah smiled and deliberately blinked hard at her Dad. Dan winked back. "Hi precious girl! How's my doll?"

Mona was more than happy to hand her off to Dan. Dan then told his wife about the visit with Matthew and gave a brief report of his time in Europe.

Shortly before Jake walked in the front door, Dan checked his emails. One was from Elder Joe who was reminding Dan of the elders' decision to forbid Dan from further involvement with a new ministry in town. The main reason they dictated this decree was that the parachurch ministry was not under any church. In fact, to be acceptable to the elders, the ministry should be under a church of their denomination or perhaps a sister denomination. Their second reason for forbidding involvement in the ministry was Dan's moral life was still suspect. The fact that his son was in public school, that he still spent time away without his wife and family, and because he disrespected Elder Dumpleton, was enough to call his character into question. Dan also suspected they had little or no confidence in his teaching ability. They never said so, but they never commended him. They did give commendations and accolades to other men who would teach from time to time, but never Dan. These things were enough to prohibit Dan from being a guest teacher with the new ministry. He complied only because he did not want to engage in yet another confrontation with the elders, even though he believed they had no grounds for restricting him like that. Besides, if Dan was that unqualified or inept then he should not be teaching anything anywhere, including at Grace.

A Saturday picnic celebrated the end-of-the-summer and back-to-school. Some kids thought it should have been a funeral event instead. The social committee reserved a spot that had plenty of trees, two barbeque grills and three tables. The escapade was scheduled from 11:00 A.M to 2:00 P.M. Everyone was to bring their own meat and a salad or dessert to share. Drinks were supplied by the church's social fund.

The social committee arrived mid-morning to set things up, and Pastor and his family showed up thirty minutes early to check on things. By 11:30 most of the people had arrived. Dan billed the event as an occasion to bring visitors, but noticed that only Melissa, a few college youth, and some teenagers did. None of Dan's neighbors showed up. Who did not show was telling, but expected. The Dumpletons, two elders and their families, two deacons and their families, and all of the antagonists except for Katrina and her children were absent. Frankly, Dan was relieved, but felt guilty for his lack of genuine love for those misfits.

What was obvious to Dan was that the fabric of the church had changed since he and his family had arrived. There were many new people and members; all of them actively involved. This upset many of the older group, which was funny in a way. When Dan was candidating they complained that the church was getting smaller. Of course it was. So many of the elderly had died or were in nursing homes, and the attrition rate was helped by member families moving away. When new families started joining, the long-term members complained that the new people did not contribute to anything. "Like what?" Dan asked three ladies.

"We're tired of always being the ones who work in the kitchen. These new people need to step in and help out."

"Okay, I'll take care of that," Dan promised, and he did.

But then the grumblers complained that the new people were coming in and taking over everything. "Like how?" the Pastor asked. One of the women protested to Dan that someone had cleaned and organized the kitchen. "Why is that a problem? Since I've been here, you all have been complaining about how disorganized and dirty it was." He found out that a teenage daughter of a new family overheard the women talking about the state of the kitchen, so she thought it would be a kind expression and surprise if she came in one Saturday to clean and organize everything, complete with new labels. No major changes were done. The kitchen looked and smelled great. But when Katrina arrived early Sunday morning to make coffee, she went ballistic. It was a surprise all right; one she hated. So did some others. It was a no-win situation.

Most of the committees were filled with the newcomers. That, of course, changed the way things were done, even though no one touched those sacred cow events. Change was happening, and a significant portion of the old guard hated it. "Change happens no matter what," Dan explained after a morning Bible study with the elderly. "I mean, just look at your own lives. Tell me you haven't changed? God expects us to change. It's the nature of life." It was to no avail. Dan soon learned that the more insecure a person is, the more he or she hates change. Grace is a church where most of the old guard are very insecure, Dan often told himself.

It was great to see Dan's favorite deacon and family at the picnic, along with the three elder nominees. Practically all of the new members were present, along with Melissa who brought her mother and a friend, Matt with six friends and a host of teens. Even Elder Joe and his wife, and another elder and his wife attended. They huddled together with some of the older members.

Dozens and dozens of multi-colored helium balloons and streamers danced in the breeze. Everyone was asked to wear a brightly colored shirt or blouse. Traditional games ensued while the serious chefs were delicately tending the meat. Children who were not playing the organized games played their own with their own rules, which required mothers to frequently referee. Dan circulated from game to game, cluster to cluster, greeting and visiting everyone. He always made a special attempt to meet and get to know guests.

After a vigorous volleyball game between the college group and the marrieds, Marty sounded a horn to summon everyone around the buffet. Though Dan was the official prayer man he delegated the task to Marcus. Marcus had no problem praying God's blessing upon the picnic and food. Then it was a mad dash to the tables.

Dan always waited to be the last one, which gave him time to continue visiting others. Someone tapped him on the shoulder and when he turned around, he was surprised to see the mayor, his wife, and an aide smiling at him. "Mayor Reed, good to see you. Won't you join us?" Dan requested.

"Who can turn down barbequed chicken and all this lovely food?" he blared. The man was as large around as he was tall, and he was tall. His petite and very feminine wife could get lost in the man's shadow. After dishing up a plate-load to sample all the recipes, the mayor and his entourage were ushered over to the Lees' blanket. The mayor was invited to sit in one of the folding chairs, but he wisely chose to plant himself on the corner of the blanket and lean against the tree. His wife curled her legs under her and sat next to Mona. The mayor's associate found familiar acquaintances with whom he could eat.

Dan and the mayor talked city politics; the man wasn't altogether interested in the church and he made that obvious. He was buttering up a constituency, and he made that even more obvious. His wife, however, expressed sincere concern for Mona, the children and the church. As the mayor was telling one of his stories, he loved to tell stories, Dan noticed Irma, Bernie, and his wife slowly cruising by. Dan watched to see if they were going to pull into the parking lot. They didn't. The mayor saw Dan's eyes following the blue Lexus and took notice of who was driving. "That's my distant cousin, you know," he announced.

"No, I didn't know that."

"They're members at your church, aren't they?" the mayor asked rather rhetorically. He already knew the place they had carved out for themselves at Grace. "Humph," he mumbled, spitting a little piece of chicken from his lips. Dan wasn't sure how to interpret the mayor's remarks, but he suspected there was bad blood.

"She stole my property right out from under me, you know? She's a beast of a woman," he blurted.

"Now Sherman! Behave yourself," his wife scolded with a soft soprano voice in a slight Texan accent.

Turned out the mayor had wanted to purchase the property where Grace was now located to erect his new business. She was crafty enough to hire high powered realtors and lawyers and snatch up the deal before the mayor could make a serious offer. It was legal enough, but the rift between the two, which started between the two families while they were in junior high school, only broadened like a massive canyon. "Your church has a bad reputation because of her and Bernie, ya know."

Dan was surprised since everything he had been told affirmed that the Dumpletons were a well-respected, very influential family in town. The mayor then leaned over toward Dan and waved his finger, beckoning the pastor to draw close. "I need to warn you that Bernie is going from business to business telling all the old-timers that you stole his church, and that you and your wife are on the verge of a divorce."

Dan said nothing as he leaned back to his comfortable position. Then he calmly stated, "Is that so? Can you prove that?"

"As sure as I got cream on my pie," he declared.

Dan did not want to be privy to gossip, even if it was about a slanderous gossiper; so he changed the subject by talking about the next election. After forty minutes with the Lees, the mayor excused himself and made sure he greeted everyone. The babies got kisses and the adults got business cards with promises to help anyone who had a need.

In spite of a sultry day and an altogether negative visit from a surprise guest, Dan and Mona declared the event quite the success. As far as they could tell, everyone had fun, with the exception of Katrina who was still stinging from Dan's gentle but firm rebuke. She found Jake climbing in a tree. It was a tree God designed for little boys and girls to climb. But Katrina believed children should stay out of trees, especially boys. So she yelled at Jake, more like screamed at him, which sent him running to his dad. With Jake's hand in his, Dan walked over to Katrina and asked what the problem was. Defensive, she raised her voice at Dan and began lecturing him about the hazards of playing in trees and Dan's irresponsibility for not keeping Jake in line.

"Katrina, stop yelling. Did Jake violate any city ordinance?"

"No!"

"Did he do anything immoral or indecent?"

"No!"

"Did he break any of God's commandments?"

"No!"

"Then you have no grounds to correct our child and you have no business being cruel. Next time there is a problem you come to me first. Do you understand me?"

"Preachers' kids are all alike; spoiled brats who always get into trouble. And boys are the worst!" she declared loud enough to attract an audience.

"Have I made myself clear to you?"

"Yes, quite so!" she said as she turned abruptly and grabbed her daughter's hand. She stormed off sobbing.

Through the drama of life mixed with the wisdom of his Word, God was teaching Dan many lessons, particularly about relationships.

After the picnic, Matt and his college crew stayed behind to help clean up. The adults were impressed by their willingness to serve. As Dan was about to pick up his family blanket, several of them came over and sat down on it. No subtle hint. The group wanted to talk. So Dan unfolded his chair and made himself about as comfortable as one can get in those things.

"We want to begin a discipleship club or something," Matt announced. Music to a pastor's ears.

"Okay. What do you have in mind?"

"Could you disciple us regularly?" Matt asked as their spokesman.

"We want you to teach us like you're teaching Matt," explained a girl.

"The purpose of my teaching would be to strengthen your faith in Christ. Do you have faith in Christ?" Dan asked.

They all said they did. "What I do with Matt is not merely teach like you might get from your professors, but I teach in a way that trains you for life. Jesus said in Luke 6 that everyone who is fully trained will be like his master. Is that what you want?"

They all concurred again.

"Fantastic! Do you know what a disciple of Jesus is?"

No one could define it. "Here it comes," Matt warned as he looked around at his friends.

"Okay, so the first lesson is on discipleship. A disciple of Jesus is a good student who follows his teaching and lifestyle. Discipling will involve private one-on-one sessions, public times like this, Sunday school, Bible studies, but most importantly at worship time. Are you willing to commit at least to worship?" They all agreed.

"A disciple-student is also one who is committed to following and doing what the discipler-teacher or mentor says. As long as it is not illegal, immoral or sinful are you willing to commit to that?" They again all agreed.

"To be a disciple means that you will be placed into situations like an apprentice. Some things you will like and others you won't. Ever see the old movie <u>Karate Kid</u>?" Most of them had. "The kid was a disciple in the fullest sense of the term." Matthew chapters 9, 10, 15 and 23 provide good examples of what I mean. Go back and read them. That's your first homework assignment."

"A true disciple is a believer in Jesus Christ who takes orders and obeys Jesus as Lord, who abides in God's Word, who submits to God's official, delegated leadership in the church and does the Father's will. A false disciple is someone who will ultimately will reject Jesus Christ or desert Him.[2] How does the Bible identify true disciples? What sets them apart? What would set you apart as a disciple of Jesus? Anyone know?"

No one offered an answer, so Dan said, "By your love for Jesus Christ and for one another. Read John chapter twenty-one. And then also by how much fruit you bear.[3] One last thing, disciples are called upon to disciple others. You ready to do that?"

"Not now," said one young man.

"Fair enough, but when the time is right?"

"Sure."

"Good! Matt, guess you are the first to take on the role as teacher-discipler. We'll get together so you can learn how." Matt enthusiastically agreed.

"Can I ask you one thing?" said a sophomore rather timidly.

"You can ask many things," Dan declared.

"Are we allowed to ask hard questions? I mean, not just about the Bible and stuff, but about other things."

"Such as something from your physics class?" Dan joked.

"Well, noooo. Like about relationships or sex or about parents and stuff."

"Of course. One way or another God's Word addresses issues of life as well as of godliness. No teacher in Christ should fear or shy away from the hard questions. We should have a love of the tough questions. When should we begin?"

Matt took the challenge and promised to arrange a mutually acceptable time between the students and Dan. Pastor Dan could not be more excited. God was expanding his ministry and his role as servant-shepherd-teacher. These wonderful blessings were beginning to override the negatives and the challenges he had been facing since he arrived; well actually, since he entered into ministry.

A CHALLENGE TO THINK AND DO

What do you think?
1. Is there anything in particular that taught you something new in this chapter?
2. What does it mean to be a disciple of Jesus Christ?
3. Are you a disciple of Jesus? If so, are you a good disciple? How do you know?
4. Define teaching.
5. What is the goal of Christian discipleship and Bible teaching?
6. Who do you consider to be a good teacher? A good disciple-maker? Why?
7. What do you think of the elders' decision to forbid Pastor Dan from being involved in the new parachurch ministry in town?
8. What would you do with the information the town's mayor gave Dan about Irma and Bernie?
9. Was Katrina justified in scolding Dan's son? Was the rebuke Dan gave Katrina right?

Some things you could do:
1. Read the Gospels for the purpose of learning what Jesus said about disciples, what he taught them, and how they interacted with and treated him.
2. Read Wilkerson's *The 7 Laws of the Learner.*

14

GIVE US AN EXAMPLE

—◠◡◠—

It was now mid-September. Alternating bouts of heat and cool fought for environmental domination, not unlike the spiritual condition at Grace Church. Pastor Dan had prearranged a meeting with Matt to continue teaching and guiding him in the skill of making disciples. Four of his college peers and one young lady were interested in discipleship. Since Matt and another woman were apparently developing a serious relationship, he was uneasy about working with Karen one-on-one. Therefore, Mona kindly volunteered to meet with the college girl on a weekly basis. Both women were excited about the newfound relationship.

Matt directed his pastor to a park with many different walking trails meandering over hill and down through dale, through thick brush or tall forests or segregated meadows. Dan parked the car in an almost empty gravel lot under a tall pine. Even though the air was warm and muggy, the two wisely wore long jeans. Matt was fearful of tics with Lyme disease. He knew a girl who had contracted a debilitating case of it which took her out of school for a couple of years. Dan, however, was more concerned with mosquitoes and West Nile Virus. Neither was concerned enough, though, to keep them from a good hike.

"Have you heard from Bill lately?" Matt asked his mentor.

"Not since the week before his wedding. Have you?"

"I got an email about the same time. He's working for his dad but is thinking about becoming a teacher. His heart is not in the business."

"Miss him?"

"Yeah…I do. He was a good disciple maker, you know."

"Yes, a very fine and gifted man, that Bill. I miss him too."

"I want to be like Bill with these dudes and Karen. I wish I could be like you too with all your knowledge and stuff," Matt moaned.

"You be your own person. You're growing, and if you keep growing the way you have been, you will be a great disciple-maker and teacher," the pastor reassured.

"At one of our campus Christian club meetings, the leader said that discipleship is nothing more than teaching. Is that true?"

"Recall what I've been teaching you? What do you think?" Dan challenged.

"Discipleship involves teaching, but more than that. Right?"

"True. What more would it involve?"

"Being involved in the disciple's life."

"Right. How so?"

"I'd get together with him…or her. I'd pray with him…or her. Stuff like that."

"Okay. Not bad. I'd say that someone who disciples another, and I'm talking about discipleship in Jesus Christ, is a teacher…and a model. In other words, he is a mentor."

"Oh…Yeah, I can see that. Did you ever have a mentor?"

"Had a couple. Still have one strong friend who is also my mentor, teacher and counselor. His name is Kent and he lives in Canada."

"He's a friend? I mean, not that you wouldn't have friends, but I've heard from several in our church that the pastor should never have a friend, at least not in the same church," Matt wondered.

"There are professors at seminaries who teach that and consequently many pastors and church people who believe that. But that's bogus. Does the Bible restrict pastors from having friendships?"

"I don't think so."

"No – it doesn't! Does the Bible restrict pastors from having friends in the same church?"

"Probably not," Matt answered correctly.

"Matt, you will learn that people come up with all sorts of ideas that sound good. Many of them come from good intentions or attempt to resolve problems. But the bottom line is if the Bible does not order it or forbid it, then it is a matter of conscience. We are free to do anything so long as it is not sinful or immoral and of course we should restrict our freedoms when they may cause another believer to stumble."

"Do you have friends in our church?"

"What do you think?" Dan volleyed back.

"I'm not sure."

"Oh? Well, then let's just keep it that way," Dan declared with a broad smile.

"So who is this Kent dude?"

Pastor explained that Kent had become a friend and mentor to Daniel during his seminary days. Though they live quite a distance apart, the benefits of technology kept their relationship connected. Contrary to what some parishioners believe, pastors need friends. In fact, they really need a mentoring relationship, at least before and at the start of their officially sanctioned pastoral ministry. Church lay people, that is, those who are not in so-called "professional ministry" or remunerated pastoral ministry, often tend to make certain assumptions about pastors. Dan had. It was different now that he was on the other side of the ministerial line.

"Let me tell you the story of my preparation for pastor-teacher," Dan remarked. "Before I pursued the call to ministry I was a dedicated lay leader. I not only made certain assumptions about pastors but even articulated those views. Views like: pastors are supposed to be leaders, pastors should be mentors, pastors do not need friends, and pastors receive all of their necessary training in Bible school or seminaries."

He went on to tell him that he had read many books and attended seminars on leadership. A common proposition from those books and seminars is that "it is lonely at the top." While that may be true, the implication is "it is lonely at the top because leaders do not have the luxury of friendships," and that is because "true leaders are supposed to be independent and unfettered by complicated or precarious relationships." Sometimes fiercely so. Tom Marshall comments:

> Leaders are therefore generally advised not to have personal friends among their congregations, because such friendships cause problems. The result is great loneliness among Christian leaders that is often a major contributory factor inleadership failure and burnout. I fear some have almost lost the capacity for friendship altogether so that they cannot be friends even with other leaders. And if leaders do not know how to be friends, how can they model that relationship before their people? How can you produce a friendly church with leaders who have no friends anywhere in sight?[1]

"My friend Kent, though quite intelligent and who always seemed wise beyond his years, is old enough to have a seasoned wisdom. I wish I were as wise, but of course without the accessories that naturally accompany age."

Matt appreciated Dan's ability to empathize.

"Because of what I had read and been told it was in my second year of ministry that I developed a false guilt about viewing Kent as a friend and mentor."

"Really? No way."

"Oh, yeah. But, once again the senior man offered wise counsel. He said, 'Dan, you are getting worked up over things you shouldn't be.'"

"How so?" I asked.

Kent said, "Consider these things: First, you are assuming that natural leadership and pastoral or spiritual leadership are synonymous. While they overlap, they aren't exactly the same. Secondly, you have adopted some of the older theories of management and leadership that are now questioned or no longer in vogue in our contemporary society. But most importantly you always need to get back to the normative standard we as Evangelicals hold to and measure your concerns against that. Do I have to repeat my favorite mantra?"

"What's his favorite mantra?" Matt questioned.

"His mantra is 'What does God's Word say about it? Base your principles and judgments upon the standard of God's Word. I know that while not everything about life is explicitly dealt with in the Bible, God's Word is 'given by inspiration of God to be the rule of faith and life.'"

Matt did not resist the temptation to run over to a tree with a branch that scooped six feet off the ground. He leaped up, grabbed the branch, swung back and forth until he flipped his feet up and over. By the time Dan arrived, Matt was sitting on it.

"You sure it'll hold you?" Dan cautioned.

"Don't know." With that, several cracks sounded from the trunk. Matt quickly jumped down. The two laughed.

"One guy at our college club said the Bible has something to say about everything."

"That's too simplistic. Our Confession explains, 'The whole counsel of God, concerning all things necessary for His own glory, man's salvation, faith and life, is either expressly set down in Scripture, or by good and necessary consequence may be deduced from Scripture.'"[2]

"Hmm. So Kent just told you that having a mentor or friend was not a problem?" Matt deduced.

"As usual, Kent assigned homework and told me to research the difference between natural and spiritual leadership, and then do a study on discipleship. The Bible doesn't talk about mentoring per se. Rather it speaks about disciples and teachers. It also speaks much to the issue of friendship. He gave me a month."

Dan told Matt that he knew the exercise would be profitable, but he was worried he wouldn't have the time. Yet he reminded himself that leaders make the time for important things. He also told Matt that early on he recognized that true mentoring was not merely a teacher-student relationship. It involves that, but more. Good training and learning happens within relational contexts. After all, that was the ancient model for parents according to the Bible (Deut. 6) and especially true for Jesus during his earthly ministry.

"Just like what's going on now?" Matt observed.

"Exactly so."

"So, what did you find out?" Matt inquired.

"Just like clockwork, one month later Kent called me. I had learned that the Bible does not have any such command against leaders or pastors having friends. In fact, it does not even remotely imply such a thing. David had Jonathan, and even Jesus had a fairly close friendship with his disciples James, Peter and John."

"What about mentoring relationships?" Matt asked, throwing pine cones down the hill.

"The same is true there. Jesus is the premier model for mentoring relationships. Like Kent once said, the Bible uses the term 'disciple' for spiritual or faith mentoring. But conceptually the two are very similar. The more notable discipling-type of relationships were Elijah with Elisha, Jesus and his disciples, and Paul to Timothy."

"Did you feel guilty about having a friend or mentor after that?"

"I learned that I'm not wrong or sinning for having friends as a pastor or even having a mentor-friend. That means I am not guilty, so I should not feel ashamed."

The two sat upon a newly fallen log. Dan reflected upon the years that had passed since this lesson gave him the freedom to have Kent as his friend and mentor. Good thing too, since he found Kent's wisdom a God-send on many occasions, particularly as a fledgling pastor. Dan had gleaned so much while at seminary. It certainly taught him how to think more clearly, solidified his theological knowledge, gave him some foundational things he needed in his pastoral tool box, and grounded him in his convictions as a theologically conservative Presbyterian. His year-long internship at a local church gave him more realistic experience in the many facets of pastoral ministry than the more clinical environment of school. He was thankful for the internship because seminary lacks the experiential opportunities for pastoring a church and in handling innumerable relational challenges. His internship was well-rounded, giving him opportunities to teach and preach in various contexts such as children's Sunday school class, at an inner city mission, and during worship. He was also able to visit the sick in hospitals; sit in on home visits with a deacon, elder, or pastor; attend deacons and elders meetings; and lead a few of the church related programs.

Out of the stillness Matt said, "And all the while I had been thinking that once a person graduates from seminary he's good to go."

Dan laughed. "I used to think that too. Still, unless one is uncharacteristically gifted and wise, most pastors need tutored experience and the ability to apply biblically informed skills to the issues of life, issues that are common to mankind, but also specific to church leadership. After seminary, I learned almost immediately that I lacked the wisdom to take on the various personalities and situations there are in church." He was thinking about the Dumpletons, Katrina and Al, the perpetually fearful Ms. Ruffles, the brilliant but arrogant and bossy Mr. Neuhmann. Those kinds of personalities absorbed more of Dan's attention and time than the ones who seemed to benefit and grow from his service. Kent was mentoring Dan through those relationships.

Both got up and headed back to the car.

"Think about it, Matt. Timothy needed a mentor, and thank God he did. We now benefit from God's inspired counsel through Paul in the two New Testament letters named after Paul's son in the Faith. Perhaps 1 Timothy should have been titled, 'Some essential and very important things a pastor needs to know and do'?

The restive young college man challenged his pastor, "Wanna race?"

Before Dan gave an answer he bolted down the path. His challenger was soon ahead of him. Matt slowed and waited for 'the old man' to catch up. The two now jogged together.

"Seminary worth it?" puffed the student.

"Definitely. But, like former pastor, and now leadership guru, John Maxwell, has stated on many occasions, seminary does not train pastors adequately in skills such as relationships, leadership, or effective communication. The debate as to the need, purpose, focus and value of Bible school or seminary training for pastors may likely go on until Jesus returns. The thing I am convinced about more than ever is the need, purpose, focus and value of solid, godly friendships and wise mentoring relationships. I'm persuaded all the more after reading books like Bill Hull's *The Disciple-Making Pastor* and Bob Biehl's *Mentoring*."

Dan stopped jogging. It dawned upon him that he had been praying for opportunities to develop mentoring relationships with budding elders and pastors, and how God answered those prayers in the arrival of the church's intern, and now in his young friend Matt.

"You are getting a great start at a young age, Mr. Matthew!" Dan declared. "I suspect the Lord has some great things in store for you someday? If you would like to read any of those books I mentioned let me know. I've got them in my library."

"Cool. Maybe during winter break I can read one?" Matt replied while stretching his legs. "What's discipleship, then? I mean what do I do as a disciple-maker or mentor or whatever?"

"Think about Jesus and how he worked with his disciples. For all intents and purposes he lived with them. As he did he taught, corrected, rebuked, admonished, nurtured, encouraged, loved and modeled a kingdom kind of life for them. Think about Paul too; how he worked with Timothy. Here, let's sit down over there," Pastor pointed to a bench in the parking lot.

Dan reached into his back pocket and pulled out his Pocket PC. He tapped a few places and opened up his New King James Bible software. He went to 2 Timothy 3:10-11. Dan pointed to the two verses and asked Matt to read them.

"But you have carefully followed my doctrine, manner of life, purpose, faith, long-suffering, love, perseverance, persecutions, afflictions, which happened to me at Antioch, at Iconium, at Lystra — what persecutions I endured. And out of them all the Lord delivered me."

"What did Paul's disciple do?" Matt's mentor asked.

"Timothy followed his teacher's manner of life, purpose, faith, patience, love... basically everything Paul went through."

"Exactly so. Now, back to Jesus. As far as we know, was there a specific manner or one style he used?"

"Uhm, I don't think so."

"No. You're right. In fact he was different than the teachers or rabbis of his day. He did not follow their method. What he did do was gather disciples, then began teaching them, and working with them through intimate and personal relationships. He taught them in practically every context you could think of. Remember what we talked about at the picnic?"

"You mean about teaching disciples?"

"Yep. Teaching is key. Modeling is second. What do you think pastors, and elders too, should model? And what is it you should model for your disciples?"

"When I think of modeling, in the biblical sense that is, I think of a person's lifestyle."

"Yes! The pastor is to model character. But his character should be an example of whose character?"

"Jesus, of course," Matt said with a pronounced confidence.

"Here, I just scrolled to Philippians 3:17. Read it for us."

"Brethren, join in following my example, and note those who so walk, as you have us for a pattern."

"Follow my example. The context is all about Paul desiring the fullness of Jesus Christ, seeking Christ as the goal of his life, living and expending himself for the cause of Christ. Then he says, follow my example. That's how pastors and elders and church leaders are supposed to be."

"You mean my friends are supposed to follow my example? To be like me?"

"Let me try to be a bit clearer. Paul qualified himself. He wasn't calling Timothy and others to follow and become like Paul, but rather to follow and become like Paul in Christ, who Paul was in relationship to his life and service to Jesus Christ. Proud and arrogant individuals will believe their lives are worthy enough for people to become just like them. Stephen Brown, I'll never forget this one, said 'The great commandment for the legalist is, 'Thou shalt be like me.'[3] Meaning, there are legalists, whether they are in office or leadership positions or not, who want people to be just like them, or think like them, or perform like them. Not so a true model of Christ. Following?"

"Pun intended?" Matt laughed.

"No. Sorry. I'm not saying that you become like Jesus and become a carpenter or wear sandals, or like Paul and become a tentmaker and travel the world. Contrary to what some think, spiritual modeling is not in things like the occupation you have, the clothes you wear, the food you eat, the place you live."

"Yeah, I get that."

"Okay, so when Jesus told his disciples to follow him, he later said that when they watched him or saw him they were really seeing someone else. Who was it?"

"Father God?"

"Absolutely! We see the Father when we see Christ. But we are supposed to follow in Christ's steps in his teaching, in his moral conduct, and in his suffering, according to 1 Peter 2. Here, I'll read another passage. This time from 2 Thessalonians 3:7-9:

For you yourselves know how you ought to follow us, for we were not disorderly among you; nor did we eat anyone's bread free of charge, but worked with labor and toil night and day, that we might not be a burden to any of you, not because we do not have authority, but to make ourselves an example of how you should follow us."

Matt was thinking hard while mixing the dirt, leaves and pine needles with a dead branch. Dan, seeing his friend was still attentive, continued. "So far we have disciples following their disciplers as they mentor and model in what?"

"Life in Christ."

"Good. Another?"

"Character."

"Yes, God's pastors, elders and disciple makers must have the character of Christ. Not perfectly, nor completely, not sinlessly, but that their character appropriately and sufficiently reflects Jesus Christ. In other words, there should be nothing about the model that is subject to impeachment. He has godly integrity. Remember, the qualities? Temperate, gentle, not violent, not contentious or argumentative, not a striker, but peaceable and self-controlled."

Dan scrolled on to another passage, Titus 2:7: "'in all things showing yourself to be a pattern of good works, in doctrine showing integrity, reverence, incorruptibility.' To be a pattern is to be a model worth mimicking. Leaders, most especially pastors and elders, are to be models of Christ's teaching that reveals integrity, a worshipful life, good works, and the like." Then he found 1 Timothy 4:12 and said, "Here's a verse that speaks to you, Matt."

"Huh? What? What d'ya mean?"

"Let no one despise your youth but be an example to the believers in word, in conduct, in love, in spirit, in faith, in purity."

"Wow! Hey, I'm going to memorize that and make it my life verse for this school year! Was Timothy young like me?"

"He was probably in his late twenties or thirties. That's still young, relatively speaking. The point, though, is that a disciple maker, a model of Christ is to be a model in word, in conduct, in love, in spirit, in faith and in purity. I have to be able to do that as a pastor. The elders must do that too."

"Really? The elders too? Oh, yeah, I guess they would." Matt said with furrowed brows and serious eyes.

"We need more who will model Jesus. Looking at my notes, here is what one author said, 'What we need are yielded followers who are conduits of the Spirit's power to bring people into the presence and kingdom of God. We need leaders who model how to submit to God and receive God's strength and cleansing for service in the world.'"[4]

The cell phone rang in Dan's pocket. He pulled it out and flipped it open. "Hello, this is Dan." Matt stood up and started walking toward the path. Dan followed, talking on the phone.

"That was Mona. She needs me to pick up a few things at the store on the way home. We're having Marcus and his family over tonight. Wanna join us?"

"Uh, naw, I can't. I've got too much homework. Thanks anyway. Ya'll sure do have lots of people over."

"We love hospitality. God calls us to be lovers of strangers, which is what hospitality literally means in New Testament Greek. But we are also supposed to love our neighbors as ourselves. It's a great way to fellowship and to get to know people."

"Well, you and your wife are great at it."

"Thanks!"

They found their way back to the car and drove over to Matt's home. As Matt was getting out of the car Dan encouraged him, "You've been given a lot to think about. Your first line of business as a disciple maker is to teach the students good solid doctrine. At the same time live the Christ-life and be an example to them for what it means to live Christ."

"I know. I'm going to memorize that verse. It's scary. I'm not sure I have it in me."

"You don't have it in you naturally. But by grace through faith in Jesus Christ, by the power of God's Spirit you definitely have what it takes to teach and model as a disciple maker. Christ-like character grows as you continue to walk in his Spirit. Bless you, Matt!"

"Same to you. See ya later!"

On the way home, Dan was thinking about how great it was to have worked with Bill and now with Matt. And through them he saw others discipled. He remembered John Maxwell's outline for training others: model, mentor, monitor, motivate and multiply.[5] *Matthew is doing many of these things. Why aren't the elders doing this too? Especially Bernie! He's the oldest and has been here the longest. How many has he discipled? How is he even a model of Christ?*

Then he began to feel guilty when he thought of the conversation he had with Katrina last year. She had cornered him and asked if Dan would be a friend to her husband Al. Dan had already been raked over the coals by Al many times, and by Katrina too for that matter. Initially Dan tried to show an interest in Al, doing things like calling him or visiting with him at church. But Al was ….well, different. He was always critical, more so than his spouse. He was a puddleglum – too depressing. Al never exhibited teachability; he always questioned what Dan said and seemed to forget what Dan taught. Then Dan decided that he was doing this for Katrina, not for Al. So to prove it in his mind he backed off from pursuing the man to see what Al would do.

As suspected, Al never took the initiative in the relationship. He was always the receiver or taker, never a giver with Dan. He never took on responsibilities at the church unless his wife told him to. He did not exhibit a humble attitude, which is a prerequisite to being a good learner or disciple. How can you teach someone who is proud? Al came to a few of the leadership classes at Mo's, but that was about it. He was rarely in Sunday School, and irregular at worship. Yet, while this convinced Dan that Al was not a serious candidate for discipleship, he was honest enough to recognize he did not love Al as he should – in Christ, sacrificially, with Al's best interest at heart.

He was somewhat pacified by the knowledge that Jesus did not disciple everyone. He had his three close-knit friends. Then he had the other nine. And one of those was Judas who betrayed the Lord, yet the Lord still loved him and discipled him. Ouch! Dan had to confess that to the Lord. But he should have had the guts to confess that to Al and be honest with Al about why he wasn't willing to try harder to develop a discipling relationship with him.

At the same time, it's like the statement by John Gilmore:

...what a contradiction it is to be a Christian, and yet to refuse to learn; for what is a Christian but a disciple of Christ? And how can he be a disciple of Christ that refuses to be taught by him? And he that refuses to be taught by his minister, refuses to be taught by him: for Christ will not come down from heaven again to teach them by his own mouth, but has appointed his ministers to keep school and teach them under him.[6]

Al wasn't actively rebellious when it came to learning. It was more of a passive rebellion. He wasn't motivated or interested. He'd prefer to talk computers or money or complain about his wife or about the church than to discuss spiritual things.

Dan forced himself not to think about it too much. Instead he poured his life into those who wanted it. After all, isn't that what Jesus and Paul did? Isn't that what Leroy Eims said? "When I observe a person who has a special hunger to learn the Scriptures and grow in grace, I must be willing to share my life with that person and pass along those things that God has taught me."[7]

At suppertime, Dan told his family and his guests how excited he was about Matthew, and the opportunity he had to disciple this young man and to see Matt discipling others. Marcus expressed excitement too. Marcus shared how he was working with two other black men at his office during lunch, doing Bible study with them. "It's more like answering their questions than a study through a book of the Bible," Marcus said almost apologetically.

"That's great! How long has this been going on?" Dan asked.

"About a month. It just kind of happened. But let me ask you this," Marcus said while serving his son another scoop of mashed potatoes. "What is a mentor? You mean a discipler?"

"Technically, a mentor is a guide. A mentor is someone who teaches you a skill. In the church a mentor is a disciple maker who trains another in the skills of life and godliness. He is a model or example, a teacher, a counselor and a guide in the way of Christ. The disciple is like an apprentice in the things of life. He is to learn the way of Jesus, to think God's thoughts about all issues of life and to apply them in the many different circumstances in life. He sees, then does, and then teaches others."

"Yeah, man! That's what I'm talkin' about. Could you mentor me too?"

Dan was floored. He was excited. This was just what he had been hoping and praying for! "It'd be a great privilege to do that with you!" Dan said waving his hand, and in the movement knocked over his water glass. Everyone laughed.

After supper, the children went off to play together, while the adults made their way to the living room for special coffee Sheree brought over. Hannah toddled from furniture piece to furniture piece, occasionally playing with a toy on the floor. Mona took the small recliner next to the couch to sit near Sheree. They talked about children. Dan sat in the winged back chair that angled off the other end of the couch where Marcus was. They finished talking about the logistics of their mentoring relationship and got into other church matters.

A fight between Jake and little brother Ben broke up the adult huddle. This was fine since it was time to serve dessert — peach cobbler with loads of ice cream on top. Everyone sat back at the table and finished off the last course of a fine meal. Mona had done it again.

It was getting late, so Sheree began to lead her family toward the door. "Hey, are you sure it's not going to be an inconvenience for you to meet with me?" Marcus asked almost apologetically.

"No way, man! Besides, it's my job," Dan confirmed somewhat sarcastically. Even though it was his responsibility and duty as a pastor, Dan genuinely considered it a great privilege and blessing. This is what beats in the heart of a pastor!

"Besides time, what does it take?" Marcus asked.

"A friend used to say it takes someone who is F.A.T. – faithful, available and teachable. I recently read an article on mentoring and one of the authors says it takes someone who is F.A.S.T. – faithful, available, Spirit-filled and teachable!"

"Cool. Just one more thing that's buggin' me," Marcus said as he grabbed Dan's elbow and pulled him out of earshot of the others.

"Now you don't go on talkin' about me!" Sheree cried out with humor. "Marcus, c'mon now. We gotta go!"

"Be right there, Sugar. Dan, real quick, what's going on with Mr. Dumpleton?"

"Which one?"

"The old man."

"What're you talkin' about?"

"He's been having meetings, and they're not Bible studies. He invited me to one last week but I didn't go."

"Did he say what it was for?"

"No. I should have gone. But rumor has it that he is trying to get a group together to vote you out of this church."

Dan was somewhat startled, but not altogether surprised. "Yeah, it would have been good if you could have gone to check it out. Bernie has never liked me. Don't know why. And he has never made it a secret that he wants me to leave."

"Nooo! Really? Are you serious?" Marcus said with great surprise.

"It's a long story."

"What about the other elders?"

"If I left, there would be no love lost. I suspect they'd be happy. Maybe even celebrate."

"You aren't leaving, are you?"

"Put it this way, there isn't anything out there that I would go to right now. But if something came up, I would give it a serious look."

"Hey man, we don't want you to go anywhere. And I can say that about most of the church."

"I appreciate that. Marcus, I appreciate you and your friendship! Just do me a favor and keep your ears to the ground. I'd keep a diary of what is going on. Who knows when it will come in handy," Dan admonished.

The two shook each other's hands and embraced. Dan rushed over to Sheree and gave her a farewell hug. He bent over to look inside the car and to say his goodbyes to their kids. It was a wonderful day for Dan. Things got bad from time to time at Grace, but it wasn't Hell. In fact, he often reminded himself what he had told the church on a couple of occasions, "For unbelievers, this is all the heaven they will ever know. But no matter how bad it gets for us as believers, just remember, this is all the Hell we will ever know!" I wish all my days were like this one, Lord! At least I had a taste of heaven today.

A CHALLENGE TO THINK AND DO

What do you think?
1. Is there anything in this chapter that challenged you? Were you able to learn something new?
2. What would you have counseled Pastor Dan if he asked you if it was wrong to have close friends once he became a pastor?
3. What is a biblical disciple-making mentor?
4. What kind of a person makes a good example of Jesus Christ? What traits would he or she have?
5. Whose example would you or do your follow? Why?
6. How important is it for a pastor to have a mentor? Why?
7. How important is it for a pastor to disciple others?

Some things you could do:
1. If you do not have a godly mentoring relationship, why not begin one soon?
2. Read Bob Biehl's *Mentoring*.

15

A PASTOR *AND* A PRIEST?

—ᴍ—

No sooner did the pastor give God's benediction at the end of the worship service and the postlude had begun playing, did Mr. Neuhman jump up from his favorite seat and rush forward toward the piano. The tall, average-built, middle-aged man was highly opinionated and nearly always convinced his perspective on things was true. He loved to argue, and he enjoyed pointing out the faults in others.

Betty was almost finished playing the last stanza of hymn #255 when Neuhman parked abruptly next to her. The single, sixty-year-old, sickly woman was a fairly accomplished pianist. She dressed well, and kept her mousy brown hair in a 1960s mushroom looking perm. Dan could not hear the conversation, but shortly after Mr. Neuhman stormed away Betty began crying.

The hard working music teacher taught choir at a local junior high school and gave private voice and piano lessons in her tiny rental. She had been in and out of the hospital numerous times. In fact, that was where she met Pastor Dan and Mona. She was so impressed by their kindness and by the help several church ladies gave her that she decided to attend. She was in the first membership class Dan taught, so she was a relatively new member.

Dan made his way to Betty and sat down next to her on the piano bench. She tried to cover her soft sobs, but tears were erasing the light tan foundation she wore to cover up her blotchy skin. "What's wrong?" Dan asked quietly.

"I've had it with this church. Some can be so mean!"

"Tell me about it."

"I really shouldn't."

"No – you really should. If someone is sinning against you then it needs to be dealt with. I saw Mr. Neuhman talking with you. What did he say?"

"It's not just him. Several men have come to me before."

"About what?"

"They keep telling me to quit embellishing the hymns. They want me to play the hymns just like they are written."

Dan's face could not hide his anger, but he restrained his fury. "Who keeps telling you this beside Neuhman?" Dan asked with a controlled, but forceful, voice. Betty noticed the flexing muscles in his jaws.

"Bernie and Walt."

"They are not your bosses. You are not doing anything wrong or sinful. I'll take care of this!" Dan declared while waving to Melissa. Melissa came over and immediately noticed a tearful pianist. "Melissa, could you stay with Betty while I take care of some business?"

"Sure. What's wrong, Honey?" she asked the broken woman.

"I'm not going to play piano here again. Not with these kinds of people treating me like this!" she said in an angry bawl. By now Mona joined the duo.

Dan found the contentious, controlling elder wannabe and pulled him to a corner of the hall. "What did you say to Betty?"

"I told her it wasn't necessary for her to embellish the music like that."

"What in the world is wrong with her embellishing the music? She's a good musician, and her playing gives a fuller expression, and it helps our singing."

"That's nonsense. She is just showing off."

"How dare you judge her like that! You had no business being critical and telling her how to play. That's the elders' and my role. Do not do that again!" Dan commanded.

"Bernie agrees with me."

"Bernie is not the elder board. He is not the king around here either."

"Oh? And you think you are?"

"Don't do that again, or I will bring you up for discipline," Dan pronounced before walking off. Betty had left by the time Dan went back into the worship hall. Mona and Melissa were trying to find ways to console an emotionally distraught woman. They feared she would not only quit playing the piano but leave the church too. Neuhman and Bernie refused to confess any wrongdoing.

It was a cool October night with a dash of sprinkles now and then. The wind swept leaves off deciduous trees and littered all the spotless, manicured lawns on Dan's street. Pastor was walking out his front door for the short jaunt to the church building when he noticed the elders pulling up. Right on time. The monthly agenda would contain the regular items of business, but Dan included two matters to be discussed under new business. The first was the matter of the men nominated for eldership. Their training was complete. Interviews by the elders and an official congregational election needed to be scheduled. The other matter pertained to Betty.

The first part of the elders' meeting went smoothly. When Dan brought up the trainees' progress and distributed copies of their written exams, he asked to set up times to interview each of the men in person. Actually the candidate would first be interviewed with his wife to see how she perceived her husband in the role of elder and if she agreed with his desire to become one.

The second meeting would ask for clarification on any of the answers the candidate wrote in his theological examination. The elders would also ask about his personal walk with Christ, his devotional life, his family life, his moral life and so forth. The prospective men were also required to retrieve three personal references: one from the wife, one from a neighbor, and one from a manager or boss at work. This was to check to see if the men had a good reputation with those outside the church.

This was a far more rigorous and comprehensive process than any of the current elders had endured. The process Bernie went through was much simpler. Back in the day when Bernie and a fellow elder were nominated it was all but a done deal. All they had to do was go through a six-week program studying their church's creed, with no interviews or exams. Being a prominent and well known man in the community, very active in the church, and relatively knowledgeable in doctrine, he had what a previous pastor and elder were looking for. Dan was convinced that only Joe would be able to survive the training and scrutiny if they had to go through the same hurdles as the new men.

Bernie was the first to speak. "I don't think all this interview stuff is necessary. I like the three men, especially Marcus. He'll be a great asset to our team."

Joe, surprisingly disagreed. At the end of the twenty-minute discussion, the elders confirmed the more rigorous process. Dan was to arrange interviews with each man.

The next item about Betty came up. Dan no sooner mentioned it when Bernie, who had already talked with Neuhman, blurted out, "There is nothing to discuss. The woman has no business playing hymns the way she does. She's a performer. I don't even think she's a good Christian lady!"

After tolerating months of Bernie's nonsense, Dan's patient veneer was very thin. He almost exploded. An old saying popped into his head which he learned from an eighty-year-old friend years before Dan became a pastor: It is better to keep your mouth shut and be thought of as stupid than to open your mouth and remove all doubt. Bernie had opened his mouth too many times, but Dan was forcing himself to be careful to only open his mouth at appropriate times. Dan also learned from Lynda, a dear family friend, that the best way to control a discussion or to get at the root of an issue is to ask questions.

Dan leaned forward and looked Bernie right in the eyes. "Is the way she plays the piano sinful?"

"She's a show-off. She doesn't need to play like that!"

"How do you know she is a show-off? On what grounds can you base your judgment?"

"Others don't like it."

"Answer my question."

"It's not right, I tell you."

"Answer my question!"

Bernie kept deflecting the question. Then he tried to turn the tables. The short man slumped over in his chair and pointed at the pastor. "You think you control everything, don't you?"

"How is it that you can judge my heart now, Bernie?"

"The elders are in charge of what goes on in worship."

"I'm aware of that."

"I move that we fire Betty and find another pianist," Bernie declared with his fist pounding the table like a gavel.

"Fair enough. Do we have a second?" Dan asked.

A weak second was offered by Bernie's ally.

"Okay, we open now for discussion. Remember, Betty is a volunteer."

Joe argued that the motion was hasty and also pointed out that there were no other pianists available. Bernie pronounced that the elderly Mrs. Dromback would play the organ again. The thought of her returning to the organ made Dan nauseous. It would be a step back into the so-called glory days, which in Dan's opinion were not only long gone, but out of touch with reality and all too stiff. The reason why Mrs. Dromback quit playing was that she could no longer keep pace with the pianists, especially with Betty's good tempo. Even hymns of praise sounded like funeral dirges. A four-verse hymn could take as long as six minutes when she played, twice as long as normal.

"Is Betty doing anything immoral or sinful?" Dan kept pushing for a definitive answer.

One of the elders admitted that she wasn't, but they just did not like her style. Dan then announced that Betty would probably leave the church.

"Good! Then that settles it!" Bernie said with hostile glee.

No vote was taken. Dan then asked, "Didn't you men tell me that I was supposed to oversee the worship service?"

"Yes," Joe agreed.

"You're doing a bad job of it, you know," said the obnoxiously cranky man.

"Bernie, your bitter vitriol is not only unbecoming of a Christian but a violation of your vows and office as an elder. You doubt Betty is a believer? Well, I have to say that based on your track record and reputation I have every reason to doubt you are a Christian!"

Dan's confrontational manner and boldness stunned everyone. Even Mr. Dumpleton. For the first time since Dan arrived, the gauntlet was thrown down. "Somebody has got to go, and it's not Betty," Dan announced. Before anyone could respond, Dan asked the question, "Am I or am I not the delegated overseer of the worship event or do you men want to take control and micromanage it?"

"The worship event? You mean the music?" asked a seemingly confused elder.

Bernie sat slouched back into his chair with folded arms. He could easily pass for Snow White's dwarf Grumpy.

240

Dan reminded them, "When we say worship we are not just talking about the musical portion of the service. In its narrow definition everything from the call to worship to the closing benediction or prayer is the official and formal part of the worship event. You should know that!"

Joe finally answered, "Yes, you are the one we've asked to oversee the worship service." A couple other men nodded with approval.

"What about Betty?" questioned Dan.

"If she will come back, then I suppose it'll be okay," Joe said looking for approval from the other men.

"Then, excuse me while I go and call her right now," Dan said as he bolted for the door. He could hear Bernie squawking as he darted up the stairs to his office. In about five minutes Dan came back down to the fellowship hall in the basement. He announced with disgust, "Men, Bernie has successfully run Betty out of the church. She said she will never return as long as Bernie and, as she put it, 'his devils' are here."

Bernie sat up with a smug sense of victory. A smile indicated this was one for his camp. It broke Dan's heart. Yet Dan could sense a growing determination on Bernie's part to maintain control of the church. Bernie knew he was losing a grip on his vision of a church made in his image.

Dan asked the men to close the meeting in prayer, lifting up concerns of the local body, but also confessing personal and corporate sins. Only Joe and Dan prayed.

At home Dan paced the floor in his office. He was too angry for Mona to correct or console him, so she wisely let him alone for the time being. Mona was never one to confront anyone, whether good or bad. She was sweet as honey. A gentle kindness oozed from her soul. Undoubtedly, she had the gift of mercy. It was a blessing to those who needed it but a bane for her and her husband. She was a magnet to needy people. It was very hard for her to believe people could be cruel, even though she would occasionally watch the news or witness the meanness of some members at church.

She even experienced cruelty first-hand when an unwed, pregnant, homeless girl stayed at the local guest house sponsored by the local churches. Mona volunteered there from time to time. This young girl was viciously caustic toward Mona like some rabid stray mutt. After the seventh visit Mona received an unprovoked verbal lashing. Mona asked her why she was so hostile toward her and not toward the other women. "Because you are just too (expletive) nice, and I hate nice do-gooders!" Her rebellious hate poisoned the home so girl was told to leave.

Dan finally sat at his computer and opened his email. He clicked on a message from a church in New Mexico asking if he would be willing to candidate there. Up until this evening Dan was ambiguous, thinking things were getting better at Grace. He typed a reply saying he would be more than happy to proceed. He hesitated a moment and then clicked on the send button.

In elder-run churches like a Presbyterian church, the elders are responsible to oversee what happens in worship. That's the delegated role they receive from God as overseers, but also in a real sense, as priests. Christians in the broad, contemporary American evangelical church think of priests as the religious officials in the Roman Catholic or other Episcopal systems of church government. They are the ones who conduct a long-established traditional service, often of the high church or high liturgical style. Depending on the denomination or appointment, the priest may or may not be a local pastor.

One of the hallmarks of the Reformation was the biblical teaching that all believers in Christ are royal priests. It is derived from 1 Peter 2:9, Revelation 1:4-6 and 5:9-10. The background for this comes from the Old Testament. Priests were set apart to God (Ex. 39:30; Ezek. 44:11), and hence enjoyed the special privilege of coming near to God. They were guardians of God's holy ways and holy things (Lev. 11-15). They were tasked with maintaining and protecting the beauty of pure worship. Priests brought sacrifices to the Lord and led others to do the same. Additionally, they taught God's holy law to the people, but also served as the people's representatives to God. Lastly, they pronounced blessings upon God's holy people (Lev. 9:22; Num 6:22-27; Deut. 21:5).

God created and ordained Israel to be a nation of royal priests (Exod. 19:1-6). The special Levitical priests were role models for what the nation of priests were to be like and to do: worship God well, live according to God's holy word, and be representatives of other people groups to God. But they defied God's will and went apostate. Consequently God warned them of his impending judgment if they did not repent and begin living up to their call as priests. The warning was explicitly pronounced through Hosea, when God said that his people were destroyed for their rejection of God's Law-Word. He also told them they were rejected as a kingdom of priests (Hos. 4:6).

With warnings of judgment and doom, God always provides promises of hope through mercy and grace. That hope would come in the form of a savior who would be the perfect priest.

The Gospel of John paints a picture of Jesus as the priest who came to fulfill all the expectations, promises and symbols of the Old Testament. He fulfilled all of the requirements and images of the old Tabernacle and Temple. He came as the new and true temple of God, pictured in Ezekiel 40 (cp. John 2). Jesus is the promised perfect, living and final High Priest (Heb. 2:17; 3:1; 4:14-15; 5; 6:20; 7, etc.). He did what all other priests failed to do and did it perfectly.

Not only was he a priest who offered a sacrifice to God, but he offered himself as the unblemished, sacrificial Lamb of God. Jesus is the final and complete sacrifice offered to atone for our sins (Eph. 5:2; Heb. 9:26; 10:12, 26).

Through this complete and perfect work of our High Priest Jesus Christ, he makes a new people to be a royal priesthood, a kingdom of priests. All those who trust and believe in Jesus Christ are priests who come to God the Father through the one priest Jesus. This is what the Reformers recaptured and promoted. In terms of our position and responsibility before God being a priest in Christ is a leveling field.

"What does it really mean for us to be priests?" asked Karen, whose mother had a Roman Catholic background. "It sounds weird to me."

The MTI, as they now called their new fraternity of disciples, were gathered in Dan and Mona's living room. The abbreviation, MTI, was taken from the first letters of the Greek words for "disciples of Jesus." Occasionally, when Matt was unable to answer their questions, they met with Dan. Dan said, "In principle, our role as priests is not unlike the role of priests in the Old Testament. But because of Jesus' work we are in a New Covenant era, so we now have a fuller sense of the priesthood. Because of the direct access we have through Jesus Christ, we enjoy the presence of God. All kinds of people can draw near to God because of our High Priest, and as his priests we lead them to God.

"It's like this: the Old Testament priests were to guard the holy temple. Today, we guard our own bodies which are temples in which the Spirit dwells. That's what we learn from 1 Corinthians 3:15 and 16. We are to maintain and protect the beauty of holy worship in our hearts and lives. In the Old the priests brought sacrifices to God. Instead of bringing animal sacrifices or grain and meal offerings we offer our whole bodies as living sacrifices to the Lord. This is what Paul is talking about in Romans 12:1-2, and in Ephesians 5:3-7."

Dan told them that as Christians we also offer up sacrifices of praise (Heb. 13:15) and bless others (Rom. 12:14; 1 Cor. 4:12). Finally, as God's new priests we have the ability to serve as mediators for people, leading them to Christ or praying for them (1 Tim 2:1–2; Jas. 5:16).

"How's that?" one of the students asked.

"We pray with and for people. As believers we can powerfully intercede for one another and for those outside the faith. We also have the privilege of acting as priest-evangelists when we lead people to Jesus Christ, and then encourage them to offer their lives up as living sacrifices to our great God."

"Awesome!" Matt said.

"Aren't you guys the priests?" Craig asked.

"What do you mean, you guys?" Dan questioned.

"You know, you pastors."

Funny he should ask. "That's what I've been saying. All believers in Jesus Christ are priests before God. Like every Christian, pastors and elders are priests. However, pastors and elders have additional priestly responsibilities. We are responsible for God's new temple, which is God's people when they come together."[1]

"That's it?" questioned Jorge.

"Oh no. As shepherds and overseers we guard the holiness of our own lives. Like all believers, we are made holy in Christ Jesus and are called upon to work out our sanctification and be holy because the Father is holy. However, we have the additional responsibility to model and guide in the way of holiness through life and lip. We must guard the holy things and holy ways of the Lord in God's Church, and monitor the spiritual walk and godliness of its members."[2]

The small group munched on chicken nuggets and pizza, drank soft drinks and tea while they listened to their pastor clarify how the Christian pastor and elder fulfill their role as priests. He went on to tell them that in their priestly roles, the pastor and elder have the responsibility to oversee the beauty and holiness of the corporate worship of God. They are to preside over corporate worship to make sure it is done in Spirit and in truth (John 4:24).

Pastors and elders are to teach (Rom.12:7; 1 Cor. 12:28; 14:19; Eph. 4:11-12; 2 Tim. 2:2). They also guard God's truth entrusted to them (Col. 1:14; 1 Thess. 2:4; 1 Tim. 1:11; 6:20; Tit. 1:3) by keeping bad teaching out of the church. They are also special stewards of the mysteries of God (1 Cor. 4:1).

What's more, the pastor and elders are at the front of the line guiding and leading others to offer up their bodies as living sacrifices to God (Rom. 12:1-2; 15:16) and to others (e.g.: Phil. 2:17, 25; 4:18). That means pastors and elders demonstrate how to take up their crosses every day. Through humility they are ready to put aside their own desires for the sake of God's will. Through humility, they are willing to lay down their lives for others. Sometimes this means they give up their rights in order to help others. Sometimes it means literally dying for the sake of others.

Pastors and elders also model and lead others how to offer the sacrifices of praises to the Lord: praising God in worship, in song, in thanksgiving, and so forth.

As leaders in the role of the priesthood they minister Christ's ministry of reconciliation (2 Cor. 5:19). They are active peacemakers, teaching and loving out what it means to be forgiven and redeemed. This is a service to non-Christians, telling them how to be forgiven by God through Jesus Christ. It is a service to fellow believers by forgiving them when they sinfully offended, and teaching them how to forgive others.

As leader-priests the pastor and elders intercede on behalf of God's people. Paul was clear about his role in this (Rom.1:8-10; 2 Cor. 13:7-9; Eph. 1:15-23; Phil. 1:3ff; Col. 1:3-14; 2 Thess. 1:11-12; 2 Tim. 1:3-7). Yet they also are to exemplify and take the lead in interceding for unbelievers (1 Tim. 2:1-8). Finally, the pastor and elders are to be a blessing and to bless others.

After the lesson, the group played board games and then watched a movie on the Lees' old television. It was nearly midnight by the time they went home. Dan and Mona experienced a happy contentment being with such an eager, hungry team of disciples. "Were the antagonists ever like this?" Dan wondered out loud. "Was Bernie or Irma ever enthusiastic about the Lord or have a vibrant, living relationship with him? If so, what happened that caused them to lose their first love?"

Mona went upstairs to get ready for bed. Dan went to his office to check his emails one last time. Nothing but junk mail. As he sat in his chair swiveling back and forth he contemplated how far off the spiritual track he and the elders were. Are we fulfilling our role as godly servants, as undershepherds, or as teachers? If we were, we would be more concerned that the drama of worship be performed in Spirit and truth, not according to petty personal preferences! If we were acting out our God ordained role as priests we would be more concerned to see people being drawn into a heavenly encounter with a holy God through various acts of worship. If we were acting like biblical priests we would take an active role in taking up our own crosses and leading people to follow after Christ with self-sacrifice. We would also be actively involved in the many opportunities to intercede for God's people as well as to have a compassionate intercession for those outside the church. What about blessing others?

Dan evaluated his own life first and admitted he didn't have a stellar report card to boast about. Yet when he thought about three of the elders, it was clear by their behavior that they failed on all points. Three of them never taught. Three of them fought for a style of worship that fit their petty preferences. Three of them showed no concern for the unbeliever, and showed contempt for self-sacrificial living. Dan never saw them in prayer meetings, and hadn't heard one little word that remotely resembled a blessing coming from their lips! In fact, they seemed too busy cursing their pastor and other people they didn't like rather than blessing anyone.

Dear God, what's to be done? We need a radical overhaul at Grace. We need major repentance and a renewed faith! Or is it too late? Have you taken the lamp stand out of our church or are you on the verge of doing so? Dan prayed, alluding to God's warnings to the churches in Revelation.

A CHALLENGE TO THINK AND DO

What do you think?
1. What did this chapter teach you, if anything?
2. How did Jesus Christ fulfill the Old Testament priesthood?
3. How is Jesus Christ the High Priest today? What relevance does that have for you?
4. If you were the pianist, how would you have dealt with Mr. Neuhman?
5. What were the roles and responsibilities of Israel's priests in the Old Testament?
6. If you are a believer in Jesus Christ, what does it mean that you are a priest?
7. What thing(s) are believer-priests called to do today?
8. In what ways does your pastor (and elders) fulfill the role of priest? How is that different from other believer-priests?

Some things you could do:
1. Read through the book of Hebrews. Highlight or list the verses that pertain to the priesthood of Jesus Christ.
2. Using the information in the chapter and the verses found in the endnotes, write down a list of things believer-priests do today. Then, write three ways to apply your priestly functions.

16

A GOOD NEWS BOY

—∿—

The sermon ended and a deep silence fell upon the congregation. This startled the pastor. He had noticed more than the usual frowns during the delivery, but couldn't spare mental space or time trying to evaluate why. It seemed awkward now to give the benediction he picked from Romans 15:13. Yet he raised his arms with hands outstretched and pronounced, "Now may the God of hope fill you with all joy and peace in believing, that you may abound in hope by the power of the Holy Spirit!" With that, the elderly organist blared the tune of a three-fold amen. She then played through "Amazing Grace" at an amazingly slow tempo.

No sooner had Dan come down from the platform than four men approached him. Two of them began speaking at once. One took control, leaning forward and almost in the pastor's face exclaimed, "Did I hear you right?"

"What are you talking about?" Dan asked, pulling his upper body away from the aggressor.

"Your sermon!"

"Obviously. What part of the sermon are you talking about?"

"Where you said it would be great to have society's rejects among us, like some homeless or former felons or homosexuals!"

The message was from Ephesians 4:1-6. What Dan preached was about the unity of God's people in Christ. The Christians in Ephesus were people who had come from all sorts of religious, political and moral backgrounds. We often tend to think of their social condition as rich and poor, slave or free. Dan said, "We tend to think of their religious background as Jewish or any number of the forms of religious Gentiles. We even tend to think of the early church being made up of people from the various political polarities: anti-Roman zealots, non-citizens, Roman soldiers to include the emperor's elite guards, and various government officials. Yet, we usually ignore the radically diverse moral conditions from which these people came. Peter talks about the Christian's former condition in 1 Peter 4:1-4. Paul does the same in Ephesians 4:17-19. Paul even paints a more graphic picture of those Christians before they were transformed by Christ in 1 Corinthians 6:9-11:

Do you not know that the unrighteous will not inherit the kingdom of God? Do not be deceived. Neither fornicators, nor idolaters, nor adulterers, nor homosexuals, nor sodomites, nor thieves, nor covetous, nor drunkards, nor revilers, nor extortioners will inherit the kingdom of God. *And such were some of you* (emphasis added). But you were washed, but you were sanctified, but you were justified in the name of the Lord Jesus and by the Spirit of our God."

At this point in the message Dan emphasized that the unity of God's people in the church of Ephesus and other early churches was based upon the redemptive work of God the Father through Jesus Christ applied by the Holy Spirit. It was not based upon artificial alliances such as legalism or moralism, far right or radical left political convictions, race or financial status. Then Dan said, "Wouldn't it be great if the work of Jesus was so impressed upon our own church that our identity would not come from our political persuasions, racial composition or economic status, but from Jesus Christ? Wouldn't it be great if we could embrace the people whom the Lord was drawing to himself, people who were of all sorts of backgrounds, even those we consider society's rejects? What if we could say with Paul that our church was composed of former fornicators, adulterers, and the like, or as we would say, former felons, prostitutes and drug addicts?" Now Dan became painfully aware that there were several in the church who did not share his biblical idealism. In fact they strongly opposed it.

The thrust of the first man's argument was that he did not want to change the social fabric of the church. He enjoyed the fact that the bulk of the church's composite was politically and socially conservative with strong patriotic overtones. It was fine by him that there were people of other races, though Dan suspected he would never feel comfortable in a fully integrated church.

Two of the men left the worship hall for the refreshment area, leaving a third man to make his protest. He could care less about the racial makeup of the church, for he was a minority. But he was also politically conservative with high moral convictions. "I, for one, would be very uncomfortable with those kinds of people in our church!"

"Oh? Even if the Lord was calling them into his kingdom and wanted our church to embrace and disciple them?"

"We can't trust them. What about our children? It is our duty to protect our children from that kind!"

Dan was heartbroken. He believed these folks did not have a biblical case to justify their beliefs, but he couldn't be the change agent. He could only provoke change through teaching and preaching God's Word. The Spirit had to change such hearts.

When Pastor entered the fellowship area to retrieve a cup of coffee, three more men gathered to him. They wanted clarification on Dan's sermon. Dan began to provide it, but he kept getting interrupted. At one point he turned the table on them and asked one of the younger men directly, "Would you be making this argument with Jesus? Do you believe he was wrong for working with the dregs of society and not the morally upright? Was he in error when he talked to a morally loose woman at the well?"

The young man and his friends said nothing. Dan turned away in order to visit with some other members, but was intercepted yet again by two more men who had no question for him. Instead, they wanted to let him know the message was way off base and offensive.

At the traditional weekly prayer meeting some of the people wanted to interact with the pastor about the sermon. Dan attempted to clarify his position, but that wasn't what they wanted. They had objections to his position. One dear lady reiterated something one of the men said on Sunday, "I would be very nervous about having those kinds of people with us! What would we do to protect our innocent children?"

"We already have a child abuse prevention policy and program. It's not as if we are going to allow people trapped in their sin or wickedness to have free reign among us, for Pete's sake!" Dan said with more than a little testiness. "So what you are saying is that if the Lord were to bring one or two or ten of 'those kinds of people' we would shun them or even kick them out?"

Nobody responded. Most eyes were down, though a few studied Dan's face. The pastor then made the same argument he had with the young man. "Was Jesus wrong for going to the immoral, half-breed woman at the well and offering his life and salvation to her?"

Almost immediately one of the elders spoke up with a firm protest, "That was Jesus! That was an exception. We are not Jesus!"

Dan was stunned that this was coming from an elder in the church of Jesus Christ who should know better! *Where is his compassion for the lost? Man! These people couldn't be any more insecure. Or any more self-righteous.*

Another man suggested to the group that Dan or some evangelist lead those people to Christ, train them up, and when they were ready they would be able to come to Grace. "So, you want a sort of half-way house?" Dan asked with disgust. He may have been justified in principle but Dan's attitude was as sinful as their views.

If only they could think through the implications of that idea. *So then, what do we say to visitors? Excuse me, but we need to fingerprint you, do a background and credit check, obtain a blood test, get ten references for your moral behavior, test your Bible knowledge, verify your political affiliation... Oh give me a break!*

"I'm speechless," Dan announced. "All I can say right now is how hypocritical we are! We only want a church filled with people of perfect moral integrity? Sorry, but no sinners allowed? God only wants the healthy and righteous in this church?"

Dan was strongly tempted to leave when a middle-aged woman spoke up. She had tears in her eyes, "I thank God that he brought me to a church who accepted me where I was in my life and loved me to Christ. You all definitely would not have liked me back then. Who knows what would have happened if I lived in this town before I was a Christian?"

"Thank you! Thank you very much, Danielle. You put it far better than I could have."

The rest of the prayer time was somewhat muted. Dan went home angry and disgusted. How can we fulfill God's purposes for us to reach the lost for Jesus Christ when so many oppose it?

Whenever Pastor taught on outreach, missions, evangelism or church planting the people seemed favorable. The church historically had a strong and active support for foreign missions. It took Dan quite some time to realize that outreach in foreign lands was very safe and relatively easy for the members at Grace.

Nevertheless, the way some members talked you would think that they viewed those missionaries as no more than spiritual mercenaries: "We will hire you to get down and dirty and go to battle for us!" It was quite acceptable for missionaries to reach the unacceptable dregs in another culture, but that sort of work could not take place in one's backyard.

Ever the idealist, when Pastor Daniel began his second year he tried to prepare the congregation for outreach, and tried to get them to see beyond their little world, beyond the comfortably safe four walls known as Grace Church. The first thing he did was ask the elders about the category in the budget labeled outreach. There were some things that did not seem to fit. "I'm having a hard time understanding your rationale for these sub-items. Help me here. How do you define outreach?"

The elders looked at each other waiting for someone to respond. After a lengthy pause, one of the elders answered, "Any activity that is outside of our church."

"Uhh...okay. I'll ask it this way: what comes to mind when I say we need to do outreach?"

Immediately another elder replied, "To find people outside of our church who are looking for what we have. To reach other people like us, other conservative Presbyterians. To work with other churches in our Presbytery."

"What if nobody is looking for what we have?"

"Oh, some people who are reading books or listening to CDs by our great teachers and preachers will be looking," said another man with pronounced confidence.

"So, let me see if I get this right? Outreach to you is doing things that connect us with others like us who are not part of our church?"

They all agreed.

"What about the lost?" Dan asked pointedly. With those quizzical looks one would think Dan was trying to talk about snow to Amazonian aborigines. He did not pursue it. The remainder of that year he taught, preached and even cast a vision for a healthy, biblical church that included outreach. To Dan, outreach was an all-encompassing thing, anything that brought the Good News of Jesus Christ to individuals, families or people groups and made disciples of some of those people. Outreach included evangelism, apologetics, church planting, local and foreign missions, and mercy ministries. Dan wrongly assumed the congregation was on board with the vision for reaching the local community for Christ. He had hoped to cast a new challenge for outreach his third year, but the sermon he delivered on unity and outreach unexpectedly put a halt to that. Many of the church, and all of the leadership was not willing to reach out.

In one Sunday school class, when Dan was teaching on the many facets of outreach, an elder commented that evangelism was the duty and responsibility of the pastor. He argued, as some do today, that Christ's command to go and make disciples was given to the apostles who in turn delegated that to ordained pastors, teachers and evangelists. Their argument also states that the book of Acts shows apostles, pastors and evangelists making disciples and establishing churches, not the lay people. It is a compelling argument, one which Dan did not totally reject. Dan also understood that some who held this position were reacting against the opposite view that all believers should be assertive, even aggressive evangelists. Some in this category had experienced high pressure to evangelize every day and had suffered a form of manipulation by guilt.

"As with all the other roles of a pastor, he takes the lead in the role of evangelism. After all, the pastor is the one who officially teaches, but that does not exclude others from teaching. He is the one who officially oversees the worship services, but that does not exclude believers from taking active roles in worship. The pastor officially preaches, but that does not exclude others from declaring God's Word, such as at a mission to the homeless. Am I correct?"

The elder admitted Dan had a valid point.

"What I am saying is that while the pastor is to model and lead when it comes to outreach, just because he is called, and may be gifted, does not preclude or forbid others from doing so. Neither does it negate the responsibility of all Christians to gossip the Good News; that's what evangelism means, you know?"

"But it is still *your* responsibility! It is still a role you must fulfill!" the elder argued adamantly.

"Don't forget, it is also your responsibility as an elder!"

"Well, I don't agree."

"Check the Scriptures," Dan said smiling. "Listen, what I am trying to get away from is the idea that the pastor is the sole professional when it comes to speaking and presenting the Good News of Jesus! Obviously we can't argue with Paul's admonition to Pastor Timothy to do the work of an evangelist in 2 Timothy 4. At the same time, I am not arguing that we all go out and become little Billy Grahams. Paul admonishes God's people to live peaceable and quiet lives among our neighbors..."

"Where does he say that?" asked Marcus.

"In 1 Timothy 2:2, I think. Peter tells us that we are all responsible to display Jesus Christ by our lives and lips. That's in 1 Peter 2:10 and 3:15. Okay, here, let's back up," Dan said as he was erasing the large white board.

"Here are notes from a course in evangelism given by our good friend Bill Vermeulen,"[1] Dan said as he wrote with a green dry erase marker:

1. *Evangelism is done by the ordained*
   Ephesians 4:11; Acts. 21:8; 2 Timothy 4:5; Romans 10:14

"This is a given. Any questions?" he asked. "Oh, and by the way, the pastor does the work of evangelism, but God gives the fruit. At the same time the pastor not only does it, he models it for others. He also teaches how and casts a vision for biblical outreach." No one responded. Then he wrote,

2. *Evangelism is done by the non-ordained.*
   Luke 8:39; 9:60; Acts 5:32; 8:1-4; 1 Thess. 1:8; Jas. 5:19, 20; 1 Peter 2:9-10.

A couple people squirmed and frowned. "Now I'll ask this, in what situations or contexts does speaking and living out the Good News of Christ happen?"

Several people offered ideas: in the neighborhood, at work, at the marketplace, at social events, on planes, and the like. Dan then printed:

3. *Evangelism is done in large gatherings.*
   Acts 2:1-41; 17:22-34
4. *Evangelism is done in small groups.*
   Acts 10:24-27; 16:15, 31-32; 18:7, 8, 26; 28:7-10
5. *Evangelism is done by visiting homes.*
   Matt. 10:11-14; Luke 19:9, 10; 10:5-7
6. *Evangelism is done through individuals and in one-on-one situations.*
   John 1: 41-45; 4:7-29; Acts 8:34, 35; Jas. 5:20
7. *Evangelism is done through mercy ministries of the church's diaconate.*
   Isa. 61:1-3; Matt. 9:35; 10:7; Acts 2:45, 47

"The church in Geneva, during the time of the Reformation under the leadership of John Calvin, is an awesome example of the effectiveness of evangelism through the deacons' mercy ministries. It is something worth studying and emulating!" Dan announced. "Frankly, in order for our church to be the healthy kind of church God wants, we ought to be active in outreach, and perhaps in some mercy ministries aimed at serving our local community." The audience was mute. After class a couple came forward to express appreciation for the lesson.

The Saturday before Thanksgiving, the monthly leadership group met at Mo's café. Being so near the major holiday season, the pastor suggested they postpone the class until January. Nobody would hear of it.

As everyone was gathering in and settling into their normal stations, Harold became aware they had not been greeted by Mo. "Where's Mo?" he asked a new waitress.

"She's in the hospital with pneumonia," she said. "What can I get you?"

Harold looked at Dan. Pastor seemed to be reading Harold's mind. "Let's go visit her after our meeting this morning," he suggested. Harold clapped his hands and with a big smile came back with, "Exactly what I was going to say! Good idea."

Marcus started the conversation once everyone had placed their orders. With his spoon he chimed his water glass and asked everyone to quiet down. Trying to conduct a decent conversation among twenty-two people in a busy restaurant was no easy task. It wasn't as if they were in their own room. A corner of the café had to do. "Before you start, Pastor Dan, could you answer this question: what is an evangelist?"

"Sure. Before I do, let me turn the question back to our class. What is an evangelist?"

Without hesitation Melissa said, "Billy Graham or Luis Palau!"

"They are indeed evangelists, but I believe Marcus was asking for a biblical definition. We Americans enjoy using illustrations when asked for definitions, don't we? I tend to do that all the time. So, let's ask it this way: What is the biblical definition of an evangelist?"

All Dan could hear was the breakfast orchestra.

"When Paul told Pastor Timothy to do the work of an evangelist, what was Timothy to do?"

The orchestra was now joined by a chorus of noise and voices from the kitchen.

"What is the evangel? What does evangelical mean?"

"Good News!" Marcus presented.

"Yes. Now, change the noun phrase to a verb form. Use your imagination. It's awkward, and we don't have such a thing in English, but someone try."

"You mean, Good News it? Like that?" Matt asked.

"Yes! Simply put, the evangel is God's good news of redemption in Jesus Christ. To evangelize is to "good news it" or give good news. An evangelist is a "good newser" or someone who declares good news. In the biblical sense an evangelist is someone who declares the good news about the person and work of Jesus Christ. Let's get back to Melissa's answer. Billy and Luis certainly are 'good newsers,' right?"

Several people responded with affirmative remarks.

"Is that the only way to evangelize?"

Harold spoke out, "No, I don't think so."

"We tend to think of an evangelist as someone who preaches a message to huge crowds, and a large number respond in some way. That traditional image came out of a practice popularized in the 1700s by John and Charles Wesley and their friend George Whitefield.

But, when we look at the Scriptures, especially the book of Acts, we see evangelists going from place to place establishing churches with the apostles. They were missionaries or church planters. Often times they would accompany an apostle, preaching and teaching and making disciples, and then remain behind for a time to get the new work established. Then the apostles or the established churches would send someone to pastor the new church. Or the commissioned emissaries, that is the apostles, evangelists and pastors, would train and ordain elders. As time wore on, a leading elder would emerge to become the church's pastor. If there were several small churches in a town or city, the emergent shepherd would usually pastor all of those churches. He was later given the name of bishop which means overseer. Any other questions?"

No one volunteered more questions so Dan started in with the lesson. At that moment three waitresses came out with the food. The teacher took the opportunity to make an announcement: "Don't forget, the third Saturday in January we are having our specially called congregational meeting to elect new elders. All three of them are here with us today." The church crowd cheered, but then a few of the men booed. They were teasing, of course.

After the brunch class, Harold followed Dan to the hospital. Mo was in a room on the second floor of a new wing. They knocked on the door jam since the door was open. Alone in a two-bed suite, Mo reclined upright in her hospital bed with an intravenous drip line stuck in her left arm. A light blue oxygen tube was clipped to her nose and additional wires slipped down the neck of her gown to monitor her heart. When she saw Harold and Dan entering her room, she lit up.

"Holy mother! What are you boys doing here?" she asked. She fumbled around for the television controls to turn it off.

"Hi, Mo!" Harold boomed.

"Hi, Mo! The question is what are you doing here?" Dan asked.

"My doctor put me in this blasted place. He thinks I'm sick," she complained.

"We hear you have pneumonia?" Harold remarked.

"So they say. They got me on all kinds of medicines, shots here, pills there. Even got my own cocktail hangin' next to me," she said tugging at the IV line. "I gots to get me one for home," she winked, "to keep my martinis in."

"You're looking pretty good. When do you go home?"

"Two more days. I'm as fit as a fiddle, but they got me locked up like some prisoner."

"For your own good!" Harold came back.

"I don't know which is worse, the sickness or the hospital. Pneumonia won't kill me but the boredom will!"

The guys laughed.

She leaned a little forward, wagging her finger for the men to come nearer, "You know what the worst part of this is?" she whispered.

"No, but I suspect you're going to tell us," Dan said.

"It's the cookin'! They're feedin' me this stuff they call food and tellin' me it's what my ticker needs. Told me my cookin' is killin' me! It's all bull, I tell ya. I grew up on good cookin' and my dear old mother did too. Look at her, she lived to the ripe old age of ninety-eight, God rest her soul," she said as she crossed herself.

"Now, now, let's not get all worked up. You'll be outta here in no time," Harold admonished.

"Yep, and the first place I'm headin' is to my café."

"Is that what the doctor ordered?" Dan asked.

"Never you mind him. He means well," she said as she lowered her voice to a near whisper, "but he's a kid, barely out of diapers. How can he know anything?"

"Don't worry about the café. We were there today and all is well," Harold announced. "It looks like your grandson is doing a fine job."

"He's a deary, that boy. God love him," she said with tears filling her eyes. "But the joint can't last long without me."

The café was her life. It gave meaning and purpose to her. Dan said, "Mo, can I read some Scripture and then pray for you?"

"Ahh, ya don't need to bother yourself with that. My priest was already here today and prayed for me, Father Dan."

"Mo, you can call me Dan."

"Oh no, that would be disrespectin' you."

"All right, then call me Pastor or Pastor Dan," he urged.

"If that's what you want," she frowned. "Don't sound right."

Harold was a little more forward. "Mo, do you know Jesus?"

"Talk to him all the time."

"Do you know him as your savior?" Harold questioned.

"Of course. Now what kind of silly question is that? Who don't know Jesus is our savior?"

"Do you mind if we have this chat?" Dan asked.

"No, no, not at all. Here, pull up those chairs and make yourselves comfy."

"What did Jesus save you from?" Harold asked.

"He'll save me from hell, I hope."

"Why would you go to hell?"

"I don't expect to."

"Why does anyone go to hell?"

"Because they deserve it."

"Who deserves to go to hell?"

She thought they were funny, so she giggled. "Hitler, that son of a butcher, and the likes of him."

"Who deserves to go to heaven?" Dan said trying a different tact.

"Good Christians."

"Are you a good Christian?" Dan asked with a smile.

"I keep you boys fat and happy, don't I?"

"Seriously, Mo," Harold pleaded.

"I go to Mass every week, unless I go out of town to visit me sister and her family."

"Are you a sinner?" Harold asked.

"I think sometimes. But confession and Mass takes care of that."

"Do you know how we know we are sinners?" Dan asked.

"When we're misbehavin'," she said. "Father, I mean Pastor Dan, for a minister you sure don't know much about theology."

They laughed at her sincere reprimand.

"Let me get to the point…"

"Don't let me stop you, Hon," she winked.

"Like your priest, we are concerned for your future, especially for your eternal future."

"No more than me. Nice to have people carin' for me" she said with a comforted smile while folding her hands.

"All of us are sinners. That means when we stand before a perfect, holy, sinless, righteous God, we come up short. We know we come up short not by comparing ourselves with anyone else but by measuring our lives against the Ten Commandments. You are familiar with the Ten Commandments, aren't you?"

She chuckled and waved him off with her right hand. "Oh yes! We had one nun, dear ol' Sister Theresa, God bless her soul. She drilled it into us."

"Sin, is failing to measure up to God's perfect standard or stepping over the line, such as we see in the Ten Commandments."

"Oh? Well that's good to know!"

"Why?" inquired Harold.

"Because then, I'm not a sinner!"

The two men looked at each other with raised eyebrows.

"You've never sinned?"

"Can't think of a day when I did."

"So you fulfilled the whole Law perfectly. Even in your heart and mind?"

"I think so."

"Let me ask you this, did you ever commit adultery?" the pastor asked.

"Ohhh, Pastor, shame on you for getting so personal. But, now that you've asked I'll have you know I never have."

"Good. Did you ever murder anyone?"

She howled, which provoked a short coughing spell. "I've got to visit your church, Harold! You've got a comedian for a minister!"

"Jesus put it this way: did you ever hate anyone or get very angry with them?"

"Sure, sure. Well, I remember this one time…"

"We don't need to know about that," Harold said. "But if so, that's a sin."

"Have you ever stolen anything?"

"Big or small? Small things don't count do they?" she winced. She raised her eyebrows, elongated her face, and drew down her puckered mouth while rolling her eyes from left, up and to the right.

"Everything counts, my dear lady."

"Oh my. My, my, my. I have to confess I did."

"Then you've broken God's law. That's sinning."

"Ever gossiped or slandered? Or coveted things other people have?"

"You caught me there. That's sin too, is it?"

"What God's Law and Jesus says. Saint Paul wrote in the Good Book, in Romans, that all of us have sinned and have fallen short of the glory of God."

"I must be a sinner. But, lad, let me assure you that I'm not one of those perverted hoodlums running around out there. And I'll never be like Hitler, that scum!" she scowled.

"The biggest question God asks is if you and I, and Harold too, love the Lord God with all our hearts, all our souls, all our minds, and all our might. If we don't, then we'll never be right with God and we will never enter heaven."

"But I go to confession and Mass, so my sin is taken care of. You need not worry about that," she said reaching over and patting Dan on his hairy hand.

"Ahhh, but here's the thing. It's not enough that our sins are forgiven," Dan responded.

"No?"

"No. We need to have a righteousness that is acceptable to God. We need to be pure and holy before God will receive us."

"I'm working on that. Maybe I can bake more cakes for our Bingo nights?" she giggled.

"Won't be enough."

"I'm sure you've got lots of good deeds behind ya, Father?"

"Won't be enough. The Bible says in places like Isaiah 64 that all of our righteousness are like filthy, dirty rags. Totally unacceptable to God."

"Ohhh, that's a bad thing. So what can you do?"

"We go to Jesus, so by his death upon the cross your sins and my sins can be forgiven. We go to him and trust in him personally."

"I believe that with my whole heart," she announced proudly. "I know what you're saying, Pastor Dan," she said lowering her voice again and peeking around the wall to see out the door. She motioned with her strong forefinger again for the two to come closer. "I watch Billy Graham all the time!" she announced with her eyes alight and her head quickly bowing down and up.

"But do you also trust in the sinless work of the God-Man Jesus for his righteousness?" Dan questioned. "Because without both his forgiveness of your sins and his righteousness given to you, God will not receive you to himself or admit you to heaven. The same is true for us all. That's where our hope comes from, not in our work but in the complete work of Jesus who paid for our sins and gives us his righteousness."

"Is – that –so?" she said with surprise and her right hand covering her mouth.

"That's what God tells us, dear heart. Right in his holy book. Do you believe that?"

"Father Dan, I'll needs to think hard on that one." Mo sat there quietly nodding her head back and forth. It was obvious she was getting tired.

"Do you have a Bible?" Harold asked.

"Somewhere at the house. But I'm not smart enough to understand all those words."

"It's not about how smart you are," Harold assured her. "It's about reading it like a child, asking God to open your heart to understand it. Here, I want you to have another Bible. It's written in a simpler English. You might read Romans first. In the New Testament."

"Or read the Gospel of John to get to know Jesus," Dan added.

He then told her they had overstayed their welcome, but enjoyed their visit. He and Harold prayed for her and told her to call either one if she needed anything.

"You're both too kind. Bless your hearts. I should be able to get out tonight!" she giggled.

"Why's that?" Harold asked.

"With three men praying for me in one day…that should do the trick."

"Have a restful day, Mo," Dan said as he leaned over to give her a quick peck on the cheek. She grabbed him and gave him a big hug.

"C'mon over here, you big lug!" she commanded Harold. They gave each other a big hug.

Riding down the elevator, Harold said, "Now that's providential, isn't it?"

"What do you mean?" Dan wondered.

"Here you've been talkin' about evangelists and giving the Good News, and that's just what happened today. Sweet!"

"It is sweet. We need to keep praying for Mo, for her health and a sure salvation."

"Dan, it was good watching you do the work of an evangelist!"

"Thanks, Harold! But you started it. You were also a Good Newser!"

"Oh yeah. Guess I was at that."

Meanwhile, Dan was actively pursuing a call to the fledgling church in New Mexico. It appeared to be a mutual thing. The chair of the pastoral search committee emailed the pastor to request a time for him to visit the church. After discussing it with Mona, Dan reported that the soonest he could fly down there would be in January. They understood. Dan wanted to know if they were looking at any other candidates. The chairman said they had only one other man.

A CHALLENGE TO THINK AND DO

What do you think?
1. What is the Gospel of Jesus Christ? Why is it good news?
2. What is true biblical unity in Christ's church?
3. What is the difference between unity and uniformity? In your opinion, are the two often confused? If yes, then how?
4. Referring to the beginning of this chapter, was the message Pastor Dan gave wrong? Why, do you think, did he receive such a negative reaction to his message?
5. How would you respond if God were to lead the "undesirables" of society into your church to give them the Gospel and to disciple them?
6. Define *evangelist* according to the Bible.
7. What do you think of Dan's definition of outreach?
8. Are you actively involved in some form of outreach? Is your church? If so, how? If not, what keeps you or the church from it?

Some things for you to do:
1. If you have not done so, write out how you know you are a Christian, giving biblical and experiential justification.
2. For practice, present the biblical Gospel to someone in your care group, study, etc.
3. Present the Gospel to someone who does not know Jesus Christ.

17

A PEACEKEEPER OR A PEACEMAKER?

—⟋⟍—

The Christmas season blew through like a winter storm, and all the fun and sentimentally warm festivities were three weeks past. Winter had a hard time breaking through. However, by January it pounced upon the region locking the town, county and the whole state in its jaws. Any place untouched by warmth surrendered to the clutches of a bitter cold, just like at Grace Church.

It seemed that nobody was talking about it, but it was no longer a secret: Bernie was spearheading a movement in the church to oust Pastor Dan. He, Irma, Mr. Schrenk, Mr. Neuhman, Al and Katrina were among the cast who had gathered at one point or another to discuss their "problem." Though informants told him now and then, Dan resisted any action. Each Sunday, many of that alliance met Dan and his family with a cool reception. Others were bitterly cold. Dan's tact was to ignore them. Mona was taking it hard. Were it not for a warm majority the Lee family might have succumbed to spiritual hypothermia.

This effect upon the whole family is exemplified by John Gilmore:

Andre Bustanoby reflects the experience of many bashed and banished ministers. As a former pastor he wrote, 'Many years passed before Fay (Andre's wife) could attend church without dissolving in tears. Even today – some twenty years later – church is no an enriching experience for her...Not only can family members be wounded in battle, but they can carry scars for life. Having a spouse become bitter toward the church or a child reject the faith because of a church conflict is a price I'm no longer willing to pay.'[1]

The year-long training with the elders was over. The elders' interviews of the candidates went well. Three new men were now waiting in the wings to be elected to church office. Everyone on both sides of the conflict seemed hopeful. Bernie was just as sure the new men would side with him as Dan was sure they would not. Marcus and the others worked hard at being fair and remaining relatively neutral.

While Bernie's vocalized contempt for Dan seethed within the church, the town's mayor made clear that it was spreading throughout the community. Bernie was telling others that

Dan caused his son's marital breakup and encouraged his daughter-in-law to flee with the children. They never did find her. He was also angry at Dan for supposedly orchestrating the vote against his son Wes's elder nomination. Wes left the church and withdrew his membership within a month of that meeting. He was no longer involved in any church. Instead he had become a regular at a town bar.

Dan attempted to visit with Wes but was told to get lost. Wes threatened Dan physical harm if Dan persisted. Bernie made sure no church discipline took place against his son, and in fact said he could not blame his boy for wanting to leave the church given the pastor's supposed role in destroying his life.

Even though elder training was over, Dan still met regularly with the candidates, since they wanted it. Since late November they had been reading and discussing *The Peacemaker*. Dan had gone through the book a couple of years earlier and had encouraged Bill, the pastoral intern, to teach it in Sunday School before he left. As with many other teachings there was a definite disconnect between the teaching and the applying. Some scholars identify this disconnect as a societal phenomenon, and not merely a church thing. Because we live in the Age of Communication, we are constantly bombarded with too much information, much of it nonessential or irrelevant. We simply do not have the mental capacity to absorb it all. Therefore, we receive it passively with little call to action. That includes what is taught or preached at church.

Marcus was first to bring it up to Dan one night: "Dan, there are many good qualities about you and you are a fine pastor…" Dan could hear the "but" coming… "But you are not handling many of these conflicts well." And Marcus was only talking about the conflicts he observed firsthand. He was not privy to the on-going challenge with the elders or the depth of the conflict with Bernie. The two other men concurred.

Though it stung, Dan humbly received the rebuke. "I have confronted these people when they have said or done something against others or me." He even told them of the time he tried to engage Ms. Dumpleton at her store.

Pointing to the graph in *The Peacemaker* book, Marcus asked, "On the scale in Ken Sande's book, what would you say is your common response when you meet conflict?"

Regarding how people respond to conflict the choices ranged from the one extreme which is to fight, to the other extreme which is to flee. The men had quite a lively dialog about the common styles people use when dealing with conflict: avoid, accommodate, compromise, compete or collaborate.

"I'd have to think about it."

"Let me suggest something. Now I can be wrong, but this is what I've seen you do. You ready?" Marcus asked. He seemed to be a natural at reproving others with truth and gentleness.

"Go ahead, shoot," the pastor said reluctantly. He needed to hear it, but he was so worn down by the constant barrage of critiques and criticisms that he didn't want to add to his growing list of failures and deficits.

"I've observed that most of the time you don't confront people who should be confronted. Yet, when someone does something to offend you, you are pretty quick to respond. It's as if you are fighting back. I have also seen that you use restraint and a firm tact, which is good. But, Dan, the rest of the time you just avoid these people."

Dan bowed his head to think about it. It didn't take long to realize that Marcus was right. "You know, I think you are right, but can I take some time to reflect on what you just said?" Dan asked with a deep heaviness. He was beginning to feel sorry for himself again. This was indeed one more of Dan's failures. There were enough people at Grace who let Dan know that he did not do enough of the right things or he did not do things right. A few of those were like this issue, in which he didn't know whether he was wrong or what to do.

Dan ended the meeting abruptly, and asked the men if they would call it a night. He wanted to escape to his office for a private breakdown. *You are a failure, nothing but a failure!* Dan kept playing over and over in his head. From childhood it was a mantra etched deeply into his mental hard drive. It kept rearing its ugly head no matter where Dan went. *Lord, show me what I need to know and do.*

Dan prepped the house for the cold winter's night, showered, then slid between chilly, gold colored, silky sheets. With his head resting on two pillows, he picked up one of the four books he was reading which were stacked on his nightstand. Providentially, the book waiting for Dan was John Frye's *Jesus the Pastor*. He opened it where he had left off. Almost immediately his eyes reached this paragraph:

'Avoid conflict' was my middle name. I was the pastorally 'nice guy' who swept through the church like the old vaudevillian crying, 'Is evvvverrrrybody haaaap-PY?' I thought I was a real peacemaker. What I really was, however, was a pain-avoider. While pain-avoiders may look like peacemakers, there is a world of difference between the two.[2]

The other book he had just finished for a second time was *The Subtle Power of Spiritual Abuse*. With regard to the way some deal with conflict, the authors say:

They are more of a 'truce-maker.' A truce is an agreement to cease fighting between people who are still at odds and who have yet to work out their differences. What the truce-maker wants to avoid, again, is any appearance that there is conflict in the system, or, in a spiritual system, that the leaders have anything wrong with them that might cause others to be in conflict with them...A true peacemaker, as noted in Matthew 5, is someone who goes where there is not peace and makes peace. It is not someone who covers over disagreement with a cloak of false peace. It is not someone who gets people who are in total disagreement to act as if they are on the same side. For real peace to happen, not just a cease-fire, there will be a change of heart.[3]

Yes, I am a pain avoider. Yes, I have been a truce-maker. Yes, I am concerned about pleasing people. God, I admit those are sins I struggle with all the time! He put the book down on his lap, rested his head back into the pillows, and sulked. Dan was emotionally spent and physically drained. He kept holding out hope that things would get better, that the ministry would improve and become more of a delight than a discouraging and disappointing burden. He was tired of the analyzing that took place in the church and in his mind. It was relentless. It seemed like people were always underscoring other's faults, mistakes, and sins. Sure, we need to have our sins exposed so that we can put them off and put on Christ (Eph. 4:24; Col. 3:10). Yet Dan wondered if the emphasis on faults, mistakes and sins wasn't equally wrong. Nobody in this place gets a break from being critiqued and analyzed, especially the pastor!

Daniel wasn't trying to skirt around a shortcoming Marcus pointed out. Marcus had done a fine job of bringing the matter to Dan's attention. It was that Dan wanted people to express appreciation for him, to give an accolade once in a while, to affirm he was on the right track or doing the right thing from time to time. He received that from his wife, from Melissa and Matt and a few others. At the same time, he had read and was told that true leaders don't need encouragement, accolades or affirmations. *Okay! So I'm an insecure wimp and a failure at leadership too! Now what?* The last time Dan looked at his clock it was 1:49 A.M. Exhaustion dragged him into sleep – with the light on.

Noises startled him awake. Mona was breathing heavily, unfazed by the commotion. There it was again! Dan got up and checked on the children. Little Hannah was snoring in her crib. Jake was motionless. Benny, as active in his sleep as awake, tossed and turned. More noises. Obviously coming from downstairs.

Dan had no substantial weapon to grab. The bat and golf clubs were in the basement. But he had to check it out. He tried to sneak down the stairs, but the old oak boards wouldn't allow it. The noise stopped when his step creaked. It started again when he stopped. He finally managed to get to the bottom and shuffle his feet toward the noise. It was coming from the kitchen. He flipped on the lights, but nobody was around. As he turned around the corner the dog barked at him; startled, Dan fell backward onto his tailbone. "Aaahhh! Owww!" he yelled out. "Dog! What are you doing here?"

Normally, during cold nights they kept the dog confined to the kitchen's entryway. Somehow had escaped and discovered the trash can under the sink. This furry member of the household disturbed the peace while making a mess of things. Its owner scolded him, put him in his kennel, and cleaned up the mess. After restoring peace and order he returned back to bed.

Surprisingly, none of the commotion disturbed the rest of the family. Because of that short adrenaline rush, Dan was wide awake. He checked his emails: all annoying junk and spam. Mostly Viagra ads. Back upstairs he slipped gently into bed, careful to keep from disturbing Mona, but mostly to pamper his painful back.

His mind picked up where he had left off. The problem is the emotional and spiritual environment of this church. We're not a grace church! We should name our church, the Perfect and Lawful Church of the Righteous! His military brother pointed out the large dose of legalists and perfectionists at Grace. He had visited many times to make that appraisal. Birds of a feather and all that. Who was Big Bird? Bernie, with Irma in a close second. It was a spiritual atmosphere established from the beginning, by a small cluster of people who wanted to form a church of holy and doctrinally sound people. Though well intentioned, it attracted self-righteous, analytical and hyper-critical individuals. His friend and professor Dominic reminded Dan about the social dynamics of an established tradition. It is very hard to break. Most people entering into an established culture end up becoming a part of it and adopting its well established traditions. Those who don't, usually leave.

In life, law is easier to deal with than grace. For one, we are a species bent on doing good works based upon our own set norms. For another, law gives us some standard by which to measure people, usually others. Dan and his family, and many of those whom he was attracting did not fit the spiritual paradigm of Bernie and his flock. Frankly Dan and his family did not share that same story with the well-established culture of Grace Church. His brother said the environment was unhealthy. Kent agreed. His Montana friend said he needed to change it, but change was ever so slow, strongly resisted, and it was exacting a heavy price on Dan, his family and the state of the church. Besides, he was stuck.

He remembered London and Wiseman's wise insight:

> People can sincerely seek healing for brokenness, however, they'll never find it if the Christian community around them isn't committed to healing. And that's one of the tragedies occurring in places where men and women have failed – the Christian community doesn't have the will to offer healthy healing.
>
> Only when the Church commits itself to restorative ministry will men and women stop acting in self-righteousness and, with the tenderness of Galatians 6:1, start being committed to getting every broken player back on the field again to serve the Kingdom.[4]

For the next hour Dan was involved in mental gymnastics doing what he was sick of doing - analyzing. He reminded himself that what he was going through was common to leaders, even in Christ's church. Moses went through it as did practically all biblical leaders. Read what M. Craig Barnes wrote an article for *Leadership Journal*:

When the Hebrews left Egypt to begin their difficult journey through the desert to the Promised Land, they brought the 'rabble' with them. They were not true believers in this journey or in the God who called them to it. The rabble's toleration for discomfort was low and their capacity for complaint was high, always an unfortunate combination.[5]

I certainly can identify with Moses on that score. But still, I'm stuck. What do I do about the rabble? Dan read further:

All the pastors I know would love to get rid of the rabble in their church. The dopey thing is that the rabble keeps threatening to leave if we don't service their needs… There is a holy purpose for the rabble. Their complaining places the pastor in the awkward position of standing between the people and the God they cannot see. The grace of that awkwardness is that it forces the pastor to pray, looking for the One who is present but not apparent.

Through most of the wilderness journey, Moses was a model of patient leadership. When the people complained about their thirst, he found water. When they complained about the lack of food, he pointed to manna. When they complained that he was gone too long on Sinai and turned to the idol of a golden calf, Moses interceded and talked God out of consuming them.

Later the people complained about their 'misfortunes.' This time God torched a few of them and would have burned up the whole camp if Moses hadn't interceded again. Immediately afterward the rabble got everyone complaining about how sick and tired they were of manna. They wanted meat! It was then that Moses finally snapped: 'Why have you treated your servant so badly, that you lay the burden of this people on me? Am I their mother? Where am I supposed to find meat for all these people? I am not able to carry this people. If you care about me at all, just kill me and get it over with' (Num. 11:11-15).[6]

This is where Dan was mentally and emotionally. He was ready to snap. That was no answer. How did Jesus deal with this issue? However, even Jesus dealt wisely and lovingly with rabble. "I remind my staff all the time that once we view certain sheep in an adversarial way, our ministry is over. That's the uniqueness of the Chief Shepherd. He loved even Judas, whom He knew would eventually betray Him. That is a mark of a true shepherd."[7]

Leighton Ford gives some insight here:

It has been said that some people are so full of grace they have no room for truth, and that others are so full of truth they have no room for grace; but Jesus was 'full of grace and truth' (Jn 1:14). He faced the various dimensions of conflict he encountered with a wonderfully creative combination of grace and truth, deciding when to increase the pressure and to probe, and when not to. As people were moved to decide about Jesus and His kingdom, the polarization increased. Some followed Him and some fought Him and some tried to ignore Him.

So the conflict deepened; and as it did, Jesus administered grace and truth in various degrees of strength and intensity, as He knew the situation called for. With the devil, from the beginning there was truth but no grace, no possibility of reconciliation.

Those of the Pharisees who responded to His message Jesus welcomed and warmly commended, like the teacher of who He said, 'You are not far from the Kingdom of God' (Mk. 12:34). But from those Pharisees who became hard and bitterly hostile He eventually withdrew, as they resisted both grace and truth. As his disciples committed themselves and grew, he gave them both more truth and more grace – not in ways that they enjoyed, but in ways that enhanced their stature.[8]

Dan knew well the stories of famous pastors. Luther, Calvin, Knox, Wesley, Whitefield, Edwards and Spurgeon all had conflicts with people in and out of the church. Larry J. Michael, reflecting upon Spurgeon's life and ministry wrote:

Any leader who if faithful to his calling sooner or later will find himself embroiled in conflict or controversy. Contrary to idealistic notions about leadership, even in the Christian context, leaders often discover resistance and reaction that they never anticipated when they accepted God's call.[9]

So I'm not alone. How do I deal with this wisely, righteously and how do I love these people the way Christ does? He flipped through *The Peacemaking Pastor* and made a promise to himself to read it again. It was 5:03 A.M. by the time the pastor dropped into slumber.

At the church office the pastor was drenched in administrative duties. It wasn't until late afternoon when Dan got back to work on the Sunday evening sermon. He was preaching through a topical series on the nature of the church. There were two sermons left. Both would address church conflict. This Sunday evening's message was "How to Kill a Local Church" taken from Romans 16:17-20 and Revelation 1-3. From the Bible and his research he would point out that all conflict is ultimately a spiritual matter. The root cause is the broken relationship we all have with God. This dates back to the sin of Adam in Eden's garden. Adam and Eve sought to do without God in all respects. They wanted autonomy from God but also equality with God. They wanted to interpret their world without reference to him and establish a world based upon their own image. This is a keynote feature of perfectionism, the counterfeit to biblical perfection.

Adam and Eve, at the same time, wanted to blame God's environment or their circumstances or other people. Adam blamed his wife for his sin, Eve blamed the serpent, and so forth. All of these conflicted dynamics are caused by sin; all are caused by breaking God's perfect standards and falling short of God's glory (Jer. 17:9; Isa. 53:6; Rom. 3:23; 6:23).

Conflict was immediately displayed in Cain's treatment of his brother Abel. We learn from the Bible that Cain's real problem was his resentment toward God, so he took it out on his brother. In his seminary class, Dr. Robert D. Stuart expressed a simple but poignant biblical truth - the source of interpersonal conflicts is conflict with God. When people are angry at God for whatever the reason, they express that anger toward others. Conflict is also due to a violation of the very command by God to love our neighbors as ourselves.[10]

Disagreements do not necessarily have to descend into serious conflicts. Paul and Barnabas disagreed about John-Mark's usefulness in ministry. The Apostles disagreed on important doctrinal matters in Acts 15. Paul had a severe, but important, disagreement with Peter, and Paul urged Euodia and Syntyche to come to an agreement in the Lord (Phil. 4:2-9). Therefore, not all conflict is evil. It provides opportunities to glorify God, to grow in Christ or to serve others. Unresolved conflict is so often more an issue of attitude toward one another than it is about the original problem itself.

From his seminary notes on the seven churches in Revelation chapters 1-3.[11] Pastor understood that unresolved matters between a local church and God were often manifested through church life. In five of the seven churches God identifies profound insights into ways a church can destroy its ministry or its life. For example, from Ephesus we learn that a lack of biblical truth, or a failure to guard orthodoxy, or a distortion of Christ's truth can kill a church. But guarding truth without love will also do the same. The church of Pergamum teaches us that a lack of holiness can destroy a church, while from Thyatira we learn that an unwillingness to address sin or to discipline those who need it can kill a church. So can a lack of faithfulness to the person and message of Christ, or a lack of unity centered upon Christ in truth and love.

The last church, Laodicea, teaches us that you can kill a church when you exclude Christ. When Jesus is not allowed to enter and commune with the local church it will die. When a church is characteristically anthropocentric or man-centered as opposed to being Christocentric it will die spiritually. This church was self-deceived like a number of the others. They believed they had a great thing going. They were rich, self-sufficient and apparently had a healing ministry. They were man-centered, and they excluded Christ from the heart of the church.

The church in Corinth was man-centered and acted fleshly, like non-believers. Richard Ganz in his book[12] describes and defines the twenty different man-centered conflicts that nearly killed that church.

The Holy Spirit speaks to the Church through many passages about sinful conflict. James 4:1-3 narrows it down and succinctly states:

Where do wars and fights come from among you? Do they not come from your desires for pleasure that war in your members? You lust and do not have. You murder and covet and cannot obtain. You fight and war. Yet you do not have because you do not ask. You ask and do not receive, because you ask amiss, that you may spend it on your pleasures.

What are these desires but idols of our hearts? When we put ourselves, our interests, our desires, our longings and expectations in place of God we go to battle. When anything stands in the way of our self-erected idols, it will suffer the brunt of our proud wrath, revealed through anger, frustration, depression, bitterness, fighting or fleeing. When we interpret our lives and local church with little reference to the Lord and try to establish our lives and local church based upon our own image, we guarantee sinful strife. Dan was given the grace of humility and saw that while his desires for a biblical church were reasonable and based upon Scripture, he had idols in his heart which were constantly being offended. What idols? Pride, the desire to be liked, admired and appreciated, the desire to be right all the time, things like that.

Because the pastor had to go to the big city for a presbytery committee meeting, he put aside his study, grabbed some old cassettes, and hopped into the car. The tape was from a series by John Maxwell on the subject of conflict in the church. In these tapes Maxwell identified several cycles of conflict.[13] At each stage there are ways to address the conflict, but if things are not addressed appropriately and the conflict continues, it develops into the next stage which makes it all the more difficult to resolve the problem or to reconcile. The first cycle is when a problem is identified and needs to be fixed. That may fold into the second cycle which is the repositioning stage. Here people ask, "Who caused the problem?" Here people tend to generalize things and focus their attention upon protecting their interests rather than upon solving the problem. The level of trust drops and communication between the parties becomes cautious and unclear.

The third stage is the "rights stage" where people assume they are right and others are wrong. At this stage people take sides and then label the others. The focus now shifts upon winning the battle. The problem tends to be overstated or distorted. If resolution does not happen at this point then the fourth stage rolls in. This is the removal stage where the intention of both parties is to get rid of the other people. Reconciliation is not the objective; indeed it is now out of the question. The two camps are clearly identified and there is a leader for each side.

The final stage is the revenge stage where it is believed that someone must pay. Even if there is a "winner" the one or the other or both parties are not happy with the results. They become fanatics, believing it is wrong to stop the fighting. Revenge is sought after.

It seemed to Pastor as he was speeding down the highway negotiating the traffic that Grace Church was at stage four. It also occurred to Dan that when he and his family entered the church a few years back that he stepped into a stage three scenario at the church. Dan was stepping into the shoes of a previous pastor or other pastors with whom Bernie, Irma and others had conflict. Same song and dance, different partner. From a stage three, within months Dan was propelled toward level four – the removal stage.

The committee meeting lasted a couple of hours. It was doubtful Daniel would be able to get home in time for supper, so he suggested some of them go out to eat. Dan learned that these particular men were more interested in talking philosophy or theology than about personal or pastoral matters. He wished he could develop a close friendship with someone, but he would be disappointed.

The slick roads and snow flurries slowed his drive home. He listened to a second tape by Maxwell.[14] The speaker outlined five types of problem people he frequently observed in his own church.

The first kind is divisive people. They are avaricious, whose hearts are always in turmoil; discontent, greedy, and at war because of it (James 4:1-3). They are also angry or bitter people because they aren't getting what they want. Divisive people are arrogant rarely accepting authority over them and therefore undermining authority. They are also attackers, who through various ploys such as gossip and slander are always attacking others, principally those who stand in their way. The Bible is clear about these kinds of people, and this struck Dan like lightning between the eyes: the church is to reject a divisive person after the first or second attempts to reconcile or admonish him. Why? Because he is a warped sinner who is self-condemned (Tit. 3:10-11). Such people are to be marked and avoided (Rom. 16:17, 18).

Dan turned off the cassette for a while to sponge in the lesson and scriptural admonitions. It was then that Dan decided Bernie and his sinful antics must be dealt with firmly and if necessary, severely. Irma also.

After reflecting about the divisive people in his church, he heard about Maxwell's second kind of problem people - the hurting or wounded people. "Hurting people hurt people," Maxwell said. In fact, Sandra D. Wilson wrote a book about the topic, entitled *Hurt People Hurt People*. These hurting, sensitive people often believe they are above being offended or hurt. Katrina fell into this category. Dan had taught on a number of occasions there are biblical ways to dealing with being offended. It's so easy to do in our culture, but even more so in churches that work hard at being perfect and righteous. Taking offense is legitimate when a sin has truly been committed. Sin is identified by the pure and perfect standard of God's Law, not based on personal preferences or desires. However, taking offense is illegitimate when no obvious sin has been committed. The Proverbs tell us that sometimes the wounds of a friend are good. Hurting or wounded people may exact revenge for being hurt by gossiping or slandering; though there are other ways too.

A third kind of people is the insecure. Pride in the heart demands an environment of stability and security. Often this is the trouble with perfectionists. These folks want the status quo more than anything. They fear the future and hate change. The more insecure they are the harder they will fight against change. Dan thought back on the family at the previous church who did not agree with his preaching. They seemed to be terribly insecure. Perhaps that explains why they asked "What did they want? or Why are they here?" when new visitors came.

The fourth is the power person, whose pride reveals itself in a lust for control and authority. Maxwell says that these people have the bully syndrome. Dan thought of them as the well-intended dragons spoken of in Shelley Marshall's book.[15] These "dragons" elevate their principles to the level of Scripture, and thereby measure others or the church against their principles.

The final character is the single-issue person who believes his or her special issue is more important than all other issues. Like the power person, this person will elevate tertiary issues to high priority status on par with the Bible. Dan thought of the church in Oregon who elevated their methodologies based upon a family-centered church to the level of God's Word. Some in that church considered any family or church that did not agree with or practice their philosophy as inferior, impure or even unChristian.

The next day the pastor sat shivering in his tepid office. He was coming down with a cold. Nevertheless, he determined to finish studying for the Sunday evening service. He would have to pamper his body later on.

Dan couldn't escape how easily his notes worked into several points. The sermon title was often difficult. This is where he wished he lived in the days of the Puritans when the pastor did not have to be clever or try and grab people's attention with sermon titles. He could be matter of fact and label it, "The Scriptural Reasons and Causes for Conflict in the Church of the Lord Jesus Christ, Exposed and Enumerated in Four Major Points with Accompanying Relevant Subpoints." Some at Grace even told him to quit coming up with clever titles and just label it plainly and clearly like the good old days. Boring. He liked "Killing us Softly with Conflict" but how many in his church would appreciate the reference to an old Roberta Flack song? The title would have to wait.

He had his points with classic alliteration: Causes of Conflict, Cycles of Conflict, Colors of Conflict and now, Contrivances for Conflict. These are the obvious ways in which conflict is displayed: First is defiance or rebellion against authority. Second is gossip – revealing or discussing personal facts about another person for no legitimate purpose. Gossip often betrays a confidence and injures a person's reputation. It is a means for revenge (Pro. 11:13; 16:28; 20: 19; 26:20; 2 Cor. 12:20; 1 Tim. 5:13).

Third is slander, which is speaking malicious words about another that also injures their reputation or damages their integrity. Slander often uses the truth to accomplish its objective. We are called upon to cease from slander but also to have nothing to do with slanderers who refuse to repent (2 Tim. 3:3).

A fourth contrivance, Dan wrote down, was grumbling and complaining (Phil 2:14; Jas. 5:9). It is falsehood (Pro. 24:28; 2 Cor. 4:2) that incites and aggravates conflict, from outright lies to misrepresentation to deceit. The other side of this wicked coin is worthless talk, which is clearly to be avoided by believers (Eph. 4:29 cp. 2 Tim. 2:16). This kind of speech is non-beneficial, put-down talk or abusive language. It could be backbiting, which is talking about another without giving that person the opportunity to defend himself, or rumors and hearsay used to diminish another's reputation.

The fifth way is presumption whereby people judge the motives of others without having hard behavioral facts or their personal admission (Jas. 4:11-12).

This is brought out by D. A. Carson:

The ways of destroying the church are many and colorful. Raw factionalism will do it. Rank heresy will do it. Taking your eyes off the cross and letting other, more peripheral matters dominate the agenda will do it – admittedly more slowly than frank heresy, but just as effectively on the long haul. Building the church with superficial 'conversions' and wonderful programs that rarely bring people into a deepening knowledge of the living God will do it. Entertaining people to death but never fostering the beauty of holiness or the centrality of self-crucifying love will build an assembly of religious people, but it will destroy the church of the living God. Gossip, prayerlessness, bitterness, sustained biblical illiteracy, self-promotion, materialism – all of these things, and many more, can destroy a church. And to do so is dangerous: 'If anyone destroys God's temple, God will destroy him; for God's temple is sacred, and you are that temple' (1 Cor. 3:17). It is a fearful thing to fall into the hands of the living God.[16]

He finished studying for his sermon. Using a variety of resources he put together checklist for his people to evaluate whether their speech was loving, truthful and godly or uncaring, false and ungodly (see Appendix P).

The cell phone chirped. It got snagged on some pocket thread, so he couldn't answer it in time. The caller ID revealed it was from Dan. Kent punched a key and the phone dialed his younger friend back. "Dan, you called? How are you? It's afternoon for you; things okay?"

Daniel updated his mentor. More than advice, he wanted to interact with wisdom. Kent had his fair share of Bernies, Irmas, Katrinas and other belligerents, but not all at once or in the same church. "I'm glad you're going through *The Peacemaker*," Kent affirmed. "You might want to go through the whole program they have for the church. Have you also read Poirier's *The Peacemaking Pastor?*"

"I have. I've been going through it again. People like Bernie and Irma are tough to deal with."

"True, but you still have to treat them rightly. Dan, what is your role in all this?"

"I'm a pastor."

"Yes, but I mean what other role do you play in this situation?"

"The role of peacemaker."

"Right. Pastors are responsible to actively take on the role of peacemaker. Here's a question for you: are you really being a peacemaker, or are you merely a peacekeeper?"

"What's the difference?"

"Are you just trying to keep the peace or are you taking the initiative and actively making peace in the way the Lord instructed? You are called to radical repentance of sin and a genuine commitment to living by faith in Christ. You are also called to building, fostering and guarding an environment of grace, mercy and peace."

"Maybe that is what Marcus was trying to say the other night?"

"Which was what?

"He told me that I wasn't handling the conflicts well. He said that when people offend me sometimes it seems that I fight back, but at other times I just avoid them."

"Maybe so."

"What do you suggest?" Pastor asked his older friend.

"That you systematically go to Irma, Katrina, and other members in the church and call them to repent of their sin and exercise faith in Christ. Then go to any deacons you need to; then go to Bernie. Follow the steps: check your own heart first, then go in person. If you are unsuccessful and they do not show a willingness to change, go back with another person or two, and so forth. You know what Matthew 18 says."

Dan took a deep breath and then thanked his mentor.

As soon as he hung up the phone with Kent Dan looked for Irma's phone number. He touched the numbers on his black phone and took another deep breath. No answer at her house. He tried again at her store.

"Dumpleton's Hardware," responded a hoarse voice, most likely raw from chronic cigarette smoke.

"Ms. Dumpleton?"

"No. This is Rose."

"Is Ms. Dumpleton there?"

"Who wants to know?" she said abruptly.

"This is Pastor Lee from Grace Church."

"Please wait." The phone turned to an airy silence.

"Yes, what do you want?" Irma answered.

"Hello Irma. How are you today?"

"I don't have time for chit chat. Get right to the point," she ordered.

"Very well. I need to meet with you. The sooner the better. I suggest for lunch at a restaurant of your choice. Next Tuesday good for you or Thursday better?"

"What about?"

"It's time you and I have a good, honest heart to heart talk and resolve this on-going conflict we have between us."

"I don't have time for this. I'm a very busy woman."

"Irma, this is a very important matter. You aren't afraid of our meeting are you?"

"Certainly not! What do you take me for? Thursday it is. Noon. Where?" she barked.

"I like Mo's Café," he said. Dan strongly suspected and hoped she would reject that idea, because he really did not want to taint his good sentiment toward his favorite eatery.

"The place is a dump. We'll meet at the restaurant inside of Hodge's Inn."

"Is that an order or a suggestion?" Dan came back.

"Would that be a good place?" she tried again.

"Acceptable. See you there at noon sharp, on Thursday. Thank you."

As was her habit she hung up abruptly.

Peacemaking it is. This is going to be torture. Maybe this will bring things to a head? Ah, well, what do I have to lose? New Mexico is a strong probability.

A CHALLENGE TO THINK AND DO

What do you think?
1. Was Bernie wrong for holding meetings to discuss Pastor Dan as "the problem."? Why or why not?
2. According to Kent, what is the difference between a peacekeeper and a peacemaker? Which one are you?
3. What does it mean to love your enemies like Jesus Christ?
4. In a time when being offended is a national or cultural sin, what is the difference between taking offense and legitimately being offended? What is the Biblical way to handle either taking offense or being offended?

Some things you could do:
1. Read Ken Sande's book, *The Peacemaker* or encourage your church to go through Peacemaker Ministries' *The Peacemaking Church* course (go to http://www.peacemaker.net).
2. Read Sandra D. Wilson's *Hurt People Hurt People*.
3. Use Appendix P to evaluate your speech habits.

18

TROUBLES AND DRAGONS

—◦◦◦—

The Saturday night was unusually frigid and brisk but thankfully it was not snowing. Consequently, there was a strong turnout to the congregational meeting. Bernie and his cohort occupied the middle left seats. Unlike the previous year's meeting, the event was without conflict. Joe and Bernie gave speeches. Bernie's was long and rambling. Dan gave a short and positive endorsement for the three candidates. They were successfully voted in by a large margin. A special ordination and installation service was set, and the fellowship committee set a date to plan out the celebration afterward.

Ironically, when Dan got home, an email from the chair of the pastoral search committee from the New Mexico church. They wanted him to fly there as soon as he could for a personal interview. Dan replied that he would try to do so in two weekends. Dan was conflicted. With the new elders and Dan's resolve to actively pursue biblical peace things hinted at hope. At the same time he was tired of the slow progress, the relentless assaults, and the perpetual conflict, so a change of venue looked more hopeful.

Twenty minutes before noon on Thursday, Dan arrived at Hodge's Inn to meet Ms. Dumpleton. He asked for a table that would allow for private conversation, but wasn't secluded. Having a meeting in a neutral place allowed both parties a level of security. Ms. Dumpleton arrived on time. The hostess showed her to her seat.

Dan stood to greet her. Ms. Dumpleton was short and stout. Her silver hair was firmly set in an elegant style. The makeup was applied with finesse and precision. Irma was too regal for someone who owned a hardware business. Everything about her portrayed class. She was the town's upscale woman, in the society of the elite. She was a big fish in a tiny pond. Her wealth would place her on the upper end of the middle class rung if she were to move to the city an hour away. But she'd be a regular folk in a place like New York or San Francisco. Here she was completely immersed in the world she made – a world where she was queen. Irma acknowledged Dan but did not offer her hand in greeting.

The waiter promptly attended to his celebrity clientele. Dan understood why she picked this place; she trained them well. They knew how to treat her like royalty. It amused the pastor to see how frightened everyone seemed to be of her. She enjoyed every moment of it too. Dan's kindness perplexed the waiter. In fact, he acted nothing like her usual luncheon partners who were either well-to-do politicians, contractors and architects or rough and tumble sub-contractors and supervisors. "I'll have my usual," she ordered. "He'll have a sirloin steak also. How would you like it?" she questioned Dan.

"No, I'll have your special steak burger, cooked medium well. Your special fries look good too. Caesar salad. And coffee. That should do it. Thank you," Dan told his waiter, while smiling and handing back the menu. He was not about to be controlled. The waiter smiled back with a glimmer of understanding.

"What is the purpose of this meeting?" Irma charged right in.

"We need to do the biblical thing and come to some reconciliation, Irma. Our relationship is wrong and unhealthy. In fact it is downright displeasing to the Lord. Are you committed to doing the biblical thing?"

"Depends on what it is," she said unfolding her rose colored napkin.

Dan was astonished. He studied her eyes. What kind of believer would not want to do God's will? James and John are clear that true believers will do what the Lord commands, even if they don't want to. Is this a clue? "What do you mean that it depends on what it is?" Dan asked forcefully.

"Just that. I think you are wasting your time here, Mr. Lee," she announced.

"Are you not interested in getting to the heart of our conflicted relationship and trying to reconcile?"

"Mr. Lee, why on earth would I want to do that? You don't get it, do you? I don't like you, neither does my brother. Neither do most others at church. The best way for us to reconcile is for you to leave."

Dan laughed. "Why don't you tell me how you really feel, Irma?" Now that she honestly expressed her contempt for Dan, it was much easier to speak directly to her.

"No, as Christians we have a duty to reconcile because of the work of reconciliation Jesus accomplished. We are to forgive because Christ has forgiven us. It is not an option for believers in Christ." He studied her. She seemed stoic, but occasionally waved to various businessmen and women who were coming and going.

"Oh, I've heard all that before. But it's not in me to forgive. I'm too old to change now."

"That's too bad, Irma, because one of the reasons why I wanted this meeting is that the Lord had placed it upon my heart that I've not been a loving pastor to you. And I want to ask your forgiveness…"

"I just told you that I'm not a forgiving person, Daniel."

H. B. London and Neil B. Wiseman tell us that:

278

Forgiveness stands at the center of the Christian faith. The gospels could easily be subtitled: God's Instructions for Giving and Receiving Forgiveness. No one has ever demonstrated forgiveness with greater consistency than our Lord. He expects no less from us.

Forgiveness shows up frequently in the Scriptures. God emphasizes forgiveness over and over again in His message to us. If we could only learn to forgive wholeheartedly, as did Christ, we would eliminate many of the frustrating issues in our lives together as human beings. Amazingly, Jesus ties the giving and receiving of forgiveness together – He tells us that no one can receive forgiveness who does not give it.[1]

Dan began to ask what it was about him that she hated. Then it dawned on him that the issue was irrelevant. She had a track record, just like Bernie, of controlling pastors or chewing them up and spitting them out. All of a sudden, he had an impulse and blurted out a deeper question. "Irma, are you even a Christian?"

Her face snapped into place, looking straight at Dan with chin up and head forward, "You impertinent fool! What do you take me for? How dare you talk to me like this!" Her elevated tone aroused the interest of most of the other patrons. Now she was as embarrassed as she was furious.

"It's a fair question. You are a member in our church. I am the pastor. It's my job. You want me to do my job, don't you? Are you a Christian?"

"I practically grew up in this church. I bought the property, built the building. I've contributed more money to that church than you will ever earn in your lifetime. My parents were good Christian folk. How can you sit there and ask me that?"

"Because your eternal destiny is at stake. You aren't a young woman. If God grants you ten more years, it'll be a wonder. I ask that because your demonstrable behavior contradicts a true life in Jesus Christ." She was squirming. Only her father and brother ever talked so boldly to her.

"I'll have you know I've been a member of that church longer than you've been alive. If they didn't think I was a Christian, how would I have become a member?"

"How and why the pastor and elders did things the way they did back then is beyond my understanding. You still haven't given an answer that indicates a saving faith in Jesus Christ. So I'll ask you this: if you were to die tonight and you were to stand at the gate of heaven, and if Saint Peter was to ask you what right you have to enter heaven, what would you say?"

"I don't have time for this nonsense."

"You don't have time to discuss the most important thing about your life? You could leave this place in a few minutes, easily slip on the ice outside and die of a brain injury. You do have time to talk about the most important thing in your life!" Dan said with pleading eyes.

Two waiters helped deliver the food. Without asking permission Dan thanked God for the food, asked him to bless it and to give Irma new life in Christ. "So? What would you say?"

She attacked her steak vigorously. Her eyes darted up and down from plate to pastor. "I've been a good person. Look at all the things I've done. Look at all I've done for the church."

Dan knew then that she was not trusting in Jesus Christ alone for her life and salvation. She trusted in her own goodness and works. Dan set his steak burger down, wiped his mouth, took a sip of coffee and proceeded to explain that anyone who trusts in his or her own works was sadly lost, but the good news is found in the mercy and grace of Jesus Christ. Irma stopped eating. Instead she finished off her wine and scooted her chair away from the table. Her composure was a mix of fear and anger.

"Irma, you are a self-made and successful woman. But that does not cut it with God. You can't earn or buy your way into a right relationship with a righteous and just God," Dan tried to explain.

She continued to stew. She was getting hotter as her meal was getting colder. "I'm a good person! Anyone can see that!"

"Irma, based on what standard? Money? Looks? Influence? Not based on God's standard. Nobody measures up to that. That is why Jesus was sent, to do the good works and fulfill the law for us. Then to die upon the cross to pay the price we are indebted to pay for our hostility and rebellion against God."

"Don't preach at me. I've heard you say that enough times in church! Everyone knows I'm good."

"Look at you! You are a bitter, manipulative, controlling, cranky old woman. People are scared to death of you. They tell you what you want them to say. Believers in Christ transformed by his supernatural work put off those attitudes and behaviors. Instead they put on Christ and live lives of forgiveness, kindness, gentleness, love, peace, and forbearance." Just then Dan thought to ask another question. "Irma, who hurt you so badly?"

Irma got up abruptly. "I will not take any more of your rude and abusive language young man!" she nearly shouted. It was obvious she was trying to embarrass Dan and solicit sympathy from the audience.

A waiter rushed over to her. "Is everything okay, Ms. Dumpleton? Can we help you?"

"You can see this man to the door!" she exclaimed.

"Oh, I'm not ready yet, Irma. I'll leave when I'm finished with my meal, thank you."

She swirled around and demanded her coat. She called for the manager who was nearby. Irma told him that Dan was never to be served in the restaurant again or else she would take all her business elsewhere; better yet, she would buy out the place and fire everyone who did not comply with her demands.

Dan sat there shaking his head.

"Shall I put this meal on her tab?" the waiter asked timidly.

"No, thanks, Jack," he replied, looking at the young man's nameplate. "I'll pay for it. You've waited on her before I take it?"

"Yes, sir."

"Ever get so riled?"

"Not like this, sir."

"I apologize for the scene."

"Not a problem, sir. I'm used to it," Jack said half smiling.

"Call me Dan. I'm Irma's pastor at Grace Church."

"You are?" Jack replied with pronounced astonishment. "Wow!"

Guy Greenfield was right on target when he commented:

I suggested to one antagonist during my last week as his pastor that he seek psycho-therapy. He was furious at my suggestion. He would do anything to avoid the pain of self-examination. Evil persons hate the light of goodness that reveals their true nature, the light of scrutiny that would expose their sins, and the light of truth that would expose their deceptiveness.[2]

Pastor watched Irma walk with a slow and careful deliberation over to her car. She probably would have screeched out of the parking lot were it not for the black ice on the road. Dan finished his large meal. What he suspected was rather obvious – the woman was not a Christian.

At home he told Mona what happened. She was dumbfounded. He then called Kent.

"Sounds like a great luncheon," Kent said sarcastically.

"I had a perfectly wonderful luncheon, but that wasn't it," Dan replied quoting comedian Groucho Marx.

"You've said you doubted she was a Christian. Sounds like she just confirmed your suspicions," Kent stated.

"Yes. Sad."

"You ready for the fall out? You know Bernie will launch an all out frontal assault against you. You've definitely crossed the line."

"I'm as ready as ever. Today's experience did surprise me."

"How's that?"

"I wasn't fearful of her. Perhaps the Spirit gave me boldness to confront her? For once I experienced power, love and a sound mind."

Dan spent some time alone on a strategy for making peace at Grace. He did the right thing by asking Irma to forgive him. Ken Sande reminds us that the first step in biblical reconciliation is to get the log out of our own eye first (Matt. 7:5). That means being willing to confess personal sins against others because when you ask another to forgive you it is asking them to pardon you for specific sins. Dan did not have the opportunity open to him to express the ways in which he was unloving to Irma.

People like Irma and Bernie are a cancer in Christ's church. There is an applicable insight from *Pastoral Politics*:

> When people substitute selfish motivation and church participation to affect their own salvation, negative repercussions will ensue, and the pastor's presence and presentation will be opposed. Rather than heeding a pastor's words of warning – rather than embracing a pastor's message, it is much easier to devise means to bring an end to his or her witness. Killing the pastor is an option that surely has been considered, but thank God that option is rarely used. Expulsion of the pastor, however, is the accepted method of choice for most disgruntled church members, although it is not always the course of action that is immediately taken. It is sometimes preferable (and fashionable) to immediately bring pressure on the pastor's personal style of ministry so that the gospel message and witness is so whittled down that offense is removed. If pastors don't watch, congregations may mold them any which way.[3]

On Sunday the church had a special service to ordain and install the new elders. All went well. Bernie kept his mouth closed and his distance wide from Dan. He at least had the courtesy to leave the conflict out of the service. The afternoon was filled with a pot luck celebration with lots of cake and decorations.

Sunday night Dan stepped into the pulpit a bit more somber than usual. It was the normal Sunday evening crowd, about a third of the Sunday morning attendance. Bernie and his wife were present, which was normal. Mr. Shrenk and Mr. Neuhman were there also. Al and Katrina attended, though their evening attendance was sporadic.

The message was from Matthew 6:1-15, titled "The Forgiven and the Forgiving." Dan began the message with, "I have a confession to make." That got everyone's attention. "I recognize and now admit that I have failed some of you as a pastor. I have not loved you as I ought. It is my plan to systematically approach those of you I know I have offended and ask each of you for forgiveness."

A soft murmur rippled in the worship hall. Dan then stated, "Many of you recognize the effect sin has upon relationships. You would no doubt agree that sin affects your relationship with the Lord, and also with others. But let's talk about sin's effects upon the dynamics of this church!" He told them that sinning against the Lord affects worship, because it is like leprosy which dulls sensitivity. "If you are sullen and dead in your sensitivities when it comes to worship, then maybe it is because sin has taken hold of your heart and dulled it. It is like what God said to his people in Isaiah 29:13: 'People honor me with their lips while their hearts are far from me.'? Sin might allow you a taste but not a fullness, a desire but not a satisfaction. Sin will rob you of the joy in the Lord; it will not allow you to overflow with joy in his fellowship."

Dan also told them that sin negatively affects true fellowship with one another, and blinds us to the fact that as believers we are called to a life of sacrificial service to one another, a life of reconciliation and peace, a life impacted by the redemption in Christ. Sin also affects believers' ability to present the love, grace and truth of the Gospel without hypocrisy. It diminishes believers' effectiveness.

"While you, dear people of God, are given many biblical names, one fundamental thing you are, if indeed you are in Christ Jesus by faith, is the Forgiven!" He highlighted that awesome reality by reading from Psalm 32:1; 85:2; 86:5; Leviticus 19:22; Ephesus 1:7; Colossians 1:14; 2:13; 1 John 2:12. "Because of the forgiveness of Jesus Christ, you are the Forgiven. Since you are the Forgiven you are to be the Forgiving too!"

True believers are forgiving people. "We are forgiven by the blood of Jesus Christ and the evidence that we are forgiven is that we are forgiving!" The pastor went on to teach the thrust of the text in Matthew 6. While the ground of God's forgiveness is always and only the work and blood of Christ and nothing else, God requires a demonstrative proof that a person is indeed in Jesus Christ. A believer will forgive others (Mark 11:25; Luke 6:37, 11:4). A proof that you are indeed forgiven of God is that you forgive others. At the same time, if you are not right with your brother or sister in Christ you cannot be temporally right with God. It is as if God is saying in Matthew 6 and other like passages that if you are not a forgiving person even after all that was done in Jesus to forgive you, then do not expect a continued forgiveness with regard to things this side of heaven. Do not expect to partake in those promises of God in your life that are conditional and are to be appropriated here and now. For example, husbands who fail to live with their wives with understanding will have their prayers hindered (1 Pet. 3:7).

Dan then asked, "Why would you or I be unwilling to forgive?" He answered the question. The first reason is due to one's sin nature. "Perhaps you have never come to faith in Christ and known the forgiveness of God. If you are a believer, then listen to this - you have never in your life experienced anything against you from anybody that is like what you did against God in your natural, sinful, rebellious condition. You were God's enemy, angry, hostile, bitter, hateful… And yet out of his mercy God forgave you for Christ's sake through Christ's death upon the cross."

Another reason for an unwillingness to forgive, Dan told them, was due to anger. As someone once said, anger is the womb that bears the monster of unforgiveness. A third reason is to seek revenge. A fourth reason is that unforgiveness is a form of manipulation (3 John 9). While there are many other reasons, the heart of the matter is idolatry of pride. Dan quoted from a message he heard years before by an undisclosed pastor who said, "No one could reasonably imagine himself to be the object of divine forgiveness who is deliberately and purposefully unforgiving toward others."

Pastor Dan made a tearful plea for God's people at Grace to commit to a lifestyle consistent with forgiveness in Christ. He asked them to seek reconciliation with others, to confess offensive sins and seek pardon, and to willingly forgive others who ask for it. Then he closed by asking God for the grace of humility and asked the Lord to grant the church a reconciling peace.

A pastor once told Dan that in the decades he served as pastor he observed that it took an average of three years from the time a new concept was introduced before the proverbial light went on and people acted on it. He also said that important things need to be repeated again and again, at different times and in different ways before people take it in and do anything about it. With that information in mind, Dan knew that if the church was going to be a forgiving, peacemaking church it would take repeating the gospel truths again and again and again.

"What if I do get a call from this new church in New Mexico? Should I take it?" Dan wondered out loud. Dan and Mona were huddled in the home office.

"I don't know," answered Mona. "The last church was a challenge. This church is a challenge. What if they are all like this? Dan, what's your biggest concern about staying here?"

"I just wonder if my ministry will ever be effective. I mean, here, read this:

A minister's peace of mind is very important to the quality of his productivity in ministry. It is very difficult to be loving, gentle, and kind toward people when a small group of nitpickers are constantly at him about trivial matters that have little to do with the overall purpose of the church. It is even more difficult to be the gentle pastor, meek and mild, when the accusations leveled at him are contrived and totally false."[4]

"Honey, all churches have nitpickers."

"This church seems to have more than its share. All of the older elders, and almost a fourth of the congregation are negative nitpickers. Remember when the elders scolded me about being under stress? 'We've noticed you are under stress. A good leader should never let on that he is under stress,' they complained. 'You are not being a good example when you show emotion like that,' they told me at another time."

"Yes, I remember."

"Maybe if I were out of this contaminated environment I might do better? Maybe I should quit the ministry altogether!"

"Honey, you can't do that. You've wanted to be a pastor for so many years, and you've worked hard to become one."

"Maybe Bernie might be successful and force me out of Grace Church?" The pastor would be in good company. Leadership magazine took a survey in 1996 which revealed 43 percent of clergy were forced out by a small faction in the church.[5]

Dan informed the elders at their monthly meeting that he needed several days off because he was asked to candidate at a church in another state. Bernie smiled. Joe said, "I'm not going to stop you." The new elders frowned. The elders approved his leave time.

The church in New Mexico was only three years old. It had two elders. The evangelist who planted the church took another church planting opportunity in the South. The church of sixty-five members had a healthy makeup of people. Most were in their thirties with young children. Almost half of the church was second-generation Latino. They were an open, warm, energetic, fun-loving group of relatively new converts to Christ. Dan immensely enjoyed his time with them, and they had more than a positive reception of him. The interviews with the search committee and the two elders seemed to go well. They invited him back, this time to meet his wife and children.

The four-day visit at the end of January was great refreshment that energized his call to ministry. Now that he was back home it was time to systematically deal with the other antagonists. It was not enough to preach grace, forgiveness and peacemaking. Dan had to get down from the pulpit and into the lives of those who needed it the most. That is a hard thing for a pastor to balance. Like Jesus, he should invest most of his time and energies with potential leaders, secondly with disciples who desire the discipleship process, thirdly with those who need urgent care, and then finally with those who are deliberately on the fringes of the church. Somewhere though, the pastor must deal with problem people whose lives and actions are harming the cause of Christ and his church. At the same time he must safeguard his life and time from those who, like leeches, would suck everything out of him and give nothing in return. For the cause of Christ and his church Dan had to confront the problem people.

Problem people are small people, so said Theodore Roosevelt, who "love to contaminate great things."[6] Leadership guru Stephen Covey is insightful when he says of such people that they spawn "...what again, I call the five metastasizing emotional cancers:

criticizing, complaining, comparing, competing and contending."[7] So, problem people are not only found in churches. It is a people thing – a sin thing.

Sometimes problem people weasel their way into leadership positions to gain a foothold, to have influence, to wield their little power sword, and if possible to take total control. These "are the people in the church who give the impression that there are only three people who can do no wrong: God, the one who has God in his or her back pocket, and the people who have canonized the teachings of the one who has God in his or her back pocket."[8]

Pastors can be small and problematic too. Gilmore discusses how sinful pettiness and negativity can be displayed in pastors:

> Even those who adhere to dress codes and clean-cut appearance may be constantly nipped at their heels for failing to cross every verbal 't' and properly accent every vowel, for such egregious faux pas as calling children 'kids,' for allowing mistyped words to get into bulletins, of for running ten minutes over in the morning worship hour. Other infringements, such as failing to get permission from the board for borrowing a projector, may also incite antagonism.[9]

But then he warns: "Pastors are often critiqued on such petty matters, yet, when a pastor nags a lay person about such matters of little consequence, he drains away energy, drives people away, and is otherwise counterproductive."[10] Such attitudes and behaviors are unacceptable, no matter who has them.

By February the town was an island in deep winter. Dan was teaching a series on how to biblically deal with attitudes and emotions such as anger, pride, depression and guilt. He taught a class on anger using resources from Jay Adams, Wayne Mack, Lou Priolo and the Christian Counseling and Educational Foundation in Laverock, Pennsylvania. As usual, the people who really needed to be at the class were absent. "Anger," Dan said, "is an emotion that God has given us in order to destroy that which is sinful, wicked or evil in order to build up something good in its place. Anger is to be controlled. Our problem is that our sin natures pervert the good emotion and changes anger into something that becomes sinful, wicked or evil."

He went on to explain that anger is not sinful, *per se*. After all, God gets angry. Jesus got angry. That is because proper anger is a righteous anger. God's righteous anger is manifested in terror or dread. Dan cataloged on the board the things that angered God and challenged his students to look up the references:

1. *Ps. 78:21, 22; Jn 3:36; Heb. 3:18, 19 –*
2. *Ps. 7:12; Pro. 1:30, 31; Isa. 9:13, 14; Rom. 2:5 –*

3. *Heb. 10: 26, 27 –*
4. *Deut. 29:20; Josh. 23:16; Psa. 78:58 –*
5. *Ps. 89:30-32; 90:7-9; Isa. 47:6 –*
6. *Ps. 2:2, 3, 5; 1 Thess. 2:16 –*

"The principle of Scripture is this: I can be and ought to be angry at the things that anger God. However, having said that, it is very hard for us as believers with residual sin to do so without sinning. Some even say we are incapable of righteous anger."

He continued, instructing on the causes of sinful anger. The ultimate and primary cause is original and indwelling sin, yet there are contributing factors for anger (Ps. 51:5; Rom. 7:21-24; Gal. 5:19; Eph. 2:3; Col. 3:8-10). He inscribed:

Internal causes include
- *fretting (Ps. 37:7-8; Pro. 30:33)*
- *jealousy or envy (Ps. 37:1; Prov. 6:34)*
- *lack of self-control (Pro. 25:28; 29:11; 16:32)*
- *pride (Prov. 13:10; Isa. 16:6; Jer. 48:29, 30)*
- *selfish ambition and idolatrous desires (Jas. 3:13-4:2).*

Certain circumstances also aggravate an angry disposition so that one is inclined to either explode (blow up) or internalize (clam up). Some examples are found in Gen. 4:1-11; 12:10-20; 16:1-6; 27:1-41; 30:1,2; 34:1-31; 37:1-4; 1 Sam. 18:6-9; 20:24ff; 25:9-35; Prov. 15:1; 22:24, 25; Jonah 4:1; Mark 5:14-29; and Eph. 6:4.

"How do we discover the trigger for a particular episode of anger?" Dan posed to the group. The class remained quiet. "Ask yourself this question: what is it I want that I am not getting? In other words, the reason why our angry hearts are triggered is because our desires and wants are frustrated."

He continued, "Angry people cause problems at times, but most assuredly problem people are chronically angry people. They are proud individuals who demand they get what they want. Angry people in the church can do great damage." He brought out that God calls upon us to repent of our angry hearts and ways and put on Christ with the fruit of his Spirit (Gal. 5:22-26; Eph. 4:24-27, 31-32; Col. 3:8-10; Jas. 1:19-20). The way we are to deal with something that angers us is to attack the issue, not each other.

"Pastor," MaryJane called out.

"Yes, MaryJane. Good to see you're better and that you were able to join us today."

"Oh, thank you. How do we deal with angry or proud or problem people who constantly cause trouble in our personal lives? And a follow up question is: should people like me just sit back and expect you or the elders to do something about them?"

"I take it you weren't able to sit in on the Peacemaker class we had about a year and a half ago?"

"No. Sorry."

"That's all right. So, who wants to help me answer her questions?"

Melissa volunteered. She was a good student. "Before we go to another person about their faults we have to look into our own lives first and repent of our own sins. Jesus said to remove the log out of our own eyes first. That's in Matthew somewhere."

"Matthew chapter seven. Very good. Yes, Judy?"

"We are supposed to go to that person and talk to them about their sin. Isn't that what Matthew 18 says?"

"Good, but how do we know when we should talk to the other person? What precipitates or justifies our going to the other person?" Dan posed.

"When they are in sin or doing something sinfully."

"Correct….and, what defines sin?"

"God's Word," Matt wisely answered.

"What if someone is just annoying, but what they are doing is not blatantly sinful? What if you get upset or offended by someone else, but it is really your heart problem and not theirs?"

The class sat silently for about twenty seconds. Brad broke the lull, "Well then, we don't go to them. We just deal with it. You know, suck it up."

"This is a good question. We are always being offended and somehow always offending others. That is the nature of life this side of heaven. But the first thing to do when offended is to determine from Scripture whether it was a sinful offense or not. Now, granted, everything we do is tainted by residual sin, but the Bible doesn't say we are supposed to go around with spiritual magnifying glasses and pick off every tiny speck of sin. Or as Jesus said, strain gnats. There are people who do that, which can be sinful in itself, because it is too judgmental. There is, after all, a difference between being offended and taking offense. However, oftentimes what someone else does may feel like a sinful offense because of your reaction to it. You might be overly sensitive and too easily offended?"

"What do you mean there is a difference between being offended and taking offense?" Neil asked.

"If a person has truly sinned against you, and remember sin is defined by Scripture, then that is a true offense. But, if the so-called offense is not sinful, then you are choosing to take offense; you are choosing to be offended. For example, what if I asked Melissa for her opinion about my purple shirt and she said she did not like it. Was her honesty a sin? No. Did she sin against me? No. But what if I was offended by it and got angry? Now it's a problem of my heart, not of her action. I wrongly took offense."

Dan explained further that we need to approach things God's way, biblically. We should not take offense when no sin was committed. Instead we should seek to repent of our own pride, We should change our own lives by applying faith in Christ, learning how to be gracious, merciful, compassionate and forgiving like Jesus.

"But what if the problem is causing a rift between you and someone else?" Marjorie asked.

"If the so-called offense is developing into uneasiness and putting a relational barrier between you and the other person, then discuss it. But discuss it only after considering your own heart, attitude and sins. Then go to the other person in order to identify the problem, if there is one, and find a biblical solution. It is preferable to find a mutually acceptable solution. Oh, and remember, attack the problem, not each other. Turn with me to 1 Peter 4:8. Matthew, please read that for us."

"And above all things have fervent love for one another, for 'love will cover a multitude of sins,'" he read from his *Thompson Chain Reference Bible.*

"Here's the point: as God's people, we are to love one another. That kind of Christ-like love will cover over a whole dumpster of personal offenses. Being loving does not mean that we fail to address the sin if it is a cause for contention, disunity, conflict, and things like that. Avoidance is not love, it's prideful cowardice. It's like Proverbs 27:5 says, 'Open rebuke is better than love carefully concealed. Faithful are the wounds of a friend…' What Peter means in his passage is that because God's love in Jesus Christ atones or covers over all of our sins and our brother's sin and our sister's sins, then we too should be gracious and merciful toward them. We should forgive them."

"What if the other person is a deacon or an elder or a pastor?" Matt's friend asked.

"Same thing applies. Except that God warns his people not to level a serious accusation against an elder or pastor without there being two or more witnesses. Check out 1 Timothy 5:19."

"What if it is an actual sinful offense?" asked Melissa.

"Then the next step is to do what?"

Marcus quickly replied, "Go to that person in private and talk to him or her about the matter. Galatians 6:1 tells us how – to go and restore such a one with gentleness."

"But, I've done that a couple of times and nothing happened," Melissa countered.

"What does Matthew 18:15 say?" Dan asked the group.

"To go back with one or two more and try again," Matt answered after reading his Bible.

"Yes. There are two ways to look at this verse. The first is that the one or two witnesses are witnesses to the sin and they are going in order to verify the sin and speak as witnesses against the person's sinning. The other way to view this is that these witnesses are going to observe and bear witness to the meeting and to whether that person repents or not. Either way, the point is we do things justly and we keep going until there is resolution."

Judy spoke up, "And if they don't repent we are supposed to tell everyone in the church?"

"Matthew 18 does say that if the person does not repent then you are supposed to tell it to the church. Yet, there is good scholarly and biblical reason to go to those who are the authority in the church and let them take disciplinary action. They are the ones given the authoritative keys to Christ's kingdom with the ability to admit people into the local church or to excommunicate them for just biblical cause."

"What if the person sins publicly, I mean, that person does something that offends lots of people or lots of people know about it?" Andres asked.

"A good rule of thumb, and I think this can be corroborated by Scripture, is that private sinful offenses are dealt with privately, while public sinful offenses are dealt with publicly."

Judy catapulted her hand up and without waiting asked, "What kinds of sins can someone be excommunicated for? Isn't it possible that they can kick someone out of the church who hasn't sinned?"

"Yes. Has happened, does happen, will happen. But it is not supposed to happen! In our denomination, the process for discipline is laid out biblically and systematically. There are checks and balances. I appreciate that because if you are disciplined at the local church level, you have a right to appeal to the regional government made up of pastors and elders in the area churches. And if you still believe you were not dealt with justly you have the right to appeal to the synod or general assembly made up of pastors and elders from around the country. Let me write down some things for which you could be disciplined." Dan marked on the white board:

1. *Unresolved sinful problems between members of the church (Matt. 18:15-17)*
2. *Disorderly and undisciplined conduct (2 Thess. 3:6-11)*
3. *Divisiveness (Rom. 16:17-18; Tit. 3:9-11)*
4. *Obvious and persistent patterns of sin (1 Cor. 5:1-13; 1 Tim. 5:20)*
5. *Adopting and/or teaching heresy*

"Okay, then let me ask this," Melissa added. "What about pastors or elders?"

"In our system they are not exempt from the process. If they are sinning in these ways, or negligent or abusive in their office, then you follow the same procedure."

"Can they ever be disciplined out of the church?" she followed up.

"Sure, but you have to remember, that just as with the discipline of members, there are various levels of sanctions. At least that is how our denomination and sister denominations interpret Scripture." Dan opened the church's Book of Church Order and listed the various sanctions on the board:

1. *Admonition.*
   "This is a formal reproof by the elders against the offender. He or she is warned guilt and exhorted to be more circumspect in his or her Christian walk."

2. *Suspension from the Lord's Supper.*
   "The second is more serious. It is suspension from the Lord's Supper whereby the person is restricted for a time from participating in Communion."

3. *A pastor or elder can be suspended from church office.*
   "This suspension can be temporary or permanent, depending upon the offense and the officer's repentance."

4. *They could also be deposed from office.*

5. *The last and most serious is excommunication.*
   "This is a pronouncement by the court that the person is living and behaving like an unbeliever. It can be due to a crime or serious sin or heresy, where the person shows him or herself to be belligerent and unrepentant. Excommunication disfellowships the guilty one and declares him or her to be an unbeliever."[11]

"Wow! So an elder can be disciplined?" Melissa wondered in amazement.

"That's good to know!" declared Judy sitting next to her with folded arms.

"Can a congregation remove an elder?" Matt asked. The class got very quiet. Tension in the air was thick.

"Again, there has to be just cause and due process. Am I in trouble again?" Dan joked trying to break the somber discussion. Everyone laughed.

"Getting back to our original discussion as we close, we have seen that God has explicit ways for us to address problem people and their problems which affect others. We should always begin from the place of the Cross, remembering who we are without Christ, and where we would be without his salvation. We must live out the Gospel by being gracious, merciful, forgiving, truthful and compassionate. We should err on the side of grace more than on the side of law. But at the same time, we should not tolerate blatant sin that seriously affects or damages personal, familial or church relationships. God calls us to maintain the peace and purity of his church, and calls us to exercise reconciliation first, but if that fails then to exercise church discipline. The Scriptures are very clear that proud, angry, abusive, manipulative, caustic people must repent or be extracted!"

At that, the class clapped enthusiastically, catching Dan off guard. What could this mean?

A CHALLENGE TO THINK AND DO

What do you think?
1. Were there any ideas in this chapter that provoked your thinking? Can you identify anything this chapter taught you?
2. How would you evaluate Dan and Irma's meeting?
3. Do you agree with Dan's personal assessment that Irma is not truly a Christian? Why or why not?
4. What do you think about the quote, "When people substitute selfish motivation and church participation to affect their own salvation, negative repercussions will ensue, and the pastor's presence and presentation will be opposed."
5. What is the difference between being sinfully offended and merely taking personal offense?
6. What did you learn about anger that was challenging or new?
7. What is your response to the statement in Dan's sermon, "Because of the forgiveness of Jesus Christ, you are the Forgiven. Since you are the Forgiven, you are to be the Forgiving too!"
8. Just what does it mean to be the Forgiven in Christ?
9. What is biblical church discipline? Does your church practice church discipline? Why or why not?
10. Greenfield said, "A minister's peace of mind is very important to the quality of his productivity in ministry. It is very difficult to be loving, gentle, and kind toward peoplewhen a small group of nitpickers are constantly at him about trivial matters that have little to do with the overall purpose of the church." How is your pastor's peace of mind?

Some things you could do:
1. One pastor said, "No one could reasonably imagine himself to be the object of divine forgiveness who is deliberately and purposefully unforgiving toward others." Who are you unwilling to forgive that you need to?
2. Read Jay Adam's *From Forgiven to Forgiving*.
3. Read Marshall Shelley's *Well-Intentioned Dragons*.

19

BY THE AUTHORITY INVESTED IN…WHO?

—◇—

Trying to negotiate an airport with three young children is not an easy task. Benny, ever the happy, carefree, fun-loving spirit had the tendency to give in to his curious impulses. Mona wished she had a leash, but the four-year-old would have resisted. Hannah, normally a quiet and passive little girl, was fussy. Her parents didn't know if it was because she was outside her secure and toy-filled environment or due to some impending illness. Jake played the little man and kept in front of his dad the entire time.

The most challenging time was going through security. Everything had to be checked. First, Benny kept trying to crawl onto the checkpoint's conveyer belt. When Dan got a pan to put his things in, Ben plopped inside. He ran through the metal detector and up to the TSA agent to ask about his badge and other equipment – twice. The man patiently helped Ben go through it – twice. The first time he set off the alarm because he had found five quarters on the floor and had stuck them in his pocket without telling anyone. Then he ran over to the woman who monitored the screen and asked if he could watch TV. Hannah started crying inconsolably when her mother took off her little shoes for inspection. Jake stayed with Dan the whole time trying to be daddy's big helper.

Thankfully, the flight was relatively uneventful. Hannah fell asleep. The boys played with and fought over toys. Dan and Mona tried to talk about the prospect of taking a call to a new church. Mona absolutely hated moving. The process of packing, leaving old friends and familiar territory, the anxiety of unknown future and place, reestablishing in a new house and town, the energies it took to make new friends, all overwhelmed her. Even though she had been the brunt of a few attacks and some unkind comments and actions, she had not endured what Dan had gone through. Neither was she embroiled in the conflict like Dan. To her the pain of making the transition was worse than the troubles in their present situation.

Not so with Dan. He was so disillusioned with the church and so beaten down and fatigued, he was ready to flee. At this point he did not care if it was the right thing to do. In fact, during the first visit he was open when the search committee asked why he would consider leaving his present call to take another. He told them he was at the point of either taking another call or leaving the pastoral ministry altogether. When they asked him why, he said that he did not want to divulge details, but he did say that it was clear he and his elders were not on the same philosophical page so it was hard to move the church forward in the same direction. He also said that the unremitting assault against his character, competencies and call by more than a handful of antagonists was getting to be too much.

One of the elders greeted the family at the Albuquerque airport in his Honda SUV. Stu Hartsteader was glad to see Dan and meet his family. He was also very surprised at how lightly they traveled. Mona was a very organized and efficient packer. The drive to town took over an hour, which was almost too much for a restless, cranky little girl. The boys were given the assignment of counting different trees or cacti or snakes or rabbits or other animals they could find. That lasted ten minutes. Mona then pulled out two rolls of masking tape and gave one to each of her boys. That helpful tip was something she learned from her good friend Carole. The elder didn't mind. The simple and cheap items entertained the boys sitting in the very back nearly forty minutes.

Kathy Hartsteader welcomed the family into their large, newly built home. Mona was impressed by the open, airy feel. It was a four-bedroom, three-bath, three-car-garage tract home on a large lot in a new neighborhood. Buyers had six Southwest models from which to choose. The elder and his family chose the ranch. Their children, a twelve-year-old daughter and a nine- year-old boy, were at school. Dan and Mona were very impressed by the Hartsteaders' warm and relaxed hospitality. They put Mona at ease.

The rest of the weekend went well. Babysitters were arranged so that Dan and Mona could visit with the pastoral search committee and elders, and to take a tour of the small city and surrounding area with the other elder and his wife. Mona felt strange in the New Mexico environment. It was so sparse compared to the other places where she had lived. The humidity was exceptionally low for this woman who had lived in moderate to high humidity areas all her life, but it didn't affect Dan.

On Saturday Mona had a luncheon with the women of the church, while Dan met with the elders. Dan taught Sunday school and preached Sunday morning. For a second time they wholeheartedly received and appreciated his ministry of God's Word, and with great appreciation. The church family had a huge Mexican style luncheon after church.

Mona was amazed by the number of families with young children. She could see making good friends with a few of the women. Dan got along very well with the elders and met a couple of men who would be strong potential friends. He especially enjoyed their music director, and was impressed by the music team.

Reserved Jake even found two new buddies to pal around with. The gregarious and cheerful Benny was everybody's friend, but he played mostly with five other little boys his age. Hannah was happy to be around other toddlers, though it was the new toys and play areas she liked most.

Because the church met in a local public school, they did not have an evening service. Instead they had community groups, but this Sunday evening they met together at the home of the architect, which Jake dubbed "the castle." Monday afternoon the pastor and his family flew back home.

Overall, everyone had a great time. The church was welcoming, upbeat, kind, gracious – and relaxed. No obvious critics, skeptics or grumpies. It seemed surreal to be in a place so uplifting and encouraging. Dan and Mona agreed they could not spot any problem people or potential antagonists, but Mona reminded Dan that they experienced the same welcome experience when they candidated at Grace Church. Dan countered that the significant difference was the overall demeanor of the church. "This group seems freer, much more authentic, and sincerely warm. I don't know, maybe it's a Southwest cultural thing, but they seem happier. None of that formal friendliness. It seems so genuine." Mona concurred.

Dan asked some tough and hard questions. Try as he might he could not find any red flags or even yellow lights for that matter.

On the flight back, husband and wife tried their best to compare impressions and notes across the aisle. Hannah fell asleep next to Mona and the boys seated by dad were playing with their small Gameboys, gifts from their hosts. As they normally did, Dan and Mona took a paper and listed pros and cons. Mona was good at coming up with the cons for leaving Grace; Dan had the pros for taking the new call. Dan told the elders they needed three weeks to decide and wouldn't be able to move until the end of May. They asked if he was inclined to accept the call. He said he could find no cause for turning it down, but the decision involved much more than that. He told them they should feel free to pursue other men in the interim, but he got a strong sense they wanted him.

"I don't want to do this anymore," Dan said with his head in his hands. It was Tuesday morning at the church office and he was looking down at his Pocket PC reviewing his schedule for the week. There was very little on the calendar that would be uplifting or enjoyable. He had scheduled a visit that evening with Al and Katrina, two of the most negative and irritable people, next to the Dumpletons, he had ever known. *Then there was Mr. Schrenk and…Oh, stop this thinking! Stop this thinking!*

Dan worked through the meeting in his mind, trying to anticipate the responses and come up with ideas for various contingencies. He expected their reception to be hostile, as always.

It was. Dan arrived right at 7:00 P.M., but the family was still eating supper in front of the television. A radio was blaring music in the kitchen. "Come in," Katrina said, opening the door. She went back to her seat on the couch. Nobody offered a drink, food, or a place to sit. Dan picked up a stack of old magazines sitting on an old recliner. "That's Al's favorite chair. You better sit over there," she pointed to an antique, dark stained wood dining room chair in the corner.

He tried to make conversation, but the foursome was mesmerized by the game show and up to their elbows in buckets of Kentucky Fried Chicken. Dan took charge. "We'll begin as soon as you are finished eating." They finished eating at twenty after the hour, but sat back to finish the game show. It was as if Dan was invisible.

When the game show was over, Dan asked if they could turn off the TV. It met with some resistance, but they submitted. The kids were sent off to play. They griped that they couldn't watch television and complained that it was totally rude.

He began the meeting with prayer and read Matthew 7:1-5, then took time to confess some of the obvious and specific ways he had been unloving toward them. The adults were quite surprised. Dan asked them to forgive him for the sins he outlined. He reminded them that forgiveness means granting a pardon and not holding the offense against the person or bringing it up again.

At first they tried to dismiss it, "Oh, no problem. Don't even think about it."

That was not granting forgiveness, so Dan explained again the importance of asking for and giving forgiveness and once more asked each to forgive him. With a long hesitation they agreed and forgave him.

"Is there any other way I have sinned against you?" Both nonchalantly shook their heads.

"Can you think of anything you might have done, Katrina, or you, Al, which was sinfully offensive toward me?" Now they were startled. Katrina stood up, fixed her strangled dress and sat down. Al, now sitting in his rocker recliner sat rocking, just staring at Dan.

"Anything at all?" Dan asked.

"Nope. I can't think of anything. Maybe you've done something, Al?" Katrina said.

"Nothing comes to mind," Al mumbled uncomfortably.

Dan then proceeded to tell them the various ways in which he believed he had been sinned against, and used illustrations and Bible references to back up his claim. They were stupefied and clearly angry. Dan told them that their caustic, vitriolic behavior, their critical manner, their gossiping and backbiting, and their association with a group of others who were willing to divide the church were sinfully wrong. "Do you have anything to say?"

"No!" declared a tearful Katrina.

"My show is on," Al said, turning the television back on.

"Can we try and resolve this before turning the TV back on, Al?"

"There is nothing to resolve," he threw back, surfing the screen for his show.

Dan said, "I'm going to read from Matthew 18. Please be considerate and turn the TV off until I am finished." He read to them the section about going in private and then if there was no resolution to return with one or two others. "Katrina? Anything you'd like to say?"

She was wiping her eyes with her sleeve. "You've hurt my feelings."

"I think it's time you went home," Al said. "It was rude of you to come in here and spout off like that. Now look at what you've done, making my wife cry like that. Why don't you just go?" he insisted while getting up.

"I need to tell you that I will be back with one or two other elders. The process will continue until there is a biblical resolution."

Katrina took off for her messy kitchen. Al stood by his chair eyes glued to the TV. Dan found his own way out.

Obviously it did not go quite the way he expected. He had hoped they would at least admit their faults, but even that did not happen. He shouldn't have been surprised. Self-centered, proud people who cause problems are rarely willing to believe they have any faults or sins. Or if they knew they had faults they rarely, if ever, admitted them. At least he had done the right thing, and with a right motive.

He walked into his house discouraged, but was greeted with a squealing little blond boy riding a piece of cardboard down the stairs. "Da –aa-aa-aa-aa-dee-ee-ee!" he cried out as he bounced down the steps. "That was fun! Your turn, Jake."

"No, Jake. You boys need to come down here and..." he paused, feigning anger, "wrestle with your Dad!" He got down on his knees and waited for them to propel them-selves into his arms. Ben was first, then Jake. They rolled around, pretending they were wrestling champions. Then Dan trapped them in a tickling lock until they were screaming with laughter. It wasn't until they knocked a table lamp from the end table that they quit the match. "Hey, look at the time! You guys need to get ready for bed."

"But Daaad," Ben protested, "we got our bath and look, we're in our pajamas!"

"Brush your teeth yet?"

"We were coming down for dessert."

"Dessert? Who said you could have dessert? You boys don't deserve dessert," he teased.

"Mommy said so," Benny complained seriously.

"Oh, well, if her majesty, Queen Mona, said so then you must obey."

Ben skipped to the kitchen. Jake took Dan by the hand. Mona had already dished up scoops of sherbet with oatmeal cookies.

Dan's joy in his family was a pleasant reprieve from a hard evening.

He phoned Bernie Wednesday morning to arrange a meeting with him. Bernie was his cold and cruel self, all the more since Dan "rudely accosted Irma." At first he refused to meet. Dan appealed to him to do the righteous thing. Bernie still refused until Dan told him that either it would be a meeting one-on-one or in front of all the elders. Friday noon was the soonest Bernie could get together.

Back at the bistro in Hodge's Inn, the two sat at a table near a window. Dan read Matthew 7 and confessed to Bernie that he didn't love him the way a Christ-like pastor should, and asked forgiveness for the times he was rude and inconsiderate toward the elderly man. He also admitted he was wrong for avoiding him, not having Bernie's best interests at heart, and for a few other things. As with the previous meetings, Bernie seemed to receive a certain satisfaction in Dan's humiliation. When Dan asked Bernie for forgiveness, he kept quiet. Then the old man said, "I don't think I could ever forgive you!"

"Scripture commands you to."

"That's your interpretation. How could you be forgiven, after what you did to my son and sister!" he said with an angry wrinkle and pursed lips.

"I did nothing sinfully offensive against either one for which I've not sought forgiveness, and you know it."

"You are an arrogant, good-for-nothing twit."

"Don't resort to name calling. That's violating the Ninth Commandment," Dan said knowing how keen Bernie was on Biblical Law. "If you have things against me, or can show how I have sinned against you other than what I've already admitted, then tell me."

Bernie kept quiet for a while. The lunch was served. The same waiter from Dan's previous visit attended their table. He looked at Dan with a curious squint, as if to indicate that he was surprised that Dan was back, and in for another beating. Dan just smiled and jerked his eyebrows up and down a couple times to communicate he understood the man's puzzlement. Perhaps he was also surprised that the manager let Dan into the bistro?

Bernie poked at his food with his knife and fork, while telling Dan nothing he hadn't heard before. It was all generic, no specific offenses were enumerated. "Why do you hate me so? You've been this way since I arrived" Dan questioned.

"Because you are not what this church needs. You are an incompetent pastor, a bad preacher, a poor theologian, disrespectful and arrogant. You are nothing like our good pastor."

"And never will be. Don't want to be. Couldn't be if I tried. We've had this conversation several times before. You aren't giving me anything specific. It's your overall caricature of me you resent, for whatever reason. I suspect it is because I refuse to conform to your image of a pastor and bow to your demands."

Bernie got up and started to leave.

"Bernie," Dan called out. "You need to hear what I have to tell you."

He shuffled back; the fury in his face could stoke the fires of hell for years. "Hurry up!" he growled.

"I'm not afraid of you," Dan said calmly, smiling. Then changing to a serious expression he announced, "Since you refuse to reconcile, I will be visiting you again with a couple of the other elders."

Bernie shuffled angrily out the door. It sounded like he was cussing under his breath.

Joe arranged the next meeting with Bernie and Dan. Marcus came along too. Against Dan's better judgment they met on Bernie's turf, in his home. His wife kept the large place sparkling clean and exceptionally organized. She served coffee and then stole away to their upstairs den.

The meeting went no better than any of the previous meetings. Bernie was feistier, probably empowered since they were in his territory. Joe tried to mediate. Marcus was stupefied by the old man's obnoxious, abusive behavior. Bernie again refused to forgive Dan, and repeated the same old sour tune. Dan declared he would be bringing charges against Bernie. Bernie claimed he would be vindicated because the elders were all on his side. "Then, we'll see who the real authority around here is!" he pronounced.

Bingo! There it was. Bernie just revealed the heart of the matter. On the way back to the church, Joe defended Bernie's behavior as coming from a man who was old, failing physically and perhaps in the beginning stages of Alzheimer's disease. "Personality changes happen with that disease, you know."

"It might contribute to his mental state, but it's not the overriding cause," Marcus wisely stated.

"Joe, you need to quit defending him. He's always been that way and you know it. He's just gotten angrier and more aggressive over the past several years," Dan said firmly.

Joe wanted to defend him because he had respect for elderly people. It just did not seem right to do anything that seemed to disrespect and elderly man like Bernie. He also admired the fact that Bernie and his family had been with the church from the beginning and had exerted much time, effort and money into the church. He was the primary leader that kept the small church together during the first several years.

"All of that is commendable. I am not dismissing any of it, but it does not excuse sinful belligerence. The man shows himself to be hatefully wicked. He must be dealt with because his poison is disrupting the church. And I fear what God will do to our church if we do not act," Dan declared.

Marcus was quite upset with what he observed. He knew people like Bernie in business related contexts, though not as mean spirited. He asked the elders if they could gather for an informal meeting to discuss the nature of pastoral and elder authority. Bernie and two of his comrades did not attend. They met at Marcus' house, where they were greeted by a dessert buffet: cakes, pies, cookies, coffee, hot chocolate, hot cider, and tea. His wife went all out.

"Didn't know we were coming to a party!" Dan said as he gave the woman a hug. "Thank you so very much."

After each of the men collected platefuls of food and drink of choice they claimed comfortable seats in the elegant living room. "I've asked us to talk about the real nature of the authority invested in the pastor or elders," Marcus started off. "I've finished reading Jay Adam's book *The Place of Authority in Christ's Church*. Ya'll need to read it."

"It's a spiritual authority, governing the citizens of Christ's Kingdom here and now. It's restricted to Christ's church," Dan said.

"Yeah, but what does that really mean?" asked Marcus.

Dan reminded Marcus and the other two new elders that they had studied this in their training. Joe had not studied the issue. Authority is not invested in a person, but in the office. That's the way it is in life. If you take a biblical perspective on things then you would understand that all are equal before God, and that we owe obedience to no other human except by virtue of their office ordained by God. "Office is the only justification and proper limitation of any human exercise of power and authority because no one has a natural right to rule over others," Dan quoted an unknown source.

"Just exactly what do you mean by office?" queried an elder.

"Any legitimate, official position with responsibility, authority, control and power: the office of parent, of teacher, of civil servant, of military officer, as well as of the elder and pastor," responded Dan.

He reminded them that the office of elder is the one office ordained by God to govern Christ's church. The three interchangeable terms for this position are *presbuteros* (elder), *episkopos* (overseer) and *poimen* (pastor-shepherd). The apostles saw themselves as elders (1 Pet. 5:1; 2 John 1; 3 John 1), and each church as having multiple elders (Tit. 1:7 cp. Acts 14:23; 20:17; Phil. 1:1; Jas. 5:14). The one elder who became prominent as a servant of God's Word and spiritual leader was the pastor, or better, the bishop (overseer).

"As someone else has said, office involves institutional power granted by God, an appointment by God to a position endowed with majesty and authority," Marcus added.

"True, but we need to understand that the power is limited in scope. It is a spiritual authority of influence by God's Word through his Spirit. The authority we see in the New Testament is derived from the clear teaching and commands of God's Word. When people begin to impose their own teachings and commands upon the church, then their authority is no longer legitimate," Dan pronounced.

The discussion continued with Dan and Marcus doing most of the talking. They had learned that God sets up church government with proper jurisdiction, with a right to govern according to the Bible. This comes through three significant words. The first, *exousia* has to do with the delegated right, duty and freedom from the Lord Jesus to exercise authority over God's flock as determined by Scripture (Tit. 3:1-2). In a general sense, all believers are to be subject to legitimate authorities over them (Luke 10:19; Tit. 3:1). Those authorities operate within their own sphere. For example, along with the sphere of the church, there is the sphere of civil government or the sphere of the family. Jesus has his sovereign sphere which is the entire universe (Matt. 9:6, 8; Mark 6:39; Eph. 1:15-23). The centurion had authority in his sphere (Matt. 8:9). Parents have authority over children, masters have authority over slaves (Eph. 6), and elders have authority over the church (Acts 5:1-13; Heb. 13:7, 17). The special authority in the church is given to build God's people up, not tear them down (2 Cor. 13:10). This delegated authority from God is the biblical duty and right to think, decide and function within the sphere of God's assigned parameters.

"Where do those parameters end? I hear about different men who claim to have the right and power to dictate pretty much anything to the people in their church," asked one of the men.

"The Word of God puts the limits on those men," Dan replied.

"Yeah, but they usually use the Bible and claim to know what God is commanding the people to do," countered the gentleman.

"Yes, and they do it by twisting the Scriptures. They have to because their abusive, manipulative dominance cannot be derived from the obvious teachings of Scripture. There is also the matter of violating a person's conscience. The line is drawn when the demands of certain individuals in the church cross or impinge upon a biblically informed conscience. Paul addresses that in Romans 14 and 15, and 1 Corinthians 8-10."

The pastor continued teaching that the other term is *hegeomai* (Matt. 2:6; Acts 7:10; 14:12) which means to lead or guide (Heb. 13:17). This is what ordained church leadership is to do (Heb. 13: 7, 17, 24). They lead or guide the church into grace and truth, biblical love and liberty, that is, into a wholesome Christ-likeness. The third word that underscores biblical church authority is *proistemi*. The context determines the translation, so it can mean to lead (Rom. 12:8), to manage (1 Tim. 3:4, 5, 12), or to rule (1 Tim. 5:17).[1]

"In our form of government there are two aspects of church rule and discipline. One is administrative, which deals with maintaining good order and government in Christ's church, seeing that everything is done decently and orderly for God's glory," citing 1 Cor. 14:40 and 10:31. "The other is judicial. This is the right, responsibility and duty to address matters of truth and practice. As God's elders we are to do what we can to prevent anything in doctrine or living that would be contrary to the Word of God."

"We're also supposed to correct sinful offenses in the church in order to protect God's people and bring the offending person back to godly thinking and doing." Marcus added.

"We've got that kind of authority?" asked one of the long-time elders. He seemed to be unfamiliar with what was being propounded.

"Hey, again, I've known certain church leaders say they are correcting the sins of people to whip them into shape, but their list of sins seem endless," argued one of the men.

Dan agreed, "I know what you mean. But the Bible is clear what sin is. The Westminster Shorter Catechism has a good definition for sin. It say that 'sin is any lack of conformity to or transgression of God's Law.' God tells us what the sins and vices are. Peter and Paul make it obvious for us in their letters. A pastor friend of mine was told he was sinning because he wore a beard. Bible doesn't say so; in fact there is strong warrant for a man to wear a beard. Other friends of ours were told that having five girls was a consequence of their sin. I've been told sending my son to public school is a sin, wearing colored shirts is a sin, eating sugar is a sin, wearing sandals to church is a sin…the list of sins men and women fabricate are endless. But God's Word is clear and simple.

"You know, this delegated authority from God is in the God-defined, legitimate office we hold, not in who we are as people. We also believe that this authority to make decisions, implement policies and so forth, comes when we sit together as a council or in session. The judgments or rulings are not mine or yours, but ours. These things must be consistent with the teachings of our final authority the Scriptures, and for the good of God's people. These things are not from our personal demands or for singular benefit. No singular pastor or elder or deacon or church member can dictate policy or rule alone," Dan stated.

The meeting continued until 10:00 o'clock that evening. What came out of it was an unofficial agreement the elders needed to charge Bernie, and try him in a church court, and discipline him if he is found guilty of any significant breach of God's Word.

At another meeting, even though they were divided five to three, the elder board formally charged Bernie, and delivered to him an official letter stating he was being summoned to a trial by his co-elders. He was being charged with violating the Ninth Commandment, being abusive, being divisive, and upsetting the peace and unity of the church. According to the denomination's rules he had a right to counsel. Bernie scoffed at the letter. He was convinced he was in the right and would be vindicated. A retired pastor, an old friend of his, volunteered to serve as his counsel.

In the interim, Bernie gathered his lot for a meeting at his house. Twenty people showed, including two of the older elders. He had them sign a petition and discuss how they were going to remove Dan from office. In order to accomplish their goal they needed to appeal to the presbytery. A letter was drafted and signed by the attendees, then sent to the clerk of presbytery.

As it turned out, the church trial lasted several evenings and two Saturdays. The evening meetings began at 7:00 P.M. and ended sharply at 10:00 P.M. The Saturday meetings lasted from 9 A.M. until 3 P.M. Part of the reason for the lengthy trial was because there were many witnesses to testify for and against Bernie. Bernie also kept trying to turn it into a trial against the pastor, but the elders would not permit it. His hot tempered belligerence got out of hand a number of times and the session had to call for a short recess each time.

Little did Dan or the elders know, Harold had gathered signatures from most of the rest of the congregation on a letter appealing to presbytery that they remove Bernie and one other elder from church office. They did not understand that the elders were systematically dealing with Bernie, and if it turned out well Bernie would repent, demit or be removed from the office of elder. The church was on the brink of a split, a sad commentary for any church of the Lord Jesus Christ.

Bernie protested the trial every time they met, and asserted his innocence. The first charge they investigated was his apparent violation of the Ninth Commandment, which says, "You shall not bear false witness against your neighbor." The Ninth Commandment, like all other commandments, has both a narrow application and a broad application. In the narrow sense this commandment primarily had to do with Israel's judicial system (Gen. 21:30; Lev. 5:1; 6:1ff; Deut. 4:25, etc.). This law was designed for the benefit and good welfare of people, to protect the name and reputation as well as to safeguard the life of the accused against false accusations and lies. Simply put, the immediate principle from this commandment is that in the administration of justice, the neighbor must be protected against false witnesses.

In the broader application, this commandment touches upon believers' witness for God. Believers are to uphold a viable and good witness for the Lord (Isa. 43:10ff), and cast off a false testimony that might defame his name (Mark 14:56; 1 Cor. 15:15). It also implies that we, as believers in Christ, should not judge rashly. One example was the case when King David believed Ziba's slander against Jonathan's son. David rendered a bad judgment without proper investigation (2 Sam. 16:4; 19:24ff). The disciples did the same with the blind man, presuming and wrongly judging that he or his parents had sinned to cause his blindness (John 9:2). This is one of the reasons why Jesus tells us not to render a personal judgment of condemnation (Matt. 7:1-3, Rom. 14:3-19; Col. 2:16).[2] In this regard, the elders contended that Bernie often rashly judged others.

Another application of this commandment says that we must investigate the facts to get at the truth, and not assume, presume or do anything that would harm our neighbor's reputation. Bernie was guilty of this too, particularly as he frequently slandered the pastor.

A further use of the ninth commandment is God's prohibition against lying (Exod. 23:1; Prov. 6:17; Hos. 4:2). A false or wicked witness is evil because he utters lies (Pro. 14:5, 25) and injures or destroys another's good name.

These were the things Bernie had been doing all along. More than ten people testified against him, while none of his friends could deny it wasn't so. Bernie's gossiping and slanderous ways, and his self-righteous judgmentalism had hurt and injured many people, and it was obvious that the elder had a goal to destroy his pastor. He denied the accusations, claiming he had a right to do what he did, that he did nothing wrong, that he was only telling the truth when he spoke, and that he never said anything to anyone else outside the church. The church people needed to know how bad the pastor was, he insisted. But then the town mayor showed up and verified that Bernie had indeed systematically gone from business to business talking to managers and owners about the pastor. Bernie was severely embarrassed.

Working through the charge of abuse took two days. Dan had already given each of the elders a copy of Richard Ganz's *20 Controversies That Almost Killed a Church*, and urged them to read Johnson and VanVonderen's *The Subtle Power of Spiritual Abuse* too. He further suggested Mike Fehlauer's *Exposing Spiritual Abuse*, Ken Blue's *Healing Spiritual Abuse,* and Dave Burchett's *When Bad Christians Happen to Good People*, and Mary Chrnalogar's *Twisted Scriptures*. Dan handed out his worksheet on abusive speech (see Appendix P) to the elders. With that they easily substantiated that Bernie had a consistent pattern of abusive language.

While the Bible does not talk about abuse, it does command elders not to lord it over or domineer God's flock (Matt. 23; 1 Pet. 5:3). Having had experience by serving on a committee to investigate charges against another pastor for being abusive, Dan was prepared to speak to this issue. Like the charge against the former pastor, this was another charge against Bernie.

When Bernie and his counsel asked for clarification, Dan was pleased to provide it. "Three passages which demonstrate abusive authority are Matthew 20:25, Matthew 23, and Luke 22:25."

After reading the passages which highlight Jesus' condemnation for abusive authority so common among unbelieving leadership, Dan said, "Lording it over is the excessive or coercive use of authority for unbiblical, sinful and/or self-serving purposes rather than for the glory of God, the edification, loving welfare and protection of God's people. Lording it over happens when leadership steps beyond the boundaries set by God's Word."

A discussion ensued about authority and submission. Bernie and his counsel tried to argue that he had a right to exercise authority and demand submission from others because he was the eldest of elders. That argument might have flown in other circles but not with those who traditionally have believed in an equal co-rulership (Acts 20:17, 28; Ti. 1:5-7). Marcus summarized for everyone present what the four elders and pastor had discussed at the previous evening's meeting.

Bernie then argued that as an elder he did not answer to the people in the congregation, but that they were answerable to him. Dan said that was only partly correct. According to such passages as 1 Corinthians 4:1-5 and Titus 1:7 the elder is not accountable to the congregation. "The Bible never teaches that the sheep or congregation has authority. Indeed many passages such as 1 Thessalonians 5:21 and Hebrews 13:17 teach otherwise."

Bernie's friend added that Christians have a responsibility to be subject to one another (Eph. 5:21; 1 Pet. 5:5). "True also, and this is what I was just going to add. However, you are not helping Bernie's case. This kind of subjection is to be done in the fear of Christ, which means that all of us are ultimately subject to the Lord. Therefore we are all subject to one another in Christ. The subjection the Word calls for is qualified by the context. It is subjection under Christ, out of love, for the highest good and needs of God's people. God's sheep place themselves under subjection of God-ordained servant-leaders in his church. Those ordained authorities are subject to the Lord and exhibit subjection to Christ by loving and serving his people justly, mercifully and with love."

"See, you agree with me!" Bernie said.

"Not with your interpretation, no. You have no authority residing in you. And you have stepped beyond the limits of biblical oversight," Dan countered. "You were selected as an elder to exercise authority from a motivation of love. As elders, we do so by teaching, urging, and appealing to people to put off sin and put on Christ, to repent and exercise faith. This is done lovingly for Christ's sake. We also exercise authority with compassion for distressed sheep. What's more, we are to exercise authority sacrificially, being willing to take up our own cross and willing to lay down our lives for God's flock."[3]

Bernie sat silently with his arms folded, legs crossed, and chin anchored to his sunken chest. His counsel had little to say. Dan watched Bernie. His heart flipped back and forth from disdain and near contempt to a sorrowful pity for the man.

Bernie accused Dan and the elders of misinterpreting Scripture. When he pronounced a number of things, which fully misconstrued Dan's definition of domineering leadership, Dan responded. "I am not saying that leaders in the church are without power and authority. I am not saying that God's officers should not or can not reprove or rebuke, or that they should never at times, reprove or rebuke severely. Indeed, they have the executive ability to come with the rod of God's Word when it is appropriate."[4] Dan continued, "Officers of God's church are not to lord it over God's sheep by ruling abusively or coercively. This abuse of authority happens when the leadership, or illegitimate power players step beyond the boundaries defined by God's Word! There is a difference between having authority and being authoritarian," Dan said looking right at Bernie.

The pastor, as moderator of the meeting, passed out two items. They were about the character and other requirements of an elder (see Appendices D and E). Dan urged the elders, including Bernie, to evaluate the defendant against the list of those character requirements. The second item was a list of questions he compiled to help the elders evaluate whether or not Bernie had lorded it over God's people at Grace Church. He passed out the paper to each elder and pastor and said, "Here are some questions for us to consider and answer:"

1. Has the elder acted in any way that has clearly violated Scripture in reference to his relationship with others?
2. Has the elder tried to enforce policies the elders never formulated, i.e., coming up with his own rules for the church?
3. Has the elder wrongfully put his or the church's rules on a level with Scripture?
4. Has the elder obviously violated another person's biblically informed conscience?
5. Have his actions built up or torn down the church (2 Cor. 13:10)?
6. Has the elder consistently said or done anything that demonstrates or proves he has not acted:
   a. With love for God's people (Jn 21:16; 1 Cor. 13)?
   b. With compassion for distressed sheep (Matt. 9:36; Mark 6:34; Jas. 5:14)?
   c. Sacrificially, for the sake of the church (Jn. 10:11, 15)?

    d. With a servant's heart (Matt. 20:25; Luke 22:26)?

    e. With a protective care for the flock (1 Tim. 3:5; Heb. 13:17)?

    f. Voluntarily without greed or without being under compulsion to serve (1 Pet. 5:2)?

7. Has he led or guided the church or an element in the church down the wrong path doctrinally or behaviorally?

8. Has he sinfully mistreated, subdued, coerced, manipulated or abused any member in the church?

9. Has he used his position in an excessive or coercive way for unbiblical, sinful and/or self-serving purposes rather than for God's glory and the loving welfare and edification of the church?

10. Can any of these items be factually, truthfully and scripturally demonstrated?

After hearing from several additional witnesses, the elders concluded that Bernie had in fact violated all of the items on the evaluation at one time or another, some to a greater degree than the others. Bernie protested and claimed his innocence.

Like his son, Bernie fit the pattern of an abusive man. Tom Marshall tells us that the classic symptoms of those who corrupt and abuse power are pride and arrogance, self-aggrandizement, insensitivity, domination and tyranny.[5] This was Bernie. Marshall speaks of this kind of tyranny:

> This is the final stage in the misuse of power, where the leader's authority is totally uncontrolled and coercive. There is no longer even the pretense of having to have good reasons for the orders given; they are to be obeyed just because they have been given, no matter how unreasonable or capricious they may be.
>
> It is clear that the people are no longer being led; they are being oppressed. They have ceased to be even means to an end; they have become the prey. They are captives who need to be rescued and prisoners who need to be set free."[6]

Just like the defrocked pastor, Bernie was guilty of being a tyrant. However, tyrants do not only come in the form of an elder or a pastor. Tyrants can also come in the form of a layman or woman, as Bill Lawrence points out:

> A major problem occurs when a church becomes a place where some laymen exercise power they can't get anywhere else. Instead of serving others they attempt to satisfy an unfulfilled drive for power. Still others use top-down authority, which is appropriate in the business world but totally inappropriate in the church. When either of these kinds of men exercise power on the board, they cease to be brothers and start to be bosses, but there is no place for a boss on any board, whether he is a

pastor or an elder. Unless the pastor is willing to confront, teach, and disciple such men in how to lead, they will constantly tell him what to do, even through they have neither the qualifications, the experience, nor the character to do so.[7]

The last charge brought against Bernie was that he was divisive. On this there was no arguing. When Bernie protested the accusation and became adamant, Marcus pulled out his notes from the meeting organized by Bernie months before, and the letter Bernie circulated among the twenty or so members of the church seeking to expel the pastor.

Even a few witnesses came in on that dreary Saturday morning to tell how they had been recruited and urged to stand against the pastor. Yet it was not merely against the pastor. Many of his actions clearly divided loyalties and polluted trusts. Bernie's gossiping, grumbling, complaining, fault-finding and backbiting was sinful in itself, but the net effect was to disrupt the peace and purity of the church and to drive a wedge into the heart of the congregation. Ganz portrays a similar scene Grace was experiencing:

> However, a quick look at the Scriptures reveals others [divisive behaviors of envy and strife which divide and ruin good churches], most notably grumbling and complaining. The most striking example in the Bible of this sin is the activity of Korah, Dathan, and Abiram. They continually grumbled and complained against the leadership of Moses. Numbers 16 said, 'They rose up against Moses. With them were two hundred fifty Israelite men.' These men had contempt and disrespect for God's ordained leadership, attitudes that could only kill and divide the congregation. In this case, Korah, Datha, and Abiram had gathered others in their cause.[8]

Bernie was the leader of a sinful rebellion, though he had other influencers who helped. God tells us that the authorities in the church are to warn a divisive man no more than two times. After that the church is to have nothing to do with him (Tit. 3:10). Paul's other warning is equally clear: "Now I urge you, brethren, note those who cause divisions and offenses, contrary to the doctrine which you learned, and avoid them. For those who are such do not serve our Lord Jesus Christ, but their own belly, and by smooth words and flattering speech deceive the hearts of the simple" (Rom. 16:17-18).

The elders found Bernie guilty on all counts. Were it not for the fact that he continued to be defiant and belligerent and deny he was guilty of anything the elders might have issued a lesser sentence. As a consequence they suspended him from the sacraments until he showed a humble repentance. They also suspended him from office and told him it was possible for him to be restored if, again, he showed a humble repentance over a period of one year. Bernie did not help himself with his closing diatribe against what he called a kangaroo court, led by a power monger disguised as a pastor. He immediately declared he would take their decision to presbytery and appeal it all the way to the denomination's national assembly.

The elders went home exhausted. The trial consumed a good portion of two weeks. Dan received a phone call from New Mexico asking if he had decided yet. Dan told them he had been tied up with a discipline case so hadn't been able to give the decision the time it deserved.

Bernie was absent from church that morning. He wasn't feeling well.

A CHALLENGE TO THINK AND DO

What do you think?
1. What lessons did you take from this chapter? In what ways has this chapter affected you?
2. How would you have dealt with Al and Katrina if you were at that meeting?
3. How would you have addressed Bernie if you were in Pastor Dan's position?
4. Just what is church office or a church officer?
5. According to the Bible, what authority and power does a church officer have? What are the limits of authority and power in the local church?
6. How would you answer the statement, "That man has the authority in this church"?
7. What is it to "lord it over" others? See Matthew 20:25, Luke 22:24, 1 Peter 5:3.
8. What should be done with domineering, abusive power players in the local church?
9. Why do you think churches tolerate domineering and abusive leadership?
10. In your opinion, why don't churches follow Romans 16:17-18 and Titus 3:10?
11. What does it mean that Christians are subject to one another in Christ? How does that apply to you and your church?

Some things you could do:
1. Read Ganz's book, *20 Controversies That Almost Killed a Church.*
2. Read Johnson and Van Vonderen's *The Subtle Power of Spiritual Abuse.*
3. Make a chart comparing what the Bible says about legitimate power and authority in the church with illegitimate, domineering authority. Then list how you should live in response to legitimate church authority, and what you should do regarding illegitimate, domineering authority.

20

THEREFORE, LET IT BE RESOLVED…

—⟋⟍—

Spring opened early. April was in full bloom. The tulips, daffodils and irises Mona planted in her front garden stood tall and colorfully proud. She enjoyed cleaning away the broken and dead branches from her shrubs and trees. Meanwhile, Dan helped her carve away the front lawn to make space for more shrubs and flowers. That suited him fine. He very much liked the fresh, perky color framing a manicured turf. It was refreshing, upbeat, and happy.

The hard winter had died away. The small town had thawed, just as Grace Church was also thawing. Dan's backyard reminded him of the church – old trees withering away and sagging with weak wood, dead branches, and sickly leaves. The newly planted fruit trees were spry with the kelly green of new growth, packed with buds, and sprinkled with flowers. Pocks in the dirt and dead clumps of grass littered a lawn trying to resuscitate itself. Like people. Two well-worn paths furrowed deeply in the yard, cut by man and beast. One ran from the door to the trash cans, and the other from the door to the dog house. The grooves were unsightly, potentially hazardous, and easily filled with water and debris. Reminiscent of bad habits turned into established traditions. And those dog-gone resilient weeds! So many, so deep, so invasive, so ugly! Like sin. On the other hand, Mona's territory reminded him of the New Life Church in New Mexico.

Trying to reconcile, Pastor Lee continued to systematically visit the antagonists. The elders summoned Katrina and Al in order to admonish them. At the meeting, Katrina seemed more broken than Al, though he looked pretty fearful. They verbally forgave Dan and promised to change their abhorrent ways. They reluctantly articulated and asked forgiveness for their obvious sins. Irma popped in and out of one worship service, but she stubbornly refused to meet with the elders.

Bernie's old friend and elder retired from the elder board. The elders had the social committee plan a small retirement event in April one Sunday after church. At the same time they urged the man not to join Bernie in his efforts to divide the church, or he too would be disciplined. His attendance was sporadic thereafter, which he blamed on his failing health.

Two of the new families left because of the strife. Two couples, both long-term members also left. They were upset that a great elder like Bernie was treated so terribly, especially by the new elders who were coming in to take over the church.

One middle-aged couple, who had been at the church for over twenty-five years, told the pastor they were leaving too. "Why?" asked a surprised Dan. They did not support Bernie. They didn't even seem to like him. "Because we are upset at how the previous pastors treated everyone at this church. Too many of them were legalistic. And we don't like the changes that are happening."

"I don't understand. Those pastors are history. Do you have a problem with me?"

"Oh no. We love you."

"You don't like the changes? If you leave and go to a completely different church, won't that be a major change?"

"Uh? Yeah, 'suppose so."

Dan gave them a copy of the handout on how to leave a church, which Dan included in the syllabus for the church's membership class (see Appendix Q). He urged them to read through it and follow its recommendations before taking their membership elsewhere.

One family who had been around for dozens of years admitted to the elders that they went along with Bernie because they feared him. He kept telling them they had to submit to their elder. On the night Joe, Marcus and Dan visited with the family, the elders explained that they were to imitate their elders (Heb. 13:7), honor them (1 Tim. 5:17-25), esteem them (Phil. 2:29), and obey them. Dan then read verses such as Hebrews 13:17, Titus 2:11-14, 3:1-3, 1 Corinthians 16:13-16 and 1 Thessalonians 5:12.

The elders also explained that Bernie was only one of several elders. He was not the singular boss. Any official directive had to come from the session and not merely from one person. Furthermore, they told the couple, no elder, not even the pastor, had a right to tell someone what to do unless it came from God's written Word. The very timid couple seemed relieved, but still feared Bernie. The elders urged the couple to come to them should they have any questions or if Bernie should confront them.

In the meantime, Bernie took advantage of the time while waiting for his appeal to be heard by the regional church. In the interim he continued his efforts to extract Dan from the church. He also demanded another vote regarding the new elders, and spontaneously called or visited people to tell them that Dan accepted a call to a new church. It provoked anger toward Dan among many of the new people. Some were confused, and others felt betrayed.

Dan called for an unofficial meeting of the congregation to dispel rumors and to answer questions. They held it in the worship hall on the second Thursday of April. Dan told them that he had indeed accepted an invitation to candidate at New Life Church in New Mexico, and that he and his family interviewed there. New Life issued a call and wanted the Lees to move in May. Yet he and Mona had not yet decided, and if they did accept the call, it would take up to eight weeks before they could leave.

Judy wanted to know why Dan would even consider leaving. Dan told them frankly that the recent turmoil surrounding Bernie, Irma and others was symptomatic of the on-going problems he experienced since he had arrived. Most people were shocked. He did his best not to put anyone in a bad light. He merely noted the disagreements with the elders over the vision and direction for the church, his preaching, and philosophy of ministry. Did Dan look at the new elders the same way? No.

Harold was angry. Judy, Melissa, and a few other women were crying. Matt was quite depressed. Marcus closed out the meeting by admonishing the congregation to practice the peacemaking lessons they had been taught. He encouraged them to pray for the peace, unity and purity of the church, for the elders and future decisions, for Bernie, and for the Lee family. Joe closed in prayer.

Dan had a message from his new friends at New Life Church to call as soon as he got in. Dan called Stu Hartsteader right away.

"Stu? Hi, this is Pastor Dan."

"Hi, Dan. Good to hear from you. How are you?"

"These are the best of times; these are the worst of times."

"Is Grace Church making any headway?"

"Yes, actually. I should be encouraged. But it's been a long and difficult battle." Dan told him a little about the congregational meeting.

"We wanted to know if you had made a decision or not?"

"Please accept my apologies, and forgive me for putting you off again and again. Had I known things would come to a raucous head, I would not have candidated at New Life. It really hasn't been fair to you."

"No apology necessary. We completely understand. How much more time do you need?" Stu asked.

"I don't see resolution...uhm...I don't think we'd be free to leave here until mid-July."

"Does that mean you are accepting the call?"

"I'd like to, but Mona isn't convinced, and there are other factors involved in the decision. Stu, look, I think you ought to go ahead and look at other candidates."

"Dan, the reason why we keep calling back is because the congregation wants you and your family."

Dan was moved to tears. Imagine that! Here I am thinking about staying at a church where a fifth of the people are trying to kick me out, where I've been the brunt of mean-spirited antagonism... so, why am I wondering if I should go to a place that wants me, likes my preaching, loves my family? Why would I waffle on a decision like this? What could possibly be so difficult about this choice?

"Dan? You still there?" Stu called out.

"Yes, I'm here. Just thinking. I'm honored and humbled. You are so kind."

"How about this, we'll give you two more weeks. Will that help you?"

"Sure, sure. Thanks. That will help, and you have my word that we will give you an answer by then. How about two weeks from tomorrow night?"

"Good. By the way, no pressure, but we really want you."

"Oh, right. No pressure at all!" Dan chuckled.

Dan told Mona they had two more Fridays, but he did not say any more. He was quite aware how distraught she was over the meeting, and knew full well she really did not want to leave.

Dan called Kent Friday morning. Kent didn't have too much more to offer than what they had already discussed, and what Dan had already figured out. Kent did remind him, however, that with the new elders the dynamics had changed. He suggested Dan think through how the three significant changes would impact the future of the church: the change with the elder board, removing or reconciling with the problem people, and the influx of new members and new believers. He told Dan he should write down a list of all the positive, encouraging things the Lord has been doing the past year. "Perhaps the intense struggle through which you've gone this past year or so was to give birth to a new life at church. The old sinful patterns had to die or be killed off, so to speak, to make way for new things in Christ."

"Good point. I hadn't considered that," Dan admitted.

"Here's another thing to consider, my friend: do you love the people at Grace?"

"Funny you should ask that. A few days ago I was working through 1 Corinthians 13, asking two questions: How does a pastor love his people, and how do God's people love their pastor? It was a hard exercise. Some people I love very much, but there are others who, admittedly, I don't love as I should" (see Appendixes R and S).

"Well, good. I believe one of the main factors in a pastor's decision to stay or leave is the level of Christ-like love he has for the people at his current church."

"Hmmm. I'll have to think through that one. Once more your advice has helped this beleaguered soul. Thanks so much, Kent."

"Always good to help out my friend. Call to let me know what you decide."

"Will do."

To the right of his old, roll-top, oak desk in his home office was a four-foot, oak bookcase. It housed a dozen or more books. Dan reached over and hooked two familiar and used ones by their spines: John R. Cionca's *Red Light Green Light* and Craig Brian Larson's

Staying Power. Mona went to bed early, but Dan decided to work through Cionca's book again. It is a book that takes the significant factors of a pastor's life and perspective, as well as the life and condition of the church, and then formulates important questions to help the pastor decide whether the conditions are favorable for him to remain or if they indicate he leave. Dan sat up until after midnight taking notes, writing down his answers in the charts, and thinking deeply about the life of the church and the condition of his own soul and ministry.

The undertaking was not easy. If he had gone through the book a year ago, and the opportunity arose to go to New Life, there would be no doubt in his mind that he and his family should leave; but changes had taken place. The church was financially healthy, even without the contributions of the Dumpletons. It was growing with new members and believers who outnumbered the old group, and there were new elders willing to work with Dan. When he finished the book by noon on Friday, he was still in a quandary. The final tally did not weigh heavily in one direction or another.

Matt called during lunch. He asked the pastor if he could meet with him and his non-Christian friend Mark around 4:30 P.M. on Saturday. Dan double-checked his calendar, and then asked Mona for clearance. The time was open and the meeting was set. Matt asked if Dan could pick them up after school at the college and then go to their favorite park. Now the place was set too.

Marcus caught him at the church office around 2:30 P.M. He said that the congregation requested another meeting for the Thursday after next. *How curious,* Dan thought. *The night before I'm supposed to call New Life Church.* "What's it about this time?" he asked.

"They all want to ask you what they can do to convince you to stay," his new elder friend said in his deep, rich voice.

"You know, this church doesn't make it easy for a minister. I'm getting pressured from both sides," Dan complained half-joking, folding his hands on top of his head. He wasn't angry. He was more emotionally numb than anything. "One group is pushing me out the door, and the other is pulling me in. At some point you all are going to rip me wide open," he sniggered.

"That might not be bad. Then both groups would get their way," Marcus laughed heartily. Dan couldn't help but laugh given Marcus' contagious belly laugh.

"Thursday next it is."

Another appointment set.

The folks at the care group did their best to lift the emotional atmosphere. They knew Dan and Mona were exhausted and discouraged. Each person arrived with kisses and long hugs to their hosts, and with special desserts and drinks. More than thirty came, filling the

Lees' front room. They asked Dan for a shorter than usual study so that they could take time to pray for him, Mona and his family. Very good idea.

Everyone was careful not to talk about the recent conflict. Not that they were trying to ignore the problems; it was that they had been talked out, and it was time to talk up. Dan took twenty minutes with the Bible lesson, and then Marcus took over the time of prayer. He directed people to spend time praising and thanking God for things. No requests or petitions yet.

The people spent thirty minutes offering praises to the Lord for his character, for the many answered prayers, for the good changes at Grace, and for new members, new visitors, and new Christians. Harold boldly thanked God for getting rid of those pesky trouble-makers. It was when people started thanking God for Dan's godly character, solid and helpful preaching, strong leadership, and for Mona's gracious spirit and limitless acts of kindness, that Dan and Mona were overcome with humble gratitude.

Then, spontaneously, people began to confess their sins. Melissa thanked God for Dan and Mona's constant support, but asked the Lord to forgive her for taking advantage of them and not coming to their aid when they needed it. Matt confessed he should have and could have found ways to serve the Lee family rather than always being served by them. He broke down in tears for being so selfish. Harold agreed, and confessed the same. Judy confessed to God she had not done enough to encourage the pastor. "His messages have meant so much to me, and I never said anything to him, Lord!" Blake admitted he liked to clown around and have fun, but that he avoided conflict; he should have told those who complained to him about the Lees, to quit grumbling and get right with God. Others joined in, some saying they hadn't shown how much they truly loved Dan and Mona, but promised to do so from here on. A few more people agreed they had the same faults, and should have told the Lee family how much they cared for them and appreciated them. Dan and Mona were broken.

When the confession time began to subside, Marcus confessed various corporate sins. "Lord, we've been a terrible church. We've not only offended our pastor and his family, we've not only failed to protect them, encourage them, love them and lift them, but we have failed you too. We have been cranky and mean. We have allowed the sins of gossip and slander, grumbling and complaining, hiding or fighting to take over us. We've been a disgrace to your name, O Lord! We put up with the cranky and the crabby too long. Allowed the goats to hurt the sheep, the tares to smother the wheat, our wayward brethren to weary our body. Forgive us, Lord! May you change our souls and the very soul of this church! We want to live by your heat and light, to be willing clay pots in your mighty hands. We want to be a people gripped by the Cross, grasped by the Spirit, grounded by your Word, and gladdened by your joy. Help us, O Lord, to be a Gospel people who live by truth and grace and love. In Jesus' awesome name!" And with him came a chorus of amens.

The little congregation embraced one another, wiped tears, laughed and cried. Dan, composing himself, requested the prayer time be over. Everyone agreed, but wanted to come together again for prayer the next week. Then, Blake called out, unwrapping his plate of chocolate chip brownies, "Let's par-tay!" Brian flipped on the stereo, turned the volume low for relaxing ambience, and forged his way to the kitchen to make the punch.

It was eleven that night before people began to leave. Dan blessed and thanked each one as they left, and told them he looked forward to seeing them on Sunday. All agreed it was a wonderful evening, and most agreed it was unbelievably refreshing and beautiful. The college and high school group, once again, cleaned house before they left.

Mona and Dan went to bed with souls much more restored. Is the evil of the past gone? Or will it rear its ugly head again? *Lord, spare the church from such wickedness happening again*, Dan pleaded.

Dan uncharacteristically decided to take Saturday morning off to play with the children and to help Mona with the front yard. Dan called it yardening. Mona called it bringing glory to creation.

Late afternoon, Dan, prompt as usual, swung by the campus to pick up Matt and Mark. As requested, they slalomed along the narrow two-lane road deep into the wood until they arrived at the wilderness park. The place was vacant, save the wild populace. Matt wanted to follow a new trail. Under partly cloudy skies, they walked the gravel lot, through a space between two old telephone poles resting atop three-foot railroad ties deeply anchored in the soil. The path was wide and pulled them to a fork.

Matt quoted one of Dan's favorites, "When you see a fork in the road, take it!"

Mark laughed.

Dan asked, "Which way, Mark?"

"Uhh, I dunno."

"Like life, isn't it?"

"Yeah? Guess so."

"You have a fork in the road of your life, don't you?"

"Oh? I think so."

"Pastor is talking about what you and I were talking about the other day; when you asked all those spiritual questions."

"Ohhh! That! Yeah, I'm not sure where I am."

"What questions do you have? But first, should we walk up this path or down that one?"

"Let's go up," Mark said with a smile.

Mark started off with the standard protest questions like – "Where did Adam and Eve's sons get their wives?" "Did the flood really happen?" "Isn't the God of the Old Testament a God of war and the one in the New Testament a God of love?"

"Those are good questions and there are so many more like them. But the real question you need to answer is the question Jesus asked his own students, Who do you say I am? Who do you say Jesus is?"

"I'm not sure."

Dan explained briefly that Jesus is the eternal God who became man. He came to save God's people from God's wrath for being guilty of rebellion against God and to pay the debt owed for sin. Jesus was brutally beaten, hung upon the cross until he died, and then was buried. But, he rose up from the dead with a new body, was seen by more than five hundred people over several weeks, and then ascended into heaven. He is there now alive and well, as the God-Man in spirit and body. He goes to bat for us as mediator and priest, he rules our lives as king, and speaks to us through his Word as prophet.

Mark asked a few more questions.

"The only way to lift the heaviness of the burden of your guilt is to trust in Jesus Christ as the one who can save you. He said, 'I am the Way, the Truth and the Life, no one can come to God the Father except through me.'"

"I don't know what to do," Mark said as they slowly hiked the hill.

"Repent," Matthew said.

"What does that mean?"

A squinting Matt looked to Dan. The sun shot scores of beams through needles and leaves, directly into their faces.

"Repent means to do a wholehearted about face. To repent is to turn away from sin, wickedness and evil, and to turn facing God," Dan said.

"Yeah, but then what?"

"Go to God in faith. Go with a wholehearted, committed trust. Faith is a grace where you receive and rest upon Jesus' life and work for salvation."

"How do I do that?"

"Go to God in prayer and tell him. Ask him to give you a saving kind of faith. Tell him you want to believe in Jesus Christ as your savior, and you want to commit your life to him," Matt encouraged him.

The three of them stopped and found some large rocks upon which to sit. They talked some more, but Mark was embarrassed to pray out loud in front of others. Neither Dan nor Matt pressured him.

It was getting near suppertime, so Matt suggested they return home. Dan asked if they would like to come over for supper. The two of them looked at each other, smiled, then turned to the pastor and said, "Sure! Cool."

Fulfilling his habit, Dan pulled into the driveway a little past the house, next to the detached garage in the backyard. The three climbed out. Dan led the way to the back door. Entering in the alcove, the place was eerily quiet. "Mona? Kids? Anyone home?"

Dan became concerned.

Matt asked, "Is everything okay? Where is everybody?"

"I don't know," Pastor said with seriousness.

The young men followed him around. As he stepped into the living room, an explosion of "Surprise!" filled the house. Dan jumped back, almost falling on Matt who grabbed him.

"What is going on here?" he said as if angry, but a smile betrayed him.

Mona led everyone in singing "Happy Birthday."

Dan never before had a birthday surprise. He was somewhat shaken. He didn't much care for surprises, but he didn't appear to mind this. Mona and the kids scooted over to him for some big hugs. Hannah kept repeating, "Happy, happy, happy." He picked up his little princess and cuddled her.

One by one people came over to shake his hand, or give him hugs or kisses. They kept streaming up from the basement, and flowing down from the second floor. More than sixty folks crowded every nook and cranny on the ground floor. Blake, once again, cried out, "Let the par-tay begin!" He liked parties.

The women retrieved the hidden plates of cookies and brownies, and the bowls of chip and dip. The college guys brought out a large assortment of drinks.

Dan locked Matt and Mark in his elbows, lightly knocking their heads together. "You were a part of this, weren't you? You knew all along!" They laughed.

Mona yelled over the crowd, "Matt's idea! Matt's fault!"

Dan let Mark go, but kept Matt in a headlock. He knuckled Matt's head, and ruffled his hair, then pushed him away. Matt turned to him, red faced, and smiled large. Dan then reached out his arms, grabbed his disciple by the shoulders, pulled him in, and gave him a big bear hug. Kissing him on his head, he proclaimed as if angry, "Matt!" Then in a soft voice, "You are something else. Thank you. I love you!"

Matt responded and gave Dan a big hug, but held him tightly for a while. "I love you too. You're my other dad, you know." He began to weep. "Please, Dan, please don't go."

Dan now got teary-eyed. "Hey, let's deal with it later, all right?"

"Okay," the wrestler huffed. Wiping his eyes, he turned around. His college friends pretended to box him, then gently tackled him and almost wrestled him to the ground. They respected him, and all the more, seeing under the clumsy and tough veneer of a short jock, a loving man who had a passion for Christ and compassion for others, especially a visible love for his mentor and friend.

A big cake was brought out with huge candles that would not blow out. Dan made the traditional first slice, and served the first piece to his wife. The mountain of gifts on the buffet sideboard required the help of Jake, Ben and Hannah. Unwrapping them was a delightfully long chore. Some gifts were practical, and others were practical jokes. All expressed generous appreciation, kindness and love. Dan could not thank them enough. He would send thank you notes to each giver within a week.

The party roared on until 11:00 p.m. when Dan chased them out the door. As Matt and Mark were leaving, Matt turned to his friend and said, "Go ahead. Tell him."

"Tell me what?" asked a curious pastor.

Mark hesitated. He fought back tears and stuttered a bit. "I believe in Jesus. Something's changed!"

"Yahoo!" Dan squealed. He grabbed his new young friend and gave him a bear hug. "That's great news! Such great news!" With his arm around Mark, he led him over to the elders to tell them the good news. Much rejoicing went on. Dan said the news was the best of the birthday gifts. He prayed for Mark, and then promised to get together with him within the week.

Almost all had left. This time the elders and their wives remained to clean up. Dan and his bride agreed the past week was the best they had experienced at Grace. Mona was reassured and pleased, but Dan was guarded. Too many dodged bullets, and leaps into foxholes, to believe all was well. He tried to encourage Mona, who was dismayed that Dan did not share her enthusiasm. Twitching and jerking, he joked that he was suffering from spiritual and emotional post-traumatic stress syndrome. She just rolled her eyes. He took her into his arms for a long embrace.

The next morning Dan and Mona observed a new energy at Grace. The Dumpletons were absent, as were quite a few of Bernie's followers. The elders huddled with the pastor after church to tell him that Bernie had a meeting at his home to start another church. This is what Bernie told Joe. Dan was disheartened. He'd prefer they stayed and reconciled; but that was his idealism tugging at his conscience. When he thought about it, it might be easier they all did leave so as to get a new start. Forgiveness is supposed to be granted, and is meant to help people forget. Yet it takes a long time to put aside long held resentments, and to develop trust.

It was a good Monday. That evening Dan burrowed himself in the home office. He learned from his brother the value of debriefing. After a military exercise, the powers gathered together to discuss the challenges they encountered, the failures they met, the successes they celebrated, the tactics that worked, and so forth. It was a time for assessment and evaluation. Dan decided to do the same. He asked himself, "What significant things have I learned since entering the ministry?" He journaled a lengthy list:

1. *There were significant skills I did not learn in seminary, but achieved through my mentors:*
   a. *Skills for equipping others*
   b. *Relational skills*
   c. *Leadership skills*
2. *Don't wait and let months pass …*

    a. *Before taking action on doing the right thing*

    b. *And assume that those sinful or negative issues will just go away by themselves*

    c. *And expect people to change without loving reproof, rebuke, exhortation*

3. *Be truthful and forthright, with gentleness, even if it hurts.*

4. *Even though a person may be placed into or assumes the role of leader does not mean he or she is in fact a leader.*

5. *Invest time in people and not merely spend time with people.*

6. *The more knowledge and skill I have, the less fearful I am and the more confident I become.*

7. *Make regular assessments of the church and my life.*

8. *Immediately address sinful, negative attitudes and behavior exhibited in meetings.*

9. *Be more assertive in working with volunteer teams. "Fire" those leaders who are not actively functioning as team leaders or who consistently fail to follow through in their delegated assignments.*

10. *Cast the vision and mission to the congregation several times a year.*

11. *Resolve not to get bogged down in doctrinal issues when the conflict(s) have to do with sinful attitudes and behaviors.*

12. *Don't waste time in pointless debates over the opinions of the overly confident.*

13. *Be an active peacemaker and work toward developing a culture of biblical peace in the church.*

14. *Insist on receiving administrative actions, policies and procedures in writing.*

15. *It's the person with a strong or the strongest point of view who influences a group.*

16. *Take significant steps to improve my communications skills:*

    a. *Choose and use words carefully.*

    b. *Attempt to be clear.*

    c. *Keep things simple and keep them short.*

    d. *Ask the questions, even the tough ones.*

    e. *Do not overuse generalizations.*

    f. *Verbally paint the big picture.*

    g. *Follow up abstract concepts with concrete examples.*

17. *If needed, enlist another person to help improve communication process between others and myself within the church.*

18. *Repent of my sin of the fear of man, refuse to be intimidated by anyone. Fear God alone.*

19. *Time invested in people should be directly proportionate to their level of commitment to grow and/or lead.*

Dan made a commitment to review, to practice, and to own these lessons in order to sharpen the skills he needed to be more godly and more effective.

On Tuesday night the cell phone yodeled in Pastor's shirt pocket. "Hello, this is Dan."
It was from Mrs. Dumpleton. Bernie was rushed to the hospital with a serious stroke. Dan was stunned. He said he would be right over.
When Dan arrived at the hospital, Wes started to get violent. The nurses called security. He left the premises, but not without yelling obscenities and threatening to shoot the man who caused his father's stroke. A nurse then called the police.
The pastor was ushered into the coronary care unit. Mrs. Dumpleton was sitting by her husband's bed. He was asleep. The doctors were running tests to determine more precisely the extent of the damage.
"It doesn't look good," she said softly with tears trickling down her cheeks. She told the pastor that he was sitting in his recliner, and as he was about to get up, he collapsed. She could not wake him up, so she dialed 9-1-1. The doctors did say that if he survived this episode it would be a long and difficult road. Dan prayed for Bernie and his wife. He stayed around a while before going home.
Dan called the prayer chain, and emailed everyone in the church in order to solicit prayers and support.

Much transpired in the days leading up to the Thursday night congregational meeting. Bernie's prognosis was not good. Wes was arrested for drunken and disorderly conduct at the hospital. The elders took turns visiting and praying for Bernie and his wife. The ladies rallied to provide meals for her. Les had come back to town to visit his father. Two couples, out of the estranged twenty, returned to the church. With Bernie no longer able to lead, the others went their separate ways. Irma now worshiped at the idol of her store. She practically lived there. The grapevine whispered she had become even more caustic. It had little effect on her business, but she could never get good help.

Joe opened the Thursday night congregational meeting with a short devotional and prayer. Then he asked Dan to come forward. "Dan, the people asked for this meeting with you for one purpose, to answer: what can we do to keep you here?"
Dan slowly approached the front of the room, swallowing the lump in his throat again and again. With a deep breath and a disciplined composure, he faced the eighty-nine teens and adults. Dan said that to keep him at Grace would require change. The terms were clear. They had to have a serious commitment to Christ, and a demonstrable love for others.

Changes would take place according to a biblical vision. That would require changes in worship and in several programs. The church would also need to take seriously Christ's mandate to reach the lost in the town and county, not merely overseas. The church would also work hard at being peacemakers. They would adopt a zero tolerance for gossip, slander, backbiting, grumbling, complaining or any other sinful, abusive and obnoxious behavior. Those were the non-negotiables. For the next twenty minutes he outlined what he believed to be the essentials for a biblical, God-glorifying church, touching upon worship, community and outreach.

Silence engulfed the place. Then Harold stood up and said, "Is that all?" The crowd burst with laughter.

Matt said, "Where's the covenant? I'm ready to sign." A rumble of agreement rose to a crescendo until Joe brought the meeting back to order.

"We have a question," Melissa said, looking at Judy.

"Go ahead," Dan responded.

"What can we do for you, Pastor? You haven't said anything about that. What can we do to encourage our pastor?"

Dan looked at them, almost with disbelief. No, not that Melissa or Judy would ask such a question. That's the kind of people they are. The fact that they had the freedom to ask it, and that eighty-seven others also wanted to know, was amazing.

"Whoa. Uhh…eh hemm. It's not about me, you know."

Judy stood. "We know that! For crying out loud, answer the question." Her finger shook at Dan.

"Okay. You asked! Get me my white board. I want you all to write this down, because either these things will apply to me or to your next pastor."

Matt and Brad ran to retrieve the large white board from the basement fellowship hall. Wheeled into place with plenty of markers and an eraser on hand, Dan began to write.

What you can do for your pastor

1. Live with him in the love of Christ, loving God with all your heart, soul, mind and might.

2. Love him in the Lord -refer to 1 Corinthians 13 notes (see Appendix S)

3. Pray for him all the time.

4. Let him rest.
"You know what this means? Give him opportunities for personal and familial rest. Be proactive to make sure he is getting spiritual, emotional, mental and physical rejuvenation.

Encourage him to take off for times of prayer, meditation and reflection. Leave him alone during his day or days off, unless of course, it is an emergency. Don't rely on him to solve all your problems, so don't keep on going to him relentlessly. Maybe even raise some funds and send him on a cruise or a study leave."

5. Honor and esteem him (Phil. 2:29; 1 Thess. 5:12, 13 cp. Acts 28:9-10, 2 Cor. 7:15).
He talked with them frankly that the esteem for a pastor or elder spoken of in Philippians 2:19-29 is a highly valued respect. It's the treatment one gives to something or someone of great and precious value.

"Esteem how? Very highly according to 1 Thessalonians 5:13. Why esteem the pastor? Because, the Bible says, he labors among you and for you as a servant who rules over you. See Hebrews 13:7 and 1 Corinthians 16:16. You know why people do not esteem their pastor, or worse, have contempt for him? Often times it is because they are rebelling against the Lord. If they are successful in undermining that delegated pastoral authority they will be successful in achieving their own selfish and sinful agenda!

Another reason to esteem the pastor is because he teaches and admonishes you in Christ. You cannot properly receive the full benefit of teaching and admonishment if you do not have humility and if you do not respect or esteem God's pastor or elder."

"You want to know how else?" Dan asked rhetorically, "you esteem him by respecting him, providing for his needs, treating him with a godly love. The opposite is despising him, which is forbidden according to First Corinthians 16:10."

"Appreciate him, says 1 Thessalonians 5:12. That means giving him a deserved recognition based upon his office and his labors.

6. Do everything you can to pump life into his soul.
"Build him up, encourage him, and communicate to him in the very many ways there are, how much his service means to you. Lift him up, inspire him, and bless him in Christ. You will reap the residual effects for it. Just as you did at the prayer meeting, lifting my family and me up to the Lord, showing your love and kindness. Just as you did when you celebrated my birthday. Be a conduit of grace, hope and love to build up your pastor.

7. Be loyal to him in Christ.
"Trust him when he is trustworthy. Treat him kindly and for who he is, and because his office."

8. Give to him as he gives to you.
"Give, not merely monetary support, but give service to him and his family. Be imaginative and think of ways you can serve your pastor: give him genuine and valuable feedback; give him moral support; give him time and prayer. Above all give him love and affection!"

9. Speak the truth in love.

"Do all you can to safeguard his name and reputation, but more than that, build up his name so that it becomes a name of honor. Certainly, the pastor must maintain his own reputation and integrity in Christ. This is not an admonition for you to pretend he is honorable if he has clearly sinned and defamed the name of Christ. But if he has a character beyond reproach, then uphold it, maintain it, and promote it."

10. Follow him as he leads with his fellow shepherd-elders.

"I've heard that an old Chinese proverb says, 'He who thinks he is leading but has no one following him is only taking a walk.' I am grateful for good followers. Church leaders are to lead God's people up the path to their personal and corporate, high and lofty calling in Christ. We are all to become the one new man in Jesus. I confess I've not been the best of leaders. At the same time I understand that I cannot expect some of you to invest more energy in service to Christ or to hike the upward climb than what your spiritual life has. I also know that there will be people who just will not follow, because for them the cost is too high. But I tell you this, as a servant-leader in the church of Christ, I'm moving ahead, and if it means leaving some behind, then so be it."

The audience clapped. Dan was astounded. He really didn't know all his people well.

"Imitate his walk in Christ. Follow his lead by obeying him. Hebrews 13:17 commands you to obey your leaders and submit to them because they watch over your souls. They have to give an account to God for you. And let their care for you be a joyful experience, not something that would make them groan!"

Dan erased and then wrote upon the board and explained:

Don'ts

1. Don't love your pastor more than you love the Lord.

2. Don't idolize or worship your pastor.

3. Don't be a living contradiction to the name and person of Christ in you.
"Don't be a hypocrite, trying to convince your pastor you are a good believer when you are thinking and behaving like the devil."

4. Don't overwork your pastor. Don't rely too heavily upon him.

5. Don't neglect the honor and respect, duty and obedience you owe the pastor in Christ that is concordant with God's Word.

6. Don't kill your pastor.

The people laughed. "I'm serious! I could write a book, '1001 Easy Ways to Kill off Your Pastor!' Of course I don't mean physically murdering the minister, though that has happened. I mean to say, don't murder him by mouth with gossip and slander. Don't beat him in the ground with the innumerable ways people can verbally assault the minister."

7. Don't allow your pastor or put your pastor in a situation that could tempt him or provoke him to immoral, unchaste thoughts, words or deeds.

"How often have we learned of a pastor who has fallen into immorality? If you know your pastor has certain vulnerabilities, then do all you can to protect him. Fellow elders, keep him accountable before the Lord in purity and holiness. If you know he is heading down a path toward sin, warn him, turn him around, stop him! Do it for his sake, for your sake, and for the good name of Christ!"

8. Don't steal from your pastor.

"Don't rob him of his devotional time, study time, down time, family time, or vacation time. Don't rob him of the double honor he is due. Pay him well so that he may be free from material concerns. Don't forbid him to exercise his God-given talents. I cannot tell you how often certain men told me I should not do things –in my own time, mind you – that exercised talents I enjoy!"

9. Don't injure the pastor's good name, and don't lie to him.

10. Don't covet another pastor when you have God's minister in your midst, and don't compare or contrast him with other pastors!

"Here's a quick way to discourage or defeat your pastor: compare him with another pastor. It doesn't matter who. Could be a previous pastor; could be a celebrity; could be a famous dead one. Don't compare! I cannot tell you how cutting it was when I was told I wasn't like Pastor X in preaching or Pastor Y in serving, or Pastor Z in personality. If you love that other person so much that you have no room for the pastor God put over you, then pack your bags and go where your hero is serving."

Before he finished, Dan suggested reading books such as Jane Rubietta's *How to Keep the Pastor You Love*. Joe allowed for a few questions, and then closed in prayer. Dan was thanked for his candid replies and insight. People were pensive and fearful that Dan would soon be announcing he took the call to another church. He would not answer their questions about the pending decision.

Friday evening rolled around. It was 9:00 o'clock. "Well, are you okay with our decision?" he asked Mona, sitting next to him.

"Yes. Are you?" she inquired back.

"I am. But I better call now and let them know." Her eyes portrayed a sympathetic smile.

He dialed Stu's number. "Hi Dan! We've been anxiously waiting your phone call. What news do you have for us? Have you come to a decision?"

"Hi, Stu! Good to hear your voice. Yes, we have made our decision."

A CHALLENGE TO THINK AND DO

What do you think?
1. Was there anything in particular that stood out to you in this chapter?
2. Read over Appendix Q on how to leave the church. Do you agree or disagree with it? Why?
3. What counsel or answers would you give Mark?
4. What responsibilities do church members have to their pastor(s) and elder(s)?
5. Look over the list Pastor Dan suggested for things you can do for your pastor. What are you good at? What things have you already done? What are the things your church does well?
6. Of the list of don'ts Pastor Dan wrote, what things are you guilty of doing? What are the things your church guilty of doing?
7. How would you advise Dan and Mona? Should they take the call to the church in New Mexico or remain at Grace Church?

Some things you could do:
1. Read through Appendix S on how to love your pastor. Put it into practice. Encourage others to do likewise.
2. Read Jane Rubietta's *How to Keep the Pastor You Love.*

APPENDIX A

A PASTOR'S CANDIDATING QUESTIONS FOR A CHURCH

—m—

A. **Tell me the history of this church**
   1. What is the history of the church?
   2. Are the founders still members of the church?
   3. What have been the attendance patterns of this church for the past three years?
   4. What is the history of your most important programs and activities?
   5. What is this church's pastoral record (I do not need personal information)?
      a. How many pastors have you had from beginning of the church?
      b. How long were their terms of service?
      c. Briefly, what were the reasons for their leaving (resigned, retired, or fired)?

B. **What demographic information about the church and community might be helpful?**
   1. What is the socio-economic composition of this church?
   2. Does this church reflect the surrounding neighborhood or local community?
   3. Is this city growing or declining?
   4. What is the economic health of the city or town?
   5. What is the socio-economic composition of this city or town?
   6. What is the housing affordability and availability?
   7. Are there zoning laws which would affect home gatherings, church's growth, potential church expansion, etc.?

C. **Tell me about the church's vision, mission and goals**
   1. Why does this particular church exist?
   2. Who is the church trying to serve?
   3. Does the church board have a vision and/or mission statement?
   4. What specific goals does the leadership of this church have?

    a. What short term goals does the leadership have?

    b. What long term goals does the leadership have?

5. How do you communicate the church's vision, mission and goals to the congregation?

6. How often do you communicate the church's vision, mission and goals to the congregation?

D. Describe the various philosophies and practices of ministry

1. Tell me about your philosophy and practice of worship.
   a. Please summarize this church's philosophy of worship
   b. How long have you practiced your current form of worship?
   c. Will adjustments or changes be permitted with the worship service(s)?
   d. What is your philosophy and practice of music in worship?
      (1) What are your views or policies regarding choir, praise team, or solos?
      (2) What do you believe about special music?
   e. What are your theological and philosophical views about baptism?
   f. What are your theological and philosophical views about the Lord's Supper?
   g. What is your philosophy of preaching?
      (1) How do you define preaching?
      (2) What styles of sermons do you expect?
      (3) Do you have any concerns about the length of the sermons?
      (4) Do you conduct formal evaluations of the pastor's preaching? By whom? How often?

2. Tell me about your philosophy and practice of the fellowship.
   a. How would you describe the relationships most of the members have with one another in this church?
   b. Approximately what percentage of the people has an active commitment to this local church?
   c. Do they faithfully pray with and for one another? Do you have congregational prayer meetings? Small group prayer?
   d. In what ways is it evident that this church expresses the love of Christ with one another?
   e. What are some ways this church practices mercy toward one another?
   f. Are there obvious exclusive cliques?
   g. Describe obvious ways that show how members enjoy one another's company and fellowship.
   h. What percentage of the church regularly practices hospitality?
   i. What kinds of things does this church do for fun and recreation?

    j.   What things do the women do for enjoyment together?

    k.   What things do the men do for enjoyment together?

    l.   How does this church promote the health of families?

    m. How does this church promote the health of singles?

3. Tell me about your Christian education philosophy and practices.

    a.   How is Christ being formed in this church?

    b.   What is your philosophy of Christian education and edification in this church?

    c.   Does this church have a written plan for Christian education?

    d.   What is your view and practice of children's ministries?

    e.   Do you have a philosophy of ministry regarding the relationship between the church and families with children?

    f.   What is your view and practice with Sunday school?

    g.   Tell me about your philosophy of youth ministry and about employing a youth director.

4. Tell me about your leadership.

    a.   Who are the official leaders in this church?

        (1) Are there elders? How many? Tell me something about them.

        (2) Are there any deacons? How many? Tell me something about them.

        (3) Are there any potential elders and deacons? Are they in training?

    b.   Who are the real power brokers in this church, the people who wield the most influence?

    c.   How does the leadership demonstrate biblical love toward one another?

    d.   How does the leadership demonstrate biblical love toward church members?

5. Describe this church's outreach philosophy and practice (i.e. local and foreign ministries of God's Word and mercy through evangelism and missions)

    a.   What is your philosophy of outreach?

    b.   How is this church fulfilling the Great Commission found in Matthew 28:18-20?

    c.   As a whole, is this church actively and regularly declaring the Good News of Jesus Christ? How?

    d.   Is there an active commitment on the part of God's people to seek and form fully devoted disciples of Jesus Christ?

    e.   What has this church done in the past five years to reach the lost in this community? Do you have any current programs oriented toward outreach?

    f.   Are there any new converts attending now?

    g.   In what ways does this church conduct Christ's work of mercy in this city?

    h.   Is there a commitment to seeing and helping new churches be planted?

    i.   What does this church do to help to encourage, to train, or to send out missionaries?

    j.   What percentage of the church's budget is committed to outreach and evangelism and missions?

    l.   What is your philosophy regarding the church's involvement in social issues?

6. Some other questions:

    a.   What is your philosophy regarding counseling within the church?

    b.   Do you have formal membership? If so, what is the process for becoming a member in this church?

    c.   What is your philosophy regarding church discipline?

    d.   Does this church have an active program to promote peace and unity among its membership?

E. Tell me about your church policies

1. Do you have a written constitution and/or by-laws? My I see them?

2. What policies (written or unwritten) do you have for:

    a.   The nursery?

    b.   Children in worship and/or children's church?

    c.   Child abuse prevention?

    d.   Who may teach in the various forums of this church?

    e.   Counseling within the church?

    f.   What ministry roles may non-members be involved with in this church?

    g.   What may women do in this church?

    h.   What may youth do in this church?

    i.   Emergencies?

F. Church Finances

1. What is the financial health of the church, now and historically?

2. Can you tell me about the congregation's pattern of giving during the past three years?

3. May I see the church budget to learn how the resources are allocated?

4. Does this church have fund raisers, pledge appeals, etc., throughout the year?

5. Is there any indebtedness?

    a. How much?

    b.   What percentage of the annual budget is the debt?

    c.   Is this related to a building program?

6. Is there a building program now or expected in the near future?

7. What is the biggest fiscal challenge presently?

8. What is your philosophy of remuneration (salary and benefits) for the pastor?

9. If the church were to receive a sizable contribution (such as $100,000.00), what would the church do with it?

G. Some questions about my fit for this church
1. What is it about my profile and resume that interests this church?
2. What are the apparent, obvious needs of the church that my gifts might serve?
3. Does this church have a job description for my position or must I develop one?
4. What expectations do you have of your pastor?
5. Can you describe your expectations for an average work-week for my position?
6. Will I have job evaluations? When and by whom?
7. Are you interested to learn about my dreams, goals or vision for ministry?
8. Are you willing to allow me to do what I do best according to my calling, gifts, talents, personality, etc.? How would I know?
9. Does the church provide time or financial provisions for my enrichment and educational opportunities?
10. What are some ways this church will help me refresh and recharge?
11. What expectations do you have for my wife?
12. What expectations do you have for my child(ren)?

H. Additional information to gather from the church
1. What do you consider to be the good thing(s) about this church?
2. What things can be improved?
3. What makes this church unique or different?
4. Are there congregational problems or issues about which the pastor will immediately need to address with the leadership?
5. What "traditions" are solidly established? Are they untouchable, unchangeable "sacred cows"?
6. What things may never be changed?
7. How big is too big for this church?
8. What reasons do new members give for joining the church?

APPENDIX B

A GUIDE FOR A PASTORAL VISIT

—m—

Date: _____

Name: _____

Address: _____

Phone: _____ **Email:** _____

Husband: _____ **Wife:** _____

Children: _____

A. <u>Questions for the Children:</u>
1. Have you been baptized yet?
2. Have you trusted in Jesus Christ as your Savior?
3. Do you read the Bible or have your own personal devotions?
4. What do you like? Dislike? What are your hobbies or special interests?
5. How is school going?
6. Do you have any questions for pastor?
7. Do you have any prayer requests?

B. <u>Questions for the Husband - Father:</u>
1. How would you describe your spiritual life?
2. Have you trusted in Jesus Christ as your Savior?
3. How is your devotional life with God?
4. How are your Lord's Days or Sundays? Do you prepare for them? How do you spend the days?)
5. Are you profiting from the messages in worship?
6. How is your giving or tithing?
7. Are you pastoring your family? Do you have daily family devotions or worship? Are you actively teaching your family spiritual truths?
8. Are you praying with and for family members?
9. Do you have regular dates with your wife?

10. Do you have quality time with your children?

11. How is your work life?

12. Do you have any goals, concerns, worries, longings you would like to share?

13. Do you have any particular problems or temptations I can help you with?

14. What are your prayer requests?

C. **Questions for the Wife - Mother:**

1. How would you describe your spiritual condition?

2. Have you trusted in Jesus Christ as your Savior?

3. How is your personal devotional life with God?

4. How are your Lord's Days or Sundays? Do you prepare? How do you spend the days?

5. Are you profiting from the messages in worship?

6. How is your giving or tithing?

7. Are you praying with and for your family members?

8. Are you actively involved in teaching spiritual things to your children?

9. Do you have quality time with your children?

10. If you work outside the home, how is that going?

11. Do you have any goals, concerns, worries, longings you would like to share?

12. Do you have any particular problems or temptations I can help you with?

13. What are your prayer requests?

D. **What do you believe are the positive things about our church? What can we do better?**

E. **Is there anything you would like to ask or discuss with me?**

Scripture Reading: _____

Close in prayer

APPENDIX C

A SERMON EVALUATION FORM

—ᗰ—

Scripture Text: _____

Sermon Title: _____

		Poor			Excellent	
I.	**Reading the Scripture**					
	A. Clear?	1	2	3	4	5
	B. Expressive?	1	2	3	4	5
II.	**Sermon Introduction**					
	A. The theme of the sermons was obvious	1	2	3	4	5
	B. Interest was aroused	1	2	3	4	5
	C. Theme was relevant (i.e. spoke to an issue or need)	1	2	3	4	5
III.	**Interpretation of the Passage**					
	A. The Bible text was explained	1	2	3	4	5
	B. The exegesis was correct	1	2	3	4	5
	C. The explanation fit the context	1	2	3	4	5
	D. The interpretation was true to the whole of the Scripture	1	2	3	4	5
	E. Jesus Christ was central to the text	1	2	3	4	5

IV. Main Structure of the Sermon

A. The main point is: _____

		Poor			Excellent	
1.	The main point was obtained from the main idea of the text	1	2	3	4	5
2.	The concern addressed in thetext is the sermon's concern	1	2	3	4	5

B. The sub-points of the text

		Poor			Excellent	
1.	The sub-points flow from the main point	1	2	3	4	5
2.	The sub-points connect to each other with a good flow	1	2	3	4	5
3.	Each sub-point was developed	1	2	3	4	5
4.	The transitions were clear	1	2	3	4	5

     5. The points and sub-points were effective   1 2 3 4 5

     6. Good overall movement   1 2 3 4 5

C. Illustrations

     1. The illustrations were appropriate   1 2 3 4 5

     2. They helped the points and did not distract   1 2 3 4 5

D. Application

     1. Application(s) came from the original application
of the text   1 2 3 4 5

     2. They spoke to where I am at   1 2 3 4 5

     3. I know now what God wants of my life   1 2 3 4 5

     4. I know why I must apply what God has said to me   1 2 3 4 5

     5. I know how I can do what I am to do   1 2 3 4 5

     6. The application flowed from the grace of God in
Jesus Christ   1 2 3 4 5

E. The Conclusion of the Sermon

     1. The conclusion came from the text itself   1 2 3 4 5

     2. There was a well-rounded conclusion of the message   1 2 3 4 5

     3. There was a summons for me to believe and/
or do something   1 2 3 4 5

     4. The conclusion highlighted the purpose of the message   1 2 3 4 5

V. Delivery

A. Verbal aspects

     1. Voice inflection was good   1 2 3 4 5

     2. Articulation was understandable   1 2 3 4 5

     3. Vocabulary was relevant and appropriate to
the audience   1 2 3 4 5

     4. Volume was appropriate and varied   1 2 3 4 5

     5. Rate of delivery was appropriate and varied   1 2 3 4 5

     6. Easy to listen to   1 2 3 4 5

     7. Good use of pictorial language (similes, metaphors,
visual)   1 2 3 4 5

     8. Concise and not filled with unnecessary words   1 2 3 4 5

     9. Tone respected the audience   1 2 3 4 5

B. Physical aspects

     1. Gestures appropriate   1 2 3 4 5

     2. Overall appearance was pleasant   1 2 3 4 5

     3. Actions were authentic   1 2 3 4 5

     4. Facial expressions appropriate   1 2 3 4 5

5. Good eye contact with audience   1   2   3   4   5
6. Presence commands attention   1   2   3   4   5
7. Distracting habits or actions were absent   1   2   3   4   5

VI. Other aspects of the sermon and delivery

A. Length of sermon was good   1   2   3   4   5
(sermon was engaging enough to make the length of time irrelevant)

B. A good sense of momentum   1   2   3   4   5

C. Had a good coherence (not many themes or 'mini-sermons')   1   2   3   4   5

D. I learned something   1   2   3   4   5

E. My faith was challenged or built up   1   2   3   4   5

F. Message offered hope   1   2   3   4   5

G. It underscored Christ's victory in life   1   2   3   4   5

H. It conveyed trust, confidence, love   1   2   3   4   5

I. I have a sense of being fed   1   2   3   4   5

J. It spoke to me personally. I "heard" Jesus Christ speaking to me   1   2   3   4   5

K. He spoke with confidence   1   2   3   4   5

L. He spoke with conviction, fire or "unction"   1   2   3   4   5

APPENDIX D

REQUIREMENTS OF A GODLY ELDER AND PASTOR

—ᴡ—

A. He must be a Christian who has repented of his sin and trusted in Jesus Christ alone for salvation, and who walks by faith in God's Word and Holy Spirit.
B. He must be pursuing godly character.
 1. He must be holy (Tit. 1:8 cp. Lk. 1:74-75; 2 Cor. 7:1; Heb. 12:14; 2 Pet. 3:11).
 2. He must be spiritually mature (1 Tim. 3:2).
    a. Not a new believer, but mature in Jesus Christ (1 Tim. 3:2, 6)
    b. Prudent (1 Tim. 3:2; Tit. 1:8)
    c. Humble (Tit. 1:7 cp. Luke 14:10; 1 Cor. 10:31-33; Phil. 2:3; Jas. 4:10; 1 Pet. 5:5)
 3. He must be temperate and self-controlled (1 Tim. 3:2; Tit. 1:8; 1 Thess. 5:6-8).
    a. Free from being drunk with the details of life
    b. Physically temperate
       (1) In the use of food and drink (not a glutton or a drunk) (Prov. 23:20, 21; 1 Tim.3:3; Tit. 1:12)
       (2) In the discipline of his body (1 Tim. 4:8; 5:23)
    c. Not quarrelsome (1 Tim. 3:2, 3; 2 Tim. 2:14)
    d. Not given to selfish anger (Tit. 1:7; Pro. 3:30 15:18; Eph. 4:26)
    e. Not pugnacious (prone to fighting) (1 Tim. 3:3; Tit. 1:7)
 4. He must be patient (1 Tim. 3:3).
    a. Marked by the fruit of God's Spirit (Gal. 5:22-24; Eph. 5:9)
    b. Gentle (2 Tim. 2:24-26)
    c. Not contentious, but rather a peacemaker (1 Tim. 3:3; James 3:18)
 5. He must not be covetous or greedy (1 Tim. 3:3; 6:5-10; Tit. 1:7)
 6. He is a lover of good (1 Tim. 1:8)
C. There are requirements for godly character before a watching world:
 1. He must be above reproach (1 Tim. 3:2; Tit. 1:5-9)
 2. He is to have a good reputation; he is respectable

3. He is to be an example of Jesus Christ
4. He is just; impartial in dealing with people (Tit. 1:8; Rom. 13:7; Col. 4:1)
5. He is respectful of employers, employees, and business associates
D. There are requirements for godliness in his home (assuming he is married):
    1. He is an example of a Christ-like husband and father.
       a. Managing his own household well (1 Tim. 3:4-5; Eph. 5:22-23)
       b. With a godly, submissive wife (1 Tim. 3:11; Eph. 5:22-33; 1 Pet. 3:1-6)
       c. If he has any children, are faithful, honoring and non-rebellious (Tit. 1:6; Eph. 6:1-3)
    2. He is hospitable (literally, 'a lover of strangers') (1 Tim. 3:2).
       a. Hospitality is not about having a cup of coffee with someone.
       b. This is a commitment, not a gift. He must be willing to have an open home for the service of others (1 Pet. 4:9)
       c. He is a pacesetter in showing hospitality (Rom. 12:13; Heb. 13:2)

APPENDIX E

IDENTIFYING AND CHOOSING A
POTENTIAL CHURCH OFFICER

—ɯ—

The positions of deacon and elder are not merely slots or duties to be filled in a church. The deacon and elder are offices in Christ's Kingdom. They serve and rule the Church, the citizens of His Kingdom. These officers are not on a par with the authoritative offices of worldly government. They are of a higher status.

According to the Bible, God calls His church to Christ-like holiness through the good order of biblical government (1 Cor. 14:40; Col. 2:5; Tit. 1:5). Jesus is the sovereign head of His Church (Jn. 15:1-14; Eph. 1:22-23; 5:23ff.; Col. 1:18). Though he sits at the right hand of God in heaven, he has chosen to serve and rule his church through believing men who have been gifted, called and ordained to those special offices (Acts 6; 15; 20:17; 1 Cor. 4:1; 1 Tim. 3:2-7; 5:17; Tit. 1:5ff; 1 Pet. 5:1ff). The nature of this authority was predicted in the Old Testament (e.g. Isa. 9:6). It resides in Christ (Matt. 16:19; 18:17; John 20:23), even though founded upon the apostles (1 Cor. 12:28, 39; Eph. 2:20; 4:11).

Therefore these offices are very important. They are high and lofty, deserving of the respect accorded by God Himself (Heb. 13:7, 17). The elders, in particular, as God's officers, hold the keys (the authoritative power) of the eternal Kingdom (Matt. 16:19; 18:15ff). Yet this position also requires a greater responsibility and accountability to God (Heb. 13:17) since the elder cares for and watches over the eternal souls of God's people.

There were certain qualifications given to elders in the Old Testament. They had to possess the credentials of godly character and wisdom (Exod. 18:21; Deut. 1:13). They had to have a spiritual disposition and enablement from the Lord, and they had to possess an authorized call or election to the office. Even more, in the New Testament era that extends to this very day, God requires His offices to be filled by male believer-priests who manifest the *right qualities* (1 Tim. 3:1-7; Tit. 1:5-9), the *right equipment* (Rom. 12:8; 1 Cor. 12:11, 28; Eph. 4:11-12), and the *right motivation* (Phil. 2:13; 1 Tim. 3:1).

With this in mind, we should regard the search and selection of a deacon and/or elder with seriousness, respect, and diligence. The purpose of this handout is to answer prevailing questions surrounding this important subject. It will guide us through the process of discovering God's man to fill the office of deacon or elder in our church.

A. The first question to ask: Does the man possess the right character?

As Kevin Reed points out, "these qualities (character qualities found in 1st and 2nd Timothy, Titus and 1 Peter) focus upon the three important aspects of a man's life: his moral behavior, his knowledge of Christian doctrine, and his family life. An elder continually will be in public view. The respect an officer receives often depends more on an example of good character than from anything else about him" (Kevin Reed, 1983, p. 9). All godly men should have these qualities, but the man who is selected for office in Christ's kingdom must be measured by these qualities to see if he is ready for the office (1 Tim. 5:22; 2 Tim. 2:2; Tit. 2:7,8).

Every person in Christ is called to put off the old sinful nature and put on these traits of Christ. Though no man, candidate or officer in Christ's Church demonstrates any or all of these qualities perfectly, it must be obvious that the officer demonstrates most of these qualities with consistent regularity. Does the man measure up to what the Word of God requires for godly character (not perfectly nor completely but obviously and substantially)?

Below is a checklist of biblical character qualities a deacon or elder must possess:
- ☐ The candidate is above reproach (1 Tim. 3:2; Titus 1:6). Can his wife, children, neighbors, work mates, boss, business associates, and fellow members at church give a good report about his character?
- ☐ He has restrained control (a balanced discipline) in his life (1 Tim. 3:2; 1 Thess. 5:6, 8)
- ☐ He is a true gentle man (approachable, kind, gracious, firm yet diplomatic) (Matt. 11:29; 2 Cor. 10:1; Gal. 6:1; 1 Thess. 2:7; 2 Tim. 2:23-25; Jas. 3:17)
- ☐ He is not pugnacious or prone to violence (Prov. 3:30; 15:18; 17:14; 20:3; 26:17; Phil. 2:3-8; 1 Tim. 3:3; Tit. 1:7)
- ☐ He is not quarrelsome (Eccles. 10:4; Matt. 5:9; Rom. 12:18; 14:19; Heb. 12:14; 1 Tim. 3:2, 3; 6:3-5; 2 Tim. 2:22-26; Tit. 3:9; Jas. 3:17)
- ☐ He is not greedy (Acts 20:33; 1 Tim. 3:3; 6:5-10; Tit. 1:7). Instead, he is content and grateful for his lot in life
- ☐ He is not given easily to selfish anger (Prov. 16:32; Eph. 4:26-27; Tit. 1:7)
- ☐ He has disciplined control over bodily appetites (Gen. 19; Prov. 20:1; Eccles. 10:17-18; Isa. 5:11; 28:1; Luke 21:34; Rom. 13:13-14; Eph. 5:18; 1 Tim. 3:3; Tit. 1:7; 2:12-13; 1 Pet. 4:1-5)
- ☐ He is self-controlled (Matt. 26:41; Acts 24:25; Rom. 6:12; 1 Cor. 10:12-13; Eph. 5:1-5, 23; Tit. 1:8; Jas. 3:2; 2 Pet. 1:5-8)
- ☐ He is truly humble and not self-willed or self-serving (Luke 14:10; Rom. 12:3, 10, 16; 1 Cor. 10:31-33; Phil 2:3; Ti. 1:7; Jas. 4:10; 1 Pet. 5:5)

- ☐ The candidate is holy (biblically devout and pious) (Lev. 11:45; Luke 1:74, 75; 2 Cor. 7:1; Tit. 1:8; Heb. 12:14; 1 Pet. 1:16; 2 Pet. 3:11). Worship is a priority for him, which is shown by his commitment to personal, family and corporate worship
- ☐ His persona and life demonstrate biblical hospitality. He has a love for people and a care for strangers, and it shows (Rom. 12:13; 1 Tim. 3:2; Ti. 1:9; Heb. 13:2; 1 Pet. 4:9)
- ☐ He is just (upright and impartial in dealing with people) (Deut. 16:20; Ps. 82:3; Prov. 21:3; Isa. 56:1; Mic. 6:8; Rom. 13:7; Col. 4:1; Tit. 1:8)
- ☐ The man is a lover of good. He has a love of virtue, people and good things (Heb.10:23-24; 1 Thess. 5:21; Tit. 1:8)
- ☐ He is prudent and wise (skilled at bringing God's thoughts to bear on matters of life) (Proverbs; 1 Tim. 3:2; Tit. 1:8)
- ☐ He is respectable (well-ordered, well-arranged, decorous in behavior and speech, with good manners) (1 Tim. 3:2)
- ☐ If he is married he is a godly leader of his wife and family (1 Tim. 3:4-5; Tit. 1:6)
- ☐ In Christ he loves his wife as he loves himself (Eph. 5:28ff)
- ☐ He loves his wife as Christ loves the Church (Eph. 5:25ff)
- ☐ He lives with his wife in an understanding way (1 Pet. 3:7)
- ☐ He is the godly pastor of his family, teaching, admonishing, and correcting them (Eph. 6:4; Col. 3:21)

B. A second question to ask: Does the man possess the right equipment?

That is, does he have the right gifts for the church office of deacon or elder?

- ☐ The man has been obviously endowed with God-given spiritual gifts suited for the office of deacon or elder (Lk. 24:49; Acts 1:8; 6:1ff; 1 Tim. 3:1-7; 5:22; Tit.1:7)
- ☐ The elder and deacon must be gifted to serve (Acts 6:1ff; Rom. 12; 15:26-33; 1 Cor. 12; Eph. 4:11ff)
- ☐ The elder and deacon must be able to show mercy (Matt. 25; 1 Cor. 12:28)
- ☐ The elder must be:
  - o Able to confront, exhort-counsel from the Scriptures (Rom. 12:8; 1 Thess. 2:11,12; 4:1-2; 2 Thess. 3:6, 14; 1 Tim. 4:13; 2 Tim. 4:1-2; Tit. 1:9)
  - o Gifted to lead (1 Cor. 12:28; 1 Thess. 5:12, 13; 1 Tim. 3:5; 5:17; Heb. 13:7, 17, 24)
  - o Able to teach (1 Thess. 4:9-5:11; 1 Tim. 3:2; 2 Tim. 2:24; Tit. 1:9)
  - o Loving (1 Cor. 13; Gal. 5:25; 1 Thess. 2:7-8)
  - o Able to shepherd God's flock (Acts 20:18; 1 Pet. 5:1-3)
- ☐ The deacon must:
  - o Exhibit a servant's heart to others and to the church (Acts 6)

o   Demonstrate a life which shows that God is doing a good work in his life, that he has a good relationship with the Lord, and it is clear that God the Holy Spirit is controlling him (Acts 6)

o   Be willing and able to share his material resources with others (Acts 4; Eph. 4:28)

o   Currently be demonstrating a heart of mercy (Matt. 25:31-46; 1 Cor. 12:28)

C. A third question to ask: Does the potential officer of God's church possess the right motivation?

☐   The man has expressed that he has a desire and an inward call from God to serve (Eph. 4:11-12; 1 Tim. 3:1)

☐   He is obviously responsive to the gifting and the call of the Holy Spirit in his life (Acts 20:28)

☐   He earnestly desires the office (Acts 6; 1 Tim. 3:1)

☐   His motives are biblical and Christ-like, not self-seeking (1 Peter 5:1ff)

☐   Not only does he have the inward call of God, but God's people in this church recognize his call as qualified and legitimate (Jer. 23:32; Acts 6; Rom. 10:15; Heb. 5:4)

D. What is the process of becoming an officer?

If a man has the right qualities or character, the right equipment and the right motivation, then is it possible God is calling him to serve as a deacon or ruling elder in our church? To find out if this is the case, there is a process for our church and the candidate.

1. Does the congregation see latent or obvious qualities in the man that demonstrate he might be fit to be called as a deacon or elder?

    a. Based upon the principle of emergence, the man who might be a candidate or who is aspiring to office is readily recognized by the elders and members of the congregation as already living, behaving and performing like or *as if* he were already a deacon or an elder. The principle of emergence says that a leader will rise to the level of recognizable leadership or rise to the occasion as a leader. His character and gift reveal themselves in ways that are apparent to the elders, deacons and a majority of the members of the church.

    b. The congregation, deacons, elders and pastor(s) observe the man and look for certain qualities:

        (1) They observe his level of maturity

            (a) Maturity – the more one is God and other-directed, and the less he is self-centered, then the greater the level of maturity

       (b) He is preferably 30 years or older, and certainly not a new believer (1 Tim. 3:6)

       (c) He is also socially, emotionally and spiritually mature

    (2) Secondly, people observe his gifts.

    (3) They also observe his life for godly character

    (4) The people also observe his leadership potential for traits such as:

       (a) He takes the initiative in things.

       (b) He serves others.

       (c) He has a genuine desire and actively pursues personal growth and development.

       (d) He is a problem solver.

       (e) Others are following him.

  c. As men begin to demonstrate maturity, giftedness, and a heart for service to God and His people, they should be encouraged and challenged toward greater growth, and to move out of their comfort zone (1 Tim. 3:1).

  d. Under the direction of the elders, potential leaders would be encouraged to go through a special training to develop and test the man's call, gifts and skills.

  e. Men in general leadership training or discipleship will be debriefed and evaluated from time to time in the appropriate areas of their natural talents, spiritual gifts, motivation and character.

2. The candidate should then be consulted

  a. Not all men who desire to become a deacon or elder are qualified.

  b. Not all men who are qualified have a desire to become a deacon or elder

  c. Individuals who intend to nominate a man must confer with him before submitting his name in order to give him the courtesy of accepting or rejecting the nomination. It is neither wise nor expedient to surprise any man with a spontaneous nomination.

  d. If individuals believe a man is qualified and gifted, they should confer with the pastor and elders to get additional input or advice.

3. Nominating qualified men

  a. Normally the nominations take place during the annual congregational meeting. However, the board could determine that nominations may be submitted at the congregational meeting and over a period of several days.

  b. The elders will announce to the congregation the date(s) of the nomination period. To safeguard against any embarrassing situations of providing names the elders could not in good conscience affirm, members are strongly advised to follow the provisions outlined above

  c. The church's governing board, by virtue of their office and duties, has the right to veto unqualified nominations.

    d. Nominating a man to the office of deacon or elder does not guarantee the person is qualified, or that he will pass the scrutiny of the exams in life and doctrine, or that will be elected by the congregation. In other words, the nomination is but one step in a systematic process toward electing a deacon or elder.

4. Confer with the elder board

    a. The elder board will meet with him to confirm that he is willing and qualified to proceed through advanced church leadership training and testing.

    b. Upon approval, the man will go through a training program in Bible, our system of doctrine and creeds (statements of faith), church history and government, godliness, and general leadership principles.

    c. At the close of the training period the nominee will be examined in:

        (1) His Christian experience, personal character and family management

        (2) His knowledge of the church's doctrine and polity.

        (3) The duties of the office to which he has been nominated, and his willingness to give assent to the questions required for ordination

5. Examine the candidate, including:

    a. An interview with his wife (if he is married)

    b. A written, take-home exam on doctrine and life

    c. Personal reference forms, to verify that he has a good reputation (1 Tim. 3:1-7) filled out by:

        (1) his spouse

        (2) a co-worker

        (3) a neighbor

        (4) a friend

    d. An oral exam in life, godliness, doctrine, church discipline, and other appropriate matters

6. Present the candidate for a congregational vote.

    a. Once a man has been nominated, trained, tested and approved by the governing board, he will be presented to the congregation for a vote of confirmation. The congregation is given at least thirty (30) days prior notice of the time and place of a congregational meeting for elections. The congregational meeting will be arrangedand conducted according to the rules of our church government and *Robert's Rules of Order.*

    b. All church members in good and regular standing, but no others, are entitled to vote in the election of church officers. A majority vote of those present is required for election.

Granted, this may seem somewhat of a rigorous process. But should it be any less than the processes through which people go to arrive at other important and authoritative positions? Consider, for example, the training and scrutiny of officers of civil law (policemen to judges).

As we pray and seek together for potential officers, men God might be raising up to serve as deacons or ruling elders, let us do so with the gravity, respect and diligence God demands.

APPENDIX F

A SELF-EXAMINATION IN GODLY CHARACTER

—m—

As you advance through this list of character traits, use the first blank line to rate yourself on a scale of 1-10: 1 meaning this character trait is lacking, almost difficult to notice in your life; 10 meaning that you are very, very strong and are a good example of this quality. Then enlist your spouse or family member to rate you on the second line. You could enlist a neighbor, workmate or friend to rate you on the third line.

1. **I am above reproach**   (1 Tim. 3:2; Tit. 1:6)
   To be above reproach means that I am blameless. There is nothing about my life that is open to rebuke. To be above reproach has to do with the general character or sum total of godly virtues. It means I am not open to censure because I have an impeachable integrity that is in accord with Biblical requirement for leadership. This does not mean I am perfect in all qualities, but that I substantially reflect godly virtues.
   Score: _____ _____ _____

2. **I am temperate** (1 Tim. 3:2; 1 Thess. 5:6, 8)
   To be temperate is to be sober, clearheaded and self-controlled. There is a restrained control and sobriety of life. I am free from excesses and not inebriated with the details of life.
   I am self-controlled because of the work of the Holy Spirit (Gal. 5; Phil. 2:13). I am to be someone who is disciplined, yet properly flexible in the use and application of all things for the glory of God.
   Score: _____ _____ _____

   a. **I am temperate in that I am not given to much wine** (1 Tim. 3:3; Tit. 1:7)
      I am not over-indulgent or a drunk. I control the wine or alcoholic drink; it does not control me. The principle has to do with having control over my bodily appe-

tites (Gen. 19; Prov. 20:1; 23; Eccles. 10:17; Isa. 5:11; 28:1; Luke 21:34; Rom. 13:13; Eph. 5:18).
Score: _____ _____ _____

b. **I am temperate in that I am not greedy** (1 Tim. 3:3; Tit. 1:7)
My life is not characterized by covetousness (Exod. 20:17; Deut. 5:21). I am not a lover of money (Lk. 6:24; 1 Tim. 6:10). The acquisition of money or things is not a central priority in my life (Lk. 12:16-21; 18:18-23). Heavenly priorities dominate (Matt. 6:33). I do not seek meaning or comfort in things.
I have a firm conviction about resisting dishonest and shady methods for acquiring money or things (1 Tim. 3:8). I recognize that one of the deadly sins of a godly leader is greed (Acts 20:33; 1 Tim. 6:5-10; 2 Tim. 3:6-7).
Score: _____ _____ _____

c. **Temperate, I am not given to selfish anger** (Tit. 1:7)
I do not have a trigger temper or an irritable disposition. I am not too easily offended, which would make me unapproachable and unpredictable in temper (Prov. 16:32).
Score: _____ _____ _____

d. **My overall character is marked by self-control** (Tit. 1:8)
In Christ I have a mastery over self. My passions and appetites are controlled. I am not lazy, gluttonous or given to filthy talk (Eph. 5:4). I have an ordered life, which reflects heavenly pursuits and priorities (Matt. 26:41; Acts 24:25; Rom. 6:12; 1 Cor. 10:12; 1 Pet.5:8; 2 Pet. 1:5-7; Jas. 3:2).
Score: _____ _____ _____

3. **I am gentle** (2 Sam. 22:36; Ps. 18:35; 1 Tim. 3:2, 3; Tit. 3:2)
Gentleness, a very important feature in a godly leader, is the quality of being gracious, kind, mild, patient, and reasonable. A gentle person is caring, considerate and has an ability to sympathize (Rom. 15:1; 1 Pet. 4:8. The gentle one shows carefulness in choosing words and expressions so as not to unnecessarily offend (Gal. 6:1).
Like Jesus Christ (Matt. 11:29), I reflect care, affection and good-will toward others (2 Cor. 10:1; 1 Thess. 2:; Eph. 4:2). I am not abrupt or critical in my communications. Gentleness is a quality the godly leader is to pursue (1 Tim. 6:11). In short, I exercise gentleness in the fruit of God's Spirit (Gal. 5:23; Phil. 4:5). Here are some characteristic ways I am biblically gentle:

a. **As a true gentle person I am**
   (1) Approachable
   (2) Firm, but diplomatic even when correcting opponents (Gal. 6:1;
       2 Tim. 2:23-25)
   (3) Kind and gracious like Jesus Christ (Matt. 11:29; Acts 24:4; 2 Cor. 10:1;
       1 Thess. 2:7)
   (4) Wise, exercising wisdom in gentleness (Jas. 3:17)
       Score: _____ _____ _____

b. **As a gentle person I am not pugnacious** (1 Tim. 3:3; Tit. 1:7)
   A pugnacious person physically hits or strikes another. Overall, I am not prone to
   violence or physical abusive. Pugnacious also has the idea of being contentious.
   Therefore, I am not one who is harsh with words. I don't lash out when hurt or
   incite arguments, nor do I alienate people by having an attacking manner. I don't
   follow through with an angry temper (Prov. 3:30; 15:18; 17:14; 20:3; 25:8; 26:17;
   Phil. 2:3).
       Score: _____ _____ _____

c. **I am gentle and therefore not quarrelsome** (1 Tim. 3:2, 3; 2 Tim. 2:14; Tit. 3:2)
   I am averse to verbal fighting, quarreling, or arguing. However, I know what,
   when, and how to properly debate. I do not delight in outdoing others or defeating
   their ideas and beliefs. There is no harsh dogmatism about my life. I do not have
   an offensive approach toward people (1 Tim. 6:3-5; 2 Tim. 2:22-26; Tit. 3:9). On
   the positive side, I have a sense of peace, tranquility, and calmness. I am a peacemaker who tries to bring calm to a stormy situation (Eccles. 10:4; Matt. 5:9;
   Rom. 12:18; 14:19; Heb. 12:14; Jas. 3:17).
       Score: _____ _____ _____

4. **God has graced me with an ever-increasing humility** (Luke 14:10; Phil 2:3;
   Tit. 1:7; Jas. 4:10; 1 Pet. 5:5)
   I know where I stand before the face of an almighty, just and holy God. Humility
   means that I am not a self-willed, self-pleasing egoist. I am not obstinate, domineering, and arrogant. That means that I do not stand hard on every minor thing I
   believe, and do not insist on having my own way, ideas, or beliefs. I have a genuine
   interest in others and in what they say.
       Being self-willed is also characteristic of one who delights too much in appear-
   ance, performance, or status to the obvious neglect of others. Humility is being teachable. It is thinking rightly and truthfully about oneself (Rom. 12:3, 10, 16).
       Score: _____ _____ _____

5. **I am holy** (Tit. 1:8; 2 Cor. 7:1; 2 Pet. 3:11)
   This word means to be religiously, biblically devout, pious. I daily offer myself as a pure and acceptable living sacrifice to God. I consistently live out the Gospel lifestyle in private and public affairs of life. I am living out the devout and Spirit-filled life of Christ before the face of an all-seeing God (Lev. 11:45; Luke 1:74, 75; 2 Cor. 7:1; Heb. 12:14; 1 Pet. 1:16; 2 Pet. 3:11).
   Score: _____ _____ _____

6. **I am hospitable** (1 Tim. 3:2; 5:10; Tit. 1:8; 1 Pet. 4:9)
   To be hospitable in the biblical sense means to be a lover of strangers. The truly hospitable one is Jesus. He gave us a parable of real hospitality in the Good Samaritan (Luke 10:27-37). The love of Christ in me exhibits itself by loving my neighbor as myself. I am kind and actively compassionate to others, even strangers. This love of heart is expressed with an open door, demonstrating a kind, compassionate, welcoming Savior. The biblical leader is a pacesetter in hospitality (Rom. 12:13; Heb.13:2).
   Score: _____ _____ _____

7. **I am just** (Tit. 1:8)
   To be just is to be fair, upright and righteous. I am impartial when I deal with people. I work hard to forget personal preferences and to seek the truth in situations especially those that involve inter-personal conflicts. I am a fair umpire over relational differences, because I have the ability to hear both sides and weigh the evidence honestly. I speak what is right and true (Deut. 16:20; Ps. 82:3; Prov. 21:3; Isa. 56:1; Rom. 13:7; Col. 4:1).
   Score: _____ _____ _____

8. **I am a lover of good**   (Tit. 1:8; Rom. 12:17; Phil. 4:8)
   To be a lover of good is to have an active compassion toward others and to promote goodness. It is to have a love of virtue, good people and good things. My affections are attached to the Lord, to good things and to godly people rather than being drawn toward worldly pleasures and gratifications. My concern is toward godliness, Spirit-empowered obedience to God's Word, and an anticipation of the world to come. I love God's good life more than such things as position, fame, abilities, and possessions, which are soon to pass away (Matt. 6:33; 12:35; Luke 6:27, 35; 1 Thess. 5:15, 21; Rev. 3:3).
   Score: _____ _____ _____

9. **I am respectable** (1 Tim. 3:2; Tit. 1:8)
   To be respectable is to be well-ordered, and decorous in dress, behavior and speech. The term may refer to manners, etiquette, and personal habits. It carries the idea of having simplicity of life-style rather than being eccentric or extravagant. It can also have a general reference to a disciplined, honorable and well-ordered life. I am modest in my dress and inoffensive in my hygiene and eating habits. I also have socially acceptable manners. My lifestyle is unpretentious and modest.

   Score: _____ _____ _____

APPENDIX G

A SAMPLE NOMINATION BALLOT FOR A CHURCH OFFICER

—ɯ—

Nomination Ballot

I believe the name(s) below fits the qualifications for a church officer:
- He possesses the right character (according to the Bible and to our secondary standards).
- He possesses the right gifts.
- He has the desire and motivation to serve.
- He is showing himself to be a godly leader.
- He is mature (physically, emotionally, mentally, and spiritually).
- He has been an active member in good standing for at least a year.
- He is willing to pursue the training. If he passes and is elected he is willing to serve in the office to which he has been called.

I have already talked with the man and he is willing to be nominated. I therefore nominate

1._____
       to the office of (circle one):   deacon   elder

2._____
       to the office of (circle one):   deacon   elder

3._____
       to the office of (circle one):   deacon   elder

4._____
       to the office of (circle one):   deacon   elder

Please write additional names on the back of this form.

APPENDIX H

GAINING ADVICE AND MAKING PLANS
(Insights from the Book of Proverbs)

—⚏—

1. In God and is Word there is great counsel and sound wisdom. Seeking it is understanding and great power for success (Prov. 8:14, paraphrased).

   Principle: An understanding of Scripture and an intimate relationship with Jesus Christ is the best foundation for any decision making. Success is always linked to godly wisdom and good counsel. The person who plans wisely will be successful.

2. Ponder the path of your feet; then all your ways will be sure. Do not swerve to the right or to the left; turn your foot away from evil (NKJV Prov. 4:26-27).

   Principle: Pursue realistic courses or options, and pursue those paths which seem to be firm. Don't be distracted by wrong goals, motives or pursuits.

   Questions:
      a. Are my options realistic?
      b. Is my heart's motive pure in this?
      c. Will this choice further my relationship with the Lord or hinder it?
      d. Do any of my options violate Scripture?
      e. Which choice will give God the greater glory, if any?

3. Make your plans by seeking advice (Prov. 11:14; 15:22; 20:18; 24:6).

   Principle: Look to those who can offer advice (biblical, common sense, etc.) and give sound guidance, such as elders or those who have gone through a similar experience and learned from it.

Questions:
   a. Who do I know who can offer straightforward advice?
   b. What elders can I seek out who can make some wise suggestions or give insight?
   c. Are there others who have gone through the same kind of experience or have had to make the same kind of decisions which might have "hindsight wisdom?"

4. Many are the plans in a man's heart, but it is the Lord's purpose that prevails (19:21).

   Principle: No matter how well I plan things, ultimately it is God's Sovereign plan for my life that succeeds.

   Questions:
   a. Have I committed this decision to the Lord? (In other words, have I told Him that I will rest in the knowledge that He is control ultimately, no matter what decision I make?)
   b. Have I purposed in my heart not to worry, but rather to give thanks for the process and for the outcome?
   c. Have I made the commitment to do what is right before the Lord?

5. Folly delights a person who lacks judgment, but one who is filled with understanding keeps a straight course (15:21).

   Principle: Being a biblically wise person (seeking to think God's thoughts after Him) will help me keep a good course of direction in a diligent manner. Wavering is a pleasure for the fool.

   Questions:
   a. Do I find more comfort and security in not making decisions than in making them?
   b. Am I seeking to think God's thoughts about this matter?
   c. Have I searched the Scriptures to see if there is anything which speaks to these issues?

6. The way of a foolish person is right in his own eyes, but a wise person listens to counsel (Prov. 12:15, paraphrased).

   <u>Principle:</u> I am willing to consider the advice I have been given, and will listen intently, even when it goes against what I want.

   <u>Questions:</u>
   a. Am I seeking the advice of others in order to find someone who will give me what I want to hear?
   b. Am I listening intently to the advice of others and seriously considering what they have to offer?
   c. Am I listening intently to the advice of Scripture and the Holy Spirit?
   d. Am I willing to take risks or make changes if this is clearly God's will?

APPENDIX I

HOW TO WORK TOGETHER TO MAKE A CORPORATE DECISION
(in the local church)

—⟋⟍—

One church leader says that his large staff operates on the philosophy of community, not necessarily on unity. By that he means that they do not expect everyone to have complete agreement of mind in all things, but they can work together as a community of godly men and women toward common things.

The genius of this is that is provides the basis and environment in which people can work together in Christ toward common things, even when there are varying views. Biblical people ought to work together in an open and deliberative body. The body discusses and debates matters until a vote is called and a decision is rendered. Unity is a worthy objective. Uniformity is not.

Ultimately, by trusting in God's providential direction, it is the consensus of the majority that will determine the direction, policies or other such matters in the local church. This is especially true of the decisions of church leadership. Those who end up with the minority opinion should submit to the final decision of the others, unless in good conscience they cannot. In such cases they should pursue the acceptable, godly and legal recourses available.

A. **How can those of differing opinions come to agreement on matters in the church?**

Below are some operating principles that might prove helpful in developing a good working relationship when there are differences of opinion:

1. First, each person should be convinced in his own mind about his position (Eccles. 7:25; Rom. 14:5).
    a. His view is best informed by the Word of God (Psa. 119:169; Rom. 14:5).
    b. He should not be double-minded (Jas. 1:5-8), but should say what he means and mean what he says (Matt. 5:37; Eph. 4:25; Jas. 5:12).

2. He should recognize that everyone has an opinion, but that not all opinions are equal, nor are they all valid.
   a. An opinion is "the judgment which the mind forms of any proposition, statement, theory or event, the truth or falsehood of which is supported by a degree of evidence that renders it probable, but does not produce absolute knowledge or certainty" (Webster's 1828 *Dictionary of the English Language*).
   b. The person should have a well-informed opinion to share, not merely one that is based upon little knowledge (Prov. 28:26), feeling or intuition (e.g.:Prov. 25:2). Well-informed opinions bring a higher value to discussion.

3. He should have the humble mind of Christ (Mic. 6:8; Phil 2:5ff; Rom. 12:3, 10; 1 Pet. 5:5).
   a. All division, discord or fighting stems from an abundance of pride and a lack of humility (Prov. 20:3; 1 Tim. 6:4ff; Jas. 4:1-3, 6).
   b. Humbleness means that the person is not seeking to please self. This means that he is not
      (1) Arrogant (Rom. 12:16; Jas. 4:16). He does not insist on his own way, ideas, or beliefs merely because they are his.
      (2) Domineering (1 Pet. 5:3)
      (3) Stubborn (e.g.: Psa. 78:8; Acts 7:51)
      (4) Unreasonable (e.g.: Gal. 6:3; Jas. 1:22)
      (5) Unyielding. He does not stand hard on *everything* he believes when the truth and facts clearly counter his position.
   c. Humility will take a genuine interest in others and in what they have to say (Rom. 12:9, 10).
   d. Humility thinks rightly about self (Rom. 12:3, 10, 16, 17), seeing oneself before the face of God.
   e. A humble person is teachable (Job 15:8; Prov. 26:12; Eccles. 7:16; Isa. 5:21; Rom. 12:16; 1 Cor. 8:2), and willing to repent or change his mind about the matter if the other view bears legitimate weight.
   f. He can be passionate about his position, without being arrogant (Prov. 11:2; 13:10; 21:4; 28:25; Mark 7:22; 1 Pet. 5:5).

4. Each person, and all the more a church leader, has a duty and a right to state his position or speak his conscience in a godly manner until a vote or decision has been rendered.
   a. If it is a matter of an on-going debate, the discourses should be tempered with humility and other Christ-like qualities. For example,

(1) He should have restrained control through gentleness
(2 Sam. 22:36; Ps. 18:35; Gal. 5:22, 23; 1Thess. 2:7; 1 Tim. 3:2, 3;
Jas. 3:17).
   (a) The idea of gentleness, a very important quality especially in a godly
      leader and precious to God (1 Pet. 3:4), is that of being patient, mild,
      reasonable, full of grace and graciousness. This is exercised by not
      defending or insisting on one's own way (2 Cor. 12:20; Gal. 5:20; Phil.
      2:3; Tit. 3:9)
   (b) Gentleness sees people as sensitive beings, deals with people where
      they are, and treats them with respect (1 Cor. 10:22-33; 1 Pet. 2:23).
   (c) The gentle one shows carefulness in choosing words and expressions
      so as not to unnecessarily offend (Gal. 6:1; 2 Tim. 2:25; Tit. 3:2).
   (d) Gentleness is a quality the godly leader is to pursue (1 Tim. 6:11).
(2) He reflects care, affection and goodwill toward others (1 Cor. 13; Eph.
   4:2). He is not abrupt or critical in his communications.
(3) He should not be pugnacious.
   (a) This means he is not a striker; not prone to violence, and not a fighter.
      He is not physically abusive.
   (b) He is not one who is harsh with words.
   (c) He doesn't lash out when hurt or incite arguments, or alienate people
      through an attacking manner.
   (d) He doesn't follow through with hot temper (Prov. 3:30; 15:18; 17:14;
      20:3; 25:8; 26:17; Eph. 4:26, 31; Phil. 2:3).
(4) He is not to be quarrelsome (1 Tim. 3:3).
   That means he is generally averse to verbal fighting or arguing.
   (a) The man knows what, when, and how to argue (read: debate) rightly.
   (b) He is not eager to make his point merely in order to get his way.
   (c) He doesn't relish or overly delight in outdoing others and defeating
      their ideas and beliefs.
   (d) With Christ-likeness there is to be no harsh dogmatism or a sinfully
      offensive approach toward people.
   (e) He is not to be a contentious disputer (1 Tim. 6:3-5; 2 Tim. 2:22-26;
      Tit. 3:9).
(5) On the positive side, the godly man has a sense of peace, tranquility, and
   calmness. He is a peacemaker- one who is able to bring calm to a stormy
   situation (Eccles. 10:4; Matt. 5:9; Rom. 12:18; 14:19; Heb. 12:14;
   Jas. 3:17).
(6) Also, the godly man is to be just (Tit. 1:8).

(a) This means he is upright, righteous, and impartial in dealing with people.

(b) He is able to forget personal interests and seek the truth in situations, in inter-personal conflicts, or as an umpire over differences.

(c) He speaks what is right, and has an ability to hear both sides and weigh the evidence honestly (Deut. 16:20; Ps. 82:3; Prov. 21:3; Isa. 56:1; Rom. 13:7; Col. 4:1).

(7) In short, the godly one exercises the fruit of God's Spirit (Gal. 5:23; Phil.4:5).

b. If, in the case of the church leadership board, a person cannot persuade others of his own position he should be content that he tried, and follow through according to a biblically informed conscience. If it is a matter of a policy decision, and one's personal perspective has been heard but not in keeping with the majority opinion and the elders rule on the issue, then the individual has several options:

(1) He should submit to the will of his brothers unless it violates his biblically informed conscience. He may not be contentious or attempt to divide the church.

(2) He has the ability and right to present (and at times have recorded) his minority opinion.

(3) Sometimes he can appeal. The appeal process takes the matter to the next higher judicatory. Once the appeal process has been exhausted the decision of the highest court stands.

(4) If the decision seriously and biblically offends his convictions, he can remove himself from the deliberative body, the court or the church.

B. How does a member express his or her opinion?

1. The member of the church group has a duty and a right to express his opinion or position within biblically acceptable parameters. Some examples:

   a. In a general discussion

   b. When permissible during a class or study

   c. When bringing an issue to an elder or the session

   d. When defending himself in a disciplinary trial

2. The biblical requirements for godliness and truth-telling apply to every member, just as it does with elders and pastors.

   a. The member should be wise, teachable, humble, submissive, etc., while holding firmly to biblical convictions.

   b. Each person should be free to graciously and truthfully express concerns or to disagree with the leadership in the church without fear of condemnation, ridicule or reprisal. Merely bringing a concern or objections or disagreeing with the leadership is not a warrant to declare the person contentious or divisive. The manner in which the issue is handled may determine that.

   c. At the same time, he or she may not be obnoxious, abusive, or contentious. Neither should the person be of such persistence as to cause dissension or division in the church. Patterns of such sins show a delinquency of life and may be disciplined.

3. There are people who tend to be one-issue type individuals. Their particular issue often becomes their litmus test for a "good church", true spirituality, holiness, etc. The person must not be arrogant, divisive, or contentious about it. He should be taught, admonished and/or forewarned that he may not become an advocate for his cause in the church if his position seriously conflicts with the biblically informed positions, practices, or policies on which the church leadership or elders have ruled.

APPENDIX J

THE PASTOR'S RESPONSIBILITIES AND DUTIES

—⟋⟍—

There are three primary divisions of the pastor's (note this is also applicable to elders) responsibilities and duties. Listed in order of priority, he answers first to God, secondly to himself and finally toward others. All too often church members reverse the order, only to the detriment of their personal and corporate well-being in Christ.

A. The pastor is responsible to serve the Lord first.
1. The pastor must exercise a saving faith in Jesus Christ as Savior and Lord (Jn. 1:12-13; 1 Thess. 1:9 cp. Gal. 1:10; Col. 1:7; 1 Tim. 4:6)
2. His first priority is to serve the Lord first and foremost, before he serves people (Acts 20:19; Gal. 1:10; 1 Thess. 2:4; Eph. 6:6-7; Col. 3:23-24). He ministers to God's people by serving and answering to the Lord first, and doing so for the glory of God (Deut. 10:12; Josh. 24:14, 15; 1 Cor. 10:31; 15:58; Eph. 6:7; Heb. 12:28; 1 Pet. 4:10-11).
   a. This was clearly the pattern of God's true prophets, priests and kings (1 Chron. 28:9; 2 Chron. 12:8; 34:33).
   b. This was also the pattern of Jesus Christ who always did His Father's will (Matt. 4:10; Luke 4:8; John 8:26-28)
   c. This was the pattern of the Apostles (Acts 4:5-21; 27:23; 1 Cor. 15:58; Col. 3:23; 1 Thess. 1:9; 2 Tim. 1:3; Heb. 12:28).
3. He is to live for Christ.
   a. He is never to be ashamed of Jesus Christ (2 Tim 1:8-11; 2:11-15).
   b. His focus is to always be upon Christ (Gal. 2:20; Phil. 1:21; 2 Tim 2:8-13).
   c. He is willing to suffer for Christ (Matt. 16:21; Lk. 21:19; Phil. 1:29; 2 Tim. 2:3-7; 3:10-12).

B. The pastor is responsible to keep his life right in relationship to the Lord.

1. All believers are called upon to keep their lives right before God (Rom. 12:1-2; 14:8; 2 Cor. 5:15; Gal. 5:17-25; Eph. 4:23-24; Col. 3:10; Phil. 2:12-13; 1 Thess. 4:1-12; 2 Tim. 2:19-21; 2 Pet. 3:1-11). They are to be faithful stewards of Christ and are accountable to him through a biblically balanced life (Rom. 14:8, 12; 1 Cor. 9:17; 1 Pet. 4:5).

2. This is all the more true for pastors, elders and deacons. The admonition to Timothy is applicable to those who take on the yoke of ministry. The pastor must guard and maintain his life, piety and gifts (Acts 20:28; 1 Tim. 4:14-16; 2 Tim. 2:19-21) so that he might have the proper capacity to serve others through Christ (2 Tim. 2:1, 6, 15; 3:16-17). Also, he should practice and devote himself to godliness in Christ so that others will see progress in his walk (1 Tim. 4:15-16).

   The purpose of taking care of his life in Christ is not for self-actualization or other self-serving goals but rather to be of greater service to others. While this might seem odd, a properly oriented life that is saturated with God through Christ is a far better blessing to others. This is because the greater, more expansive capacity one has for God, the greater is his capacity for a fruitful ministry.

   Jesus is a model of one who, though sinless, maintained and nurtured his relationship with the Father, understood God's will and was strengthened from on high in order to accomplish all that God set out for him to do. He always made it a priority to spend time with the Father before serving others, yet he was the perfect servant (Matt. 20:28; Luke 22:27; John 13:5; Phil. 2:7ff).

3. The pastor is called to train and discipline himself for godliness (1 Tim. 4:7-11) so as to become more and more like Jesus Christ (2 Cor. 3:18; Col. 3:10; 1 Tim. 6:11-16; Ti. 2:12; 2 Pet. 1:4). After all, the pastor is to model the life of Jesus Christ (2 Cor. 12:18; 1 Thess. 2:10-12; 1 Tim. 4:12; 1 Pet. 5:3), a very profitable pursuit (1 Tim. 6:6). At minimum, this would include the nurture and improvement of the godly character required according to 1 Timothy 3:1-9 and Titus 1:5-9, but he should also cultivate and strengthen other qualities God desires of him as Christ's under-shepherd. These include:
   a. Humility (John 13:14; Acts 20:19; 1 Cor. 10:12)
   b. Being free of or fleeing the love of money (1 Tim. 3:3; 6:7-11)
   c. Being a vessel of honor that is set apart from sin (2 Tim. 2:20-21)
      (1) Actively pursuing biblical righteousness, godliness, faith, love, perseverance and gentleness (1 Tim. 6:11)
      (2) Fleeing youthful lusts, pursuing righteousness, faith, love (2 Tim 2:22)
   d. Fearing no one or nothing except God (Deut. 10:12; Eccles. 12:13; Psa. 118:6; Prov. 29:25; Isa. 12:2; Isa. 51:12; 2 Tim. 1:7; 1 Pet. 1:17; 2:17)
   e. Being sober-minded about everything (2 Tim. 4:5; 1 Pet. 5:8)

  f. Maintaining a clear conscience before the Lord (Acts 24:16; 1 Tim.1:19; 1 Pet. 3:16)

4. He is to put to use the good gift(s) God has placed upon him. In fact, he is called upon to fan the flame or rekindle the gift(s) of God in his life (1 Tim. 4:14; 2 Tim. 1:6).

5. The pastor is to saturate his life with and properly handle God's Word (1 Tim. 5:17; 2 Tim. 2:15; 3:14-16), by:
  a. Always growing in grace and truth (2 Pet. 3:18).
  b. Holding fast to and being nourished by the Word of God (1 Tim 4:6; 2 Tim. 1:13; 3:14-17; Ti. 1:9).
  b. Rightly handling God's Word so as to be approved by God (2 Tim. 2:15).
  c Contending for the truth of God's Word (1 Tim. 1:18-19).
  d. Guarding the truth (1 Tim. 6:20; 2 Tim. 1:12-14)

6. He should bear fruit (Jn 15:8; Gal. 5:22-23; Eph. 2:8-10; Col. 1:10; Ti. 2:7; 3:8, 14)

7. He is to take care of his physical life (1 Tim 5:23).

8. He should not be concerned about the judgments of others (1 Cor. 4:1-5); neither should he compare himself with others (1 Cor. 3; 2 Cor. 10:12-16). At the same time he should defend a biblical and righteous ministry in the cause of Christ against false accusations (1 Cor. 1:6-23; 2:4, 17; 3:6, 12; 4:1-8; 5:14, 21; 1 Tim. 4:12).

9. He must keep his family life in order (1 Tim. 3:4-5; Ti. 1:6).

10. Finally, he and others must understand that his life and ministry is a living sacrifice to God (2 Sam. 24:24; Acts 20:24; 21:13; Phil. 2:17; 3:7-8; 2 Tim. 4:6).

C. After serving God and attending to his life in Christ, the pastor or elder then serves others, particularly God's people.

1. The pastor or elder serves through self-sacrifice (Jn. 10:11, 15; cp. Matt. 16:24-25; Lk 10:34-37; Rom. 12:1-2; 15:1; Phil. 2:4) as a faithful steward of God's ministry (1 Cor. 4:1-2; Ti. 1:7), in a manner like Jesus Christ (Matt. 20:25-28; 23:11-12; Mark 10:43, 44; Luke 22:26-27; John 13:1-20).

2. He prays for others (Acts 6:4; Rom. 15:30; 2 Cor. 1:11; Col. 1:9; 4:12; 1 Thess. 1:2; 1 Tim. 2:1).
  a. His priority is to pray, especially for God's people (Acts 6:4; Eph. 1:16-23; Col. 1:9; 4:12; 1 Thess. 1:2-4).
  b. He also prays for those who are not believers in Christ (1 Tim. 2:1-8).

3. As an undershepherd to the Great Shepherd he pastors through God's Word (Jn. 21:15ff; 1 Pet. 5:1ff); ministering the Word of God (Mk. 6:34b; Rev. 7:17; 1 Tim. 5:17; 1 Thess. 5:12; Col. 1:28; Jas. 3:1) in a variety of ways. In fact, the

bulk and thrust of his labors is in the power of God's Spirit through the Word of God, by:

a. Publicly reading, preaching, explaining and applying the Scriptures (1 Cor. 1:17; 1 Tim. 4:13-14; 2 Tim. 2:15)

b. Preaching in season and out of season reproving, rebuking and exhorting (2 Tim. 4:1-2)

c. Teaching boldly the Word of God (Matt. 28:18-20; Mark 6:34; Acts 20:20; 1 Cor. 12:28, 31; Col. 1:28; 1 Tim. 1:3; 3:2, 16; 4:11-13; 6:2-5; Jas. 3:1) in these things:

  (1) Apostolic truth, particularly to faithful men who would teach others the same (2 Tim. 2:2).

  (2) Godliness in Christ (1 Tim. 5:24-6:6)

  (3) Older men to be sober, reverent, self-controlled, sound in faith, sound in love, patient (Tit. 2:1-2).

  (4) The rich to be rich in good works and generosity (1 Tim. 6:17-19)

d. Feeding God's people in the Truth (1 Pet. 5:2)

e. Edifying or building up believers in Christ (2 Cor. 13:10-11; Eph 4:12-16)

f. Convicting the contrary (2 Tim. 2:25; Tit. 1:9)

g. Bringing comfort to hearers of the Word (1 Cor. 14:3, 31; 2 Cor. 1:4-6; 1 Thess. 4:18)

h. Confronting Sin (1Tim 5:1-2; Gal. 6:1)

  (1) Warning of the consequences of sin (Acts 20:31)

  (2) Rebuking sin (2 Tim. 4:1-2; Tit. 1:13; 2:15)

j. Admonishing wayward believers to obey God's Word (Gal. 6:1; 1 Thess. 5:14; 2 Thess. 3:15)

k. Exhorting or confronting the opposition with sound doctrine in love (1 Cor. 13:1; Eph. 4:15; 2 Tim. 2:24-26)

4. He trains them in spiritual warfare, resisting Satan and calling them to their role as godly warriors (2 Cor. 11:13-15; Eph. 6:10-18; Jas. 4:7; 1 Pet. 5:8-9).

5. He delegates to others, such as deacons, administrative tasks of lesser priorities for his vocation in order to concentrate on the ministries of prayer and the Word of God (Act 6:1-7).

6. The minister's godly office was created by Christ (2 Cor. 3:9; 4:6). Therefore, the minister is responsible with other elders in the church to perpetuate the office with sound, godly and faithful men who are gifted, called, and qualified (1 Tim. 1:11; 3:1-7; 4:14). It is perpetuated through the laying on of hands by ordained elders of the church (Acts 6:6; 13:3; 14:23; 19:6; 1 Tim. 1:5; 2 Tim. 1:6).

7. He must always keep before him the biblical goals of his God-ordained ministry, which are:

    a. To form Jesus Christ in the community of God's people through love (Eph. 1:15-23; 3:14-21; 4:13; Col 1:224-29; 1 Thess. 3:11-13; 1 Tim. 1:5) until that community is like one mature man(Eph. 2:15) who lives:

      (1) In the unity of the Faith (Eph. 4:13)

      (2) In an intimate full-knowledge of the Son of God, deeply in love with Christ and is becoming more like him in every way (Eph. 4:13)

      (3) In truth that is spoken and expressed through love (Eph. 4:15)

    b. To equip the saints to do the work of ministry (Eph. 4:11-12) in the faithful exercise of their gifts (1 Cor. 12; Rom. 12).

D. The pastor's duties are enumerated through the many roles he has:

1. As an evangelist (Matt. 28:18-20; Acts 20:21; 21:8; 1 Tim. 5:22; 2 Tim. 4:5; Tit. 1:5)

    a. By faithful testimony of Christ in life and lip (Acts 20:21; 1 Thess. 2:2)

    b. By giving the Gospel of Christ (Rom. 3:21-28; 11:6; Gal. 3:1-9; 1 Pet. 4)

2. As a model of godliness (Psa. 101:2; 1 Cor. 4:6; 11:1; Phil. 3:17; 1 Thess. 1:6; 2:10-11; 2 Thess. 3:7, 9; 1 Tim. 4:12; Ti. 2:7; Heb. 12:2; 13:7; 1 Pet. 2:11-25; 5:3; 1 Jn. 2:6; etc.)

3. As a parent

    a. Like a father (Matt. 13:52; 1 Cor. 4:12-21; 1 Thess. 2:10-12; 1 Tim. 3:5; Philem. 10)

      (1) Who sees to it with fellow elders and the deacons that widows in need are taken care of (Acts 6:1ff; 1 Tim. 3:5-16; Jas. 1:27)

      (2) Who also oversees with elders and deacons the needs of orphans (James 1:27)

      (3) Who, with the elders through the service of the deacons, takes care of the needy in the church (Luke 14:13; Acts 2:45; 4:35; Rom. 15:26; Gal. 2:10; Eph. 4:28; Jas. 2:2-6)

    b. Like a mother who nurses her little ones (1 Thess. 2:7)

    c. Who is a nurturer and disciplinarian (Matt. 18; 2 Cor. 7:8-13)

4. As a peacemaker or reconciler (Matt. 5:9; 2 Cor. 5:18-19)

5. As a preacher of the gracious Word of Christ (Rom. 10:14-15; 2 Pet. 2:5)

6. As a priest. Even though he is like all other Christians who are believer-priests, he models for others and takes the lead in:

    a. Interceding and praying for God's people (e.g.: 1 Sam. 12:23; Acts 12:5-9, 12; Rom. 10:1; Eph. 1:18; Col. 4:12; 1 Tim. 2:1, 2; Jas. 5:16)

    b. Worship

7. As a professor-teacher (see B.3.c above)

8. As a servant-ruler with fellow elders over Christ's church (1 Thess. 5:12, 13; 1 Tim. 5:17; Heb.13:7, 17)
   a. Overseeing the church of Christ with servant-authority (Acts 20:28; Rom. 12:8; Tit. 2:15; 1 Pet. 5:2)
   b. Exercising restorative church discipline (Matt. 18:15-19; Rom. 16:17; 1 Cor. 5; Thess. 5:14; 2 Thess. 3:6-15; 1 Tim. 5:20; 6:3; Ti. 1:13; 2:15; 3:10-11)
   c. Exercising Christ's authority, but not lording it over God's people (Matt. 20:25-26; Mk. 10:42-43; 1 Pet. 5:3)
9. As a self-sacrificing servant (Matt. 20:27; John 10:11, 15; Lk. 10:34, 35; 1 Cor. 4:1)
   a. Of God (2 Cor. 6:4; Ti. 1:1, 7) and of Christ (Phil. 1:1; 2 Tim. 2:24)
   b. Of God's people (2 Cor. 4:5)
   c. Who serves God and his church well (Rom. 12:8; 1 Thess. 5:12; 1 Tim.5:17; 2 Tim. 2:15; 2 Pet. 3:14)
10. As a caring undershepherd of the flock of God (Jer. 3:15; John 21:15ff; Acts 20:28; 1 Pet. 5:1-2)
    a. Who leads (Mark 6:34; Heb. 13:7, 17, 24) and guides (Matt. 2:6; Acts 7:10, 14; Heb. 13:7, 17, 24)
    b. Who protects (Acts 20:28-30; Jn.10:12; Ti. 1:9; 2:1; Eph. 4:14; 1 Pet. 5:8; 1 Jn. 4:1-3)
       (1) From enemies within (2 Tim. 2:16-18; Jude 12f)
       (2) From enemies without (Mt. 13:24f; 2 Cor. 11:12-15)
11. The pastor is also described in roles as a messenger (2 Cor. 8:23), a good worker (2 Cor. 6:1; Phil. 2:25), a soldier (Phil. 2:25; 2 Tim. 2:3-4), an athlete (1 Cor. 9:24-25; Phil. 3:14; 2 Tim. 2:5; 4:7-8; Heb. 12:1) and a farmer (2 Tim. 2:6).

APPENDIX K

A PROPOSED BIBLICAL VISION FOR THE LOCAL CHURCH

—〰—

Picture something radically different: a church that reflects and applies some of the metaphors God uses for his church. This vision is the ideal to which we are called as Christ's church.

AS A BODY OF CHRIST
(Rom. 12; 1 Cor. 12; Eph. 1:15-23; 4:4ff; Col. 1:18ff)
- This is a church where Jesus Christ is obviously preeminent (Acts 14:23; 2 Cor. 4:5; 1 Thess. 1:9; Rev. 1:13).
- The people obviously have an observable vital and loving relationship with Jesus Christ and for one another (John. 13:34; 15:12-17; Rom. 13:8; 1 Thess. 4:9; 1 Pet. 1:22; 1John. 3:11, 23; 4:7-13; 2 John. 1:5,6).
- The members glorify and enjoy Jesus (Ps. 42:1; 73:25,26; Rom. 15:5-7; 2 Thess. 1:12).
- Christians have opportunities to use their gifts and talents for the benefit of one another (where the majority of the people participate in some capacity in the work of the Church) (Rom. 12; 1 Cor. 12; Gal. 5:13; Eph. 4:7-16).
- Those "one-another" passages in the NT are exercised in a genuine, loving way. This is a people-loving and people-serving church.

AS A FAMILY OF GOD
(Ex. 4:22; Deut. 14:1; Isa. 1:2,4; 63:8; Jer. 31:9; John. 1:12; 11:52; Rom. 8:14-16; 2 Cor. 6:18; Gal. 3:7,26; 29; Eph. 3:14-21; 1 John 3:1)
- Each Christian individual and family is looked upon and treated as part of the greater family of God; not as separate little units serving self-interests (Matt. 12:50; Rom. 12:3-5; Eph. 2:19; Tit. 1:4; Jas. 2; 1 Pet. 5:5).
- Hospitality is part of the culture of the church. People come and are warmly welcomed and incorporated (Acts 2:42ff; 1 Pet. 4:7-11).

- Families are refreshed, encouraged, and nourished in Christ's truth and love (1 Cor. 13:6; Eph. 4:13; Phil. 3:15-16; Col. 2:19).
- The place known for its comfort, refuge, healing, and unity (1 Cor. 1:9-10; 2 Cor. 1:2-7; 13:11-14; Eph. 3:14-21; 1 Pet. 4:7-11).
- Men learn to be godly leaders, loving husbands, and Christ-like fathers (Eph.5:23-31; 1 Tim. 6:11; 2 Tim. 3:16ff).
- Women grow as godly women, loving wives and nurturing mothers (Prov. 31; 1 Cor. 11:12; Eph. 5:22; 1 Tim. 2:15; 5:14).
- Biblical and godly "family" is taught and caught (1 Cor. 4:15,16; 11:1; 2 Thess. 3:7,8).
- The pastor and elders live out their genuine role as spiritual fathers (2 Thess. 3:7-8; 1 Tim. 4:12; 5:1; 1 Pet. 5:2-4), and older women mentor younger women in the Faith (Prov. 31; Acts 12:12-13; Rom.16:5,6; 1 Tim. 3:11; 5:2-5; Tit. 2:3-5).
- "Motherly" exhortation and counseling happens in a spiritual hospital for the hurt and wounded. It is a haven of rest (1 Cor. 12:25-26; Gal. 4:26; 6:1; 1 Thess. 5:11; 2 Pet. 1:3-11).
- We encourage one another in hope through various ministries of mercy, including the ministries of deacons. (Mark 10:43,44; Acts 6; 11:29; 12:25; 2 Cor. 8:4-5; Col. 1:24; 1 Tim. 3:8-12; 4:11).
- The church has a reputation of love for one another (John. 13:35; Rom. 12:10ff; 1 Cor. 12:26; 13; 1 Thess. 3:11-13; 5:11).

AS A FLOCK OF GOD

(Ps. 23; 78:70-72; Ezek. 37:23-24; Mic. 2:12; Matt. 25; Jn. 10:1-18; Heb. 13:20; 1 Pet. 2:25; 5:2, 3)

- We are Christ's sheep who no longer wander aimlessly about, but head in the same direction.
- Shepherds (pastor and elders) are models of wisdom, who exercise caring oversight in the local church (Acts 15:6; 20:17-38; 1 Tim. 5; 2 Tim. 4:5; Heb. 13:7,17; I Pet. 2:25; 5:2,3).
- Sheep are being prepared for service; and who are willing to be led through dark valleys and quiet waters (Ps. 23).
- This flock of sheep is filled with the full-knowledge of God (Eph. 1:17-19; 3:16-21; 2 Pet. 3:18).
- The flock is known as a people who know and hear God speaking through the preached Word (Psa. 46:10; 100:2-3; John 6:68-69; 10:27ff; 17:3; Acts 17:11; Rom. 10:14; 15:4; 1 Thess. 2:13; 1 Tim 4:13).

AS A HOUSE OF GOD
(Matt. 16:18; 1 Cor. 3: 9, 16-17; Eph. 2:19-22; Heb. 10:21; 1 Tim. 3:15; 1 Pet. 2:4-10; 4:17)

- In God's house, the people are in a growing relationship, an active commitment, and loving service to God (1 Pet. 2:5; Rev. 1:6; 2:1-7; 5:10).
- Worship is distinctly God-centered, Word-regulated, and spiritually alive (with wonder, joy and reverence) (1 Chron. 16:29; Ps. 2:11; 29:2; 95:6; John. 4:24; 1 Cor. 14; 2 Cor. 4:5; Gal. 6:14; Rev. 14:7).
- Each person knows how to and enjoys personal, family, and community times of worship (Deut. 16:13ff; 31:12; Psa. 5:7; 34:11; Joel 2:16; Matt. 19:13; John. 4:24).
- Each person is spiritually growing; building one another up in the Faith through God's Word, baptism and the Lord's Supper (Matt. 28:19-20; Acts 2:42; 1 Cor. 3:10,11; Col. 2:6-7; 1 Thess. 5:11; 2 Tim. 4:1ff; 2 Pet. 3:18; Jude 1:20-21).
- In God's house prayer is key: spontaneous (praying for someone right then and there), vigorous (with great expectations and enthusiasm), and dedicated (regular times, a prayer ministry, frequent at home and church) (Matt. 21:13; Acts 4:24; Rom. 15:30; Eph. 6:18-20; Col. 1:3; 1 Thess. 1:1-3; Philem. 1:3; Jude 1:20).
- In this house the members truly glorify God and enjoy Him (Psa. 20:5; 32:11; Isa. 29:19; Hab. 3:18; 1 Cor. 10:31)!

AS A PEOPLE OF GOD
(Ex. 6:7; Deut. 27:9; 2 Sam. 7:23; Jer. 11:4; Rom. 9:25; 2 Cor. 6:16; Eph. 4:12; 5:3; Phil. 3:20-21; 2 Thess. 1:10; Tit. 2:14)

- These people with a solid, biblical orthodoxy of the historic Christian Faith (1 Tim. 6:3; 2 Tim. 2:2), are keenly aware of their spiritual and historical heritage (2 Thess. 2:13-17; 3:6; 2 Tim. 1:2ff; Heb. 11).
- In this covenant community, which means they understand who they are in Christ: God is their living God and they are God's special people (Gen. 17:8; Ex. 19:5; Deut. 7:6-14; 14:2; 2 Tim. 2:10; Ti. 2:14; Heb. 8:10; 1 Pet. 2:9-11; Rev. 21:3).

AS A PEOPLE OF THE KINGDOM OF GOD
(John. 3:5-6; 7:38; Matt. 16:18-19; Phil 2:9-11; Col. 1:13; Jude 1:25)

- A church that clearly lives out the mandate from King Jesus to make disciples of all peoples (Matt. 28:19,20; Acts 28:31; 2 Cor. 4:5; Eph. 3:8-12; 2 Tim. 4:1ff)
- Where there is a growing relationship and active commitment to seeking out and making fully devoted disciples of Jesus Christ (Matt. 10:37ff; 28:18-20; John. 13:35; 1 Thess. 1:1-6; Jas. 5:19,20; 2 Pet. 3:18)

- With a reputation for conducting Christ's work through a passionate demonstration of His truth, mercy, and love in our city (e.g.: Jer. 29:4-7). The impetus for God's grace to see true reformation take place in our local community (Rom. 13:8ff; Gal. 1:3-5; 2 Pet. 1:8).
- A people characterized by kingdom principles who actively promote a culture of Christ's kingdom (Matt. 5-7) where:
- The proud are scattered, but the humble are exalted (James 4:10)
- The greedy are excluded but the hungry are satisfied in God (Prov. 16:26; Psa. 17:15: 42:1-2; Matt. 5:6)
- The prisoners are freed, because sin, guilt and evil no longer binds them
- The blind can now see and the deaf can now hear Truth and God
- The poor have good news to celebrate: there is restoration, comfort, encouragement, and riches!
- God gives power to establish justice, mercy, grace and righteousness
- People are not takers, but givers of good things. They are servants of one another.
- A culture of righteousness, peace, and joy in God's Spirit (Romans 14:7)
- It is a realm of true empowerment and abundant living (Mt. 19:17, 23-24 cp. John. 3:5, 16:4: 14; 5:21,24)
- Love is the principle and core value that is embraced and sincerely practiced by all (1 Cor. 13)
- Kingdom work is from love, mercy and grace that produces real fruit; not for personal consumption but to give to God and to others:
  - Being comforted we comfort others (2 Cor. 1:3-7)
  - Having received mercy we show mercy to others (Matt. 18:21-35)
  - God's glory reflects His light through us in the world (Matt. 5:14ff)
  - Because we have been rescued we rescue others (Lk 10:25-37)
    (Leithart, 1993)

APPENDIX L

HOW TO GROW IN GRACE THROUGH THE PREACHED WORD

—w—

Preaching is an incarnational event: it involves both the Holy Spirit and whole soul.

A. Granted, the Holy Spirit has a most crucial and vital role through the Word in the life of a believer. Some of the ministries of the Holy Spirit through God's Word include:

C onvicting us of sin (John 16:8-11; 2 Tim. 3:16,17)

A ssuring us of our place in Christ (Romans 8:16; 1 John 3:19; 5:11-13)

T eaching us (Luke 12:12; John 14:16; 16:12-15; 1 Cor. 2:10-16; 1 Thess. 4:9; 1 John 2:27)

A nointing us (1 John 2:20-27; 2 Cor. 1:21)

G uiding us into all truth (Psa. 25:9; 31:3; 32:8; John 16:13; Rom. 8:14-17)

I nterceding for us (Rom. 8:26, 27, 34; 1 John 2:1)

C omforting us in Christ (John 14:16; 15:26; Acts 9:31; 2 Cor. 1:3)

   (Ron Merryman, n.d.)

B. Nevertheless, believers also have a very active relationship and role with God's Word.

1. Preaching is an operational event. It is a functional, active, working experience in the life of the believer.

   a. Using the metaphor of the seed and soil, let's observe how this is so. Read Matthew 13:1-9.

   b. What does it take to harvest a good crop or to produce good fruitful plants from start to finish?

   (1) Prepare the soil

   (2) Plant the seed

   (3) Provide the circumstances (light and heat)

   (4) Pick the fruit

   What does it take to harvest and produce good fruit in your life?

2. As a believer you need to prepare the soil of your heart
    Note: It is the character of the soil, not the sower, which makes the difference! Almost everything in Scripture points to the responsibility of the listener, and very little upon the preacher. The emphasis given in the Scriptures for the preacher is little upon *how* to preach, but upon *what* is preached. This is so unlike a common view about today's Christian and preacher where the emphasis is upon *how* and very little upon *what* is preached.
    a. What were the types of soil about which Jesus speaks in Matthew 13?
        (1) Stony, rocky ground – it is resistant hostility to the Word. It is rebellious or unwilling to hear what God says.
        (2) Soil not deep enough for plants to grow – this is the superficial, shallow heart of a casual listener. You might say that radical change is the last thing this person wants.
        (3) Soil filled with weeds that choke out the growth of the Word. Perhaps this is where the weeds of worry and greed choke out growth.
        (4) The good soil – open, ready, willing, teachable, humble and fertile.
            (a) This soil has a fresh, child-like predisposition with a sense of wonder and a willingness to receive (Matt. 18:3).
            (b) This person is an active, aggressive, intentional listener (Prov. 18:15 versus Ezek. 3:31ff; Heb. 5:11-15).
            (c) This person is a discerning listener (Ps. 119:104).
    b. What does it take to prepare *good soil* of your heart?
        (1) Confess yourself empty.
            Humble yourself before the Lord (Jas. 4:10; 1 Pet. 5:6). Confess sin and sinful attitudes such as indifference, lukewarmness, anger, pride, bitterness, lack of love, lack of zeal, etc., so as not to quench or grieve the Holy Spirit (1 John 1:9; 1 Thess.5:19; Eph. 4:30). Repent of and put off known sin (Ezra 9:5-15; Neh. 9:1-38; Dan. 9:1-20; 1 Kings 8:31-53; Ps. 51).
        (2) Pray yourself full.
            (a) Pray for your own heart that God would teach, convict, anoint, humble and grant you the physical and spiritual ability to hear and receive God's Word. Pray too that God's Spirit would do a mighty work in you from His Word read and preached.
            (b) Pray for the preacher of the Word.
        (3) Read yourself ready.
            Read and meditate upon the passage(s) of Scripture the pastor will be preaching.
        (4) Bring yourself expecting.

Don't expect to hear merely a sermon, but rather expect to hear a particular message from Christ to you (Rom. 10:14, 17). Come with expectant faith.

3. The next thing after preparing the soil is to plant the seed.

    a. The Holy Spirit is the primary agent by which God's Word is implanted (1 Cor. 2).

    b. The preacher has the responsibility to faithfully and soundly declare God's Word.

    c. But you are to <u>attend</u> to the Word (concentrate, focus) (Heb. 2:1-4).

        (1) Come willing, ready, and expecting to hear God speaking to you (Isa. 55:7-11; Matt. 18:3).

        (2) Do not be a passive, lazy listener (Ezek. 33:31ff; 1 Cor. 3:1-3; Heb. 5:11-15).

        (3) Instead, be an active listener (Ps. 78:1; Pro. 18:15; 25:12; Matt. 11:15; Luke 8:15; Rev.13:9).

            (a) Read Proverbs 18:15 – the terms in this passage imply an intense desire to

hear and learn.

            (b) Daniel 10:12 – God's person sets his or her heart to understand God's truth!

            (c) Hebrews 2:1 – we must pay attention to God's Word.

    d. You are to receive the Word by faith (Luke 18:12, 13; John 5:38; 17:20; Acts 15:7; 1 Cor. 2).

        (1) Do not be one who disbelieves or refuses to hear God's Word, or you may suffer some dire consequences (Ps. 50:17; Isa. 5:24; 30:12; Jer. 6:10; 8:9; 18:18; 20:8; 36:23; Zech. 7:13; Mal. 2:2; Mark 7:13; Rom. 2:8, 9; 1 Thess. 1:8; 2 Tim. 4:3; 1 Pet. 4:17).

        (2) Romans 10:17 reminds you that faith comes by hearing God's Word.

        (3) Believe and receive God's Word (Deut. 6:3; Pro. 8:34; 15:31; Eccles. 5:1; Matt. 7:24-26; Acts 15:7; Rev. 2:11)

            (a) Heb. 4:2 says that some did not receive nor benefit from God's message because they did not unite faith to their hearing.

            (b) 1 Thess. 2:13 tells us that the Word of God was at work in believers at Thessalonica because they received and accepted God's Word not as the word from men, but as from God.

4. Provide the circumstances for spiritual light and heat

    a. Examine the Word through investigation, exploration, analysis and assessment

        (1) Actively listen and go through the investigative process by asking yourself good questions about the text and the message.

(2) Be a discerning listener. This means that your focus is upon hearing the truth first rather than merely or always seeking to detect error (Ex: Psa. 119:104)

(3) Later examine what was heard in the reading and preaching by measuring it against other Scriptures (Ezra 7:10; Acts 17:11).

   b. Meditate upon the Word (Joshua 1:8; Ps. 1; 19:14; 104:34; Mal. 3:16; Luke 9:44; 1 Tim. 4:15)

   c. Talk about the Word read and preached to others (Luke 24:14; Deut. 6:6-7; Mal. 3:16; Eph. 5:18-19). For example:

(1) Do a "search" with others (friends, family, etc.)

    (a) Search how did the Lord minister to you today during worship?

    (b) What did you learn?

    (c) What will you do because of it?

(2) Discuss the sermon with others in church, with your family or others:

    (a) Some general questions you can ask:

      (a.1) What was the main point(s)?

      (a.2) Could you recall the sub points?

      (a.3) What was the overall theme or purpose of the sermon?

      (a.4) Was there something that stood out particularly to you?

      (a.5) Was there something you did not understand in the sermon? If so, what?

      (a.6) How was the Lord portrayed in the message?

      (a.7) Was I convicted, comforted, or challenged?

    (b) Additional specific questions:

      (b.1) Is there any temptation that you ought to flee?

      (b.2) Any judgments threatened that should make you tremble?

      (b.3) Any duties commanded that God calls you to obey?

      (b.4) Any comforts or promises that you ought to embrace?

      (b.5) How was your faith encouraged to receive and rest on Christ alone for your salvation and needs in life, and in your life to come (cp. 2 Tim. 3:16-17; 2 Pet. 1:3-11)?

5. Hide the Word in you heart (Prov. 2:1; Ps. 119:11; Eph. 5:18b-19)
To hide the Word hearts means more than merely memorizing portions of Scripture. It means to retain the truth in your mind and keep on thinking it over and reflecting on its relation to every sphere of our life.

6. Pick the fruit (Matt. 13:8; Luke 8:15; Jn 15:18; Jas. 1:25).
Bring the Word forth, practice it, apply it, and perform it.

APPENDIX M

HOW TO BE AN EFFECTIVE HEARER OF GOD'S WORD

—ɱ—

These Biblical recommendations for becoming a more effective listener to the reading and preaching of God's Word at the time of worship are taken from the Westminster Confession's Larger Catechism, Question #160:

1. Attend to the preaching of God's Word with diligence, preparation and prayer (Prov. 8:34; I Pet. 2:1-2; Luke 8:18; Ps. 119:18; Eph. 6:18-19).
2. We test the message against the Scriptures (Acts 17:11).
3. We are to receive God's truth with faith, love, meekness and readiness of mind (Heb. 4:2; 2 Thess. 2:10; Jas. 1:21; Acts 17:11).
4. That truth is to be received, not as a mere matter of human opinion, but as the Word of God with divine authority. (1 Thess. 2:13).
5. We are to meditate and confer concerning it (Deut. 6:6-7; Mal. 3:16; Psalm 119; Luke 9:44; 24:14; Heb. 2:1).
6. We are to hide the Word in our hearts (Prov. 2:1; Ps. 119:11).
7. We are to see to it that the Word is fruitful in our lives (Luke 8:15; Jas. 1:25).

APPENDIX N

HOW TO PRAY FOR YOUR PREACHER

—ɯ—

Dr. Dave Eby in *Power Preaching for Church Growth* (1996) suggests that you pray to God for your preacher and his preaching in these specific ways:
1. Help him to realize his absolute dependence on the Lord, that apart from God he can do nothing (John 15:5);
2. Help him to pray for his preaching continually and depend on God's Spirit for power;
3. Anoint him and fill him with the Spirit for preaching. Bring him under complete the submission to the Lord;
4. Enable him to preach the Word with accuracy, clarity, boldness and love;
5. Anoint the ears of listeners to be humble, hungry hearers of the Word;
6. Bring conviction of sins and true conversion by the preached Word to unbelievers;
7. Bring conviction of sin, on-going repentance, edification, encouragement and growth/sanctification to believers.

You could also take the words of Westminster's *Larger Catechism* Question 159 and pray: "Lord, help our preacher to preach sound doctrine
1. Diligently
2. Plainly
3. In the power of the Spirit
4. Faithfully
5. Wisely
6. Zealously, with fervent love to God and His people
7. Sincerely, aiming at God's glory, and the conversion, edification and salvation of all who listen to the Word."

Remember that power preaching is what our church needs. You can be used by God to promote the powerful preaching of His Word.

APPENDIX O

COMPARATIVE VIEWS ON PREACHING

—m—

The purpose of this comparative chart is to demonstrate the many, and often conflicting, expectations that are placed upon a preacher. Both lists are drawn from seminary class notes, books on preaching, articles on preaching, and the expressed opinions of various people.

SOME SAY THAT YOU MUST:

1. Preach about Christ from the text

2. Not use application because that is the Holy Spirit's role

3. Preach only one verse at a time

4. Preach from only one verse and give plenty of application

5. Give non-specific application

6. Have only one central point

7. Not include any Law, we are in an age of grace

8. Use many Bible verses in each sermon

9. Plan out the illustrations

OTHERS SAY THAT YOU MUST:

1. Preach only Christ from the text

2. Always use application and exhortation

3. Preach a section of Scripture at a time

4. Preach from a section but let the Bible determine explicit application

5. Give specific application that people can apply that week

6. Have many points (and subpoints)

7. Always include Law to bring out God's grace

8. Use few Bible verses

9. Let the Spirit give you illustrations while you are preaching

SOME SAY THAT YOU MUST:

10. Use your life experiences for illustrations

11. Preach no more than 20 minutes

12. Make the major point clear at the beginning of the sermon

13. Give all your points at the beginning of the sermon and repeat them

14. Use big theological terms to increase people's vocabulary

15. Make sure sermons are deep and heavy

16. Preach didactically, like a lecture

17. Preach with eloquence, good grammar, and formal English

18. Keep gestures to a minimum

19. Use no technology

20. Always preach from a pulpit

21. Preach like the best preachers

22. Never use handouts or sermon supplements

OTHERS SAY THAT YOU MUST:

10. Never use your life experiences for illustrations

11. Preach as long as you want

12. Make the point clear any time during the sermon or wait until the end

13. Give your points as you progress through the sermon

14. Keep the sermon simple and speak at the level of the audience.

15. Be simple and as clear as possible

16. Preach dialogically, engaging the people

17. Preach in the vernacular of the people

18. Use appropriate and expressive gestures

19. Use any technology you need

20. Pulpits may be useful but not required.

21. Preach from your own personality

22. Use handouts or supplements if helpful

APPENDIX P

CHECKING MY SPEECH AGAINST GOD'S EXPECTATIONS

(Check the boxes that are true for you most of the time.)

—ɯ—

Is my speech false, uncaring or ungodly?

These are sins I am called to put off:
- ☐ I am consistently slow or unwilling to listen; I have a habit of interrupting
  (Prov. 18:13; Jas. 1:19).
- ☐ I do not listen to others well and then react or draw improper conclusions
  (Prov. 25: 8; 18:17; 27:2; 18:13; Job 13:5).
- ☐ I refuse to try to understand the other person's opinions
  (Jas. 1:19 cp. Prov. 18:2, 13, 15; Phil. 3:15,16).
- ☐ I am too quick to speak
  (Ps. 106:33; Prov. 15:23, 28:29:20; Jas. 1:19).
- ☐ I talk too much
  (Job 11:2; 16:3; Eccles. 5:3; 6:11; 10:14).
- ☐ My words are rash
  (Prov. 12:18; 29:20).
- ☐ I flatter to manipulate people
  (Ps. 12:3)
- ☐ I lie in order to manipulate things in my favor
  (Exod. 23:1,7; Ps. 34:13; 58:3; 109:2; Prov. 6:16-19; 12:19; 14:5, 25; 26:24; 28:24; Hos. 4:2; Mk. 7:21-22). Note: liars hate those to whom they tell lies (Prov. 26:28).
- ☐ I am generally or often argumentative, quarrelsome or contentious
  (Prov. 15:18; 17:14; 20:3; Rom. 13:13; Eph. 4:31; 1 Tim. 3:3; 2 Tim. 2:24).
  - o   Argumentative means to bicker, dispute, squabble, wrangle
  - o   Contentious means to compete, to engage in controversy, to be adversarial
    (Prov. 18:6; 21:19; 22:16; 25:24; Jer. 15:10; 1 Cor. 11:16; Gal. 5:19-20).

❒ I nag
  (Prov. 10:19; 16:21, 23; 18:6,7; 21:19; 27:15).
❒ I brag
  (Ps. 94:4; Jer. 9:23, 24; 48:29,30).
❒ I respond verbally to others with uncontrolled anger
  (Prov. 14:29; 15:1; 25:15; 29:11; Eph. 4:26, 31).
❒ I attack those who criticize or blame me
  (Ps. 10:7; 64:3; Jer. 18:18; Rom. 12:17, 21; 1 Pet. 2:23; 3:9).
❒ I call other people names, mock or make fun of them
  (Prov. 12:18; 16:24; Matt. 7:12; Eph. 4:29, 30; Col. 4:6).
❒ My words are biting; they reveal my anger and bitterness
  (Ps. 10:7; 64:2ff).
❒ I use language or tone of speech that provokes children to anger
  (Eph. 6:4).
❒ 'Grumble and complain' could be my middle name
  (Phil. 2:14; Jas. 5:9).
❒ I use words that discourage
  (Prov. 18:1; Ps. 10:7; 64:2ff cp. Heb. 3:13; 10:24-25).
❒ What comes from my mouth is often cursing instead of blessing
  (Ps.10:7; 64:2-4; 109:17).
❒ I use rotten talk. This is speech that tears down, is non-beneficial, or presumptive
  (Eph. 4:29; 2 Tim. 2:26; Jas. 4:11-12).
❒ I "murder" with my mouth
  (Prov. 11:9; 18:20, 21; Matt. 5:21, 22; Jas. 4:11; 5:9).
    o By cutting others with gossip. Gossip means to reveal or discuss personal facts about another person for no legitimate purposes; it often betrays a confidence. It is used to diminish a person's reputation in the eyes of another (Prov. 11:13; 16:28; 20:19; 26:20; 2 Cor.12:20; 1 Tim. 5:13).
    o By slander – speaking false or malicious words about another, also used to diminish a person's reputation in the eyes of another (Lev. 19:16; Ps. 15:3; Prov. 10:18; 50:20; 2 Tim. 3:3; Tit. 2:3; 3:2; Jude 1:10)
    o By destroying with words rather than building up (Ex. 20:16; Prov. 11:19; 12:18; Jas. 3:5-6 cp. Acts 20:32; Rom. 14:19; 15:2; 1 Cor. 14:26; Eph.6:18-19; 1 Tim. 2:1-4).
    o I cut others down behind their backs (Ps. 15:2,3).
❒ I use words that speak down or cut down another
  (Jas. 4:11).
❒ I condemn instead of commend
  (Psa. 94:21; Luke 6:37 cp.1 Thess. 1:2; 2 Thess. 1:3).

- ☐ I speak harshly
  (Pro. 15:1).
- ☐ I scold
  (Prov. 15:1; Matt. 16:22, 23; Mark 14:3-5; Col. 4:6).
- ☐ I make rash judgments. That is condemning another without proper investigation
  (2 Sam. 16:4; 19:24ff; Matt. 7:1-3; John 9:12ff; 1 Cor. 4:5).
- ☐ I tell stories (tale bearing) that are injurious to another
  (Prov. 11:13; 17:9; 18:8; 20:19; 26:20).
- ☐ I am a false witness against others (Exod. 23:1; Deut. 5:20; Prov. 21:28).

Am I verbally abusive?

When the preponderance of the above qualities is evident and my overall demeanor and the overall tone of my home is sinfully negative and oppressive because of my words, then I would be considered verbally abusive.

Is my speech truthful, loving and godly?

These are qualities I am called to put on:
- ☐ I have a love of God's truth rather than such things as position, fame, abilities, possessions, etc., which are soon to pass away
  (1 Thess. 5:21; Heb.10:23; Rev. 3:3).
- ☐ I desire to please God in my speech
  (1 Cor. 10:31; 2 Cor. 5:9).
- ☐ Words have power of death and life, so I am careful with how I talk
  (Prov. 18:21).
- ☐ I recognize that I must not be careless in the use of my words, since I will give an account of them in the Day of Judgment (Matt. 12:36).
- ☐ I struggle and work to guard my mouth (Ps. 39:1; 141:3) so as to avoid all kinds of problems (Prov. 21:23).
- ☐ I am careful to use the right words at the right time
  (Prov. 10:19).
- ☐ I think before I talk
  (Prov. 15:28).
- ☐ I am slow to speak and quick to listen
  (Prov. 15:23, 28; 29:20; 18:13; Jas. 1:19).
- ☐ Wise speech brings healing. Often what I say brings healing and refreshment to others
  (Prov. 8:7).

- ☐ I work to grow in my life that I might be wise, so that my words are words of wisdom (Ps. 35:28; 37:30).
- ☐ I speak truthfully (Ps. 34:13; Prov. 8:7; Eph. 4:25).
- ☐ I speak the truth with love – gently but firmly, with the intention of helping (Prov. 15:4; 1 Cor. 13; Gal. 6:1; Eph. 4:15; 5:9).
- ☐ My speech is often without bitterness, anger, wrath, yelling, slander or malice (Ps. 10:7; 64:2-4; Eph. 4:29-32).
- ☐ When I speak, it is often gracious, courteous, helpful, tender, sympathetic, forgiving (Eph. 4:29-32).
- ☐ My speech serves grace to others and is helpful for the moment (Eph. 4:29).
- ☐ My speech is gracious, so that it can be readily received and preserved (Col. 4:6).
- ☐ I speak appropriately and with straight-forwardness (Matt. 5:37; James 5:12).
- ☐ I exhorting and encourage others with my speech (Heb. 3:13; 10:24-25; 1 Thess. 4:18; 5:11).
- ☐ I teach others (Deut. 6:4-9; Col. 3:16; Heb. 5:11-14).
- ☐ I admonish when necessary (Rom. 15:14; 1 Cor. 10:11; Eph. 6:4; Col. 1:28; 3:16; 1 Thess. 5:12, 14; 2 Thess.3:15).
- ☐ I build others up in Christ (Acts 20:32; Rom. 14:19; 15:2; 1 Cor. 14:26; Eph. 4:12-13; 1 Thess. 5:11).
- ☐ My words at times are firm, but diplomatic even when correcting opponents (Gal. 6:1; 2 Tim. 2:23-25).
- ☐ I often pray that God would deliver me from an evil tongue (Ps. 120:2).

APPENDIX Q

HOW TO GRACEFULLY LEAVE A CHURCH

—ᴡ—

Being a member means you have made a serious commitment to Jesus Christ and his local Body. There may come a time when because of circumstances you either must leave or have a desire to leave the church. We expect that all members of this particular church will do so with love, truth and grace.

A. **What are some good reasons and circumstances for leaving this local congregation?**
    1. When you need to relocate to another geographical area that would make it a burden to
        travel and participate in the life of the church.
    2. When you have come to a different and informed conviction about certain doctrines where in good conscience you cannot support the teachings of the church.
    3. When it is apparent the Lord is directing you to actively serve in another congregation of like faith and practice. Leaving under this circumstance should be done in consultation with the pastor, elders and other godly individuals.
    4. When the philosophy of ministry or the direction of the church violates your biblically informed conscience.
    5. Of course there are other legitimate reasons. Transferring to another church should not be so much a matter of running away from a problem or conflict but rather being led to another congregation.

B. **What are some wrong reasons and circumstances for leaving the local congregation?**
    1. To avoid coming under church discipline or following through with the discipline process (which is to restore you to Christ and his church). Once the discipline process has begun and is a matter of record, the pastor and elders are duty and conscience bound to complete it.

2. When you have a conflict with someone in the church and you have not taken the steps to resolve the conflict and reconcile. Biblically, you are free to leave after you have taken the correct steps to make things right.
3. When you don't *feel* like being a part of the church, but do not have any good biblical or moral grounds for leaving.
4. When your children are bored with church.

C. What is a gracious way to exit the church?
1. Don't let problems or convictions linger or fester indefinitely. Speak to the pastor and/or elder(s) to resolve the issues as soon as possible. It would be sinful to exit the church without reconciling. Furthermore, you would just be bringing the problem(s) with you to the next church.
2. No matter what the circumstances are, be courageous and do the righteous thing by talking in person with the pastor or elder(s).
    a. Do not send a letter or email. If need be, write a letter and bring it with you when you dialog in person.
    b. Let them know what you are thinking and where your heart is.
    c. Be willing to listen and receive sound, biblical advice from them.
3. Make arrangements with the elders to exit and do so graciously.
    a. The elders will be able to give instructions on how to transfer.
    b. If you leave sinfully or with unresolved conflict, the elders will not be able to give you a letter of transfer or a letter of good standing. Should the other church inquire as to the circumstances the elders are obliged to speak the truth.

APPENDIX R

HOW A PASTOR CAN LOVE GOD'S PEOPLE
(An application of 1 Corinthians 13)

—ᨕ—

All of these qualities of love find their source and perfect expression in God through Jesus Christ. If I am truly in Christ, I should express these loving qualities more and more toward God's people under my care. Fill in the blank spaces with your member's name.

1. Does my communication with _____ come from a heart of love or am I just all talk and an irritating noise maker (1 Cor. 13:1)?

2. Do I use the gifts God has given me to lovingly serve _____ (1 Cor. 13:2)?

3. Do I love _____ sacrificially? In what specific ways do I do so (1 Cor. 13:3)?

4. Am I patient with _____? In other words, do I show an enduring restraint with him or her even when I have a right to act? Do I restrain my words and actions when wronged or provoked when I have a right to act, unless there is a particular sin I need to address through gentle rebuke (Matt. 18:15-22; Gal. 6:1).

5. Am I kind toward _____? Kindness proceeds from a tender heart that contributes to the good will and happiness of others (1 Cor. 13:4).

6. Am I envious of _____? Do I feel uneasiness with the excellence, reputation or happiness he enjoys? Do I have a desire to depreciate him or her (1 Cor. 13:4)?

7. Do I brag about myself to _____? This means that I do not have an anxious display of myself for the purpose of elevating my own life, especially at the

expense of putting him or her down. Do I campaign for the center of attention (1 Cor. 13:4)?

8. Am I arrogant, puffed up or swollen with a proud vanity with _____ (1 Cor. 13:4)?

9. Am I considerate and not rude with _____? Do I act unbecomingly or unseemly toward him, or unnecessarily embarrass him (1 Cor. 13:5)?

10. Do I seek _____'s greatest good and benefit (1 Cor. 13:5)?

11. Am I easily provoked or angered by _____? Do I have a trigger temper that stems from bitterness (1 Cor. 13:5)?

12. Do I keep a record of the wrongs suffered by _____ from which to make a plan for retaliation? Do I really apply the fact that Jesus Christ took the registry of my sins and their sins, and paid for them with his own sacrificial life and death (1 Cor. 13:5)?

13. Do I rejoice in unrighteousness or evil done by or done to _____? Do I find pleasure in his or her demise, nor in rumors about his or her sin, rather than seek out the truth (1 Cor. 13:6)?

14. Am I able to bear all things with _____? Is it true that I protect his or her reputation, welfare or life (1 Cor. 13:7)?

15. Do I put the best construction regarding _____ and see things about him or her from a good and positive light, unless there is sufficient evidence to believe otherwise (1 Cor. 13:7)?

16. Do I have a positive and sure expectation that through Jesus Christ God will work all things together for _____'s good? Am I actively promoting the hope of Christ with others (1 Cor. 13:7)?

17. Does my love endure and persevere? Do I find ways to encourage others to persevere in their life, walk and service in Christ (1 Cor. 13:7)?

APPENDIX S

HOW TO LOVE MY PASTOR

(An application of 1 Corinthians 13)

—ⱳ—

All of these qualities of love find their source and perfect expression in God through Jesus Christ. If I am truly in Christ, we should express these loving qualities more and more, even toward my pastor. Fill in the blank spaces with your pastor's name.

1. Does my communication with Pastor _____ come from a heart of love or am I just all talk and an irritating noise maker (1 Cor. 13:1)?

2. Do I use the gifts God has given me to lovingly serve _____ (1 Cor. 13:2)?

3. Do I love _____ sacrificially? In what specific ways do I do so (1 Cor. 13:3)?

4. Am I patient with _____? In other words, do I show an enduring restraint with him even when I have a right to act? Do I restrain my words and actions when wronged or provoked when I have a right to act, unless there is a particular sin I need to address through gentle rebuke (Matt. 18:15-22; Gal. 6:1)?

5. Am I kind toward _____? Kindness proceeds from a tender heart that contributes to his good will and happiness (1 Cor. 13:4).

6. Am I envious of _____. Do I feel uneasiness with the excellence, reputation or happiness he enjoys. Do I sinfully desire to depreciate him (1 Cor. 13:4)?

7. Do I brag about myself to _____? Do I anxiously display myself for the purpose of elevating my own life, especially at the expense of putting him down. I do not campaign for the center of attention (1 Cor. 13:4)?

8. Am I arrogant, puffed up or swollen with a proud vanity (1 Cor. 13:4)?

9. Am I considerate and not rude with _____? Do I act unbecomingly or unseemly toward him, or unnecessarily embarrass him (1 Cor. 13:5)?

10. Do I seek Pastor _____'s greatest good and benefit (1 Cor. 13:5)?

11. Am I easily provoked or angered by _____? Do I have a trigger temper that stems from bitterness (1 Cor. 13:5)?

12. Do I wrongfully keep a record of the things suffered by _____ from which to make a plan for retaliation? Do I really apply the fact that Jesus Christ took the registry of my sins and my pastor's sins and paid for them with his own sacrificial life and death (1 Cor. 13:5)?

13. Do I rejoice in unrighteousness or evil done by or done to _____? Do I find pleasure in his demise, or in rumors about his sin, rather than seek out the truth (1 Cor. 13:6)?

14. Am I able to bear all things with _____? In other words, do I protect his reputation, welfare or life (1 Cor. 13:7)?

15. Do I put the best construction regarding _____ and see things about him from a good and positive light, unless there is sufficient evidence to believe otherwise (1 Cor. 13:7)?

16. Do I have a positive and sure expectation that through Jesus Christ God will work all things together for _____'s good. Do I actively promote the hope of Christ with my pastor (1 Cor. 13:7)?

17. Does my love endure and persevere? Do I find ways to encourage my pastor to persevere in his life, walk and service in Christ (1 Cor. 13:7)?

NOTES

—m—

Introduction
1. London, JR. & Wiseman, *Pastors at Greater Risk*, pp. 205-206.

Chapter 1: Unqualified Applicants Need Not Apply
1. Rediger, *Clergy Killers*, p. 20.
2. Statistics come from Jack L. Arnold, "A Pastor's Perspective,"Class lecture in DM875 The Pastor's Private and Professional Life, New Geneva Theological Seminary, 2002; and Stephanie Wolfe, "The Most Valuable Partnership, Part One." *The Pastor's Coach* Volume 5, Issue 10 (May 2004) : np. Available from http://www.injoy.com/Newsletters/pastors/Archives/ 2004/05_ 2.txt. (accessed May 25, 2004).
3. Clowney, *The Church,* 1995.
4. Joseph A. Pipa, Jr., "Pastoral visitation Questionnaire," Lecture notes presented at a Pastoral Internship Class at Trinity Presbyterian Church, Escondido, CA, 1995 (photocopied).
5. The two main sources for the sermon evaluations were derived from Joseph A. Pipa, Jr., "Sermon Evaluation Form," Class notes with the Pastoral Internship Class at Trinity Presbyterian Church, 1995; and David Schuringa, "Student Preaching Evaluation Form," Class lectures in Preaching Style and Audience Analysis at Westminster Seminary California,1995.
6. Matthew 22:37-38.
7. Ken Sande, "Strike the Shepherd,"2004, p.1. Available from http://www/hispeace. org/html/ artic50. htm?pfriend= Yes (accessed May 13, 2004).
8. Michaels, *Spurgeon on Leadership*, p. 191.

Chapter 2: Did God Really Call?
1. The Old Testament elders had to possess the credentials of godly character (Exod.18:21; Deut. 1:13). In the New Testament God requires His offices to be filled by male believer-priests who manifest the right qualities (1 Tim. 3:1-7; Tit. 1:5-9), the right equipment (Rom. 12:8; 1 Cor. 12:11, 28; Eph. 4:11ff) and the right motivation (Phil. 2:13; 1 Tim. 3:1).
2. God endows men with certain gifts and gives the men to His church (Mark 16:15-18; Luke 21:15; 24:49; Acts 1:8; Eph. 4:11; 1 Tim. 5:22; 3:1-7; Tit. 1:7). A pastor must be gifted and able to exhort (1 Thess. 2:11, 12), to lead (1 Cor. 12:28; 1 Thess. 5:12, 13; 1 Tim. 3:5; 5:17), to serve (Acts 20:24f; Rom. 15:26-33), to share his resources with others (Acts 4; Eph. 4:28), and to show mercy (Matt. 25; 1 Cor. 12:28).
3. Reed, *Biblical Church Government,* p. 9.
4. See 1 Timothy 5:22; 2 Timothy 2:2; and Titus 2:7, 8.
5. He is responsive to the gifting and the call of the Holy Spirit in his life (Acts 20:28), and hence he desires the office (1 Tim. 3:1). Often times this call or desire is so compelling that he cannot do anything else. But it takes other people and wisdom test whether his motives are biblical and Christ-like (1 Pet. 5:1ff), or if they are self-serving.

6. He must also be properly called of God through the appointed means in God's church (Jer. 23:32; Rom. 10:15; Heb. 5:4).

7. Lutzer, *Pastor to Pastor,* p. 11.

8. Michaels, *Spurgeon on Leadership*, p. 68.

9. Ibid., p.38.

10. His ministry was not accepted by his home town or even his own family, with perhaps the exception of his mother (Matt. 13:57; Mark 6:4; Luke 4:16-30; Jn. 7:3-5). That is, not immediately so (Acts 1:14).

11. Regarding character and life see 2 Pet. 1:10; Eph. 1:18; 2:8-10; and Eph. 4:1.

12. All believers in Christ have been given special gifts to work out their particular role in the church body. For examples, see Rom. 12; 1 Cor. 1:26-29; 12; Eph. 4:11-16.

13. Donald Grey Barnhouse, *God's Covenant: Romans 9:1-11:36*. Eerdmans, 1963, np. Quoted in http://www.preaching.com/newsletter/archive_2004/05_25.htm, 2004.

14. Ibid.

15. They have an official appointment to serve (Acts 13:1-3; 14:23; Tit. 1:5). You see, ordination is an act that sets a man apart to the office. There are unique situations where one is called and ordained by the very hand of God. Jesus, of course was the prime example of this (Luke 3:21-4:21). Abraham was such a man (Gen. 12:1), as was Moses (Exod. 28:1), Elisha (1 Kings 19:19), Isaiah (Isa. 6:1-13), Ezekiel (Ezek. 1:4-28), and Jonah (Jon. 1:1-2). But those were special circumstances. Jesus called and commissioned his disciples (Matt. 28:18-20; Mark 1:20; John 15). In the New Testament we see Barnabas being called by God for ministry (Acts 13:2), along with Saul who became Paul (Rom. 1:1; 1 Cor. 1:1; 2 Cor. 1:1; Gal. 1:1-24; Eph. 1:1; Col. 1:1; 2 Tim. 1:8-12). Paul, like the other apostles, received his call and ordained commission from Jesus. Then, the apostles appointed and ordained elders in various churches (e.g.: Acts 14:21-23).

16. Larson, *Staying Power*, pp. 119-120.

17. Lutzer, *Pastor to Pastor,* p. 11.

18. Larson, p. 49.

Chapter 3: Is He a Character or Does He Have Character?

1. The resources used for the different terms of the various age groups are BibleWorks 5, 2002; Brown, *The New Brown-Driver-Briggs-Gesenius Hebrew and English Lexicon*, 1979; and Harris, Archer, and Waltke, *Theological Wordbook of the Old Testament*, 1980.

2. The resources consulted for the different terms are Bauer, Arndt and Gingrich, *A Greek-English Lexicon of the New Testament and Other Early Christian Literature*, 1979; BibleWorks 5, 2002; and Brown, 1979.

3. Glancy, *Slavery in Early Christianity*, pp. 21-24.

4. See www.peacemaker.net.

5. London and Wiseman, *The Heart of a Great Pastor*, p. 64.

6. Marsden, *Jonathan Edwards*, pp. 341-374.

Chapter 4: Only a Saint Will Do

1. International Standard Bible Encyclopedia, Vol. 2, p. 516.

2. BibleWorks 5, 2002.

3. Ibid.

Chapter 5: A Wise Guy
1. See Psa. 90:12; Prov. 2:3; Eph. 1:17; Col. 1:9.
2. Heb. 2:18; 4:15.
3. Proverbs 2:7-9.
4. Proverbs 1:23, 3:11 and Proverbs 3:11; 19:25; 23:13.
5. Col. 2:3.
6. The Messiah would have the Spirit of God resting upon him with all wisdom and understanding (Isa. 11:2). When Jesus went to his home town and taught in the synagogue, the people were amazed and wondered where he got his wisdom and power (Matt. 13:54).
7. God grants us wisdom through faith (1 Cor. 2). He gives believers the mind of Christ (1 Cor. 2:16). Therefore, this special wisdom is given by the Spirit of God through the Word of God by faith (Prov. 3:19; 8:30; 28:7-9; 30:5; Jer. 8:8f; Acts 6:3 I Cot. 1:24, 30; 2:6-16; Col. 2:3; 3:16; 2 Tim. 3:15). This kind of spiritual wisdom pertains to the skill of Christ-like living (Jas. 3:13-17).
8. The natural person without Christ rejects this wisdom of God because he rejects God (Rom. 1; 1 Cor. 1:18-21). Everyone needs a change of heart to turn from this natural, sinful condition (Prov. 3:7, 8:13, 9:10), and from his or her cherished independence (Prov. 14:12). Every person must turn to the Light of true wisdom (Prov. 9:4-6, John 1).
9. We should also become devoted disciples of wisdom (Prov. 2:1-5, 10, 8:34), who treasure it to the end (Prov. 9:9).
10. Wisdom gives you understanding about things and insight into life (Prov. 1:22, 2:2). Wisdom has the ability to discern between right and wrong, good and evil (1 Kings 3:9; Phil. 1:9-10). Is there any calling or line of work that isn't covered under what I've just mentioned?"
11. First, such a person deals wisely with others (Prov. 1:3, 10:5, 12:8). This kind of wisdom is what we would classify as success (Prov. 8:18; 9:1-6, 12; 16:20). Second, a wise person does the morally good and right thing (Prov. 10:21; 11:19; 12:18; 16:17; 21:21).
12. "He is like Jesus Christ who walks in the way of righteousness and the path of justice (Prov. 8:20). Jesus taught that we are to hunger and thirst after righteousness. This righteousness is not only moral and religious but also very practical…Third, a wise person is both shrewd and discreet (Prov. 1:4; 2:11).
13. With wisdom God gives you good sense and discernment (Prov. 6:32, 10:13)…A wise person has sound judgment (Prov. 3:21-22). The biggest thing, I would say, is that a wise person is able to bring to bear what God is revealing and teaching to the small and the big concerns in life, and…and…he trusts in God's direction and will for his life (Prov. 3:5,6, 20:24). Why would that be important? Because we have a difficult time wrapping our heads around things that happen in our own lives, let alone what's beyond us. Even when we can't get it, whatever it is, we can trust that the Lord is ever directing our steps because he has ordained those steps according to his wonderful plan (Prov. 20:24).
14. The Lord is in control and will continue to direct him (Prov. 19:21). He trusts that God is sovereign and such a mastermind that he will use good and evil, good decisions and disobedient ones, for the ultimate good of those who love him and are called according to his purposes (Rom. 8:28-39).
15. Meek (Jas. 3:18), morally pure (Matt. 5:8), peace-loving (Rom. 12:18; Matt. 5:9), considerate, delights in mercy, justice and faithfulness (Matt. 5:5; 23:23), submissive and obedient, full of mercy (Matt. 5:7), full of good fruit, impartial and fair, authentic.

Chapter 6: If Books Could Skill
1. London and Wiseman, *Pastors at Greater Risk*, p. 195.
2. Gilmore, *Pastoral Politics*, p. 174.

3. John C. LaRue, Jr., "Pastoral Gifts and Calling," *Your Church,* (November/December 2003) : 72.
4. Ibid.
5. George Barna, *Leaders on Leadership*, p.23-24.
6. Fitch, *The Great* Giveaway, p. 80.
7. Wagner, *Escape From Church, Inc.*, p. 142.

Chapter 7: All in a Day's Work
1. Rubietta, *How to Keep the Pastor You Love*, p. 90.
2. London and Wiseman, *Pastors at Greater Risk,* p. 62.
3. Rubietta, p. 57.
4. Rediger, p. 23.
5. London and Wiseman, *Pastors at Greater Risk,* p. 63.
6. Carson, *The Cross and Christian Ministry,*, p. 98.
7. London and Wiseman, *The Heart of a Great Pastor,* p. 201.
8. Wagner, pp. 176-183.
9. London and Wiseman, *Pastors at Greater Risk*, p. 72.
10. Ford, *Transforming Leadership*, p. 92.
11. London and Wiseman, *The Heart of a Great Pastor*, p. 44.
12. Ibid., p. 78.
13. Ibid., pp. 73-74.

Chapter 8: At Your Service, Master
1. Dodd, *Empowered Church Leadership*, p. 57.
2. Lawrence, *Effective* Pastoring, p. 88.
3. Gilmore, pp. 53-54.
4. Bauer, 1979; BibleWorks 5, 2002; Brown, 1979.
5. The following resources were consulted: BibleWorks, 2002; Cowell, *Life in Ancient Rome,* pp. 95-107; Davis, *Readings in Ancient History*, pp. 90-97; Frame, 2006; Gill, 2006; Glancy, 2006; Stark, *For the Glory of God*, pp.295-300.
6. London and Wiseman, *Pastors at Greater* Risk, p. 225.
7. Frye, *Jesus the Pastor*, p. 95.

Chapter 9: Sheep Herding 101
1. Wagner, p. 46
2. Ibid, p. 48-49
3. Damazio, *The Making of a Leader*, p. 18.
4. See: Gen. 26:24; Exod. 14:31; 33:11; Num. 12:7, 8; 1 Sam. 3:9; 29:3; 1 Chron. 17:4. See also Clinton, *The Making of a Leader*, pp. 18-19.
5. Sanders, *Spiritual Leadership*, p.17.
6. Wagner, p. 47.
7. Ibid., p. 42.
8. Sanders, p. 21.

Chapter 10: The Roles We Play
1. Bowling, *Graceful Leadership*, p. 109.
2. Barna, *Leaders on Leadership*, p. 53.

3. Dodd, p. 119.
4. I am thankful for George Meisinger's *The Local Church and Its Leadership,* which provided the basis for much of the information in this chapter.
5. Armstrong, *Reforming Pastoral Ministry*, p. 148.
6. See: 1 Cor. 16:10-11.
7. Read Rom. 13:1-2 and 1 Pet. 2:18.

Chapter 11: More Than Lip Service
1. David Eby, "How to Encourage Your Pastor," Church Membership Syllabus for North City Presbyterian Church, Rancho Bernardo, CA, 1991, (Photocopied).
2. Ibid.
3. Eby, *Preaching for Church Growth*, 1996.
4. Bauer, 1979; BibleWorks 5; Brown, 1979.
5. BibleWorks 5; Pipa, 1996.
6. BibleWorks 5; Harris, Archer, Waltke, 1980.
7. Azurdia, *Spirit Empowered Preaching*, p. 19.

Chapter 12: What a Great Message!
1. MacNair and Meeks, *The Practices of a Healthy Church,* p. 99.
2. Sidney Greidanus, *Modern Preacher and the Ancient Text*, (Grand Rapids, MI: William B. Eerdmans Publishing Company, 1988), np.
3. Carson, *The Cross and Christian Ministry*, p. 34.
4. Ibid. 1993 p. 113
5. Michael, *Spurgeon on* Leadership, p. 26.
6. Ibid. p. 142
7. Dallimore, *George* Whitefield, p. 421.
8. Frank Charles Thompson, *Thompson Chain Reference Bible*, (Michigan: Zondervan Bible Publishers, 1983).
9. Carson, *The Cross and Christian Ministry*, p. 13.
10. Schuringa, 1995.
11. Eby, 1996.

Chapter 13: Yes, But Can He Teach?
1. Wilkerson, *7 Laws of the Learner*, p. 26.
2. A true disciple is a believer in Jesus Christ who takes orders and obeys Jesus as Lord (John 14:15, 21; 15:10; 1 John 2:3,4; 3:22-24), who abides in God's Word (John 8:31), who submits to God's official, delegated leadership in the church (Matt. 14:22; 18; Mark 6:45; Heb. 13:7, 17), and does the Father's will (Matt. 12:50). A false disciple is someone who will ultimately will reject Jesus Christ (John 12:4) or desert Him (John 6:66).
3. See John 15:8.

Chapter 14: Give Us an Example
1. Marshall, *Understanding Leadership*, p. 143.
2. See Westminster Confession of Faith 1.6 in *The Westminster Confession,* (Glasgow: Free Presbyterian Publications, 1976).
3. Brown, *No More Mister Nice Guy!*, p. 193.

4. Dodd, *Empowered Church Leadership*, p. 32.
5. Maxwell, *Developing the Leaders Around You*, pp. 99ff.
6. Gilmore, *Pastoral Politics*, p. 125.
7. Eims, *Be the Leader You Were Meant to Be*, p. 138.

Chapter 15: A Pastor and a Priest?
1. Eph. 2:21.
2. Heb. 13:17.

Chapter 16: A Good News Boy
1. Vermeulen, 1996.

Chapter 17: A Peacekeeper or a Peacemaker?
1. Gilmore, *Pastoral Politics*, p. 179.
2. Frye, *Jesus the Pastor*, p. 124.
3. Johnson and VanVonderen, *The Subtle Power of Spiritual Abuse*, p.91.
4. London and Wiseman, *Pastors at Greater Risk,* p. 103.
5. Craig Barnes, "Leader's Insight: Rabble Roused," *Leadership Journal* (November 2004) : np.
6. Ibid.
7. Wagner, *Escape From Church, Inc.* p. 50
8. Ford, *Transforming Leadership*, pp. 270-271.
9. Michael, *Spurgeon on Leadership*, p. 163.
10. Robert D. Stuart, Class lecture notes from DM 855 Pastoral Counseling, New Geneva Seminary (Feb. 2004).
11. Dominic Aquila, "Lessons from the Seven Churches of Revelation," Class ledture notes presented in Foundation for Ministry, New Geneva Seminary, Colorado Springs (Aug. 2001).
12 Richard Ganz, *20 Controversies That Nearly Killed a Church* (Phillipsburg, NJ: P&R Publishing, 2003).
13 John Maxwell, "Relationships: A New Beginning or a Bitter End" No. 12, (Injoy Inc., 1997) (cassette).
14 John Maxwell, "How to Leader the Seven Most Difficult Personalities," 1-4, (Network Twenty-One, 1995) (cassette tapes).
15 Shelley Marshall, *Well-Intentioned Dragons* (Minneapolis, MN: Bethany House Publishers, 1985).
16. Carson, *The Cross and Christian Ministry*, pp. 83-84.

Chapter 18: Troubles and Dragons
1. London and Wiseman, *They Call Me Pastor*, p. 82.
2. Greenfield, *The Wounded Minister*, p.53.
3. Gilmore, *Pastoral Politics*, p. 39.
4. Greenfield, p.104.
5. Rediger, p. 13.
6. Stock, *Theodore Roosevelt on Leadership*, p. 185.
7. Covey, *The Eighth Habit*, p. 135.
8. Brown, *No More Mr. Nice Guy!*, p. 206.
9. Gilmore, p. 119.
10. Ibid.

11. See 1 Cor. 5:6; 2 Cor. 2:5-11; and 2 Thess. 3:14-15.

Chapter 19: By the Authority Invested In…Who?
1. Information sources were gleaned primarily from BibleWorks 5 and George Meisinger, *The Local Church and its Leadership* (Minneapolis, MN: privately printed, 1981).
2. John Frame, "The Decalogue," class lecture in ST323 Doctrine of the Christian Life (Westminster Seminary California, Feb.1988) (photocopied).
3. You were selected as an elder to exercise authority from a motivation of love (John 21:16). As elders, we do so by making appeals to people to put off sin and put on Christ, to repent and exercise faith. This is done lovingly for Christ's sake (Philemon 8-9). We also exercise authority with compassion for distressed sheep (Matt. 9:36; Mark 6:34; Jas. 5:14). What's more, we are to exercise authority sacrificially, being willing to take up our own cross and willing to lay down our lives for God's flock (John 10:11, 15).
4. I am not saying that God's officers should not or can not reprove or rebuke (2 Tim. 4:2), or that they should never at times, reprove or rebuke severely (Tit. 1:13; 2:15). Indeed, they have the executive ability to come with the rod of God's Word when it is appropriate (1 Cor. 4:21).
5. Marshall, *Understanding Leadership*, pp. 45-60.
6. Ibid., p. 55.
7. Lawrence, *Effective Pastoring*, p. 117.
8. Ganz, p. 51.

REFERENCES

Adams, Jay E. *From Forgiven to Forgiving*. Wheaton, IL: Victor Books, 1989.

_____. *Handbook of Church Discipline*. Grand Rapids, MI: Zondervan Publishing House, 1986.

_____. *Shepherding God's Flock*. Grand Rapids, MI: Zondervan Publishing House, 1975.

_____. *The Christian Counselor's Manual*. Grand Rapids, MI: Baker Book House, 1973.

_____. *The Place of Authority in Christ's Church*. Stanley, NC: Timeless Texts, 2003.

Allen, Blaine. *When People Throw Stones*. Grand Rapids, MI: Kregel Publications, 2005.

Aquila, Dominic. "Lessons from the Seven Churches of Revelation." Class lecture notes presented in Foundation for Ministry, New Geneva Seminary, Colorado Springs, CO, Aug. 2001. Photocopy.

Armstrong, Chris. "Preacher in the Hands of an Angry Church." *Leadership Journal* 25 (Winter 2003) : 52.

Armstrong, John H. edit. *Reforming Pastoral Ministry*. Wheaton, IL: Crossway Books, 2001.

Arnold, Jack L. "A Pastor's Perspective." Class lecture in DM875 The Pastor's Private and Professional Life at New Geneva Theological Seminary, 2002.

Ayling, Stanley. *John Wesley*. New York, NY: William Collins Publishers, Inc., 1997.

Azurdia, Arturo III. *Spirit Empowered Preaching*. Great Britain: Christian Focus Publications, 1998.

Bainton, Roland H. *Here I Stand: A Life of Martin Luther.* Nashville, TN: Abingdon Press, nd, Reprint, New York, NY: The New American Library, 1950.

Banks, Robert. *Paul's Idea of Community.* Peabody, MA: Hendrickson Publishers, 1994.

Barna, George. *Leaders on Leadership*. Ventura, CA: Regal, 1997.

_____. *Today's Pastors*. Ventura, CA: Regal Books, 1993.

Barnes, M. Craig. "Leader's Insight: Rabble Roused." *Leadership Journal* (November 2004): n.p.

Barnhouse, Donald Grey. God's Covenant: Romans 9:1-11:36. Eerdmans, 1963. Quoted in http://www.preaching.com/newsletter/archive_2004/05_25.htm, 2004.

Bauer, Walter. Arndt, William and Gingrich, F. Wilbur, trans. *A Greek-English Lexicon of the New Testament and Other Early Christian Literature*, 2nd Edition. Chicago, IL: The University of Chicago Press, 1979.

Baxter, Richard. *The Reformed Pastor.* Great Britain: 1656. Reprint, Carlisle, PA: Banner of Truth Trust, 1994.

Beeke, Joel R. "Take Heed to Your Attitude to Ministry – Part 1." *The Ordained Servant* 13 (nd) : 28-30.

Bennis, Warren, and Nanus, Burt. *Leaders*. New York, NY: HarperBusiness, 1997.

Berghoef, Gerard, and DeKoster, Lester. *The Elders Handbook*. Grand Rapids, MI: Christian's Library Press, 1979.

BibleWorks for Windows, Version 3.5. Big Fork, MT: Hermeneutika Software, 1996.

BibleWorks 5, Revision 2. Big Fork, MT: Hermeneutika Software, 2002.

Bickel, R. Bruce. *Light and Heat: The Puritan View of the Pulpit*. Morgan, PA: Soli Deo Gloria Publications, 1999.

Biehl, Bobb. *Mentoring*. Nashville, TN: Broadman and Holman Publishers, 1996.

Biehl, Bobb and Maxwell, John. *Senior Pastor Profile 1-6*. INJOY TT1138, 1996. Cassettes.

Bixby, Douglas J. *Challenging the Church Monster*. Cleveland, OH: The Pilgrim Press, 2002.

Blue, Ken. *Healing Spiritual Abuse*. Downers Grove, IL: IVP Books, 1993.

Bowling, John C. *Grace-Full Leadership*. Kansas City: MO: Beacon Hills Press, 2000.

Brandt, Henry. "How to Deal with Anger." *The Journal of Biblical Counseling* 16 (Fall 1997) : 28-31.

Breen, Mike and Kallestad, Walt. *The Passionate Church*. Colorado Springs, CO: NexGen, 2005.

Bridges, Charles. *The Christian Ministry*. Carlisle, PA: The Banner of Truth Trust, 1991.

Bridges, Jerry. *The Crisis of Caring*. Phillipsburg, NJ: P&R Publishing, 1985.

_____. *The Practice of Godliness*. Colorado Springs, CO: NavPress, 1983.

_____. *The Pursuit of Holiness*. Colorado Springs, CO: NavPress, 1996.

Briner, Bob and Pritchard, Ray. *Leadership Lessons of Jesus*. New York, NY: Random House, 1998.

Brown, Francis. *The New Brown-Driver-Briggs-Gesenius Hebrew and English Lexicon*. Peabody, MA: Hendrickson Pub., 1979.

Brown, John, ed. *The Christian Pastor's Manual*. Morgan, PA: Soli Deo Gloria Publications, 1991.

Brown, Mark R., ed. *Order in the Offices*. Duncansville, PA: Classic Presbyterian Government Resources, 1993.

Brown, Peter. *Augustine of Hippo*. Berkeley, CA: University of California Press, 1967.

Brown, Stephen. *No More Mr. Nice Guy!* Nashville, TN: Thomas Nelson Publishers, 1986.

Brown, Steve. *A Scandalous Freedom.* West Monroe, LA: Howard Publishing Co., Inc., 2004.

Bruce, A. B. *The Training of the Twelve.* Grand Rapids, MI: Kregel Publications, 1988.

Burchett, Dave. *When Bad Christians Happen to Good People.* Colorado Springs, CO: Water Brook Press, 2002.

Callahan, Kennon L. *Effective Church Leadership.* San Francisco, CA: Jossey-Bass, 1990.

Calvin, John. "Harmony of Matthew, Mark, Luke." *Calvin's Commentary Vol. II.* Grand Rapids: Wm. B. Eerdman Publishing Company, 1949.

Carson, D.A. *The Cross and Christian Ministry.* Grand Rapids, MI: Baker Books, 1993.

Carrick, John. *The Imperative of Preaching.* Edinburgh, UK: The Banner of Truth Trust, 2002.

Chapell, Bryan. *Christ-Centered Preaching.* Grand Rapids, MI: Baker Books, 1994.

Chrnalogar, Mary Alice. *Twisted Scriptures.* Grand Rapids, MI: Zondervan, 2000.

Cionca, John R. *Red Light Green Light.* Grand Rapids, MI: Baker Books, 1994.

Clinton, J. Robert. *The Making of a Leader.* Colorado Springs, CO: NavPress, 1988.

Clowney, Edmund P. *Called to the Ministry.* Phillipsburg, NJ: P&R Publishing, 1964.

_____ *The Relation of Ministers to Ruling Elders.* <http://hornes.org/teologia/papers/eclowney_ministers_ruling_elders.htm> (8 Mar 1999) : 1-6.

_____ *Living in Christ's Church.* Philadelphia, PA: Great Commission Publications, 1986.

_____ *The Church.* Downers Grove, IL: Intervarsity Press, 1995.

Cohen, William A. *The Art of the Leader.* Englewood Cliffs, NJ: Prentice Hall Press, 1990.

Coppes, Leonard J. *Who Will Lead Us.* Chattanooga, TN: Pilgrim Publishing Company, 1977.

Coughlin, Paul. *No More Christian Nice Guy.* Minneapolis, MN: Bethany House, 2005.

Covey, Stephen R. *The Eighth Habit.* NY: Free Press, 2004.

Cowell, F. R. *Life in Ancient Rome.* New York, NY: Perigee Books, 1980.

Dallimore, Arnold A. *George Whitefield: The Life and Times of the Great Evangelist of the Eighteenth-Century Revival.* Carlisle, PA: Banner of Truth Trust, 1970.

_____. *Spurgeon.* Carlisle, PA: Banner of Truth Trust, 1985.

Damazio, Frank. *The Making of a Leader.* Portland, OR: Bible Temple Publishing, 1988.

Davis, William, ed., *Readings in Ancient History: Illustrative Extracts from the Sources,* 2 Vols. (Boston: Allyn and Bacon, 1912-13), Vol. II: *Rome and the West.* http://www.fordham.edu/halsall/ancient/slavery-romrep1.html.

Dawn, Marva and Eugene Peterson. *The Unnecessary Pastor.* Grand Rapids, MI: William B. Eerdmans Publishing Company, 2000.

Decker, Rodney J. "Polity and the Elder Issue." *Grace Theological Journal*, 9 (Fall 1988) : 258-279.

Derrett, J. Duncan M. "Binding and Loosing." *Journal of Biblical Literature* 102 (1983) : 112-117.

Dickson, David. *The Elder and His Work.* Dallas, TX: Presbyterian Heritage Publications, 1990.

Dillenberger, John. *Martin Luther: Selections from His Writings.* Garden City: Anchor Books, 1961.

Dodd, Brian J. *Empowered Church Leadership*. Downers Grove, IL: InterVarsity Press, 2003.

Domokos, Robert L. "Pastoral Theology in the New Testament." ThM. Diss., Grace Theological Seminary, 1972.

Dudley-Smith, Timothy. *John Stott–The Making of a Leader*. Downers Grove, IL: InterVarsity Press, 1999.

Eby, David. *Power Preaching for Church Growth*. Great Britain: Christian Focus Publications, 1996.

_____. "How to Encourage Your Pastor." Church Membership Syllabus for North City Presbyterian Church, Rancho Bernardo, CA, 1991. Photocopied.

Edwards, Gene. *Preventing a Church Split*. Scarborough, ME: Christian Books, 1987.

Edwards, Jonathan. *Charity and its Fruits*. Carlisle, PA: The Banner of Truth Trust, 2000.

Eims, LeRoy. *Be the Leader You Were Meant to Be*. Colorado Springs, CO: Victor, 2001.

Ellsworth, Wilbur. *The Power of Speaking God's Word*. Great Britain: Christian Focus Publications, 2000.

Eyres, Lawrence R. *The Elders of the Church*. Phillipsburg, NJ: Presbyterian and Reformed Publishing Co., 1977.

Fairbairn, Patrick. *Pastoral Theology*. Edinburgh: T&T Clark, 1875. Reprint, Audubon, NJ: Old Paths Publications; 1992.

Fehlauer, Mike. *Exposing Spiritual Abuse*. Lake Mary, FL: Charisma House, 2001.

Fenton, Horace L. Jr. *When Christians Clash*. Downers Grove, IL: InterVarsity Press, 1987.

Finzel, Hans. *The Top Ten Mistakes Leaders Make*. Colorado Springs, CO: Victor, 2000.

Fischer, John. *12 Steps for the Recovering Pharisee*. Minneapolis, MN: Bethany House Publishers, 2000.

Fisher, David. *The 21ˢᵗ Century Pastor.* Grand Rapids, MI: Zondervan Publishing House, 1996.

Fitch, David E. *The Great Giveaway.* Grand Rapids, MI: Baker Books, 2005.

Fitzpatrick, Elyse. *Idols of the Heart.* Phillipsburg, NJ: P&R Publishing, 2001.

Ford, Leighton. *Transforming Leadership.* Downers Grove, IL: InterVarsity Press, 1991.

Forman, Rowland, Jones, Jeff, and Miller, Bruce. *The Leadership Baton.* Grand Rapids, MI: Zondervan Publishing, 2004.

Frame, John. "The Decalogue." Class lecture in ST 323 Doctrine of the Christian Life, at Westminster Seminary California, (photocopy) Feb. 1988.

_____. "The Doctrine of the Christian Life, Book One: Living Under God's Law: Christian Ethics, Part Three: Christian Ethical Methodology, Section Three: The Ten Commandments, Chapter 34: The Fifth Commandment: Equalities, Racial and Otherwise." *Reformed Perspectives Magazine,* Volume 8, Number 51, December 17 to December 23, 2006. http://reformedperspectives.org/newfiles/ joh_frame/ PT.joh_frame. dcl.4.3.34.html.

Frye, John W. *Jesus the Pastor.* Grand Rapids, MI: Zondervan, 2000.

Furniss, George M. *The Social Context of Pastoral Care.* Louisville, KY: Westminster John Knox Press, 1994.

Galloway, John Jr. *Ministry Loves Company.* Louisville, KY: Westminster John Knox Press; 2003.

Ganz, Richard L. *20 Controversies That Almost Killed a Church.* Phillipsburg, NJ: P&R Publishing, 2003.

Gardner, John W. *On Leadership.* New York, NY: The Free Press, 1990.

Getz, Gene A. *Elders and Leaders.* Chicago: Moody Publishers, 2003.

_____. *Sharpening the Focus of the Church.* Chicago: Moody Press, 1969.

_____ *The Measure of a Man.* Ventura, CA: Regal Books, 1974.

Giles, Kevin. *What on Earth is the Church?* Downers Grove, IL: InterVarsity Press, 1995.

Gill, N. S. "Categories of Roman Slaves based on Plautus" *Ancient/Classical History.* http://ancienthistory.about.com/cs/romeslavery/a/slavetypes.htm.

Gilmore, John. *Pastoral Politics.* USA: AMG Publishers, 2002.

Glancy, Jennifer A. *Slavery in Early Christianity.* Minneapolis, MN: Fortress Press, 2006.

Glasscock, Ed."The Biblical Concept of Elder.*" Bibliotheca Sacra* 144 (Jan 87) : 67-78.

Goldsworthy, Graeme. *Preaching the Whole Bible as Christian Scripture.* Grand Rapids, MI: William B. Eerdmans Publishing Company, 2000.

Goleman, Daniel, Boyatzis, and McKee, Annie. *Primal Leadership.* Boston, MA: Harvard Business School Press, 2004.

Grant, Bernard. *First Class Leaders.* Huntsville, AL: Milestones International Publishers, 2004.

Greenfield, Guy. *The Wounded Minister.* Grand Rapids, MI: Baker Books, 2001.

Greenway, Roger S. ed. *The Pastor-Evangelist.* Phillipsburg, NJ: Presbyterian and Reformed Publishing Company, 1987.

Greidanus, Sidney. *Preaching Christ from the Old Testament.* Grand Rapids, MI: William B. Eerdmans Publishing Company, 1999.

_____. *The Modern Preacher and the Ancient Text.* Grand Rapids, MI: William B. Eerdmans Publishing Company, 1988.

Gundry, Robert Horton. *The Use of the Old Testament in St. Matthew's Gospel.* Leiden, Netherlands: E.J. Brill Co, 1975.

Hagopian, David G. *Back to Basics.* Phillipsburg, NJ: P&R Publishing, 1996.

Haile, H. G. *Luther.* Garden City, N.Y.: Doubleday & Company, Inc., 1980.

Hall, David W. and Hall, Joseph H., eds. *Paradigms in Polity*. Grand Rapids, MI: William B. Eerdmans Publishing Company, 1994.

Hansen, David. *The Art of Pastoring*. Downers Grove, IL: InterVarsity Press, 1994.

Harris, R. Laird, Gleason L. Archer, and Bruce K. Waltke, edits. *Theological Wordbook of the Old Testament*, Volumes 1 and 2. Chicago, IL: Moody Bible Institute, 1980.

Hay, E. M. "A Project to Enable Designated Church Leadership to Understand Stress in The Minster's Professional Life and Develop Church Strategies to Enhance its Effective Management During Times of Relocation, Work Overload, and Organized Opposition." D.Min. diss., Midwestern Baptist Theological Seminary, 1994.

Hayward, Steve F. *Churchill on Leadership*. Rocklin, CA: Prima Publishing, 1997.

Hegg, David W. "Proven Character: Prelude to Position." *Reformation and Revival Journal,* 7 (Winter 1998) : 35.

Hellerman, Joseph H. *The Ancient Church as Family*. Minneapolis: Fortress Press, 2001.

Heyns, J.A. *The Church*. Translated by D. Roy Briggs. Goodwood, Cape, South Africa: N.G. Kerkboekhandel, 1977.

Hiebert, D. Edmond. "Pauline Images of a Christian Leader." *Bibliotheca Sacra* 133 (Jul 76) : 214-229.

Hoge, Dean R., and Jacqueline E. Wenger. *Pastors in Transition*. Grand Rapids, MI: William B. Eerdmans Publishing Company, 2005.

Horton, Michael. "What About Bob? The Meaning of Ministry in the Reformed Tradition." *Modern Reformation*. (March/April 1997) : 1-7.

Hughes, R. Kent. *Disciplines of a Godly Man*. Wheaton IL: Crossway Books, 1991.

Hughes, Kent and Barbara Hughes. *Liberating Ministry from the Success Syndrome*. Wheaton, IL: Tyndale House Publishers, Inc., 1987.

Hull, Bill. *The Disciple-Making Pastor*. Old Tappan, NJ: Fleming H. Revell, 1988.

Jaugk, Kenneth C. *Antagonists in the Church*. Minneapolis, MN: Augsburg Publishing House, 1988.

Jethani, Skye. "All We Like Sheep." *Leadership* Summer 27 (2006) : 28-32.

Johnson, David, and Jeff VanVonderen. *The Subtle Power of Spiritual Abuse*. Minneapolis, MN: Bethany House Publishers, 1991.

Johnson, John E. "The Old Testament Offices as Paradigm for Pastoral Identity." *Bibliotheca Sacra* 152 (Apr. 95) : 189-200.

Jones, O. Garfield. *Parliamentary Procedure at a Glance*. NY: Penguin Books, 1990.

Jones, Robert D. "Anger Against God." *The Journal of Biblical Counseling* 14 {Spring 1996) : 15-20.

_____. "Redeeming the Bad Memories of Your Worst Failures." *The Journal of Biblical Counseling* 22 (Fall 2003) : 40-47.

Jordan, James B. "Eldership and Maturity Part 1" *Rite Reasons* 39 (May 1995) : np.

_____. "Eldership and Maturity Part 2" *Rite Reasons* 40 (May 1995) : np.

Keller, Timothy J. *Ministries of Mercy*. Grand Rapids, MI: Zondervan Publishing House, 1989.

Kellerman, Barbara. *Bad Leadership*. Boston, MA: Harvard Business School Press, 2004.

Kelly, J.N.D. *Golden Mouth*. Ithaca, N.Y.: Cornell University Press, 1995.

Kistler, Don, ed. *Feed My Sheep*. Morgan, PA: Soli Deo Gloria Publications, 2002.

Kotter, John P. *Leading Change*. Boston, MA: Harvard Business School Press, 1996.

Kouzes, James M., and Barry Z. Posner. eds. *Christian Reflections on the Leadership Challenge*. San Francisco: Jossey-Bass, 2004.

Kuiper, R. B. *The Glorious Body of Christ*. Grand Rapids, MI: Wm. B. Eerdmans Publishing Co.,1966.

LaRue, John C. Jr. "Pastoral Gifts and Calling."*Your Church.* (November/December 2003) : 72.

Larson, Craig Brian. *Staying Power.* Grand Rapids, MI: Baker Books, 1998.

Lawrence, Bill. *Effective Pastoring.* Nashville, TN: Word Publishing, 1999.

Leithart, Peter J. *The Kingdom and the Power.* Phillipsburg, NJ: P&R Publishing, 1993.

Lenski, R.C.H. *The Interpretation of St. Matthew's Gospel.* Minneapolis: Augsburg Publishing House, 1964.

Littleproud, J. R. *The Christian Assembly.* Denver, CO: Wilson Foundation, nd.

Lloyd-Jones, D. Martyn. *Preaching and Preachers.* Grand Rapids, MI: Zondervan Publishing House, 1971.

_____. *Spiritual Depression.* Grand Rapids, MI: Wm. B. Eerdmans Publishing Co., 1965.

Logan, Samuel T. Jr. *The Preacher and Preaching.* Phillipsburg, NJ: Presbyterian and Reformed Publishing Company, 1986.

Lohse, Edward. *The New Testament Environment.* (Trans.: John E. Steely). Nashville: Abigdon Press, 1976.

London, H. B. Jr., and Neil Wiseman. *Pastors at Greater Risk.* Ventura, CA: Regal Books, 1993.

_____. *They Call Me Pastor.* Ventura, CA: Regal Books, 2000.

_____. *The Heart of a Great Pastor.* Ventura, CA: Regal Books, 1994.

Lowry, Rick. "Mentoring That Produces Mentors." *Leadership Journal* (Summer 2003) : 42-45.

Lucas, Sean Michael. *On Being Presbyterian.* Phillipsburg, NJ: P&R Publishing, 2006.

Lutzer, Erwin. *Failure the Backdoor to Success.* Chicago, IL: Moody Press, 1975.

_____. *Pastor to Pastor.* Grand Rapids, MI: Kregel Publications, 1998.

MacArthur Jr., John. *The Body Dynamic.* Colorado Springs, CO: Victor Books, 1996.

_____. *The Book on Leadership.* Nashville, TN: Nelson Books, 2004.

_____. *Twelve Ordinary Men.* Nashville, TN: Nelson Books, 2002.

MacArthur Jr., John, 'let al. *Pastoral Ministry.* Nashville, TN: Thomas Nelson, Inc., 2005.

Macchia, Stephen A. *Becoming a Healthy Disciple.* Grand Rapids, MI: Baker Books, 2004.

MacDonald, Gordon. "When it's Time to Leave." *Leadership Journal* (2002) : 1-5.

MacDonald, James. "I'm In Charge Here." *Leadership Journal* 12 (Spring 2001) : 34.

Mack, Wayne. *Down, But Not Out.* Phillipsburg, NJ: P&R Publishing, 2005.

Mack, Wayne, and David Swavely. *Life in the Father's House.* Phillipsburg, NJ: P&R Publishing, 1996.

MacNair, Donald J. *The Birth, Care, and Feeding of a Local Church.* Decatur, GA: Committee for Christian Education and Publications, 1971.

_____ *The Living Church.* Philadelphia, PA: Great Commission Publications, 1980.

MacNair, Donald J., and Esther L. Meek. *The Practices of a Healthy Church.* Phillipsburg, NJ: P&R Publishing, 1999.

Malphurs, Aubrey. *Leading Leaders.* Grand Rapids, MI: Baker Books, 2005.

_____. *Ministry Nuts and Bolts.* Grand Rapids, MI: Kregel Publications, 1997.

_____. *Pouring New Wine into Old Wineskins.* Grand Rapids, MI: Baker Books, 2000.

Malphurs, Aubrey, and Will Mancini. *Building Leaders*. Grand Rapids, MI: Baker Books, 2004.

Mappes, David. "The 'Laying on of Hands' of Elders" *Bibliotheca Sacra* 154 (Oct. 97) : 474-479.

_____ "The New Testament Elder, Overseer, and Pastor" *Bibliotheca Sacra* 154 (Apr. 97) : 162-174.

Marcel, Pierre Ch. *The Relevance of Preaching*. Translated by Rob Roy McGregor. New York: Westminster Publishing House, 2000.

Marsden, George M. *Jonathan Edwards*. New Haven: Yale University Press, 2003.

Marshall, Tom. *Understanding Leadership*. Kent, EN: Sovereign World, Ltd., 1991.

Mawhinney, Bruce. *Preaching With Freshness*. Grand Rapids, MI: Kregel Publications, 1997.

Maxwell, John C. *Be a People Person*. Colorado Springs, CO: NexGen, 2004.

_____. *Dealing with Discouragement*. Network Twenty-One RT370. 1995. Cassette.

_____. *Developing the Leaders Around You*. Nashville, TN: Thomas Nelson, Inc., 1995..

_____. *How to Lead the Seven Most Difficult Personalities, 1-4*. Network Twenty-One, 1995a. Cassettes.

_____. *Relationships: A New Beginning or a Bitter End,* 12. Injoy, Inc.,1997. Cassettes.

_____. *The 10 Commandments of Conflict Resolution*. Network Twenty-One, 1995b. Cassette.

_____ *The 21 Indispensable Qualities of a Leader.* Nashville, TN: Thomas Nelson, Inc., 1999.

_____ *The 21 Irrefutable Laws of Leadership*. Nashville, TN: Thomas Nelson, Inc., 1998.

Maxwell, John C., and Jim Dornan. *Becoming a Person of Influence*. Nashville, TN: Thomas Nelson, Inc., 1997.

McGrath, Alister E. *A Life of John Calvin*. Malden, MA: Blackwell Publishers, 1998.

McIlvaine, Charles P. *Preaching Christ*. Edinburgh, UK: The Banner of Truth Trust, 2003.

McIntosh, Gary L., and Samuel D. Rima, Sr. *Overcoming the Dark Side of Leadership*. Grand Rapids, MI: Baker Books, 1997.

Meisinger, George. *The Local Church and Its Leadership*. Minneapolis, MN: privately printed, 1981.

Merryman, Ron. "Experiential Ministries of the Holy Spirit" unpublished notes, (photocopy), 1977.

Michael, Larry J. *Spurgeon on Leadership*. Grand Rapids, MI: Kregel, 2003.

Miller, Calvin. *The Empowered Leader*. Nashville, TN: Broadman & Holman Publishers, 1995.

Miller, C. John. *Outgrowing the Ingrown Church*. Grand Rapids, MI: Zondervan Publishing House, 1986.

Miller, David W. "The Uniqueness of New Testament Church Eldership." *Grace Theological Journal* 6 (Fall 85) : 315-327.

Miller, Kevin A. "Why Do They Love/Hate Me?" *Leadership Journal* 24 (Fall 2003) : 10.

Miller, Paul E. *Love Walked Among Us*. Colorado Springs, CO: NavPress, 2001.

Morley, Patrick M. *The Man in the Mirror*. Grand Rapid, MI: Zondervan Publishing House, 1997.

Murphy, Thomas. *Pastoral Theology*. Audubon, NJ: Old Paths Publications, 1996.

Murray, Ian H. *The Forgotten Spurgeon*. London: The Banner of Truth Trust, 1966.

New American Standard Bible. Carol Stream, IL: Creation House, Inc., 1960, 1971.

New Geneva Study Bible, New King James Version. Nashville, TN: Thomas Nelson Pub., 1995.

Olyott, Stuart. *Ministering Like the Master*. Carlisle, PA: The Banner of Truth Trust, 2003.

Parker, T.H.L. *John Calvin*. Batavia, IL: Lion Publishing Company, 1975.

Parrott, Les III. *The Control Freak*. Wheaton, IL: Tyndale House Publishers, 2000.

Peck, T. E. *Notes on Ecclesiology*. Greenville, SC: GPTS Press, 1994.

Pfitzner, Victor C. "Purified Community – Purified Sinner." *Australian Bible Review* 30 (1982) : 34-55.

Phillips, Donald T. *Lincoln on Leadership*. NY: Warner Books, Inc., 1992.

_____ *The Founding Fathers on Leadership*. NY: Warner Books, Inc., 1997.

Piper, John F. *The Supremacy of God in Preaching*. Grand Rapids, MI: Baker Books, 1990.

Pipa, Joseph A., Jr. "Pastoral Visitation Questionnaire." Lecture notes presented at a Pastoral Internship Class at Trinity Presbyterian Church, Escondido, CA, 1995. Photocopied.

_____. "Preaching." Class notes for the Pastoral Internship Class at Trinity Presbyterian Church, Escondido, CA, 1996. Photocopied.

_____ "Sermon Evaluation Form." Class notes with the Pastoral Internship Class at Trinity Presbyterian Church, Escondido, CA, 1995. Photocopied.

Plyant, Todd. "New Ideas, Old Church" *Leadership* <http:/www.christianitytoday.com / le/2005/001/15.51.html> (12 April 2005) : 1-2.

Poirier, Alfred. "The Cross and Criticism." *The Journal of Biblical Counseling* 17, (Spring 1999) : 16-20.

_____. *The Peace Making Pastor.* Grand Rapids, MI: BakerBooks, 2006.

Poole, Matthew. *Commentary on the Holy Bible.* Vol. 3. McLean, VA: Mac Donald Publishing Company, nd.

Powlison, David. "Anger Part 2: Three Lies About Anger and the Transforming Truth." *The Journal of Biblical Counseling* 14 (Winter 1996) : 12-21.

_____. "Getting to the Heart of Conflict: Anger." *The Journal of Biblical Counseling* Vol. 16 (Fall 1997) : 32-46.

Prime, Derek, and Alistair Begg. *On Being a Pastor.* Chicago: Moody Publishers, 2004.

Priolo, Lou. *How to Help Angry Kids.* Alabama City, AL: S.E.L.F. Publications, 1996.

Rediger, G. Lloyd. *Clergy Killers.* Louisville, KY: Westminster John Knox Press, 1997.

Reed, Kevin. *Biblical Church Government.* Dallas, TX: Presbyterian Heritage Publications, 1983.

Richards, Lawrence O., and Clyde Hoeldtke. *Church Leadership.* Grand Rapids, MI: Zondervan Publishing House, 1980.

Richardson, Ronald W. *Creating a Healthier Church.* Minneapolis, MN: Fortress Press, 1996.

Roberts, Henry M. *Robert's Rules of Order, Newly Revised.* Glenview, IL: Scott, Foresman and Company, 1970.

Robinson, Haddon W. *Biblical Preaching.* Grand Rapids, MI: Baker Book House, 1980.

_____ *Making a Difference in Preaching.* Grand Rapids, MI: Baker Book House, 1999.

Robinson, Theodore H. "Gospel of Matthew." *The Moffatt New Testament Commentary.* London: Hoddor & Stoughton, Ltd., 1947.

Robinson, Stuart. *The Church of God.* Greenville, SC: GPTS Press, 1995.

Rozakis, Laurie. *New Robert's Rules of Order.* NY: Smithmark Publishers, 1994.

Rubietta, Jane. *How to Keep the Pastor You Love.* Downers Grove, IL: InterVarsity Press, 2002.

Rusaw, Rick, and Eric Swanson. *The Externally Focused Church.* Loveland, CO: Group, 2004.

Ryle, J. C. *Christian Leaders of the 18th Century.* Great Britain, England, 1885. Reprint, Carlisle, PA: Banner of Truth Trust, 1997.

_____. *Holiness.* Great Britain: Bath Press 1879. Reprint, Durham, England: Evangelical Press, 1993.

Sande, Ken. *The Peacemaker.* Grand Rapids, MI: Baker Book House, 1991.

_____. "Strike the Shepherd" <http://www/hispeace.org/html/artic50.htm?pfriend= Yes> (13 May 2004).

Sanders, J. Oswald. *Spiritual Leadership.* Chicago, IL: Moody Press, 1967.

Schmidt, Wayne. *Lead On.* Indianapolis, IN: Wesleyan Publishing House, 2003.

Schuringa, David. "Hans va der Geest's Study on What Makes a Good Sermon." Class lecture in Preaching Style and Audience Analysis at Westminster Seminary California, 1995.

_____. "Student Preaching Evaluation Form." Class lecture in Preaching Style and Audience Analysis at Westminster Seminary California, 1995.

Scott, Stuart. *Anger and Repentance.* Institute in Biblical Counseling and Discipleship, ibc0006, 2000. Cassette.

_____. "Pursue the Servant's Mindset." *The Journal of Biblical Counseling* 17 (Spring 1999) : 9-15.

Shaw, John. *The Character of a Pastor According to God's Heart Considered.* Don Kistler edit. Morgan, PA: Soli Deo Gloria Publications, 1998.

Shelley, Marshall. *Well-Intentioned Dragons*. Minneapolis, MN: Bethany House Publishers, 1985.

Shelp, Earl E., and Ronald Sunderland, Edts. *A Biblical Basis for Ministry*. Philadelphia: The Westminster Press, 1981.

Sietsma, K. *The Idea of Office*. Translated by Henry Vander Goot. Jordan Station, Canada: Paideia Press, 1985.

Sinclair, Gary. "Seduced by Power." *Leadership Journal* Fall 2001 23 (Fall 2001) : 99.

Skinner, Betty Lee. *Daws*. Colorado Springs, CO: NavPress, 1974.

Smith, William P. "I've Had it With You! Learning to Be Tender When People are Tough." *The Journal of Biblical Counseling* 22 (Fall 2003) : 31-39.

Sproul, R.C. ed. *The Reformation Study Bible*. Lake Mary, FL: Ligonier Ministries, 2005.

Spurgeon, C. H. *An All Round Ministry*. Carlisle, PA: The Banner of Truth Trust, 1972.

_____. *Lectures to My Students*. England, 1875. Reprinted, Lynchburg, VA: Old Time Gospel Hour, nd.

Stanley, Andy. *The Next Generation Leader*. Sisters, OR: Multnomah Publishers, 2003.

_____ *Visioneering*. Sisters, OR: Multnomah Publishers, 1999.

Stark, Rodney. *For the Glory of God*. Princeton, NJ: Princeton University Press, 2003.

Steer, Roger. *J. Hudson Taylor*. Singapore: Overseas Missionary Fellowship, 1990.

Stock, James M. *Theodore Roosevelt on Leadership*. Roseville, CA: Prima Publishing, 2001.

Stonehouse, Ned B. *J. Gresham Machen*. Carlisle, PA: The Banner of Truth Trust, 1987.

Stott, John. *Basic Christian Leadership*. Downers, Grove, IL: InterVarsity Press, 2002.

Stott, John R.W. *Between Two Worlds*. Grand Rapids, MI: William B. Eerdmans Publishing Company, 1982.

Strauch, Alexander. *Biblical Eldership*. Littleton, CO: Lewis and Roth Publishers, 1995.

_____. *Meetings That Work*. Littleton, CO: Lewis and Roth Publishers, 2001.

Strock, James M. *Theodore Roosevelt on Leadership*. Roseville, CA: Prima Publishing, 2001.

Stuart, Robert D. Class lecture notes from DM 855 Pastoral Counseling, New Geneva Seminary; Colorado Springs, CO, Feb. 2004.

Swavely, Dave. *Decisions, Decisions*. Phillipsburg, NJ: P&R Publishing, 2003.

_____. *Who Are You To Judge?* Phillipsburg, NJ: P&R Publishing, 2005.

Swindoll, Charles. *Stress Fractures*. Portland, OR: Multnomah Press, 1990.

The American Heritage College Dictionary 3rd edition. New York: Houghton Mifflin Company, 1993.

The Book of Church Order of the Orthodox Presbyterian Church. Willow Grove, PA: The Committee on Christian Education, 2000.

The Book of Church Order of the Presbyterian Church in America. 6th Edition. Lawrenceville, GA: The Office of the Stated Clerk of the General Assembly of the Presbyterian Church in America, 2005.

The Holy Bible English Standard Version. Wheaton, IL: Crossway Bibles, 2001.

The New International Version of the Holy Bible. East Brunswick, NJ: International Bible Society, 1973, 1978, 1984.

The Practical Works of Richard Baxter. Morgan, PA: Soli Deo Gloria Publications, 2000.

The Westminster Confession of Faith. Glasgow: Free Presbyterian Publications, 1976.

Thompson, Frank Charles. *The Thompson Chain Reference Bible*. Michigan: Zondervan Bible Publishers, 1983.

_____. *The Thompson Chain Reference Bible, New International Version*. Indianapolis, IN: B.B. Kirkbride Bible Co., Inc., 1983.

Thompson, James W. *Pastoral Ministry According to Paul*. Grand Rapids, MI: Baker Academic, 2006.

Thornton, Paul B. *Be the Leader –Make the Difference*. Torrance, CA: Griffin Publishing Group, 2000.

Tripp, Paul David. *War of Words*. Phillipsburg, NJ: P&R Publishing, 2000.

Tucker, Austin B. *A Primer for Pastors*. Grand Rapids, MI: Kregel Publications, 2004.

Umidi, Joseph L. *Confirming the Pastoral Call*. Grand Rapids, MI: Kregel Publications, 2000.

Van Gelder, Craig. *The Essence of the Church*. Grand Rapids, MI: Baker Books, 2000.

Vermeulen, William. "Evangelism Seminar, 1996. Ada, MI: (photocopy).

Wagner, E. Glenn. *Escape From Church, Inc*. Grand Rapids, MI: Zondervan, 1999.

Welch, Edward T. "Counseling Those Who Are Depressed." *The Journal of Biblical Counseling* 18 (Winter 2000) : 5-31.

Wemp, C. Summer. *Guide to Practical Pastoring*. Nashville: T. Nelson Pub., 1982.

White, John. *Excellence in Leadership*. Downers Grove, IL: InterVarsity Press, 1986.

White, William, Jr. *Van Til*. New York: Thomas Nelson Publishers, 1979.

Whitney, Donald S. *Spiritual Disciplines within the Church*. Chicago, IL: Moody, 1996.

Wilkerson, Bruce. *Seven Laws of the Learner*. Sisters, OR: Multnomah Publishers, 1992.

Wilson, James L. "Few and Far Between." *Leadership Journal* 22 (Spring 2001) : 45.

Wilson, Sandra D. *Hurt People Hurt People*. Grand Rapids, MI: Discovery House Publishers, 2001.

Wolfe, Stephanie. "The Most Valuable Partnership, Part One" *The Pastor's Coach*, May 2004, Volume 5, Issue 10. Database on-line. Available from http://www.injoy.com/ Newsletters/ pastors/Archives/2004/05_2.txt. Accessed May 25, 2004.

Wright, Eric. *Church – No Spectator Sport*. Durham, England: Evangelical Press, 1994.

Young, Jerry R. "Shepherds, Lead!" *Grace Theological Journal* 6 (Fall 85) : 329–335.

Zachman, Randall C. *John Calvin as Teacher, Pastor, and Theologian*. Grand Rapids, MI: Baker Academic, 2006.

Zaspel, Fred G. "The Apostolic Model for Christian Ministry: An Analysis of 1 Corinthians 2:1-5" *Reformation and Revival Journal* 7 (Winter 1998): np.

Printed in the United States
93602LV00005B/39-62/A

9 781602 666566